BERLITZ®

CITIES
of

E

1989/1990 Edition

By the staff of Berlitz Guides
A Macmillan Company

How to use our guide

- The choice of cities in this guide is based on those most favoured by visitors from English-speaking countries. Any tour of Europe should take in a selection, according to individual interests.

- The general introduction will help visitors make their choice, and paints a broad picture of each destination.

- Each of the thirty-four cities is made up of an introduction, a brief history and a where to go section, plus hints on what to shop for and what to look out for on local menus.

- Suggestions, where relevant, are made of possible excursions to outstanding sights nearby.

- The colourful, accurate city maps help orientate yourself.

- Finally, an index will help locate places around the cities not noted in the table of contents.

- For more detailed information on the destination, check the list of Berlitz' complete range of travel and country guides on the inside front cover.

Although we make every effort to ensure the accuracy of all the information in this book, changes occur incessantly. We cannot therefore take responsibility for facts and circumstances in general that are constantly subject to alteration. Our guides are updated on a regular basis as we reprint, and we are always grateful to readers who let us know of any errors, changes or serious omissions they come across.

Printed in Switzerland by Weber S.A., Bienne.

2nd Printing 1989/1990 Edition

Contents

6

Layout: Doris Haldemann
Falk Cartography: Falk-Verlag, Hamburg

Photos: Cover Photo by KEY-color/ZEFA.
Loomis Dean pp. 22, 400; Jürg Donatsch pp. 245, 251, 421, 425, 427; Herbert Fried pp. 405, 410, 415; Dany Gignoux pp. 253, 258, 260, 261, 262, 266, 301, 305, 308, 309, 312, 313; Roy Giles pp. 165, 167, 170, 171, 173, 176, 179; Jeremy Grayson pp. 269, 275, 278, 283; Roselyne Hanhart pp. 323, 324; Claude Huber pp. 27, 77, 82, 83, 85, 91, 101, 108, 109, 112; Walter Imber pp. 229, 230, 233, 238, 241, 243, 373, 374, 380, 383, 385, 386; Monique Jacot pp. 117, 120, 125, 129, 130, 131, 207, 357, 362, 366, 368, 369, 371; Eric Jaquier pp. 11, 149, 155, 158, 162, 336, 337, 343, 345, 346; Geraldine Kenway pp. 2–3, 55; KEY-color p. 293; KEY-color/Brännhage p. 317; KEY-color/Wälterlin pp. 221, 225; KEY-color/Wiederk p. 321; KEY-color/ZEFA pp. 197, 203, 210, 298, 352; KLM Aerocarto p. 33; Suki Langereis pp. 29, 39; Erling Mandelmann pp. 9, 133, 134, 136, 137, 140, 144, 147, 389, 397; MARKA, Milano p. 349; Jean Mohr pp. 17, 181, 188, 193; Reflejo/Susan Griggs, London pp. 52–53; Salmer, Barcelona p. 61; Georg Stärk p. 333; Jean-Claude Vieillefond pp. 445, 446, 449, 452, 454, 457, 459, 477, 486, 491; Daniel Vittet pp. 14–15, 45, 47, 50, 57, 59, 93, 99, 213, 285, 291, 329, 461, 464, 468, 470, 472, 475, 493, 496; Ken Welsh pp. 62, 68, 73, 429, 433, 435, 437, 440, 443.

Acknowledgements

We would like to thank the Berlitz correspondents throughout Europe and team of authors for their contributions, in particular Jack Altman, Adrienne Jackson, Ken Bernstein, Hugh Oram. Our thanks also go to the tourist offices of each city that have provided invaluable help.

Maps

Amsterdam pp. 34–35, Athens p. 49, Barcelona pp. 66–67, Berlin p. 81, Berne p. 96, Brussels pp. 106–107, Cologne p. 123, Copenhagen pp. 138–139, Dublin p. 153, Edinburgh p. 168, Europe pp. 18–19, Florence p. 185, Geneva p. 217, Helsinki pp. 234–235, Innsbruck p. 248, Lisbon p. 255, London pp. 272–273, Lucerne p. 289, Madrid pp. 306–307, Munich pp. 338–339, Nice (French Riviera coastline) pp. 360 and 365, Oslo pp. 378–379, Paris pp. 392–393, Rome pp. 412–413, Seville p. 438, Stockholm pp. 450–451, Venice p. 467, Vienna pp. 482–483, Zurich p. 496.

Introduction

Looking back over their history, it's hard to find a time when they weren't killing one another, grabbing each other's land, sinking ships, burning churches, stealing works of art. Even today, when they've made what for want of a better word they call peace, they can't help fighting over the price of olive oil, wheat and codfish or whether to put clean gasoline in their cars. No, Europeans are not exactly one big happy family.

But they do have fun. The land they grabbed is marvellously fertile, the churches they left standing are magnificent and the works of art eminently worth stealing. And when you taste your first Genovese *tagliatelle al pesto* or crusty French *baguette*, you'll understand that the olive oil and wheat are worth fighting for.

Touring some of the three dozen cities we propose in this book, you'll soon sense that the good things of European life derive from its sheer diversity.

Take the city parks. When you walk around the geometrically arranged lawns bordered by regiments of chestnut trees in Paris's Tuileries Gardens, you couldn't possibly mistake them for the rolling expanses of grass scattered with sturdy oaks, deck chairs and loving couples in London's Hyde Park. Paris's poets and philosophers meditate along right-angled or diagonal gravel paths while their London counterparts proclaim their wisdoms corralled in one corner of their park on dilapidated soapboxes. Even the so-called Englischer Garten of Munich has as its centrepiece a decidedly un-English beer garden.

Or the cheeses. France may have 400 different kinds (the figure seems to change as often as the Dow Jones average), but the serious gourmet should not neglect the scores of others to be found in Italy, Britain or the Netherlands, each of them subtly different in aroma, texture and taste. The Baroque palaces of Austria do not resemble those of Italy; the beaches of Greece and Spain are as different as chalk and cheese.

The diversity of urban landscape, cuisine or architecture is of course an inevitable expression of the endless variety in the people themselves, not just the obvious differences between, say, Swedes and Italians but also between Prussian and Bavarian Germans or Parisian and Mediterranean Frenchmen. These national and regional differences are occasional causes of international and civil wars, but a permanent source of pride for the natives and a joy for the foreign visitors. The ideal places for you to sample the flavour and spice of this variety are the major cities, natural magnets for the best talents in Europe.

Well, where do you start? If you don't want to add too much culture shock to your jet lag by confronting a foreign language as soon as you land, it may be a good idea to start with an English-speaking city. So unless the "old country" demanding your undivided allegiance is Ireland or Scotland, which we'll get to in a minute, your first choice is likely to be **London.**

The old lady is looking good. Since Britain's entry into the European Common Market in the 1960s, London has become a top tourist destination not just for Americans but for all of Britain's European partners. This has forced London, at last, to raise the standards of its restaurants and the comfort of its hotels. The internationalization of the job-market has brought in

Italian, Spanish, Greek and even French chefs and the competition has improved the quality of English food, too.

The theatre is as good as ever, whether in the venerable West End houses around Shaftesbury Avenue or in the ultra-modern performing arts centre at the Barbican and the prestigious new National Theatre on the South Bank of the River Thames. The monuments and museums of London's historic past are remarkably unforbidding, but you still won't get the guard at Buckingham Palace to give you a kiss. Shopping is a delightful adventure both in the imperturbable department stores of Oxford Street and Knightsbridge or the elegant arcades of Piccadilly.

Only the most adventurous drivers should think of renting a car in London. Driving on the left may prove too much of a challenge in the crowded city. If you're not planning to tour the surrounding countryside, wait till you get to the Continent.

But before you cross the English Channel, why not take a plane or train up to **Edinburgh?** Scotland's dashing, cobblestoned capital charms visitors with its graceful Royal Mile stretching from

Edinburgh Castle to the palace of Holyroodhouse. The couple of dozen courses in and around the city limits make it a heady delight for golfers, and the pure malt whisky served in the cheerful taverns does a similar job for the rest of us.

Dublin is for poets, professional and amateur, romantic and cynical. The professionals bear names like W.B.Yeats, James Joyce and George Bernard Shaw and the amateurs are to be seen and heard any night of the week in the pubs around St Stephen's Green. They are at their most entertaining on "cabaret night". For your moments of meditation, walk the quadrangles of Trinity College and in the evening enjoy the splendid Irish drama at the grand old Abbey Theatre.

After the acclimatization in Britain and Ireland, your choices are infinite. In Scandinavia, where they speak very good English, too, **Stockholm** is a pleasant mixture of historic and modern, sexy and strait-laced. The medieval charm of Gamla Stan has been lovingly restored to house art galleries, covered and open-air markets, and nightclubs for every taste. For a sense of traditional Swedish life, visit the open-air folklore museum at Skansen.

If you like the variety of *smörgåsbord,* check out the giant market at Östermalms Saluhall to see just how many different kinds of herring the Swedish can put together (almost as many as the French with their cheeses).

Copenhagen is of course the home of Hans Christian Andersen and you'll find his old house down at the harbour, along with a lot less whimsical nightlife for sailors and other lonelyhearts. But there's still something of Andersen's fairytale atmosphere in the Tivoli Gardens ablaze with the colours of 160,000 flowers, particularly spectacular when illuminated at night.

Oslo, big capital of a small country, is spacious enough for dozens of cross-country ski-runs inside the city-limits, much favoured by businessmen commuting in the wintertime. In a beautiful setting of moorland, lakes and fir-tree forests, the town has grown prosperous through Norway's North Sea oil and you can watch construction of the gigantic oil rigs down at the city docks.

The museums of this seafaring people will also show you their ancient Viking long-

boats and the Kon Tiki balsa raft that crossed the Pacific a few years ago. In the Vika shopping district, you'll find some terrific ski-sweaters or mink coats, and art-lovers will appreciate the Edvard Munch Museum to which the great Norwegian neurotic bequeathed the bulk of his work.

Finland is attached to, but not strictly speaking part of, Scandinavia. Its capital **Helsinki** acts as a kind of bridge between the Russians and the Swedes, Danes and Norwegians. The city's roots in the western world are clear in the striking modern architecture of Aalto Saarinen. Aalto's splendid Finlandia Hall is the ideal place to hear a concert of the great Finnish composer Sibelius. The onion domes of the Orthodox churches are an equally clear indicator of the Russian presence in Finnish life.

Helsinki boasts the cleanest air of any capital in Europe and broad spacious avenues to enjoy it. The shopping is much appreciated by the wives of Moscow-based Western diplomats who fly in for the hairdressers and boutiques around Esplanadi Park. Connoisseurs insist that the local vodka is the best in the world, bar none, and their children love the pancakes with raspberries.

If you may, from the purely practical point of view, have some legitimate hesitation about driving in London, on the Continent a rental car can be a real asset. European freeways are first class, and the secondary roads, with some exceptions in Spain, Portugal, Italy and Greece, are excellently paved and signposted. The important thing is to have the right means of transport at the right moment.

For instance, as fast and convenient as it may be, instead of flying to **Paris** from London, you could take the cross-Channel ferry and then the train to see something of the beautiful Normandy countryside on the way into the French capital. For visiting Paris itself, the local subway (Métro) and bus systems are efficient and a lot of fun, too, but you should consider renting a car for your excursions outside the city to, say, the magnificent château at Versailles or the horse-racing in idyllic Chantilly.

A car will make it easier for you to plan a picnic and so give you an excuse to take full advantage of Paris's marvellous streetmarkets for your provisions. For the best way to enjoy Paris is to try, for however brief a time, to participate in the Parisians' daily life rather than make your stay there just another sightseeing tour. Visit those bakeries, cheese-shops and wine-merchants. Don't always take your breakfast at the hotel, get out early to a corner café and have your coffee and croissants with the locals.

But don't neglect Paris's traditional sightseeing, either. There are some tricks: get your first view of the Eiffel Tower and Notre Dame cathedral from a Seine riverboat, *bâteau mouche*. Go to the Louvre Museum early Monday morning, not Sunday, to the super-modern Pompidou Centre in the evening, not the afternoon, to the flea market at Clignancourt at *dawn* with the early-bird antique dealers.

In Paris you'll be able to sample all the regional cuisines of the country—the snails of Burgundy, oysters of Brittany, goose of the Périgord—and of course the wines, not just the great labels of Bordeaux and Burgundy, but also the lesser known regional wines of Cahors, Provence or the Loire. There's something here for all five senses, plus that sixth intuitive sense for adventure.

Fly or drive down to the French Riviera. From **Nice** east to the Italian border via Monaco and Menton, or west through Antibes, Juan les Pins and Cannes to Saint-Tropez, you pass through towns whose names evoke lazy luxury, easy fun in the sun, sea and sand. After years of pollution, the French Mediterranean beaches have cleaned up their act. Nice has a pebble beach, but superb white sands are to be found in and around Cannes, home of the international film festival in May, or outside Saint-Tropez, where the girls look like film stars all summer long.

In Nice, take a walk along the stylish Promenade des Anglais (the English are credited with "discovering" the Riviera) to the old town and its Italian-style fish, fruit and vegetable market. As Nizza, Nice was for long an Italian possession, and its older neighbourhoods still have a certain Italian atmosphere. Monaco is famous for its Grand Prix motor race through the downtown streets of Monte Carlo (also in May) and the casino gambling. Choose between the old-fashioned elegance of crystal chan-

deliers over the roulette and baccarat tables or the more recent Las Vegas-style rooms with craps and slot-machines.

Since the death of General Franco, Spain has taken on a new lease of life. Things are a lot more exciting these days, even in the once rather staid and melancholy **Madrid**. The flamenco from Andalusia but also the Castilian fandango and bolero are danced in the cabarets of the capital till the early hours of the morning. Every other *bodega* claims to be an old Hemingway watering-hole. Most of them are.

Nonetheless, despite the heightened bustle at the Puerto del Sol, the prevailing tone of Madrid is still one of dignity. Its Prado museum has one of the great art collections of the Western world, proud not only of its Velazquez, El Greco and Goya, but also of the triumphant return of Picasso's *Guernica*. You'll find the stately essence of old Madrid in the narrow streets tucked away behind the Royal Palace. And if you're an *aficionado* of bullfights, the best are to be found at the Plaza Monumental and Vista Alegre.

For some easy and rewarding excursions around Madrid, drive out to Toledo with

its fantastic cathedral and colourful old Jewish quarter, to Avila for its fascinating ramparts or to El Escorial for the grand domes of King Philip II's royal palace-city.

Capital of the Republican government during its valiant struggle against fascism in the Spanish Civil War, **Barcelona** stands with pride and independent spirit apart from the rest of Spain. The feisty Catalonians have made it the country's liveliest cultural centre, the gathering place for writers, artists and eccentrics.

The centre of town is around La Rambla, where high and low gather to discuss the future of the nation, the fortunes of the local soccer team or how to carry on a torrid affair without wife or husband finding out. The port district behind La Rambla, the Barri Chino, is raunchy but exciting for the bold and brazen. Plan your evening stroll or *paseo*, like the Spanish, before a late dinner. Catalan cuisine is robust rather than refined—try the *zarzuela* fish soup and *escudella* meat stew, with a fruity *sangría* wine punch to help it down.

Besides the impressive cathedral in the medieval Barri Gótic, Barcelona's great architectural attraction is the bizarre 19th-century work of Antonio Gaudí, plant-like extrusions covering his church and apartment buildings.

Seville was the commuter-terminus for the Spaniards' voyages of discovery to America. Testimony to the famous "mistake" they made about where they thought they were going can still be seen today in the Archivo General de las Indias, the museum where you can see original documents of Columbus, Cortés and Magellan.

But Seville is now above all a great centre of Spanish Catholicism. Its great cathedral is the third biggest church in Europe, after Rome's St. Peter's and London's St. Paul's.

It's also the home of the country's best flamenco dancing, often right there in the streets of the Barrio de Santa Cruz (once the old Jewish quarter). Together with the minaret of the Giralda, remains of the mosque that the cathedral replaced, the Moorish fortress of the Alcazar and its tropical gardens are an intriguing reminder of the varied exotic elements of Spain's beginnings. You're a long way from Oslo.

Important wherever you are in Spain (or, for that matter, in any other of the hot countries of southern Europe): participate in the life-saving local custom of the *siesta*. A half-hour nap in the afternoon will work wonders—it makes late nights and early starts a lot easier.

First thing to remember when in **Lisbon** is not to mistake the Portuguese for Spaniards, they really don't appreciate it. But you'll find them a polite and friendly people, for the most part more easy-going than the Spanish. But note, too, that touch of melancholy in their music, the heart-rending *fado* sung as you sip a glass of chilled semi-sparkling young white wine known as *vinho verde*, literally "green wine", not sweet, not dry. And they don't kill their bulls at the bullfight. Enigmatic bunch.

Walk through the ancient Alfama neighbourhood and you'll encounter vestiges of the Greeks, Romans, Visigoths and Moors who created this intriguing cocktail. Built on hills overlooking the Tagus River, it's a great walking town, with sudden dramatic views, best of all from Castelo Sao Jorge (Saint George's Castle).

The special richness of Italy for the tourist is that centuries of regional rivalries have left

the country with no dominant capital like London in Britain or Paris in France. Rome may be the political capital, but culturally, other major cities—Florence, Venice, Milan or Naples—in no way feel overshadowed.

But let's start in **Rome** anyway, since so much of Europe itself started there, too. It's certainly not a town to 'do' in a couple of days. Take its cultural riches slowly—the ancient splendours of the Colosseum, the Roman Forum in its noble ruins; the artistic treasures of the Vatican, not just Michelangelo's ceiling in the Sistine Chapel, but also the serenity of the Raphael Room and the grandeur of St. Peter's and its vast square.

Combine them with the enjoyment of Rome's wonderful street life, from the famous Spanish Steps of Piazza di Spagna and the lovely Piazza Navona, to the old working-class neighbourhood of Trastevere, Fellini's Rome "across the Tiber river". Throw your three coins in the Trevi Fountain, seek out the last vestiges of a few *dolce vita* dinosaurs along the Via Veneto.

You should shop or at least window-shop around the stylish luxury of Via del Corso,

Via Condotti, Frattini or Borgognona—for knitwear, silks and leather goods. Cool off with a *granita di caffè* (iced coffee). Fill up with one of the great simple Roman pasta dishes, *olio, aglio, peperoncino* (spaghetti with oil, garlic and pepper) or *carbonara* (bacon-bits, egg and cheese), together with a local Frascati white wine.

Above all, try to see this town at dawn and sunset, when the light is mellow, mellow, mellow.

Milan is the country's major business centre, home of its stock exchange, but also a leading focus for fashion and the arts. The Milanese tend to regard themselves as more sophisticated than the "provincials" of Rome or Florence. These days, men will find "English" suits and coats on the Via Monte Napoleone better cut than in most shops in London.

When you visit the cathedral, get up on the roof to wander around the, yes, 135 white marble steeples. The Pinacoteca di Brera has a magnificent collection of old Italian masters and in the little galleries of the surrounding neighbourhood, you'll find the country's principal avant-garde artists.

Do it right and **Venice** will never disappoint you. Even at the busiest moments of the year, in July and August when you might think that La Serenissima, as she is known, will succumb to the onslaught of the hordes of her admirers, you walk just 100 yards away from the crowds and you'll find yet another blessed quiet spot of Venetian magic. For this town perched on a lagoon *is* magic, like no other on earth, and its canals and bridges, palaces and little churches, artisan's workshops and galleries, all contain a part of the potion.

Your gondolier—you must try one at least once—is well enough paid to know exactly where to take you away from the mob. If the Piazza San Marco with its cafés and bandstands, splendid basilica and cheeky pigeons, is too crowded in the middle of the day, go back at midnight or first thing in the morning. The shopping district of the Rialto is nearly always packed but it would be much less fun when deserted, so just plunge in.

The great Venetian artists—Giorgione, Titian, Tintoretto and Veronese—can be seen at the Accademia, but also in the Doge's Palace. One painter, Carpaccio, had a famous beef dish named after him, another, Bellini, is honoured with a peach-champagne cocktail.

There's something awe-inspiring about the towering reputation of **Florence**, but there's no better place to go to sense Europe's achievements.

Less boisterous than the Romans and less bustling than the Milanese, the Florentines today have an elegance and dignity appropriate to their city's prestige. Women travellers insist that there is no more handsome man in the world than an upright, silver-haired 60-year-old Florentine gentleman strolling on the fashionable Via de Tornabuoni with his cashmere coat nonchalantly draped like a cape over his shoulders, a Medici reincarnate.

Each visitor comes away with his own favourite memory—the Masaccio frescoes in the church of Santa Maria del Carmine, the Ghiberti bronzes on the Baptistery's Doors of Paradise, the Fra Angelico paintings for the monastery of San Marco. The masterpieces of the Uffizi and Pitti galleries are beyond counting—don't try to 'do' them all, just seek out a dozen and you'll still leave dazed and happy.

For your best first—or last—view of Florence go up to the hillside town of Fiesole. From here, you'll get a taste of the rest of Tuscany of which Florence is the capital. The vineyards and cypress trees will lead you west to Pisa, where you'll find the leaning tower more poetic than comic in the cathedral square understandably named Piazza dei Miracoli (Square of Miracles). A few miles north of Pisa, Lucca offers a charmed moment in the exquisite medieval streets inside its ramparts.

Don't be frightened of **Naples**. Cynics say that the old adage "See Naples and die" is exaggerated and should really only be "See Naples and have your pocket picked." In this respect, Naples is in fact not so very different from American port-towns. You'll avoid trouble with the elementary precautions of leaving your valuables in the hotel safe-deposit and holding firmly on to your handbag. The rewards of a visit to this unique south Italian city far outweigh the risks. Many of Pompei's treasures are on display in the museum.

The bay really is as beautiful as the poets and singers say, the Mount Vesuvius volcano makes a spectacular backdrop and the people are the most colourful in all Italy. The Certosa (charterhouse) di San Martino gives you a lovely view of the bay.

Lovers, young and old, will swoon at the *bel canto* singers, both in the backstreet tenements and the great Teatro San Carlo opera house.

Athens has long basked in its reputation as the cradle of Greek and indeed Western civilisation. Greece's return to the democracy it invented 2,500 years ago, along with its more recent entry into the European Common Market, has shaken the capital out of its torpor, persuaded it to clean up its ancient monuments and at least make a start on the problematic air pollution.

If you're headed for a rest on the Greek islands, stop off in Athens to see the great Acropolis, with its Parthenon temple, and the unrivalled classical collections of the National Archaeological Museum. The Plaka district of boutiques, bars and restaurants has a slight air of 'tourist trap' about it, but the Monastiraki is a lively flea market. Watch the Greek world go by from a sidewalk café on Syntagma Square.

Switzerland offers a cool relief from that unrelenting Mediterranean sun. The political capital, **Bern,** is a pleasantly sleepy town which doesn't take its politics too seriously. The many 16th-century fountains create a refreshingly old-fashioned atmosphere; a more modern note is struck by by the superb Paul Klee paintings at the Fine Arts Museum.

Zurich is the business centre of Switzerland, seat of the financial 'gnomes' and laid out with clean, clean homes. Bahnhofstrasse is its elegant main shopping street, the place to buy the best of Swiss jewellery and watches. See the work of Edvard Munch and Marc Chagall at the Kunsthaus and take a lazy cruise on the lake.

But **Lucerne** has probably the most spectacular of the many Swiss lakes—the Vierwaldstättersee. A steamer takes you around its coves, inlets and bays. Picturesque symbol of the town is the Kapellbrücke, a 14th-century roofed bridge across the Reuss river.

If only international diplomacy could be infected with the tranquillity of one of its principal focuses, **Geneva,** the earth would be a much safer planet. With its lake and the parks and bandstands and flower-clocks, and nothing more troublesome than a little spray from its fountains, Geneva is a world away from hijackings and riots. The only explosions come from the August fireworks display on the lake.

Grand-Rue is the centre of the old part of town, as spotless as the new. Out at the Palais des Nations you can see where they created the ill-fated League of Nations and still bring together the representatives of the great powers.

Vienna is one of those dreams that do come true. In Austria's capital, the music is everywhere, the chocolate cake terrific, the coffeehouses reviving, the old world charm still operative. With the departure of the Emperor, tradition stayed on as king. The imperial palaces of Schönbrunn and Belvedere have been preserved as magnificent Baroque monuments to the glory of the Habsburg dynasty. And the unmatched skills of their cavalry live on at the Spanish Riding School.

In the Kunsthistorisches Museum, you'll see the world's finest collection of Brueghels, and other town museums house the turn-of-the-century Viennese masters, Klimt and Schiele.

Stephansdom cathedral is the centre of this still

very Catholic capital. Twice burned down, once by negligence, once by bombs, the Opera House resounds again to the sublime music of Mozart and Wagner. The Grosser Musikvereinssaal is the concert home of that inimitable warm sound that the Vienna Philharmonic Orchestra imposes on all its conductors. On the city outskirts, in Heiligenstadt, you can see where Beethoven composed his masterpieces. If your taste is less highbrow, walk a little further to the hillside Heurige winegardens to hear a waltz and polka on violin or zither.

Before or after your evening music, have a *Wienerschnitzel* (veal cutlet) and don't forego a dessert of chocolate Sachertorte or Apfelstrudel with whipped cream.

At the other end of Austria, **Innsbruck** is the capital of the Tyrol, centre of some of the best skiing country in Europe, but also a great summer resort for mountain hikes. The Altstadt (Old Town) is a colourful hodgepodge of Baroque houses, and you'll see the locals still wearing the traditional regional costume of dirndl skirts and peasant blouses, or *Lederhose* and *loden* jackets.

Salzburg is Mozart's birthplace and doesn't let you forget it. There's of course his house, with his first violin and last piano, a Mozartplatz, Mozartkugel (chocolate and hazelnut candy-balls). But most important is his music, at the annual summer festival, completely booked a year in advance. The cheerful town is well worth a visit outside festival time, too: elegant shopping on Getreidegasse, the imposing cathedral and archbishop's Residenz palace, and a bonus of Austria's most devastating dessert—Salzburger Nockerl, something halfway between a soufflé and meringue.

Like Italy, West Germany is a country of many rival big towns rather than one all-powerful capital. However, let's start with the old German capital of **Berlin**, not totally politically integrated into the Federal Republic, but culturally and socially a part of West German life. West Berlin is a bright and bouncy town, undaunted by that formidable Wall which separates it from East Berlin, capital of the German Democratic Republic.

The western sector is a colourful mixture of an older generation of dyed-in-the-wool Berliners, witty, sardonic, long-suffering and younger artists, writers, moviemakers and other jolly misfits who find a special stimulus in the air of this exceptional city. The main street is Kurfürstendamm, which you'll soon know as Ku'damm, symbol of West Berlin's boisterous prosperity. The art galleries on and off the Ku'damm, the museums of European art at Dahlem, ancient Egyptian art near the Charlottenburg Palace or modern art at the Nationalgalerie, the Philharmonie concert hall, are all testimony to the vitality of West Berlin's cultural life.

You should also visit East Berlin, not only for the curiosity of crossing the Wall, but also to get at least a glimpse of both how the most prosperous of the East bloc countries lives, and what this great city used to look like, architecturally at least, in its roaring twenties. The eastern sector has kept much more of that old world intact.

Hamburg is the pride of Germany's north, a thriving port-city of great civic dignity. Its opera, theatre and art galleries belie the somewhat tawdry reputation it has acquired through the red light district of the Reeperbahn. The curious and bold will seek it out, down by the docks, but the more prudent or less prurient will stick to the nearby Sankt Pauli fish market early in the morning.

If you're planning a Rhine river-cruise, pay a visit first to **Cologne**. Not only does it have a grandiose Gothic cathedral and fine museums of Roman and German art, but it's the ideal place to sample the best of the Rhine and Mosel wines—perfect with the locally hunted venison. It still may not look like it, but **Bonn** is the political capital of the Federal Republic. It's also a pleasant university town and most famous as Beethoven's birthplace. His well-preserved home is certainly worth a visit.

At the junction of the Rhine and Main rivers, **Frankfurt** is West Germany's financial centre, and its mammoth Book Fair every October has contributed towards making it capital of world publishing. Badly bombed in World War II, its 15th-century Römerberg square has been meticulously restored. The town's prosperity has enabled it to replenish the great art museum, Städelsches Kunstinstitut, with some of the best European and American works on the market. The attractive town of Heidelberg,

animated by lively student taverns and dramatic firework displays in the ruins of the old castle, is an easy drive down the Autobahn.

Munich is the capital of Bavaria and often likes to think of itself as a place apart from the rest of the country while remaining resolutely the most German of cities. It's both a rollicking town for lovers of beer and sausages at the annual Oktoberfest and a magnet for the most creative talents in German art and cinema, concentrated in the neighbourhood of Schwabing.

Luxembourg is the charming capital of a country of the same name, which is not much bigger than the city itself. The old part of town is perched up on a plateau overlooking the Alzette river and you get a superb view of the surrounding forests and meadows.

To the extent that the Common Market represents a European unity, **Brussels** is its capital. The imposing Grand-Place is the centre of town life and civic pride. Gourmets agree the Belgians produce the best French fries in Europe (in curious combination with mussels).

Let's finish in style with **Amsterdam**, one of the most cheerful cities in the world.

True, it's a rich repository of Dutch culture. The Rijksmuseum is famous for its Rembrandts, the Van Gogh Museum is the perfect place to contemplate that tormented Impressionist's work and life, the Stedlijk is an admirable museum of our modern era. But above all this is a town to see the people and their homes.

Start your visit with a boat trip along the canals—Singel, Herengracht, Keizersgracht and Prinsengracht—and you'll float past delightful mansions of the 17th century. This is a town of noble bourgeois and bumptious youngsters. Get out there walking or rent a bike and join in the fun.

Seek out the floating flower market, beautifully arrayed on sturdy old barges near the Munt (Mint). Wheel around the lively popular neighbourhood of Jordaan, peep into the sleepy courtyards. This town manages to be bright and clean without the sterility of excessive hygiene. The people are friendly, witty, they speak good English and they're curious about the whole world.

If you have something of the same attitude as the people of Amsterdam, you're all set to go to Europe.

Bon voyage!

AMSTERDAM

The Netherlands

Introduction

Amsterdam is a remarkable mixture: a capital without a government (the latter is 40 minutes down the road in The Hague); a city of canals and houseboats where the bicycle is king; a mecca of art, where the Rijksmuseum and the Van Gogh collection vie with the red-light district as prime tourist attractions; prim plant-filled suburban homes contrasting with city-centre sex-shops and gay bars; a gourmet's delight, with anything from traditional raw herring to an Indonesian *rijsttafel* on the menu.

Along with London, Paris and Rome, Amsterdam is one of Europe's most popular tourist cities—thanks, certainly, to the warm-hearted welcome its inhabitants extend to foreigners but, above all, to the picturesque Golden Age look of the town's central canal area.

This area is a unique 17th-century museum, often called the Venice of the North. Row upon row of gabled houses lean crazily against one another along a network of tree-lined canals. Vistas of venerable churches stretch beyond white wooden drawbridges, narrow cobbled streets and myriads of barges.

And this is the way City Hall likes it. The Golden Age character is preserved by statute. At last count, 7,000 buildings were classified as protected monuments. Complete 17th-century residential areas are renovated, rather than replaced with office blocks. No excuses—there's even an official yard where surplus old doors and window frames can be purchased, to replace woodwormed or irreparable originals.

A negative side to the city has been growing, for sure: a severe housing shortage has created a whole population of squatters. The tolerant city's violence has greatly increased. The drug problem has reached heady proportions, and graffiti have been scrawled all over Amsterdam's once clean and tidy walls. Problems familiar to most of today's major cities, however. Amsterdam will take it all in its stride, and find solutions, reasonable and equitable, like it always has.

A Brief History

Early times
Frisians and other primitive tribes are scattered throughout the region. Franks, Saxons and warlike Germanic tribes invade the area in the 5th century A.D. largely eclipsing the tenuous Christian influence of the Roman Empire. As they die out, the Netherlands develop into a loose amalgam of small states ruled variously by counts, dukes and bishops. One group, the Waterlanders build a settlement on a sandbank where the River Amstel flows into the IJ. They construct a dam to prevent flooding. The settlement becomes known as Amstelredamme.

13th–15th centuries
In 1275, Count Floris V grants privileges to the local citizenry. It is from this date that Amsterdammers traditionally count the founding of their city. After a miracle occurs, Amsterdam becomes a place of pilgrimage for Christians of the Middle Ages. Commerce increases. Refugees fleeing from Spanish domination in neighbouring states pour in.

16th century
Charles V, Holy Roman Emperor and King of Spain, introduces the Inquisition to his Netherlands' realms in the 1520s. His heir, Philip II of Spain, pursues his father's anti-Reformation policy in order to retain his temporal power.

The struggle for independence begins in earnest, with Prince William (dubbed the Silent) of the House of Orange leading the Dutch rebellion. In 1579, the Treaty of Utrecht between the seven Protestant provinces north of the Rhine estranges the southern provinces. The split later leads to the separate existence of the Netherlands and Belgium.

17th century
The Dutch Golden Age flowers in the Netherlands. Merchants, scientists, artists and craftsmen thrive in the Renaissance atmosphere. The Dutch East Indies Company (*Verenigde Oostindische Compagnie*—VOC) expands into a powerful commercial monopoly establishing trading posts throughout the Far East, Africa and Australia. The Treaties of The Hague and of Westphalia in 1648 (marking the end of the Thirty Years' War in Europe) gain more territory for the Dutch. The

independent state of the Netherlands, almost as it stands today, is internationally recognized.

18th–19th centuries

Dutch fortunes decline as French and British influences begin to increase. Napoleon's armies overrun the United Provinces in 1795 and the Netherlands are annexed by France. Independence comes in the early 19th century, as Napoleon's fortunes begin to turn. Prince William of Orange is proclaimed king. New houses, museums and schools are built. Canals are improved.

20th century

Land is reclaimed from the tidal Zuyder Zee area in a mammoth project that transforms it into a freshwater lake enclosed by a 19-mile-long dike.

Germany invades Holland in 1940. Five years of bitter resistance and hardship follow. Queen Wilhelmina, exiled in London, broadcasts messages to her people, bolstering their valiant will to survive as an independent nation.

Post-war developments include a highly advanced welfare system and vigorous support for the European Economic Community. Despite the unemployment problem, as in neighbouring countries, the economy flourishes.

Sightseeing

The one-hour **canal tour** is a must. It's the best introduction to the city and shows you Amsterdam in a nutshell—historic and charming, pragmatic and businesslike and always with a touch of liberalism that borders on the bizarre.

Singel, the inner canal, was once the city's fortified boundary. Look out for No. 7, a real oddity—the narrowest house in Amsterdam. It's only as wide as its front door and is jammed between two 17th-century buildings. Three bridges down, at the junction with Oude Leliestraat, note the iron-barred windows of a quaint old jail set into the bridge itself and just above water level. Approachable only by water, it's said to have been used to keep drunks quiet overnight.

From the Singel, the town spread outwards in the early 1600s to **Herengracht.** This was the No. 1 canal on which to live during the city's Golden Age. The wealthiest merchants vied with each other to build the widest homes, the most elaborate gables, the most impressive front entrance steps. The patrician houses are still here in all their glory, though most are now too big for private residence and are occupied by banks and offices.

Keizersgracht was named after Holy Roman Emperor Maximilian I, whose realm also included the Netherlands. The houses on this canal are not quite so grand as on Herengracht, but still charming and solid middle-class.

Prinsengracht, the last main canal of the horse-shoe, is much more down-to-earth, with smaller homes and many warehouses still in their original condition. The ubiquitous Amsterdam hoisting-beam is still in daily use by the warehousemen as they haul goods from the cobbled street below up past a vertical succession of gaping wooden doorways.

Looking around you from your canal boat seat, you'll see a kaleidoscopic jumble of houseboats like nothing else on earth. The 2,000-plus houseboats range from luxury living to hippy rafts, from a cats' home to a floating pottery.

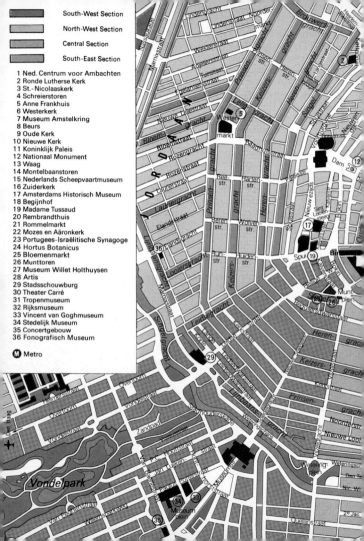

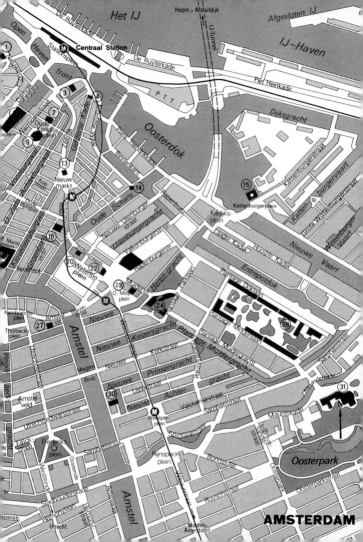

Only about half are actually licensed to moor.

Because the central part of Amsterdam is relatively compact, it's also easy to visit on foot. A good idea is to split the centre into four sections and cover one at a time.

South-West Section

Leidseplein (*plein* = square) is the site of the old city gate on the road to Leiden. Today, the gate, the markets and the carriages have gone, and in their place is a multitude of restaurants and sandwich shops, outdoor cafés and cinemas, discotheques, nightclubs and bars.

The north-west side of the square is dominated by the Stadsschouwburg (Municipal Theatre) with its pillared entrance. Built in 1894 to replace an earlier edifice which had burnt down, it now houses the Dutch Public Theatre.

The American Hotel, virtually next door to the theatre, is something of a city tradition. A building full of character, begun in 1880, it has a magnificent **Jugendstil restaurant,** protected by the authorities as an architectural monument. This has become a meeting place for artists, writers, students and anyone who likes to chat and to be seen. Dutch-born Mata Hari, the legendary World War I spy, held her wedding reception at the American in 1894.

Vondel Park is only 200 yards (182 m.) away, to the south-west. This "lung" for the densely built city centre is named after Holland's foremost poet, the 17th-century Joost van den Vondel. Its 120 acres (49 hectares) include lawns, lakes and flower displays.

Nearby Museumplein, a broad grassy square wild with crocuses and daffodils in spring, is bordered by three major museums and the city's main concert hall.

Looking down the square from its rightful place at the top is the palace-like **Rijksmuseum,** designed by Petrus Cuypers and opened in 1885, home of one of the world's great art collections.

Whether your interests extend to porcelain, Asiatic or Muslim art, Dutch history, 18th-century glassware or 17th-century dolls' houses, the Rijksmuseum has something for you. Highlight is, of course, the European art section, and Dutch painting in particular.

On the right-hand side of the square, looking down

from the Rijksmuseum, are the new **Vincent van Gogh Museum** designed by Gerrit Rietveld, its glassbox exterior looking something of an anachronism on the square, and the **Stedelijk Museum** (Municipal Museum) containing the city's rich collection of modern art.

Make your way back to the top of Leidsestraat along the Singel canal to see the **floating flower market** *(drijvende bloemenmarkt)*. Here for more than 200 years Amsterdammers have stepped aboard the gently swaying, floating shopboats moored at the canalside to buy the profusion of plants and flowers that you'll see in the windows of their homes, all around.

The **Munttoren** (Mint Tower) overlooks this colourful scene, its 17th-century carillon adding an extra touch of gaiety by chiming out an old Dutch tune every half-hour. The tower was originally a medieval gate in the fortified wall of the Singel canal.

A few hundred yards north of the floating flower market is the **Begijnhof** (Beguine Court), a charming haven of quiet in the heart of the busy city. Inside is a neat quadrangle of lawn surrounded by perfect 17th- and 18th-century alms-houses, two small churches and a 15th-century wooden house. English Pilgrim Fathers who fled to Holland before joining the *Mayflower* prayed regularly in the Beguine Court church dating originally from 1392 and known since 1607 as the Scottish Presbyterian Church. Opposite is the Catholic church which nuns were allowed to install in two of the almshouses during the Calvinist domination of Amsterdam in the 17th century.

North-West Section

Leaving the Beguine Court by the rear gate, you are straight into the vast **Amsterdams Historisch Museum** (Amsterdam Historical Museum), newly restored after serving as an orphanage for almost 400 years. Its many rooms and galleries tell the city's fascinating story from 1275 to 1945, with exhibits ranging from prehistoric remains and the city's original charter to audio-visual slide shows on land reclamation.

Dam Square (called, simply, Dam in Dutch) is the city's heart and *raison d'être,* a no-frills area always throbbing with life. Exactly here the river Amstel was dammed some time before 1275, eventually to be filled in completely along Damrak and Rokin.

Dam Square is dominated by the **Koninklijk Paleis** (Royal Palace). Opened as the Town Hall in 1655 in the prosperous Golden Age, it was converted into a palace by Louis Bonaparte, the emperor's brother, during his brief sojourn as king in Amsterdam (1806–10).

Just across the narrow Mozes en Aäronstraat stands the **Nieuwe Kerk** (New Church). This simple, late-Gothic basilica whose origins date back to the 15th century was built without a tower, the willowy, miniature, neo-Gothic steeple dating from the mid-19th century only. The church's glory is its Baroque woodcarving and 16th- and 17th-century organs.

The energetic visitor may like to climb the tower for an incomparable **view** of the city. Aloft, the carillon of 47 bells, some cast by François Hemony, strikes out merry tunes each half-hour of the day *and* night.

The white, stone column on the other side of the square is the **National Monument** erected by subscription in 1956 to commemorate the Dutch role in World War II. In a small curved wall at the back of the monument there are 12 urns—11 filled with soil from each Dutch province, and the 12th with soil from Indonesia.

A few hundred yards behind the palace is the **Westerkerk** (West Church). Begun in 1619 by Hendrick de Keyser and finished in neo-classical style after his death by Jacob van Campen, it's distinguished not only by its tower, Amsterdam's tallest at 273 feet (82 m.), but also by the shining, multi-coloured crown and orb on top of it, a replica of the crown presented to the city by Holy Roman Emperor Maximilian I in 1489.

The **Anne Frankhuis** (Anne Frank House) is just around the corner at Prinsengracht 263. Here, for the two years from 1942 to 1944, this young Jewish girl hid from the occupying power, writing her now-famous diary. At the top of the steep stairway you can still see the bookcase wall which apparently closes off a corridor, but which in fact swings out and gives access to the secret *achterhuis*, or concealed part of the house behind, where Anne, her family and four friends eked out an existence until they were betrayed just nine months before war's end.

The **Jordaan** area across the

canal has become a sought-after area for artists and designers, a trendy quarter that has blossomed with a number of new and fascinating small shops, boutiques and restaurants alongside the area's traditional "brown bars". Over 800 of its 8,000 houses are protected monuments.

The **Ronde Lutherse Kerk** (Round Lutheran Church) is located on the Singel canal. Its 146-foot (44-m.) copper dome has dominated the old herring-packers' quarter here since 1671. The church was rebuilt after being gutted by fire in 1822, and in 1830 a handsome organ was installed.

Over the next century, however, congregations dwindled to such an extent that in 1935 the church was deconsecrated and for a while was used as a warehouse.

At Nieuwendijk 16, is the **Nederlands Centrum voor Ambachten** (Holland Art and Craft Centre), where you can watch local craftsmen make cheese, cut diamonds and chisel wooden clogs.

Central Section

Railway stations are rarely tourist sights, but Amsterdam's **central station,** dominating the Damrak boulevard vista, merits a moment of admiration as both a considerable engineering feat and a fine 19th-century neo-Gothic monument. It was built by Petrus Cuypers, architect also of the Rijksmuseum, on three artificial islands and 8,687 wooden piles.

At the waterfront opposite the station is the NZH (Noord-Zuid Hollands) Koffiehuis, a protected monument, newly restored, housing the VVV tourist office and a restaurant.

Just a few yards down Damrak from the station, the stock-exchange building, the **Beurs,** designed by Hendrik Petrus Berlage, has always excited controversy. It was one of Berlage's ultra-modern masterpieces when first unveiled to the world in 1903.

The **Oude Kerk** (Old Church) is located just behind Beursplein and across Warmoesstraat.

This, the city's biggest and oldest church, was consecrated around 1300. It is the burial place of Rembrandt's wife Saskia. Though a wealth of decoration and statuary was disposed of by 17th-century Calvinists as "Catholic pomp", there remains a lot of Gothic stone carving to be admired both inside and outside, as well as some fine stained-glass including a window commemorating the Peace of Westphalia which, with the Peace of The Hague, brought an end to the 80 years' Spanish war in 1648.

Museum Amstelkring, otherwise known as Ons' Lieve Heer Op Solder (Our Lord in the Attic church), at Oudezijds Voorburgwal 40, is the only one of Amsterdam's 60 once-clandestine Catholic churches of the Calvinist era left in its original condition. Tucked away up a series of steep stairs and winding corridors, it contains numerous relics of interest from the 18th century.

The 1482 **Schreierstoren** is across the small Chinese quarter of the lower Zeedijk. Henry Hudson left from here to discover Manhattan in 1609, and a plaque hailing the event is one of many on the tower.

Within sight of Schreierstoren lies the **Nederlands Scheepvaartmuseum** (Netherland's Maritime Museum), appropriately blessed with a panoramic view of the harbour, and housed in vast old Admiralty supply buildings called 's Lands Zeemagazijn. It's full of model ships, charts, instruments and the fascinating paraphernalia of sailing. The old **Montelbaanstoren**

(Montelbaan Tower) on the Oude Schans canal, is said to be the city's best-proportioned tower. It was built as part of the 15th-century defences and bristled with cannon on its then flat roof. In 1606, the architect Hendrick de Keyser added the present 143-foot (43-m.) spire, with clock and bells, in the same neo-classical style of his other towers.

The **Waag** (Weigh House) stands like a medieval, seven-turreted castle on Nieuwmarkt square. It was built in 1488 as a city gate, but was little used as such. It then had a varied career as weigh house, fire station, guildhouse and museum.

The nearby **Zuiderkerk** (South Church), constructed in the early 17th century, was much admired by Christopher Wren, and is said to be the prototype for many of his London steeples.

The brick and glass **Muziektheater** (Music Theatre) facing the River Amstel is home to the Netherlands Opera and to the National Ballet.

The **Rembrandthuis** (Rembrandt's House) at Jodenbreestraat 4–6, red-shuttered and three storeys high, is a 1606 brick building with a typical Amsterdam step gable. It was the home of Holland's greatest painter from 1639 to his bankruptcy 20 years later.

South-East Section

The **Portugees-Israëlitische Synagoge** (Portuguese Synagogue) was built in 1675 by the city's large community of Sephardic Jews, descendants of refugees from Spain and Portugal in the late 16th century. It's said to have been patterned on the plan of King Solomon's temple.

On Jonas Daniël Meijer Square in front of the synagogue is the **Dockworker Statue** by Mari Andriessen. Revered by Amsterdam Jew and Gentile alike, this rough figure of a man in working clothes commemorates the events of February 1941, when Amsterdam's dockworkers staged a 24-hour strike in protest against the deportation of Jews.

The cheery, impudent stall-holders of Amsterdam's **flea market** in Valkenburgerstraat will happily sell you anything, from a fur coat to a twisted piece of lead piping, a fine old wind-up gramophone to a cheap modern lock.

Overlooking Waterlooplein is the **Mozes en Aäronkerk** (Moses and Aaron Church), an 1840 Catholic church. It has an imposing classical façade with a pillared entrance surmounted by a statue of Christ, and twin towers at each end of the balustraded roof. Two gablestones of "Moyses" and "Aaron" from an earlier church on this site are set into the wall.

The River Amstel, from which Amsterdam takes its name, is only a minute's walk away, and the best river view in town is from the **Blauwbrug** (Blue Bridge). Built in the 1880s, and named after a former blue-painted wooden drawbridge on the site, it is a copy of the Pont Alexandre in Paris, richly ornamented with golden crowns and ships' prows.

Some consider it the city's most beautiful bridge, but look down-river to see its immediate rival, the white wooden drawbridge with nine graceful arches, the **Magere Brug,** or "Skinny Bridge", as it can be colloquially translated. This is unique and totally Amsterdam—a bottle-neck for the single-file traffic but a delight for every photographer.

Rembrandtsplein (Rembrandt Square) and the adjoining Thorbeckeplein are Amsterdam's scaled-down version of Times Square, New

York, or Leicester Square, London. Covered with advertising, cinema, restaurant, bar and nightclub signs, they form a brash fun area offering everything from strip-shows to a cup of coffee at one of the many outdoor cafés.

A **view** of 14 bridges makes a tranquil finale to this active, four-section tour of town. From the far end of Thorbeckeplein, look down Reguliersgracht to see six of them in a row. To the left down Herengracht are six more, and to the right another two. It's a particularly memorable view in summer after dark, when all the bridges are lit.

Eating Out

The claim is made that Amsterdam offers more variety in food and restaurants than any other European city. Pride of place goes to Indonesian cuisine, well ahead of the native Dutch in popularity.

There are up to 32 items in a *rijsttafel* (literally, rice-table). Tackle the feast this way: put a mound of rice in the centre of your plate, and build around it with spoonfuls from your dishes of *babi ketjap* (pork in soya sauce), *daging bronkos* (roast meat in coconut-milk sauce), *sambal go-*

reng kering (spicy pimiento and fish paste), *oblo-oblo* (mixed soya beans), etc.

Even the dish of mixed fruit in syrup, *rudjak manis,* will be spicy hot. All in all, what with the crisp, puffy shrimp bread, sour cucumber, cut-up chicken, the nuts, the fried banana—not forgetting the skewers of cubed meat with peanut sauce called *sateh*—the rice-table is an unforgettable eating experience.

Dutch specialities include pea soup *(erwtensoep);* red kidney bean soup *(bruine bonensoep);* potato and vegetable hash *(stamppot)* with fat Dutch sausage *(worst)*. Fresh sea fish and vegetables are also plentiful in Amsterdam.

The Dutch are not great dessert-eaters, but that's no reason for you to follow suit. Dutch apple-tart *(appeltaart)* is usually available, with its filling of apples, sultanas and cinnamon. So is fresh fruit. And if you like a spicy-cool dessert, try the typical Dutch *gember met slagroom* (lumps of fresh ginger with cream).

Second to coffee, beer *(pils)* is the national drink. Dutch brandy *(vieux)* is half the price of cognac and milder. Jenever is a juniper-flavoured drink along the lines of English gin.

Shopping

Amsterdam shopping is done in any of hundreds of small shops scattered through the central area. Best buys:

Antiques—Plenty of antique shops, especially in the Nieuwe Spiegelstraat, contain bargains. But be aware that up to 50 per cent of the goods may come from Britain or France.

Cigars—renowned throughout the world for their aroma.

Diamonds—a girl's best friend, are all over town. The city has a well-deserved reputation for their cutting and polishing.

Dutch gin, Jenever—a special taste; made from juniper berries is less fiery than English gin.

Pottery—Delft and Makkum pottery; delicate and distinctively different.

Silver and **Pewter**—provide any number of useful or decorative gifts from bracelets to ashtrays.

Souvenirs—clogs, tea, spices, bottles, candles, bamboo basketwork; dozens of colourful keepsakes to take home.

Practical Information

Banks: Open from 9 a.m. to 4 p.m., Monday to Friday, and Thursday also from 4.30 p.m. to 7 p.m.

Currency: The unit of Dutch currency is the *gulden,* usually called the guilder, or more rarely the florin, in English. It's abbreviated *f, fl, gld.* or *DFL.,* and is divided into 100 *cents* (abbreviated *cts.*). Coins include 5, 10 and 25 cents and 1, 2½ and 5 guilders. Banknotes come in denominations of 5, 10, 25, 50, 100, 250 and 1,000 guilders.

Public transport: A good idea if you are planning to spend a day in Amsterdam is to buy a day ticket *(dagkaart),* valid for one day and the next night, entitling you to unlimited rides on any of the city's public transport systems.

ATHENS
PIRAEUS

Greece

Introduction

For every visitor, Athens holds an undeniable fascination—so many centuries spanned, so much of Western civilization rooted in a single city.

The city centre, just 4 miles from the sea, is scanned by a gentle audience of hills. Crowning Athens—as it has since the dawn of Greek history—the Acropolis with its breathtaking Parthenon.

Considering the very real ravages of man and time, the wonder is that any of the city's venerable monuments have survived at all. They have though—even if the ancients would hardly recognize Athens today. Suburbs of cement and steel sprawl chaotically over its historic basin, and the crystal-like quality of Attica's light, famous since Homer, has become little more than a memory. Swollen by unrelenting floods of Greeks migrating from the countryside, Athens' population has soared to some 3 million. The entire country contains only 9 million people.

Despite the congestion, this city will inevitably delight. Life is an outdoor extravaganza, a blend of classical and cosmopolitan. Parks, squares, even roof gardens are cluttered with statuary.

During the white-hot afternoon hours, the city's bustle dies away, the streets are shuttered. Athens drowses in ritual observance of that most logical of Mediterranean traditions, the siesta—just as it doubtless did under Pericles.

When the sun starts its downward curve, the pace picks up again. Offices and boutiques reopen, often until 8.30 p.m. Shopping streets throb with activity, cafés fill up, neon blinks on, the first strains of bouzouki music are heard from the labyrinth of bars under the Acropolis.

Generally Athenians are short in stature and dark-haired. Some could pass as replicas of their discus-throwing ancestors who pose classically in the museums. They are a volatile, talkative and irrepressibly curious people.

The Athenians' surpassing kindness to foreigners reflects the tradition of generous hospitality instinctive to all Greeks. At the same time you'll come to respect the local business acumen: shoppers beware!

Powerful Poseidon, the sea god, in a dramatic pose illustrates consummate artistry of Ancients.

A Brief History

2000–776 B.C.	First Hellenic races (Achaeans, Aeolians and Ionians) descend from north and settle on Greek mainland (Mycenaean civilization). Siege of Troy (1400–1390 B.C.). Invasion of Dorians who destroy Mycenaean culture (1100 B.C.).
776–500 B.C.	776 B.C. first recording of Olympic Games. Although city-states of Athens, Sparta, Thebes and others are often at war, they share common sense of identity: they are all Greeks with same language and religion. Athens dominates entire peninsula and experiences all forms of government—from monarchy to democracy to dictatorship and back to democracy. The country produces great poets, law-makers, generals, statesmen and philosophers.
500–176 B.C.	Persian wars which influence entire history of Europe. 490 B.C. Athenians defeat Darius' vastly superior forces at Marathon. 480 B.C. a few Greek troops under Leonidas hold up enormous Persian army un-

der Xerxes at pass of Thermopylae long enough for Athens to be evacuated, before Xerxes plunders the city and burns all wooden constructions. In same year Greece's much smaller fleet under Themistocles trounces Persians in the bay of Salamis. In final and decisive battle at Plataea, Persians beaten and Greek independence ensured (479 B.C.). Athens reaches its Golden Age of art, literature, philosophy and science under rule of Pericles. Parthenon built. 431–407 B.C. Peloponnesian War between Athens and Sparta won by latter with naval help from Persians. Philip II of Macedon, father of Alexander the Great, takes political lead after battle of Charioneia (338 B.C.). Macedonian troops occupy Athens in 322 and again in 262 B.C. while the city continues to decline.

176 B.C.– A.D. 326	Macedonia becomes Roman province (146 B.C.). In 86 B.C. Roman General Sulla sacks Athens in retribution for its alliance with one of Rome's enemies, and many Athenian treasures are taken to Rome. After visit of St. Paul (A.D. 50) Christianity starts to take root in Greece.
326–1204	Emperor Constantine chooses Greek colonial town of Byzantium as his "New Rome" and calls it Constantinople. During Byzantine rule, Athens sinks into provincial obscurity. In 529 Emperor Justinian puts definite end to Greek polytheism by closing last "pagan" temples and Athenian schools of philosophy.
1204–1821	After being ruled by adventurers from Burgundy, Catalonia and Florence, Athens and Attica fall to Turks in 1456. Venetians briefly take Athens from Turks in 1466 and again in 1687 when they damage the Parthenon. The Ottoman rule is Greece's darkest age, and only the Orthodox Church provides people with a sense of continuity with the past.
1821–1913	Greek war of independence. With foreign help (Lord Byron has popularized cause abroad), Greeks finally win against Turks. 1834 Athens becomes capital of Greece. Great Powers install Bavarian Prince Otto as king. He and Queen Amalia deposed in 1862 and after European diplomatic bargaining, William

of the Danish royal house takes Greek throne as George I, King of Hellenes, until his assassination in 1913.

1913– Cretan politician Venizelos, several times prime minister, helps Greece regain Macedonia, most of Aegean Islands and Epirus. Under population exchange agreement with Turkey (1922), many repatriated Greeks flood into Athens. 1934–40 Greece under dictatorship of Metaxas. During World War II Greece invaded and controlled by Germans, until freed by Allied forces in 1944. 1947–49 Civil War which ends with Communist defeat. 1967 Military dictatorship seizes power forcing King Constantine into exile. 1974 regime of the colonels crumbles. With King Constantine still in exile, popular referendum abolishes monarchy, and democracy with free elections is restored.

---

1 Post Office   2 National Library   3 Byzantine Museum   4 Parliament
5 National Gardens   6 Temple of Olympian Zeus   7 Tower of the Winds

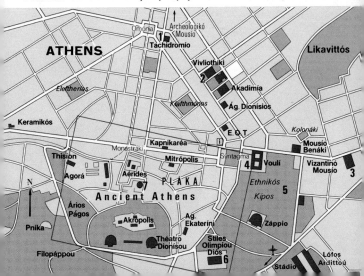

Piraeus and Modern Athens

More than half a million people live in Piraeus, the Mediterranean's third-largest port and part of greater Athens.

You may not recognize the Piraeus that soared to fame with the film *Never on Sunday* —seamen's cafés and down-and-out port-front bars are dying out, and the streets once peopled by ladies of the even-ing and bosun's mates now are lined with marbled banks catering for big shipping and oil clients.

But you can still find local colour especially at **Tourkolimano** (officially called Mikrolimano). Here you can eat at one of the enticing seafood restaurants ringing the tiny yacht basin, and watch the fluffing of brightly coloured canvas and the bobbing of masts. Included in your outdoor dining programme will be a stream of

gardenia vendors, fortune tellers, guitar players strumming Theodorakis tunes, pistachio salesmen. None will press too hard. The only thieves you'll encounter on this enchanting waterfront will be the overfed cats (if you give something to one, you'll end up with 30 or 40 around you).

In Athens, you can get your bearings from the two great squares: elegant **Syntagma** and dowdier **Omonia.** They're perhaps a ten minute stroll apart, linked directly by two major streets, Stadiou and Venizelou.

On Syntagma (its name celebrates the March 1844 Greek constitution) are de luxe hotels, expensive cafés, and tall glass-and-concrete buildings containing air terminals, travel agencies, banks, post offices and international business concerns.

Across the upper, east side of the square is Greece's Parliament, until 1935 the royal palace. Soldiers in traditional uniform guard a memorial to the nation's unknown warrior in the forecourt.

The oldest quarter of Athens —and by far the most charming—is the **Plaka.** People have lived continuously for more than 3,000 years in this picturesque maze huddled against the northern slope of the Acropolis. Ancient ruins, Byzantine churches, shops, cafés, hotels, bars and nightclubs are packed into less than one quarter of a square mile.

Ancient Athens

The Acropolis

This 10-acre (4-ha.) rock rising 300 feet (90 m.) above the plain of Attica was the making of ancient Athens. Battered and incomplete though it may now be, the Acropolis possesses such majesty that it still ranks among the world's true wonders. The name means "high town", from the Greek *acro* (highest point) and *polis* (town or city). Alternately it means "citadel", which it was originally—a place of defence shared by gods, kings and heroes.

The visitors' entrance is the Beulé Gate (a 3rd-century-A.D. Roman addition named after the French archaeologist who discovered it in 1852).

The Propylaea. Six Doric columns mark this monumental entranceway to the Acropolis. The Propylaea was planned by Pericles and his architect Mnesicles as the most spec-

tacular secular building in Greece, more complex than the Parthenon which it was designed to complement. Construction began in 437 B.C. but was halted five years later by the Peloponnesian War and never finished.

The central and largest of the gateways was for chariots and approached by a ramp; steps lead up to the four other entries destined for lesser mortals. The well-preserved building on the north (left) side housed a gallery of paintings by famous artists offered to Athena.

The Temple of Athena Nike. High on a terrace off to the right (south-west) of the Propylaea perches this enchanting temple, the work of architect Callicrates. It enjoys a glorious panorama of the sea and distant mountains. Tiny compared with the Parthenon towards which it points, the temple of Athena Nike (also called Wingless Victory) now

standing is a piece-by-piece modern reconstruction of what remained after the Turks tore down the original in 1687.

Passing through the Propylaea, you emerge onto the great sloping plateau of the Acropolis. Try to imagine what it was like 2,400 years ago, when these masterworks of architecture and sculpture were going up. Scores of stone cutters, carpenters, founders and others swarmed over this site.

Dominating the immediate foreground was a gigantic bronze statue of Athena under another guise—Athena Promachos, the Defender. This statue of the goddess holding shield and spear was created by Phidias to honour the victory at Marathon. The great statue stood here for 1,000 years, until it was carted off to Constantinople in the 6th century A.D. You'll see no more than scattered fragments of its base near an upright slab-relief of a maiden.

The Parthenon. This miracle of marbled harmony was inspired by Phidias, the sculptural, architectural and artistic genius of classical Athens. It was executed by architects Ictinus and Callicrates and commissioned by Pericles to replace the Acropolis sanctuaries destroyed by the Persians.

Work on the Parthenon (which means Temple of the Virgin) began in 447 B.C. Two-hundred and twenty-eight feet long and 101 feet wide (68 × 30 m.), its 46 exterior columns rise 34 feet, each consisting of about a dozen fluted marble drums placed one above the other.

The columns swell gently at the middle and lean slightly inwards. It is no optical illusion: the Parthenon is an unfinished pyramid with an apex projected to achieve itself at an altitude of about 3,000 feet.

Originally the Parthenon was decorated with sculptures at three levels. Very little of this remains. The renowned "Elgin Marbles", removed by the British ambassador to Constantinople at the beginning of the 19th century with Turkish permission, can be seen in the British Museum.

During its current restoration, the Parthenon is out of bounds to tourists.

The Acropolis Museum. Here you will be able to enjoy outstanding pieces of archaic and classical Greek sculpture at your ease—and get out of the sun. Every exhibit in the cool interior of this outstanding museum was found on the Acropolis.

The Erechtheion. Across the Acropolis plateau at the northern wall stands the Erechtheion. The identity of the chief architect remains something of a mystery. His task certainly was not easy. First he had to house three cults—those of Athena, Poseidon and Erechtheus—in one building; he had to work on irregular ground, meaning sharply different foundations; and finally, though much smaller than the Parthenon, his temple had to be able to hold its own. One additional difficulty: the Erechtheion, the last temple to go up on the Acropolis, was built entirely in wartime. Construction took 15 years, with dedication in 406 B.C.

The north porch is considered a work of great architectural genius. Note its dark-blue marble frieze, panelled ceiling and the bases and capitals of its distinguished columns.

Those six bigger-than-life-sized maidens holding up the roof of the south porch are the famous **Caryatids**. These days models stand in for the originals. Four of the Caryatids—together with what remains of the fifth—are recovering in the Acropolis Museum.

Before leaving the Acropolis, succumb to the temptation to linger over the view: Athena Nike's temple faces west towards the Bay of Salamis above which Xerxes watched his fleet sink. Far beyond that are the mountains of the Peloponnesus, nestling the citadel of ancient Corinth. To the left, islands of the Saronic Gulf. Behind the violet shoulder of Hymettos to the east is Cape Sounion.

Other Major Sights
The Temple of Olympian Zeus.
As was only fitting for the ruler of the gods, this temple was the largest in ancient Greece. But it took a Roman to complete it—almost 700 years after construction started.

Back in the 6th century B.C., they say, the tyrant Pisistratus and his sons conceived of the monumental building project to keep the population too busy to plot against their rule. But the temple was only finally finished off by Roman

Models replace Erechtheion's maidens, now on view in the Acropolis Museum.

Emperor Hadrian in A.D. 132. It had 104 Corinthian columns, each 56 feet (17 m.) high and more than 7 feet (2 m.) thick. Today only 15 remain upright.

To mark the separation of his own Athens from the ancient city of Theseus, an arched gateway was erected facing the temple. Relatively modest in size, **Hadrian's Arch** is thought to have been a donation from the people of Athens.

The Agora. The Agora is almost as old as Athens itself. Originally the word meant "a gathering together", later the place where people met and conducted business. Sprawling under the northern walls of the Acropolis, it was the heart of the ancient "lower city", the market-place and civic centre.

Today only rubble and foundations remain of the marble or stone altars, temples, law courts, state offices, public archives, shops, concert hall, dance floor and gymnasium that stood here. A panoramic, pictorial reconstruction on a pedestal by the main entrance on Odos Adrianou helps you visualize the Agora in its golden days.

The Olympic Stadium. In the hollow of Arditos Hill, the modern Olympic Stadium is on the site of the stone original built by Lycurgus in 330 B.C. In the 2nd century A.D. Emperor Hadrian introduced Rome's favourite sport here: he imported thousands of wild animals to be pitted against gladiators.

The stadium, built for the first modern Olympics in 1896, seats 70,000 people. Its length is just over 600 feet (180 m.) or one *"stadion"*. In form it's identical to the ancient U-shaped stadiums at Olympia and Delphi.

Sounion

Poseidon's renowned temple crowns this promontory 45 miles (70 km.) south of Athens, as beautiful a place to watch the sun set or rise as there is in the Aegean.

The marble temple, with 15 of its original 34 Doric columns now standing, was built about 444 B.C. Another of stone had been started in this obviously commanding location, but the Persians destroyed it in 490 B.C. The precipice is a sheer 197-foot (60-m.) drop to the sea.

Lord Byron, whose name you'll see carved on one of the pillars, was so inspired by Sounion that he wrote a famous poem about it.

Eating Out

Although Athens can hardly claim to be a gourmet's paradise, you'll find eating here very satisfying, perhaps even exciting—and often in a pleasant outdoor setting.

Most restaurants will serve the following specialities:

Appetizers

Melidzanosalata: a baked aubergine purée flavoured with garlic, onions and herbs.

Dzadziki: a yoghurt dip of sliced cucumber, flavoured with garlic.

Taramosalata: a spread of *tarama* (grey mullet roe), mashed potatoes, bread, olive oil and lemon juice. Dip bread in it as an appetizer or have it on lettuce as a salad.

Soup

Soupa avgolemono: a soup of chicken or meat, eggs and rice, flavoured with lemon.

Fish

Astakos: spiny lobster; *barbouni:* red mullet; *fagri:* sea bream; *garides:* prawns; *glossa:* sole; *kalamaraki:* squid; *kefalos:* grey mullet; *lithrini:* spotted bream; *marides:* similar to sprats; *chtapodi:* octopus.

Meat

Dolmades: grape leaves stuffed with lamb and rice, seasoned with wine, grated onion and herbs. Often served hot with lemon sauce.

Kolokithia gemista me rizi ke kima: marrow (zucchini) stuffed with rice and meat.

Keftedes: meatballs, flavoured with onion, cinnamon, oregano, mint and wine. Baked or deep-fried in oil and served with a sauce.

Moussaka: sliced aubergine and minced meat, baked with a white sauce and grated cheese.

Salads

Don't miss the delicious "village" salads *(salata choriatiki),* sliced vegetables topped with *feta,* a cheese made from sheep's milk.

Wine

The first time you sip Retsina, you may get a shock; it's flavoured with resin and has a turpentine-like taste but it rarely causes hangovers and helps digest rich, oily foods.

Of the unresinated wines Demestica, white or red, is popular, and Santa Helena and Pallini are pleasant, dry whites. Reds are Naoussa and Santa Laoura, and some refreshing lighter rosés can also be found.

Other Drinks

The national aperitif is *ouzo,* a clear, aniseed-flavoured spirit. Greek brandy is sweet and quite agreeable. Metaxa is the best known; Kamba is a little drier. Greek beer *(bira)* is excellent.

Snacks

Ask for *souvlakia,* meat and vegetables grilled on a skewer; spicy sausages *(giros)* and *doner kebab,* meat cooked on a spit, or *souvlaki me pitta,* grilled meat, tomatoes, peppers and onions in a flat bun *(pitta).*

Shopping

Try not to buy on impulse: things are not always what they seem in Greece. The best bet is to stick to handmade items. Labour costs are still low, and the quality of rural

and island handicrafts remains high.

Rugs and Carpets. *Flokati* rugs—priced by the kilo (a square metre weighs about 2½ kilos)—come machine-made or, preferably, hand-woven. They are made of pure sheep's wool shag, spun from fibres into yarn and then looped together to be processed under water.

Furs. If purchased intelligently, fur coats, stoles, capes and hats—made from pelts hand-sewn together—can be a handsome bargain. You'll find mink, muskrat, beaver, red fox, stone marten and Persian lamb.

The secret of the pelt-strip coat lies in the sewing, which varies in quality. Shop carefully around Syntagma, and verify the quality and origin of the pelt.

Jewellery. Reproductions of museum jewellery in gold and silver are definitely worth a second look.

You'll find the best jewellery shops in the Voukourestiou and Panepistimiou area. Gold and silver are sold by weight; each item should be weighed in front of you. Some gold rings are made from two different purities; check for hollowness and correct weight-price equivalents. Enamel cannot be graded for quality, so cast a suspicious eye on anything which seems too spectacular.

Icons and Folk Art. Buying icons is a tricky business. Warped and cracked wood doesn't necessary mean that it's old or Byzantine. Note that you must have government permission to export authentic originals and that icon smuggling is a jailable offence in Greece.

For genuine folk art, some antique shops display **tamata,** the silver votive offerings you'll see attached to church icons. They're mainly aluminium now, but still fashioned in the shapes of the parts of the body. Origins of this practice date to the ancient world of Zeus and Athena.

Brightly coloured **plates** with ship, fish and floral patterns, from Lindos on Rhodes, are good value in Athens.

Practical Information

Banks and currency exchange: Generally 8 a.m.–2 p.m., Monday–Friday. Currency can be changed at some banks' foreign-exchange bureaux until 7 or 8 p.m. In Syntagma Square, the National Bank of Greece is open 8 a.m. to 8 p.m., Monday–Friday, and 9 a.m. to 4 p.m. on Saturdays and Sundays.

Credit cards and traveller's cheques: Major names of both are usually accepted by those shops selling anything of substantial interest to the visitor. For dining out, however, you're better off relying on cash.

Currency: The *drachma*. Coins: 1, 2, 5, 10, 20, 50 drachmas. Notes: 50, 100, 500, 1,000, 5,000 drachmas.

Post offices: The post office at Syntagma is open weekdays from 7.30 a.m. to 8.30 p.m., Saturdays from 7.30 a.m. to 3 p.m. and Sundays from 9 a.m. to 2 p.m. Stamps can also be purchased at news-stands and souvenir shops, but at a 10% surcharge. Letter boxes are painted yellow.

Restaurants: Lunch 12 to 2 p.m., dinner 8 to midnight. Service is included but you should leave a bit extra for the waiter.

Shops: Open Monday, Wednesday, Saturday: 8 a.m. to 2.30 or 3 p.m.; Tuesday, Thursday, Friday: 8 a.m. to 1.30 and 5 to 8 p.m. (Tourist-oriented shops stay open much later.)

BARCELONA

Spain

Introduction

Close on two million people live within the boundaries of Barcelona, a centre of banking, publishing and industry. Another million live in the surrounding metropolitan area. The city's attractions for visitors are renowned—the mighty cathedral, the port, gracious promenades and distinguished museums. You have to be alert for the smaller delights: a noble patio hidden from view, a tiled park bench moulded to the anatomy, a street-light fixture lovingly worked in iron, a sculpted gargoyle scowling down from medieval eaves.

The lively people of Barcelona know how to make money. They spend it on flowers

Plaça del Rei, King's Square, recalls the era of Columbus.

and football, music and books, and gooey pastries for their children. They enjoy the bull-fights and dancing in the street. They go to gourmet snack-bars and sexy floor-shows, and wear formal evening dress to the opera house.

In the Middle Ages Barcelona was the capital of a surprisingly influential Catalonia. Thirteenth-century Barcelona, ruling distant cities of the Mediterranean, was building the ships commemorated today in the Maritime Museum, and living by Europe's first code of sea law.

The next great era, economically and artistically, came with late 19th-century industrialization. Politically, the 20th century witnessed a brief revival. In 1931, Barcelona became the capital of an autonomous Catalan Republic that came to an end in 1939 when General Franco triumphed.

After Franco's death, the Catalan spirit was unshackled and regional power restored to Barcelona. The capital of Wilfred the Hairy and James the Conqueror remains an outward-looking, eminently European city.

A Brief History

4th century B.C.–5th century A.D.	Phoenicians and Greeks bring commerce and culture to Catalonia. The Carthaginians give Barcelona its original name, Barcino, in honour of General Hamilcar Barca, father of the legendary Hannibal. In the 2nd Punic War the Romans defeat Carthage; they rule Iberia for the next six centuries. By the 5th century A.D., Rome's grip slackens and Spain is overrun by Vandals and Visigoths.
8th–12th centuries	The next invasion occurs in 711 when Moorish forces from Africa assail the Iberian Peninsula. As Muslim civilization takes root, Christian efforts to reconquer Spain begin. Charlemagne captures Barcelona from the Moors and Catalonia becomes a Frankish dependency called the Spanish March. Count Wilfred the Hairy wins the independence of Barcelona from the Frankish king, Charles the Bald, in 878, ushering in a period of prosperity commercially, politically and intellectually. Count Ramón Berenguer I of Barcelona draws up a constitution called the *Usatges* in 1060.

Ramón Berenguer IV (1131–62) marries a princess of Aragon, an expansionist tactic which creates a sizeable joint kingdom.

13th–16th centuries

With the addition of two dukedoms in Greece, the seizure of Sardinia and annexation of Corsica, Catalonia dominates the Mediterranean. Catalan culture flourishes, great churches are constructed and works of art created. The discovery of the New World proves disastrous for Catalonia. The Mediterranean loses much of its importance as a trading zone and Barcelona declines as a commercial centre.

17th–19th centuries

Seventeenth-century Catalonia rebels against Philip IV of Spain. Violent struggles continue for more than a decade, until a besieged Barcelona finally surrenders and Catalonia renews its allegiance to the Spanish crown. In the War of the Spanish Succession (1701–1714), Catalonia sides with Archduke Charles of Austria. The Bourbon King Philip V triumphs and Barcelona is overrun. The Catalonian parliament is disbanded and the Catalan language banned. Catalonia becomes little more than a satellite of France. Throughout the 19th century, Catalonia is embroiled in a succession of disastrous wars, beginning with the War of the Third Coalition in 1805 and ending with the Spanish American War of 1898. In the first, Spain was defeated by Nelson at the Battle of Trafalgar, and in the latter it lost the colonies of Cuba, Puerto Rico and the Philippines.

20th century

Three decades after the empire fades away, King Alfonso XIII goes into exile as confusion and disorder grow in Spain. The Republicans, who favour socialist and anti-clerical policies, gain control in several Spanish cities. Catalonia is proclaimed an autonomous republic. But Spain is a divided nation, and civil war breaks out between the conservative Nationalists and the Republicans. Barcelona falls to the Nationalists in January 1939 and Catalonia is absorbed into General Franco's Spain. On Franco's death in 1975, King Juan Carlos I is crowned. After the years of repression, the language and culture of Catalonia flourish anew, and regional autonomy has been granted.

Sightseeing

The Barri Gòtic
(Gothic Quarter)

The nucleus of old Barcelona, the Barri Gòtic is concentrated round the cathedral. Here are elements from just about every century since Iberian tribesmen first settled on the site over 2,000 years ago.

On the spot where the cathedral stands today, the Romans dedicated a temple to Hercules (you will see three remaining columns in nearby Carrer del Paradís). Two early Christian basilicas occupied the area before construction of the present **Catedral de Santa Eulalia** between 1298 and 1454. Don't be taken in by the façade, however—it dates from the end of the 19th century, when new work on the cathedral began, thanks to a subsidy from a rich industrialist.

The interior is laid out in classic Catalan Gothic form, with three aisles neatly designed to produce an effect of grandeur and uplift. Impossibly slender columns soar upwards to support the nave; muted golden light filters through 500-year-old stained-glass—one of the most striking characteristics of Catalan Gothic architecture.

Below the altar lies the Crypt of St. Eulalia, the 13-year-old martyr to whom the cathedral is dedicated. Bas-relief carvings on the 14th-century alabaster sarcophagus supply vividly gruesome details of her torture and execution. Behind the altar, in the Chapel of the Holy Sacrament, have a look at the Christ of Lepanto. Juan de Austria carried this sacred image during the decisive sea battle of Lepanto (Spaniards and Venetians versus the Turks), and legend has it that the image of Christ moved its body at precisely the right moment to escape a bullet.

Pride of the **Cathedral Museum,** with its religious paintings and sculpture from the 14th century onwards, is undoubtedly the *Piedad del Arcediano Desplá,* executed in 1490 by Bartolomé Bermejo on commission from an egocentric archdeacon, who is pictured kneeling in the foreground of this transcendental Biblical scene.

The nearby Carrer de la Tapineria—where cobblers made shoes called *tapín*—leads to Plaça de Berenguer el Gran. Behind the modern equestrian statue of Ramón Berenguer III (who ruled Catalonia from 1096 to 1131) stands a reconstructed Roman wall. You can follow the wall for a fair dis-

CASA MICENC

La Pedrera

Carrer de Provença

Temple Expiatori
de la Sagrada
Família

Avinguda Diagonal

Carrer de València

Carrer de València

Conservatori
Municipal
de Música

Carrer d'Aragó

Casa Batlló

Carrer del Consell del Cent

Plaça de Toros
Monumental

Universitat Central

Gran Via   de les   Corts Catalanes

Ronda Universitat

Oficinas
de Turismo

Plaça de
Catalunya

Carrer d'Ausias Marc

Ronda Sant Pere

Carrer de Ribes

Palau de
la Música

Arc del
Triomf

Sant Pere
Puelles

Palau
de Justicia

Pt. Nova

Pg. de Pujades

Pl. Berenguer
el Gran

Parc
de la
Ciutadella

Gran Teatre
del Liceu

C. de Ferran   C. de la Princesa
Plaça de St. Jaume L'Angel

Pg. de Picasso

Rambla

Plaça
Reial

Sta. Maria
del Mar

Museu d'Art
Modern

Palau
Güell

Correus

Llotja

Estació
Terminal França

Museu
de Cera

Esglèsia
de la Mercè

Colom

Monument   de   Colom

Avinguda d'Icària

Passeig Colom

Duana

Transbordador Aeri

Estació
Marítima

Acuario

1 Antic Hospital
   de Santa Creu
2 Palau de la Virreina
3 Esglèsia de Betlem
4 Palau Episcopal
5 Palau de la Generalitat
6 Catedral
7 Plaça del Rei

8 Casa de la Ciutat (Ajuntament)
9 Museu de l'Indumentaria
10 Museu Picasso
11 Museu de Zoologia
12 Museu Martorell
13 Zoo
14 Drassanes (Museu Maritim)

tance on either side of the Plaça de l'Ángel.

Not far away is the **Museu d'Història de la Ciutat** (Museum of City History), housed in a stately 16th-century palace. There are paintings, tapestries, maps and documents of municipal import. But the real spectacle is below ground, for beneath the museum are the remains of a settlement the Romans called Julia Faventía Augusta Pia Barcino. Houses, a drainage system, roads and marketplaces have been excavated. The well-lit, clearly documented underground archaeological zone now extends as far as the cathedral.

A typical street of old Andalusia is transplanted to Poble Espanyol.

The museum windows face onto **Plaça del Rei** (King's Square), where, in the Middle Ages, farmers sold their produce and locksmiths made bolts. Here, too, is **Saló del Tinell** (Tinell Hall), where Columbus may have been welcomed by Ferdinand and Isabella on his return from America. The extraordinary span of the meeting hall's ceiling, without a column or support, represents a remarkable technical feat.

Beside the hall, the Archives of the Crown of Aragon contain documents dating back to the 9th century, as well as some very ancient books.

Two other highly important buildings of medieval civic architecture remain to be visited: the Generalitat (Provincial Council) and Casa de la Ciutat or Ajuntament (City Hall), facing one another on Plaça de Sant Jaume. The **Palau de la Generalitat** is the seat of the Catalonian Parliament. This ceremonial 15th-century structure hides a surprise or two: the overpowering ornamentation of St. George's Room and an upstairs patio with orange trees. The **Casa de la Ciutat** still serves, from time to time, for meetings, and the impressive 14th-century Saló del Consell de Cent (Hall of the Council of One Hundred) does honour to any assembly.

La Rambla

Barcelona's best-now promenade, **La Rambla,** descends gradually but excitingly from Plaça de Catalunya to the port, a distance of about a mile. Like the women of Barcelona, La Rambla is full of life, self-assurance and charm. Almost every visitor succumbs to the attractions of this boulevard, thronged day and night with a fascinating crowd of people, animals and things.

Every couple of cross-streets, the Rambla's character changes. So does its official name: Rambla dels Estudis, Rambla dels Caputxins, Rambla de Santa Mónica and others—five in all—which explains why very often it's simply referred to as Les Rambles.

To walk down La Rambla's full extent from the Plaça de Catalunya to the Monument a Colom (Columbus Monument) is an experience, an entertainment and an education. You can buy a canary, a monkey, a mouse or a turtle; a carnation, an orchid, a potted plant or a bird-of-paradise flower, a packet of nuts or one cigarette from a news-stand. Here the bookstalls stock all the papers and magazines of Europe, gypsies insinuate hot watches, lottery sellers flutter tickets practically guaranteed to win you a million.

Visit the **frontón** to see a game of *pelota* (called *jai-alai* in the Basque country). The ball flashes around the court at speeds of up to 125 miles per hour. The betting around you is even more frantic; split tennis balls stuffed with gaming slips whizz overhead.

Need a rest? Stop at one of the multitude of bars and cafés lining La Rambla while traffic streams by in a seemingly endless flow, barely noticed—except by the waiters, brandishing their trays aloft, who dodge to and fro to their sources of supply between serried ranks of cars.

Alternatively, leave bustling La Rambla, go through a small arcade and find yourself in the quiet, stately **Plaça Reial,** the city's finest square. Or simply hire a chair on the Rambla. People-watching is a cheap entertainment by any standards, and there's hours-worth to watch.

The **Mercat de Sant Josep** (Boqueria), St. Joseph's Market, faces La Rambla. You have to wander among the eye-catching displays to appreciate the wealth of fresh fruit and vegetables, meat and seafood available here. The fish are lovingly laid out on crushed ice.

The **Palau de la Virreina** is one of the most sumptuous buildings on the Rambla. It houses the city hall Department of Culture, as well as the Postal Museum and the Numismatic Cabinet. Other floors of the palace are used for topical exhibitions.

The Rambla leads on down to the Columbus monument

and the port. Whether you stay in the shade of the tall plane trees on the promenade or cross the traffic to window-shop along the edges of the street (where you can buy anything from a guitar to a deep-sea diving-bell), you'll want to walk the Rambla from beginning to end and back again. For this is surely where it's all happening.

On the other side of La Rambla, entering at the Plaça del Teatre, are the noisy streets of the infamous **Barri Chino** ("Chinatown"). Al-

The Sardana

The energetic yet graceful national dance of Catalonia, the *sardana,* with its haunting woodwind accompaniment, hypnotizes Catalans wherever they may be. The exact origins of this disciplined ring dance are unknown. But in the *Iliad,* Homer describes a Greek dance very like the *sardana,* and researchers suggest that Greeks may have introduced it to Catalonia when they were established in Ampurias and elsewhere on the coast.

The deceptively simple-looking *sardana* is danced in normal everyday clothes, except on special occasions, and very often Catalans simply put their satchels, bags or briefcases in the centre of the circle. The dancers form a circle which grows as newcomers join it. If it proves unwieldy, they simply form another. If they run out of room, they make circles within circles. Each group has a leader who keeps meticulous time and signals changes. If he makes one error his ring loses its rhythm and can't complete the final step in time with the band.

The wonder of the *sardana,* quickly noted by visitors, is the spirit it generates. The dance—performed in many resorts on weekend evenings—cuts all barriers. Doctors and farmers dance together; long-haired students join the same circle as middle-aged housewives. They may have little in common in everyday life, but the *sardana* reminds them that, whatever their social differences, they are Catalans. Even tourists can, technically, join in. In actual fact, prudence is advisable. There is a fairly strict rule that puts an end to most tourists' ambitions: no local would ever move into a circle that has a much higher standard of dancing than he is capable of, and the uninitiated visitor might thus find himself edged out.

though prostitution was outlawed in Spain in 1956, the colourful denizens of Barri Chino's bars have, one might gather, yet to be notified, and the area has a classic air of portside low-life.

Montjuïc

Montjuïc (pronounced mon-ZHWEEK) is a modest mountain less than 700 feet (some 200 metres) high. It long had only military significance. But Barcelona's World Exhibition of 1929 saw hundreds of buildings planted upon its hillsides. One of them, the Palau Nacional, houses the **Museu d'Art de Catalunya** (Museum of Art of Catalonia), a great collection of medieval art; another, the Palace of Graphic Arts, has been turned into the **Museu Arqueològic** (Archaeological Museum), displaying prehistoric finds from Catalonia and the Balearic Islands.

The **Museu Etnològic** (Ethnological Museum) of Montjuïc is devoted to specimens gathered by expeditions to exotic far-off places. While the newest museum on the mountain, opened in 1975, goes under the name of **Fundació Joan Miró**. This complex of original concrete-and-glass buildings, the work of architect Josep M. Sert, pays tribute to

the great Catalan artist Joan Miró.

Perhaps the most popular sight of Montjuïc is **Poble Espanyol,** a five-acre exhibition of Spanish art and architecture in the form of an artificial village designed to show off the charms and styles of Spain's regions.

The Waterfront

Glass-and-steel commercial castles may come and go, but the Drassanes, or medieval shipyards, are special. From these royal dockyards were launched the ships which carried the red-and-yellow Catalan flag to the far corners of the world as it was known before Columbus. Since 1941 the **Museu Marítim** (Maritime Museum) has occupied the site. An annexe of the Maritime Museum is moored at the wharf of Portal de la Pau (Gate of Peace): a full-sized replica of the *Santa María,* Columbus's own flagship. You may board the floating mini-museum any time during the day.

The **Museu Picasso** is located in three contiguous 13th-century palaces in Carrer de Montcada, a short walk inland. Though Pablo Ruiz Picasso was born in Málaga, he came to Barcelona at the age of 14 to study art. The museum displays

"Aerial ropeway" over Barcelona's port offers panorama of lively city.

examples of his early work, as well as a selection of paintings, drawings and prints spanning the decades from the 1920s through the '60s.

Gaudí and "Eixample"

The "Eixample"—the new city which grew beyond the medieval walls in the 19th century—contains some of the most creative buildings ever designed, the work of Barcelona's inspired *art nouveau* architects at the turn of the century.

The greatest of them all was Antoni Gaudí, a controversial genius who died in Barcelona in 1926, run down by a tram.

Take a look at some of Gaudí's famous projects: **Palau Güell,** just off the bustling Rambla, is noted for its innovative façade, decorated with imaginative ironwork. **Casa Milá ("La Pedrera")**, a block of flats on the corner of Passeig de Gràcia and Carrer de Provença, has an undulating façade and a roof-terrace with weird formations covering chimneys and ventilators. **Casa Vicenç**, Gaudí's first big commission, sports the distinctive ironwork and tile that became the hallmark of his style.

Parc Güell started out as a suburban real estate development which failed. Count Güell and Gaudí wanted to create a perfect garden city for 60 families. But only two houses were sold (Gaudí bought one of them). Explore the grounds and discover that the plaza is in fact the roof for what would have been a market-place supported by a thicket of mock-classical columns. The last column in each regiment is playfully askew.

Temple Expiatori de la Sagrada Familia (Holy Family), Gaudí's eternally unfinished "sandcastle cathedral", must be seen; you may not believe it. Wild and wonderful, it is an extravagant hymn to one man's talent and faith. Many Catalans look on this stupendous church as an extension of their own faith and strivings; their donations keep the construction work going.

Eating Out

The Catalans appreciate hearty dishes based on honest ingredients fresh from the farm—and the sea. If you share this enthusiasm, some memorable treats are in store.

Since the Mediterranean is near at hand, the accent is on fish. Here are some of the varieties you'll be offered, normally fried or grilled: *lenguado*—sole; *mero*—sea bass; *salmonetes*—Mediterranean red mullet; *calamares*—squid; *gambas*—prawns (shrimp); *langosta*—spiny lobster.

Perhaps the greatest speciality of Catalonia is *zarzuela,* a triumphant concoction of up to a dozen different kinds of seafood, including prawns, shrimp and clams, octopus, squid and various white fish, all topped by a brandy-and-wine sauce. *Esqueixada* (pronounced eskay-SHA-da) is a stimulating salad of cod, beans, pickled onions and tomato.

Xató (pronounced sha-TO) *de Sitges* is a related, but more complicated salad including anchovies, tunny fish or cod and a hot sauce made of olive oil, vinegar, red pepper, diced anchovies, garlic and ground almonds.

Pa amb tomàquet goes well with any salad. Peasant-style

bread, in huge slices, is smeared with fresh tomato and grilled.

Butifarra, a rich pork sausage, may be served with chips, vegetables or eggs. *Habas a la catalana* are broad beans cooked with ham and *butifarra.*

The sweetest temptation of all is *crema catalana,* custard with a glazed caramel topping.

Wines

The provinces of Barcelona and Tarragona produce good wine. Priorato is a well-known red wine of the region. White or rosé Tarragona wines are notable. Penedés can be red or white. In Sitges a dessert wine, malmsey (*malvasía* in Spanish), is produced. And the Penedés region is a major source of the world's best-selling white sparkling wine, called *cava.* Sangría, a mixture of red wine, lemon and orange juice, brandy, mineral water, ice and slices of fruit, is rather like punch.

Shopping

Barcelona, with its fashionable shops, offers variety and quality, but no single street or neighbourhood will satisfy your window-shopping. The commercial area is so extensive that you might have to walk miles to compare quality and value.

Tourists from abroad will be refunded the value-added tax (called IVA) they pay on purchases over a stipulated amount. To obtain the rebate, you have to fill in a form, provided by the shop. The shop keeps one copy; the three others must be presented at the customs on departure, together with the goods. The rebate will then be forwarded by the shop to your home address.

Best Buys

Catalonian **ceramics** range from the primitive to the sophisticated—and they're always original.

An intensive cottage industry along the coast produces **leather goods,** mainly handbags and items of clothing. The quality of the leather and the workmanship is erratic and so is the style—you have to look around. High fashion shoes and boots are top-class but expensive.

Embroidery, lacework and **woven goods** such as rugs and bedspreads are produced in coastal villages which keep alive the old patterns and skills.

Jewellery, either simple modern designs or traditional styles with lots of silver or gold fili-

76

gree, can include bargains for the knowledgeable.

For less expansive budgets, there are **records** of Catalan music—the *sardana* played by those reed bands, or emotional choral works. Or local **glasswork,** such as the *porrón,* from which wine is projected through the air to the consumer.

Among the best buys of any trip to Spain are **alcohol** and **tobacco,** which remain inexpensive by European and American standards.

Look for **antiques** in the shops concentrated around the cathedral. Dealers carry the real thing, as well as reproductions; sometimes the dividing line becomes blurred.

Practical Information

Banks: Business is transacted from 9 a.m. to 2 p.m. Monday to Friday, till 1 p.m. on Saturday. Money can be changed outside normal banking hours at hotels, travel agencies and other businesses displaying a *cambio* sign. Always take your passport with you when changing money.

Currency: The monetary unit of Spain is the *peseta* (abbreviated *pta.*). Coins: 1, 2, 5, 10, 25, 50, 100, 200 and 500 pesetas. Banknotes: 500, 1,000, 2,000, 5,000 and 10,000 pesetas.

Post offices: Branch offices open from 9 a.m. to 1 or 2 p.m. and 4 or 5 to 6 or 7 p.m. Monday to Friday, mornings only on Saturdays. Barcelona's main post office is open from 9 a.m. to 9 p.m. Monday to Friday, 9 a.m. to 2 p.m. on Saturdays.

Shops: Open from 9 a.m. to 2 p.m. and from 4 to 8 p.m. or later. Apart from the big department stores, all businesses observe the midday pause.

Restaurants: Lunch is served from about 1 to 3 or 4 p.m., and dinner from 8 or 9 to 11 p.m. or later.

Tipping: Since a service charge is normally included in restaurant and hotel bills, tipping is optional. However, it is appropriate to give something to porters, lavatory attendants, taxi drivers, tourist guides and so on.

BERLIN

Germany

Introduction

More than a place, Berlin is an idea: few cities have a more dramatically evocative name.

Brandenburg Gate, with its goddess of Victory on her chariot, continues to honour the formidable Prussian past. The Kurfürstendamm, at once elegant and garish, offers an ebullient echo of the wildly creative 1920s. The restored Reichstag recalls united Germany's brief attempts at parliamentary democracy, while the gigantic Olympic Stadium still proclaims the bombast of Hitler's dictatorship. The chaos and destruction that followed finds a quite deliberate reminder in the bombed-out shell of the Kaiser Wilhelm Memorial Church.

The serene green spaces (largest of any city in the world) are West Berlin's lungs, but the heart, the centre around the Kurfürstendamm— or Ku'damm as it's popularly known—has an urgent, urban beat. Here are the shops, cafés, cinemas and theatres that have always appealed to both the Berlin bourgeoisie and intellectual community.

Since the Wall put a stop to the drain of East German manpower to the West, East Berlin—or as the signposts say: *Berlin, Hauptstadt der D.D.R.* (Capital of the G.D.R.)—has become one of the most prosperous capitals in Eastern Europe. With a population of over a million, it has that most visible and audible proof of a (relatively) thriving economy, rush-hour traffic jams. The East German capital makes an effort to provide its citizenry with an alternative to the West Berlin "shop window" they can see on daily television programmes picked up on their East Berlin TV sets, and to what they hear about from visiting relatives and friends living in the West. As a counterpart to the Ku'damm, Alexanderplatz or "Alex", the heart of pre-war Berlin, has been transformed into a vast pedestrian zone with cafés brighter and shops better stocked than "before the Wall".

"East, West, home's best", they say. Whichever side of the Wall you happen to be on, that old adage will take on poignant new meaning for every visitor to Berlin.

A Brief History

Early times | The settlements of Cölln (on an island in the middle of the River Spree) and Berlin (on the north bank) develop as trading centres within the German empire, and later they merge.

Friedrich II, Prince Elector of Brandenburg, assumes greater control over Berlin in 1447. The town retains virtual autonomy within the empire.

During the Reformation, the people persuade the Prince Elector, Joachim II, to accept the Reformed rituals taught by Luther.

17th century | The Thirty Years' War causes widespread strife. The Great Elector, Friedrich Wilhelm (1640–88) dreams of one united state of Brandenburg and Prussia. His efforts prepare Berlin to become a strong capital. Jewish refugees from Vienna and Huguenots fleeing France add to the city's cosmopolitan population.

18th century | In 1701 the Kingdom of Prussia is proclaimed under Friedrich I. His successor, Friedrich the Great, concentrates on building up the Prussian empire. Wars against revolutionary France begin in 1792.

19th century | Napoleon's Grande Armée defeats Friedrich's successors. The French advance through Eastern Germany in 1806. Napoleon rides unimpeded through the Brandenburg Gate into Berlin. After the two-year occupation the Prussian rulers are left to contend with liberal nationalism. Workers revolt in 1848 and are brutally suppressed by Prussian cavalry.

In the Franco-Prussian War of 1870–71, the Germans under Bismarck, the Iron Chancellor, overcome the French. In the aftermath of the conflict he creates a united Germany. Berlin booms as the centre of the machine industry.

20th century | Berlin's university and research institutes bring new prestige to the city but fortunes turn with World War I. Afterwards the Weimar Republic lasts fourteen years only to be overcome by economic difficulties and mass unemployment, ultimately causing a return to power of the National Socialist (Nazi) Party in 1932. Hitler becomes chancellor in 1933.

Starting in 1939 after Germany's invasion of Poland, World War II ends on May 7th, 1945 with the unconditional surrender of German troops. Four-power control of Berlin is formalized at Potsdam by Churchill, Truman and Stalin. Soviets try to incorporate Berlin into East Germany, blockading West Berlin in 1948; but this is circumvented by airlifting supplies into the city. In 1961 Soviets construct the Wall to prevent refugees leaving East Germany.

West Berlin

Running through the centre of town is West Berlin's most important street, **Kurfürstendamm** (Prince-Elector's Embankment), perhaps the liveliest avenue in all of Germany. This is one place which pulsates with traffic late into the night. The street is known widely as "Ku'damm" and, like the Champs-Elysées in Paris, it plays a more popular role as the town's preferred promenade.

When Ku'damm window-shopping expeditions take you as far as Fasanenstrasse, you might like to visit the **Jewish Community Centre** (Jüdisches Gemeindehaus) at number 79/80. Framing the entrance is the portal from the synagogue that once stood here. It was burned to the ground in 1938.

From the hub of the Ku'damm at Joachimstaler Strasse, move on to Breitscheidplatz and its monumental fountain and street theatre troupes. The sombre **Kaiser-Wilhelm-Gedächtniskirche** (Memorial Church) here has been preserved as a ruin, never to be restored. There is no more eloquent symbol of the city's suffering from bombardment and postwar rebirth. The war-scarred tower with the broken stump of its steeple is flanked by a new octagonal church to the east and a chapel and six-sided tower to the west.

Beyond the church is the 22-storey **Europa-Center,** which extends from Tauentzienstrasse to Budapester Strasse. There are scores of boutiques, a cinema, a casino, and, best of all, a rooftop café with a splendid view of the whole city.

KaDeWe (short for Kaufhaus des Westens), Berlin's phenomenal department store, lies a stone's throw away in Tauentzienstrasse.

The **zoo,** or Zoologischer Garten, in Budapester Strasse contains such beguiling attractions as Indian and African elephants, giant pandas from China and rare, single-horned rhinoceroses from India. Next door is the **Aquarium,** with fascinating ocean and river life.

Tiergarten Area

Despite its name, the **Tiergarten** ("Animal Garden") is not another zoo. For the Brandenburg princes, it was a forest for hunting deer and wild boar. Friedrich the Great cleared away the trees and turned it, as was his Francophile wont, into a French-style park of formal gardens and geometrical avenues.

The north-west side of the Tiergarten constitutes **Hansa-Viertel,** a chic residential neighbourhood damaged during the war and rebuilt in 1957 for an international exhibition.

To the south, just off Strasse des 17. Juni, you'll catch sight of a whimsical architectural landmark: the Technical University's **Institut für Wasserbau und Schiffbau** (Hydraulic and Ship-Engineering Institute). The building, despite its earnest name, is painted blue, pink and green

—technology with a smile.

Climb the 285 steps of the soaring **Siegessäule** victory column on the circle of the Grosser Stern for a magnificent **view** of the city.

Between the canal and Tiergartenstrasse, in rubble-strewn wasteland not far from the Wall, is a **cultural centre,** where some of Berlin's most prestigious institutions can be found: the Nationalgalerie, Staatsbibliothek and Philharmonie. In the nearby **Strasse des 17. Juni** you'll see a gloomy **Soviet war memorial** *(Soviet-Denkmal)* made of marble from the Reich Chancellery, topped by a huge bronze statue of a Russian soldier. The figure is flanked by two T-34 tanks, the vanguard of the 1945 Soviet invasion of Berlin, and a permanent Russian honour guard. Several hundred yards away, the street ends abruptly at the Wall, in sight of **Brandenburg Gate.**

Crossing the Border

If you bear in mind the following, you'll encounter no more difficulty in going from West to East Berlin than at any other national border.

● *Do* take with you the obligatory amount of money to exchange for East marks (25 DM per person over 14, 7.50 DM per child age 14, no exchange for children under 14) plus the 5 DM visa fee.

● *Don't* carry any additional East German money.

● *Do* fill your petrol tank in West Berlin, if you're driving over, as it's a complicated business buying petrol in East Berlin.

● *Don't* take in radios, tape recorders or cassettes, western books, newspapers or magazines, children's war toys or, of course, anything remotely resembling a weapon.

● *Do* keep cool and calm in dealings with the authorities.

● *Don't* photograph railway stations, factories, the Wall or border installations, military installations or activities.

● *Do* enquire in East Berlin shops about export regulations before making a purchase.

● *Don't* engage in any unofficial currency transactions with East Berliners; the penalties are severe.

The Wall

It's difficult to conceive of a structure that more explicitly conveys its historical meaning than the Berlin Wall. This barrier against free passage from East to West traces West Berlin's 100-mile border with East Berlin and the East German hinterland. It has the feeling of a medieval rampart, except that it is aimed at keeping people in rather than out. On the western side of the Wall, you'll see graffiti that emphasize its grotesqueness with humour, pathos or anger— *Lieber Rotwein als Totsein* (Better Red Wine than Dyin'), *Menschen, ich habe euch lieb* (People, I Love You)—and unprintable curses against East Germany. Dozens of wreaths and wooden crosses mark the places where refugees were shot trying to get across.

Checkpoint Charlie, the crossing point on Friedrichstrasse, became the celebrated focus for confrontations between American and Soviet tanks in the weeks following the Wall's construction. Close to the border, a café that once served as a press centre for correspondents covering the momentous events of 1961 has been converted into a small museum documenting the Wall's history.

Once the focus of cold war tensions, the Wall is taken for granted now.

Schloss Charlottenburg

After the harsh realities of the Wall, you may well feel like escaping to a more serene world, another century altogether. With the havoc wrought by war, few buildings have been preserved from Berlin's distinguished past. But one vestige remains: the carefully restored Schloss Charlottenburg, a representative example of Prussian Baroque and Rococo architecture and decoration.

In the palace courtyard is a splendid **statue** of the Great Elector Friedrich Wilhelm on horseback, designed by the prolific Baroque sculptor and architect Andreas Schlüter.

The palace interiors have been restored to recapture the gracious atmosphere of royal life in the 18th century. You are free to roam at will through the ornamental world of the Hohenzollerns, except for Friedrich I's and Sophie Charlotte's apartments in the central building and west wing (join one of the guided tours offered daily at regular intervals). The rooms occupied by the king and queen echo the Baroque grandeur of Versailles.

Do not miss the incomparable **Rococo paintings** in the concert room.

Like the Tiergarten, the **Charlottenburg gardens** were originally laid out in the formal French style. English landscaping was introduced later. Several outbuildings can be visited. The nearest is the compact little **Schinkel-Pavillon,** just behind the New Wing of the palace proper, where you can see three major early **works by Caspar David Friedrich,** the great German Romantic painter.

Further exploration of the gardens takes you to the Belvedere, a tea house at the northern end of the carp pond, and the Mausoleum in the form of a Doric temple, put up in 1810 and enlarged some 30 years later. Here lie the remains of 19th-century members of the Prussian royal family.

Olympic Stadium and I.C.C.

Sightseeing in Berlin never ceases to be a graphic exercise in contemporary history. Nowhere is this more evident than in the area around **Olympiastadion.** The stadium provides a supreme example of Hitler's *folie de grandeur* in all the bombastic gigantism of his favourite architecture and sculpture.

As you approach through the main Olympic Gate, the stadium looks surprisingly "low-slung". But once inside, you see that the field itself lies 40 feet (12 m.) below ground level. Built originally for 120,000 spectators, the stadium now holds 96,000. The huge Olympic complex has facilities for soccer, hockey, tennis, riding and swimming.

South-east of the stadium in Masurenallee there is a colossus of more recent apparition, the **I.C.C.** *(Internationales Congress Centrum)*, completed in 1979 as an audacious gamble on West Berlin's economic viability. The giant complex boasts 80 conference halls and meeting rooms. You may want to take a guided tour of this ultimate in buildings; the ingenuity and efficiency of it are fascinating, almost frightening.

Grunewald and the Havel

Before World War II, **Grunewald** forest was a rather melancholy woodland of dense pines. Wartime bombardments and the Berliners' post-war needs for fuel stripped an estimated 45 per cent of the forest, now replanted with a number of varieties—18 million pines, but also six million chestnut, linden, beech, birch and oak trees. The grassy clearings make pleasant picnic grounds, while the wooded areas form a reserve for deer, wild boar, marten, foxes and myriad rabbits.

You can reach this greenery by bus or car. Take the Avus road, turning off half-way at the Grosser Stern. From here Hüttenweg runs to the **Grunewaldsee**, a lake which offers good swimming from delightful, sandy beaches. On the east shore, set impressively against the lake and surrounded by beach trees, stands **Jagdschloss Grunewald,** a hunting lodge built in the 16th century for Prince Elector Joachim II of Brandenburg.

Havelchaussee, a more leisurely route than the Avus, skirts the Grunewald on the west side, bordering the broad River Havel. Several ferry stations along the way offer boat rides on the river and lakes.

Museums

Some of West Berlin's fine museums which shouldn't be missed are the **Nationalgalerie** (Potsdamer Strasse 50) which displays 19th- and 20th-century art, the **Bauhaus-Archiv** (Klingelhöfstrasse 13), showing progressive architecture and design from the Weimar period, and the **Ägyptisches Museum** (across the street from the Charlottenburg palace): three millennia of Egyptian art in all its diversity. The **Antikenmuseum** (opposite the Egyptian Museum) contains artefacts from Greek and Roman antiquity, and the **Berlin Museum** (Lindenstrasse 14) tells the story of the city from early times to today.

The museums housing the major part of the Prussian State art collections are situated to the south of the city centre (Dahlem-Dorf U-Bahn station). In addition to European painting, sculpture and engraving, Dahlem groups the museums of ethnography (noted for its pre-Columbian holdings) and Indian, Islamic and Oriental (Chinese, Japanese and Korean) art. These last will take over the entire Dahlem installation when the European collections are moved, eventually, to the Tiergarten.

East Berlin

Travel agencies in West Berlin organize guided bus tours of East Berlin. They take care of all the red tape for you, providing the best introduction to the city and the people. You can always return on your own afterwards for an evening at the opera or a closer look at Unter den Linden. Crossing the border independently is in itself worthwhile—if only for the view of no-man's land from the S-Bahn to Friedrichstrasse and the disquieting experience of transit.

Unter den Linden:
In and Around the Avenue

Brandenburg Gate *(Brandenburger Tor)* has been the supreme symbol of the city, unified or divided, since its completion in 1791.

Sweeping east from the gate, **Unter den Linden** (literally "Beneath the Linden Trees") was once Berlin's grandest avenue. Friedrich the Great saw it as the centrepiece of his royal capital, and for the aristocracy and wealthy bourgeoisie it became the most prestigious address in town.

The renewed importance of Unter den Linden can be seen at the western end in embassy row. This part of the avenue fairly bristles with diplomats, functionaries and East Berlin police. The most visible delegation, the Soviet, is ensconced in a huge building on the righthand side of the street as you walk away from Brandenburg Gate.

A little further along, beyond the crossing with Charlottenstrasse, you come to Friedrich the Great's "Forum Fridericianum", today known simply as **Lindenforum.**

The East Germans have done an admirable job of restoration and these buildings once more form an impressive classical architectural perspective. Knobelsdorff's **Deutsche Staatsoper** (German State Opera), in the style of a Greek Corinthian temple, lies opposite Humboldt University, East Germany's biggest academic institution, which began life in 1810 in Prince Heinrich's old Baroque palace.

Rather paradoxically, the most elegant building on Unter den Linden may well be the old Baroque **Zeughaus** (Arsenal), next door to the Neue Wache. It was built at the end of the 17th century to hold the Prussian Army's munitions and weapons. Now it houses the **Museum für Deutsche**

Geschichte (German History Museum), which traces the nation's history from earliest times to the present day from a consistently Marxist point of view.

A short distance from Unter den Linden stands Schinkel's **Schauspielhaus** (Playhouse), notable for its imposing Ionic-columned entrance. After refurbishing, the playhouse is once again an exciting place, though nowadays it serves as a concert hall.

To the north of the Schauspielhaus is the **Französischer Dom** (French Cathedral), and to the south the classically inspired **Deutscher Dom** (German Cathedral), forms its natural counterpart.

Karl-Liebknecht-Strasse

Marx-Engels-Brücke, designed by Schinkel, links Unter den Linden to Karl-Liebknecht-Strasse. As you cross the bridge, you'll catch a glimpse of **Museumsinsel** off to your left. This is the site of East Berlin's most prestigious museums (see p. 90). On the opposite side of the bridge lies **Marx-Engels-Platz,** focus for May Day military parades and mass rallies.

The **Palast der Republik,** completed in 1976, houses the Volkskammer (Parliament) and a 5,000-seat conference hall for Communist Party congresses.

The outsize and somewhat ponderous **Dom** (cathedral), erected at the turn of the 20th century, stands across the street from the Palast der Republik.

Further along, in the square beyond the crossing, you'll see the venerable 13th-century **St.-Marien-Kirche,** a sober brick edifice.

The neo-Gothic bulk of the **Rotes Rathaus** (Red Town Hall) stands on the opposite side of the square. And in the centre lies the massive Neptune fountain, stranded in a sea of concrete.

Monumental in their own right, the fountain, church and town hall are nevertheless completely dwarfed by the soaring 1,197-foot (365-m.) **Fernsehturm** (Television Tower).

Alexanderplatz

"Alex", as the square is universally known, remains the undisputed heart of the city, despite relentless post-war "modernization". (It would probably be the centre of *both* halves of town if Berlin were ever reunited.) Now it is a bustling pedestrian area of cafés, hotels, small shops and apartments.

Köpenick

Köpenick, with its delightful **Altstadt** (old town) of 18th- and 19th-century houses, lies on the edge of the city to the south-east of East Berlin's centre. The solid 17th-century **Schloss Köpenick** occupies an island in the River Dahme.

From Köpenick, a branch of the Spree leads to the **Grosser Müggelsee,** Berlin's largest lake and a very pleasant place for picnics. You can get a good view of the surrounding countryside from the 98-foot-high (30-m.) **Müggelturm** nearby.

Museums

Most of East Berlin's museums are to be found on **Museumsinsel** (Museum Island), just across from Marx-Engels-Platz in a fork of the Spree.

The **Pergamon Museum** is outstanding by any standards; containing works of classical antiquity, the art of the Near East and Islam as well as German art. The **Bode Museum** displays Egyptian, Early Christian and Byzantine art, European painting and sculpture; the **Nationalgalerie,** 19th and 20th century art, and the **Märkisches Museum** has a pleasant collection of Berliniana: the first bicycles, sewing machines, telephones, etc.

Eating Out

Some local specialities are *Soljanka,* East Berlin's Russian mixed vegetable soup; *Soleier,* eggs pickled in brine served with seasoning and mustard; and *Havelaal grün,* eel boiled in dill sauce.

Eisbein mit Sauerkraut und Erbsenpüree is pig's knuckle with pea purée and spicily seasoned sauerkraut, and *gebratene Leber* is liver fried with apple and onion rings.

Dessert favourites are *Schwarzwälder Kirschtorte,* Black Forest cherry cake, *Haselnuss-Sahne,* hazelnut cream cake; and *Käsekuchen,* cheesecake.

Snack bars and mobile stalls sell *Bulette* (meatballs) and *Schaschlik* (skewers), as well as *Currywurst* and *Thüringer Rostbratwurst* and other tasty German sausages.

The most highly reputed Rhine wines are those of the Rheingau, the birthplace of the Riesling—the pick of the crop being Schloss Johannisberg, Schloss Vollrads, Kloster Eberbach, Hattenheim and Rüdesheim.

Berlin, like any other self-respecting German town, can offer you a good glass of beer on tap *(vom Fass),* or bottled in several varieties.

Shopping

If West Berlin is one big shop window for western culture, then the main branch is undoubtedly Ku'damm. Fashionable boutiques and big department stores line the avenue itself, while KaDeWe (Kaufhaus des Westens), a cherished Berlin institution, is situated close by in Tauentzienstrasse. The Europa-Center near the Gedächtniskirche gathers together a variety of small shops under one roof.

Some articles to look out for in West Berlin:

Antiques. Objects from the era of Kaiser Wilhelm; Art Nouveau and Art Deco glassware.

Cutlery and electronic gadgets. These are of very high standard and design.

Linens. Whether traditional or modern in design, German linens are noted for their good old-fashioned quality.

Porcelain. The manufacture of tableware and decorative objects continues a great German tradition.

Precision instruments. Many people appreciate German binoculars and telescopes.

Turkish products. A delightful side-effect of the *Gastarbeiter* (immigrant worker) colony.

Shopping east of the Wall is a more ticklish business because of the restrictions on exporting certain items from East Germany, particularly antiques and works of art. Ascertain whether the goods you wish to buy can be taken out of the country before completing your purchase.

Practical Information

West Berlin

Banking hours: From 9 a.m. to 1 p.m. Monday to Friday. Most banks remain open two afternoons a week (often Tuesday and Thursday from 3.30 to 6 p.m.).

Currency: West Germany's monetary unit is the *Deutsche Mark (DM)*. The mark is divided into 100 *Pfennig (Pf.)*. Coins: 1, 2, 5, 10 and 50 Pf. and DM 1, 2, 5, 10. Notes: DM 5, 10, 20, 50, 100, 500 and 1,000.

Post offices: West Berlin's main post office is situated in the Bahnhof Zoo. It is open 24 hours a day to deal with mail, telegrams and telephone calls. Branch offices open from 8 a.m. to 6 p.m. Monday to Friday and to 12 noon Saturdays.

Shops: Open from 9 a.m. to 6 or 6.30 p.m., Monday to Friday, till 1 or 2 p.m. on Saturdays (until 6 p.m. on the first Saturday of the month).

East Berlin

Banking hours (for supplementary exchange): 8 a.m. to 3 p.m. Monday and Friday, 9 a.m. to 3 p.m. Wednesday. 8 a.m. to noon and 2 to 6 p.m. Tuesday and Thursday.

Post office: The most convenient branches are to be found in Bahnhof Friedrichstrasse (open Monday to Friday 7 a.m. to 9 p.m., Saturday 8 a.m. to 1 p.m.) and S-Bahnhof Alexanderplatz (Monday to Friday 7 a.m. to 9 p.m., Saturday 8 a.m. to 7 p.m., Sunday 8 a.m. to 2 p.m.).

Shops: Open from 10 a.m. to 7 p.m. Monday to Friday, 9 a.m. to 1 p.m. Saturday.

Border formalities: The border crossings for non-Germans are Checkpoint Charlie (Friedrichstrasse by the Kochstrasse U-Bahn station) for pedestrians and vehicles and Bahnhof Friedrichstrasse for passengers riding the U-Bahn or S-Bahn. Note that you must return to West Berlin via the same crossing point. Be sure to verify the closing hours of border posts: at present, all one-day visitors must be out by midnight. At least half-an-hour should be allowed for formalities. (See also p. 8.)

BERNE

Switzerland

Introduction

In many ways, Switzerland is like its famed watches—small, compact, reliable and aesthetic. And its capital city is no exception. "Compromise" choice it may have been, but an indisputably fine setting, gracious old buildings and a quiet allure make Berne a worthy seat for Switzerland's federal government.

Berne looks back on nearly 800 years of often tempestuous history. Tradition claims that the town was founded in 1191 by Duke Berchtold V of Zähringen as an impregnable bastion on the western edge of his domain. The city's strategic position is still striking: it stands on a high, rocky peninsula formed by a loop in the River Aare. After a fire in 1405, which almost completely destroyed the wooden houses, Berne was rebuilt in sandstone. Today, bedecked with flowers and flags, the town retains such a medieval appearance that the old duke himself wouldn't look out of place riding down one of the wide, arcaded streets.

Were he to do so, he would find the Zähringen bear portrayed everywhere: in statuary, on flags, and very much alive in the ever-popular Bear Pit. According to legend, at the time of the town's foundation the duke vowed he would name the place after the first animal caught in a hunt in the nearby woods. A bear (*Bär* in German) was first to fall.

In 1353, having fought the Habsburgs for its freedom and independence, Berne joined the Swiss Confederation. The city grew in power and influence. Its westward expansion ultimately drew the French-speaking part of the country into the Confederation. When the constitution of 1848 was drafted, Berne was chosen as the centre of the federal government.

Despite this honour, there is practically no political pomp and very little ceremony. The seven members of the Federal Council carry on like ordinary citizens; you might see them walking to work, or sitting in a café in the Bärenplatz opposite the parliament building.

Don't bother looking for heroic monuments or grandiose boulevards in Berne. But the site and architecture of the city make it one of Europe's most charming and pleasant capitals.

A Brief History

400 B.C.–5th century A.D.	The Helvetians (a Celtic tribe) arrive in Switzerland, and in 58 B.C. leave to seek new territory in the south-west. They are stopped by Julius Caesar's Roman legions, who follow them back, and colonize the region. Relative peace follows.
5th–9th centuries	Alemannic tribes invade north-eastern and central areas of Switzerland. This effectively divides the country into two parts along the River Sarine. The Burgundians in the west assimilate the customs and language of Rome, while the Alemanni fiercely maintain their own language and customs. Under Charlemagne, the Franks subdue both the Alemanni and the Burgundians, and Switzerland is incorporated into the Holy Roman Empire.
10th–15th centuries	The Carolingian dynasty dies out in 911, and struggles for power begin between the Zähringen, Kyburg and Habsburg families. Duke Berchtold V of Zähringen founds the town of Berne in 1191, but, during the 13th century, the Zähringen family dies out and the town becomes self-governing. On August 1, 1291, farmers from three valley communities (Uri, Schwyz and Unterwalden) meet and form a pact against the Habsburgs, thus forming the Confederation. Berne joins the Confederation in 1353, and is instrumental in drawing French-speaking parts of the area into it.
16th–18th centuries	After defeat at the Battle of Marignano, at the hands of the French, Switzerland signs a treaty of perpetual peace with France, and begins to follow a policy of neutrality. During the Thirty Years' War (1618–1648) Swiss neutrality is preserved. The Treaty of Westphalia in 1648 grants legal recognition to Swiss independence—with Berne as the dominant canton. But independence is challenged in 1798 when Bonaparte's armies occupy the country, and call it the Helvetic Republic. After three years of anarchy, Napoleon gives the Swiss a constitution based on the old Confederation, plus another six cantons, bringing the total to 19.

19th–20th centuries	The perpetual neutrality of Switzerland is established in 1815 at the Congress of Vienna, and Geneva, Neuchâtel and Valais join the Confederation. In 1848 the constitution is drafted (revised 1874) and Berne is chosen as the seat of government. Switzerland manages to retain neutral status during the two world wars.

Sightseeing

Start at the railway station (one of the most modern in Europe). In the pedestrian underpass you'll find the remains of the Christoffelturm, part of the wall of the town gates dating back 600 years.

Taking the escalator to street level, you come out at the beginning of the **Spitalgasse**, a lively shopping street whose thriving department stores take refuge behind elegant old façades. The solid-looking arcades are characteristic of the architecture—the city has over 5 miles of them!

Before walking down the Spitalgasse, notice the **Heiliggeistkirche** (Holy Ghost Church) on the left. Built between 1726–29, it is considered by many to be the most beautiful Protestant Baroque church in Switzerland. But to visit it you'll have to come 30 minutes before a service on Sundays as otherwise it's closed to the public.

The first fountain you come to is the Pfeiferbrunnen (Bagpiper Fountain). Berne's numerous **fountains** were almost all built in the 16th century and are as much a symbol of the city as the arcades, bears and red geraniums. The little bagpiper atop the column was probably by Hans Gieng, who designed many of the fountains.

Pass through the 300-year-old **Käfigturm** (a prison tower) into the **Marktgasse** where you'll find two typical fountains; the first of hospital foundress Anna Seiler in a flowing blue gown and a little further on the Schützenbrunnen (Musketeer Fountain).

Not so charming is the 16th-century Kindlifresserbrunnen (Ogre Fountain) on the left as you come out into the Kornhausplatz. On a slender column the child-eater sits poised to bite off the head of one victim, while others wait in his sack.

Back to the famous **Zytgloggeturm** (Clock Tower). Pass through to the other side and try to get there 3 minutes before the striking of the hour for a fascinating display of 16th-century Swiss clockwork.

About 60 yards from the Zytglogge in the upper part of the **Kramgasse** is the Zähringerbrunnen (Zähringer Fountain)—a warrior bear in armour with a tiny bear at his feet—dedicated to the city's founder.

Down the Kreuzgasse on the left you come to a little square where you can sit and admire the **Rathaus** (Town Hall), a lovely Gothic building (1406–17). The colourful Vennerbrunnen (Flagbearer Fountain) shows a Bernese standard-bearer in full uniform.

Rejoin the **Gerechtigkeitsgasse** to get to the finest fountain in the city: the **Gerechtigkeitsbrunnen** (Justice Fountain), an allegory of justice holding a sword and a delicately balanced set of scales with the Pope, emperor, sultan and mayor at her feet.

The **Nydeggkirche** (Nydegg Church), in the oldest part of town, dates back to the 14th century although the interior was completely renovated in 1953.

Continuing downwards, the street levels out at the Läuferplatz, and directly in front of you is the Untertor-brücke (1461–89), Berne's oldest bridge. On the left, the Läuferbrunnen (Messenger Fountain) honours a Bernese herald who had the audacity to reply to a French king's complaint that he didn't speak French, "Well, you can't speak German!"

Turn right after the Untertorbrücke and walk up the gradient to the **Bärengraben** (Bear Pits). If you're lucky enough to be in Berne on Easter Sunday, weather permitting, you'll be able to see the bear cubs let out with their mother for their first spring outing.

Berne's late-Gothic **cathedral** *(Münster)* took centuries to build. Started in 1421, the nave was completed more than 150 years later and the tip of the filigreed steeple (nearly 300 ft. (90 m.) tall) added in 1893. In the interior the 15th-century **stained-glass windows** are impressive and the Renaissance **choirstalls** magnificent.

If you've only limited time and want to stay near the city, the **Gurten** is well worth the 25-minute tram and funicular ride. From this high spot (2,815 ft.; 845 m.) above the city, there is a magnificent panorama of the Bernese Alps in one direction and Berne itself in the other.

Museums

Bernisches Historisches Museum (Historical Museum) at Helvetiaplatz 5. The mock-16th-century building, actually constructed between 1892–94, houses various collections from arts and crafts to furniture, but the most interesting is the treasure taken from the Duke of Burgundy in the Battle of Grandson (1476). Closed Mondays.

The **Kunstmuseum**, Hodlerstrasse 12, is famed for its Paul Klee collection—the artist was born and grew up in Berne. Closed Mondays.

For an overview of the whole country, go to Ballenberg, near Brienz, to the **Schweizerisches Freilichtmuseum** (Swiss Open-Air Museum). Here you can see full-size reconstructions of farmhouses, chalets and homes from all over Switzerland. Open daily between April and October.

The Bernese Oberland

A one-day excursion from Berne can cover some of the loveliest countryside in the Oberland.

Around the lake of Thun, in beautiful surroundings, are the towns of **Thun** and **Spiez**, and between the lakes of Thun

and Brienz is **Interlaken**. This famous summer resort has huge Victorian hotels, nostalgic grandeur and an incomparable **view** of the Jungfrau. The Jungfrau railway line from Kleine Scheidegg (the train is actually *inside* the Eiger for half the trip) leads to Europe's highest railway station, **Jungfraujoch** (11,330 ft.; 3,454 m.), with wild and craggy scenery all the way up.

Grindelwald, at 3,360 feet (1,008 m.), is the largest mountain resort in the Bernese Oberland, known as "Glacier Village" because of the two nearby glaciers.

are irresistible. Try *Zuger Kirschtorte* (Kirsch brandy cake from Zug), *Rüeblitorte* (carrot cake), and *Kirschtorte mit Schokolade* (chocolate and brandy cake).

Eating Out

A typically Swiss meal can be had at almost any corner restaurant. Cheese *fondue* (bread dipped into a bubbling cheese and wine mixture) is famous the world over. Another variation on the melted cheese theme is *raclette* with boiled potatoes.

Among meat dishes, you'll find *Geschnetzeltes Kalbfleisch* (diced veal in cream sauce) and the *Berner Platte* ("Bernese board") is loaded with local meat, sausage, sauerkraut and potatoes.

Swiss pastries and desserts

Shopping

Shopping is expensive in Switzerland, but standards are high. Look out for **watches;** the shop assistant will provide an international guarantee and an address in your country where the watch can be sent for repairs.

Chocolates are a Swiss speciality and make a fine present to take home. **Cheese**, likewise, makes a good present if you don't live too far away; try *Emmentaler* or *Appenzeller*.

Swiss Army knives, either miniature or full-size, come with numerous gadgets.

Practical Information

Banks: Open from 8.30 a.m. to 12.30 p.m. and from 1.30 to 4.30 or 5.30 p.m., Monday to Friday.

Currency: The Swiss *franc* (in German *Franken*), abbreviated *Fr.,* is divided into 100 *centimes* (in German *Rappen*). Coins: 5, 10, 20, 50 centimes, Fr. 1, 2, 5. Banknotes: Fr. 10, 20, 50, 100, 500, 1,000.

BRUSSELS

Belgium

Introduction

Life in a European melting-pot is nothing new for the people of Brussels. Through the centuries invaders and occupiers have come and gone, some with a whimper and others with more of a bang, but the natives have developed a healthy, good-humoured cynicism that helps see them through the crises and pervades every-day life.

It is no shock nowadays, of course, to catch the babble of a dozen foreign tongues as you revive yourself with a glass of beer at one of the myriad pavement cafés, for Brussels has established itself as the capital of NATO, the European Economic Community and Western capitalism. This newly found international status has swept in with it a flood of bureaucrats, Eurocrats, businessmen, army chiefs and property developers, with a host of attendant offshoots. But though some 230,000 foreigners—almost a quarter of the total population—now mingle multiculturally on the broad cosmopolitan avenues of modern Brussels, the enigmatic spirit of the heart of Belgium is still very much in evidence.

The idiosyncrasies of a thousand years of European culture have helped to shape both people and city—they look back on invasions by Roman legions, Spanish Inquisitors, the Habsburg armies, Napoleon, the Kaiser and Hitler. But Brussels has not been cowed into insipidness. Tucked away behind the skyscrapers there is a lively brew of boisterous old-fashioned working-class districts and elegant bourgeois neighbourhoods, lusty taverns and superb restaurants, museums steeped in history and parks aglow with colour.

The people of Brussels have a deep-seated allegiance to Catholicism—but forces sacred are balanced by an exuberantly profane attitude to life. They revel in revelries, especially if they involve dressing up and cavorting through the colourful past. Many of the festivals and processions stem from religious roots, but the most flamboyant are the purely secular, which date back to proud civic parades before visiting rulers during a Joyeuse Entrée, or Ommegang.

Brussels' architectural glories reflect the importance attached to the municipal, material side of life—the spirit of prosperity in the shape of the magnificent Town Hall and fascinating guildhalls of the Grand-Place. And the symbol of modern Brussels—the enormous molecular model known as the Atomium, erected for the 1958 World Fair—encapsulates its progressive 20th-century prosperity. The Fair's slogan was *Bâtir le monde pour l'homme* ("Building the World for Mankind"), with the emphasis on *building*.

In keeping with its international political and economic role, Brussels is officially bilingual, with both Flemish and French street signs and public notices. Bilingualism is also a reflection on the Belgian split, between Dutch-speaking Flemings in the northern region and French-speaking Walloons in the south—although the official equality in language does not prevent somewhat stormy relations between the two groups.

Despite internal French-Walloon squabbles and the bureaucratic invasion, Brussels remains a city of good beer and good cheer, the province of the happy cartoon adventurer Tintin and the great painter Pieter Breughel, whose solid, serene, yet sceptical subjects are still personified in the city's narrow backstreets four centuries later. To appreciate the real Brussels, you have to appreciate the combination of prosperous modern living and the power of tradition; the festive rituals of historical pageantry, which are played out with such relish beneath the gleaming skyscraping symbols of post-industrial success.

A Brief History

10th century	Charles de Lotharingie, brother of King Lothaire of France, erects a fortress on the site, in 979.
11th century	Count Lambert II of Louvain builds a new castle on the Coudenberg heights (today the Place Royale), surrounded by houses inside a walled-in compound.
12th–13th centuries	Brussels establishes itself as a prominent trading centre on the commercial route between Bruges and Cologne. The city is renowned for skilled goldsmiths and silversmiths, as well as the flourishing textile industry based on wool imported from England. It is ruled by an oligarchy

of seven patrician families under the wing of either French or German leadership—sometimes both.

14th–15th centuries

The dukes of Burgundy become the feudal overlords, and high living is the order of the day—for the patrician families and their cronies at least. Life is hard for the textile artisans in the face of English competition, but the more resourceful turn their skills to tapestry and rapidly establish a far-reaching reputation. The great Town Hall and the guildhouses built in the Grand-Place proclaim the prosperity of the town, while the arts, too, enjoy a golden age with the emergence of a number of magnificent Flemish painters.

16th–17th centuries

Under the Habsburg King Charles V, who is also King of Spain and Holy Roman Emperor, Brussels becomes a great European centre and capital of the Low Countries, with trade in luxury goods and the arts continuing to thrive. The Ommegang becomes established as a dazzling riot of finery, as the nobility parade around the Grand-Place in an assertion of their civic authority.

Times become turbulent as the Calvinist movement takes hold. Spiritual rebellion against the Catholics is rapidly identified with nationalist sentiments against Spanish rule. Charles V's son, Philip II, responds with the bloody repression of the Spanish Inquisition, which eventually provokes a successful rebellion against the Catholics. This is crushed by the Counter-Reformation and its reassertion of the Catholic presence, mainly in the southern provinces of Belgium. Peace and prosperity are restored for a time. In 1695 much of the city is destroyed in two days of ferocious French bombing—Louis XIV's revenge for Dutch and English actions—but it is painstakingly rebuilt in its old Renaissance and Baroque style.

18th–19th centuries

After the old patrician families lead a revolt against Austrian rule, France re-occupies and annexes Belgium. Napoleon visits Brussels in 1803 and introduces plans for broad avenues and airy boulevards. His defeat at Waterloo leads to a period of Dutch rule fraught with the old tensions between Flemings and Walloons, until riots erupt in 1830. In 1831 Belgium achieves independence and, with industrial growth and successful colonial exploits in Africa, again enjoys great material prosperity, in spite of the continuing bitter squabbles between Dutch-speaking Flemings and French-speaking Walloons.

20th century   Brussels is occupied by Kaiser Wilhelm's German troops in 1914. The Germans are back again with the brewing of World War II. Fascist movements have been afoot since the early thirties, and many Belgians die with the German troops on the Eastern Front—but a powerful underground organized resistance, which includes the Légion Nationale among its members, plays its role in the war against the Nazis.

The post-war years see Brussels' establishment as the headquarters of the EEC in 1957 and of NATO in 1967. Internal strife between the Flemish and the Walloons is balanced and ameliorated by international responsibilities—a set of marriages in which the in-laws have to get on for the sake of the children.

Sightseeing

On any meanderings through the streets of Brussels keep an eye open for the details, for there are many delightful minutiae in the most unlikely places. Old shop-signs; delicate wrought-iron railings, banisters and even butchers' hooks; streetcorner shrines in the walls holding effigies of the Virgin Mary and the saints —all offer further insights into the reality of Brussels.

Grand-Place

The focal point of Brussels' daily life and history, the

Grand-Place is a joyous architectural celebration of the city's civic pride. Sit outside in one of the cafés and absorb the riot of colour in the flower market and the throngs of natives and tourists. If you visit in early July you may catch the **Ommegang,** the great dressing-up parade of the patrician families' descendants, while at any time you're likely to see an open-air theatre performance or concert held there.

The square's harmony of Gothic, Renaissance and Baroque styles was achieved when it was planned and re-

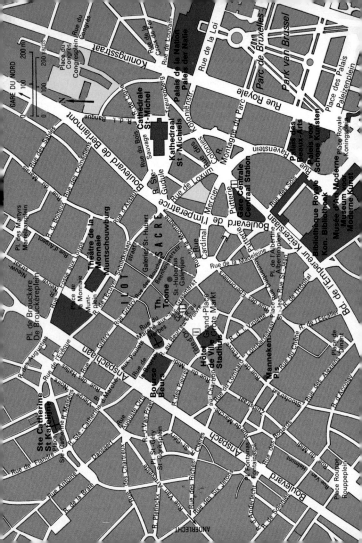

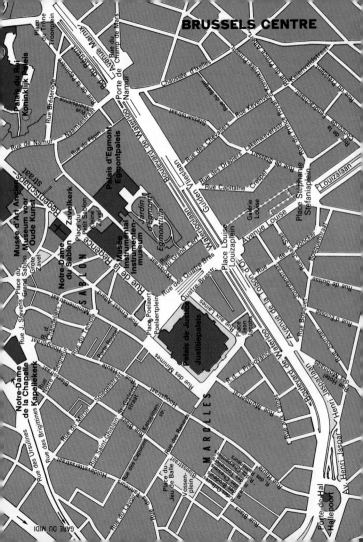

built after Louis XIV's attack on the city in 1695. Only the graceful 295-foot (90-m.) tower of the **Hotel de Ville** (Town Hall) somehow escaped destruction and still soars over the square as a testament to the 15th-century architectural talents of Jan van Ruysbroeck. The Town Hall's Gothic bulk derives much of its charm from the off-centre placing of the door and tower. Its carving also merits close inspection, and a breath-taking view of the city makes the long haul up the tower well worth while.

The magnificent Renaissance **guildhouses** around the Town Hall are the most concrete evidence imaginable for the historical importance of the craftsmen and merchants. Number 10, **L'Arbre d'Or** (The Golden Tree), once housed the brewers' guild and is now the home of the brewery museum. Opposite the Town Hall is the **Musée Communal,** displayed in the inelegant 19th-century neo-Gothic **Maison du Roi,** a must for any visitor to Brussels. On prominent view are the original carvings preserved from the façade of the Town Hall, and a selection of Brussels tapestries and a fine collection of 18th-century Brussels pottery to

rival that of Delft. The top floor, however, draws the biggest crowds—it contains the vast and ever-growing wardrobe of **Manneken-Pis,** contributed by visitors from all over the world. the Manneken-Pis, an irreverent little statue, can be found relieving himself into a fountain on the Rue de l'Etuve; he has become the world-wide mascot of Brussels—as is all too evident from the plethora of souvenir bric-à-brac on which he cheekily displays himself.

Just north of the Grand-Place is **L'Ilot Sacré** (The Sacred Isle), a treasured enclave of historic Brussels pres-erved from the ravages of the property developers. Many of the tiny backstreets are now for pedestrians only, hiding a veritable profusion of delights for any sensualist—beautiful Renaissance houses, many converted into excellent restaurants, others containing art galleries and craft shops. In the summer, strolling musicians, acrobats and flower-sellers add to the pleasures of this little haven.

Wander through the complex of glass-vaulted arcades of the **Galeries Saint-Hubert,** a fascinating array of shops and restaurants off the Rue de l'Ecuyer; then past the

Théâtre de la Monnaie back to the realm of 20th-century Brussels—the main shopping streets, Boulevard Anspach and Rue Neuve.

The **Cathédrale Saint-Michel** is worth a visit too. The choir of this imposing Gothic edifice dates back to 1226; the nave and chapter are from the 14th and 15th centuries, and the chapels were added later. The two towers, designed by Jan van Ruysbroeck, echo his soaring masterpiece on the Town Hall, while inside, in the diffuse light of the fine stained-glass windows, is the **Chapelle du Saint-Sacrement.** This artistic gem was built in 1540 to commemorate a miracle now acknowledged as "false and unjust" by the archbishopric. The legend is that in 1370 some Jews stole the sacraments and on Good Friday they stabbed them in ritual defilement, whereupon blood spurted from the sacrament's "wounds". Accused of this crime, four Jewish families were burned at the stake in Brussels (hatred of the Jews was rife at this time). In spite of the loathing that motivated their construction and the gruesome facts that surround them, the tapestries and stained-glass windows are magnificent pieces of artistry.

Le Sablon

South of the Grand-Place lies an elegant and peaceful relic of pre-19th-century Brussels, the Sablon area. Around the **Place du Grand Sablon** nestle antique shops and chic restaurants, while on the other side of the church of **Notre Dame du Sablon,** the **Square du Petit Sablon** is a welcome garden retreat in which to sit and muse upon the Sablon of days gone by. The 19th-century bronze inhabitants of the square include the great martyrs of Belgium, Counts Egmont and Hoorn (who were executed for their part in the resistance movement against Spain), as well as forty-eight little statues representing the medieval guilds, each identifiable by the item he is clutching. The church itself, which took a hundred years to build, is a masterpiece of the 15th and 16th centuries and worth savouring in its own right, rather than for any particular treasures inside. However, don't miss the charming **statue** of the patron saint of huntsmen, St. Hubert, accompanied by a stag with a hanging Christ between its horns. This stands just beyond the porch; there is also a beautiful Baroque **pulpit** inside the church.

Les Marolles

To the north and west of Le Sablon is the working-class area of the **Marolles,** whose street-names indicate the types of crafts once practised there—for instance, Rue des Orfèvres (goldsmiths) and des Chaisiers (chair-makers). The streets themselves are always fascinating places in which to watch the vigour of daily goings-on in the district, and to try to identify the hotch-potch of languages— Flemish, French, Spanish, with Italian, German and Hebrew thrown in—that make up the rich dialect of the inhabitants.

This is the area where the great populist painter Pieter Breughel lived and died. His home was probably no. 132. rue Haute, a fine gabled **house** restored in the beamed style of the period (1563–69). His marble mausoleum is just up the road, in the Gothic church of **Notre-Dame de la Chapelle.** Wandering south, you'll come across the enormous Palais de Justice, the biggest building erected in the 19th century; the bombastic epitome of Belgium's golden age of expansionism. Down the Rue de la Régence is the **Place Royale** with the **Musées Royaux des Beaux Arts**—the homes of some of the Low Countries'

most stunning and valuable art treasures.

The **Musée d'Art Ancien** contains pieces dating up to the end of the 18th century, and began life in 1799 as a depository for everything the French couldn't carry back to Paris. Much was retrieved from France after Waterloo, and there are now around 1200 paintings, mostly from the great Flemish schools. The celebrated names represented there include **Roger van de Weyden** (1399–1464), **Dirk Bouts** (c. 1415–75) and **Hieronymus Bosch** (c. 1450–1516), whose *Crucifixion* is a relatively modest and conventional work compared with his usual macabre style. There is a fine collection of **Pieter Breughel's** work, including *The Fall of Icarus,* while **Peter Paul Rubens** (1577–1640) is displayed in strength. The morbidly fascinating imagination of **Ribera** may or may not be characteristic of the 16th-century Spanish occupiers—one hopes not, looking at his *Apollo Flaying Marsyas.* Apollo has discarded his lyre and is calmly and gracefully skinning Marsyas alive.

A passageway takes you to the refurbished, subterranean **Musée d'Art Moderne,** also accessible via Place Royale.

—those whose fancy lightly turns to other civilizations and cultures should not miss the astonishing panorama of ancient and modern arts on show in the **Musées Royaux d'Art et d'Histoire** in the Parc du Cinquantenaire. Music lovers should make time for the **Musée Instrumental** on the Rue de la Régence, which contains rare European instruments dating back to the 16th century, and some weird and wonderful pieces from China, Java, Sumatra and Mexico.

Further out of the city, the **House of Erasmus** in the borough of Anderlecht is a charming and tranquil combination of Gothic and Renaissance architecture. It houses a fascinating museum of the philosopher's career. Also in Anderlecht is the **Béguinage,** a 16th-century nunnery where eight nuns lived and worked at the budding lace industry.

Among the Belgian masters on display are **Rik Wouters, René Magritte** and **Paul Delvaux,** each taking a pot-shot at the bourgeoisie in characteristically satiric or surreal fashion. There are also a number of fine French painters.

Brussels' other museums span a wide range of interests

Parks

You will find yourself spoilt for choice, as far as parks in Brussels are concerned. The **Parc de Bruxelles** lies in the centre of the city, an elegant area of fountains, and Baroque and Rococo statues. The botanic gardens of the **Domaine Royal de Laeken** are a delight in spring and summer, and the royal greenhouses are beautifully illuminated at night during May. But the favourite of the inhabitants of Brussels is the **Bois de la Cambre** at the far end of the Avenue Louise, merely the municipal tip of the gigantic **Forêt de Soignes,** which extends across the south-eastern corner of Brussels. The Bois offers boating lakes, tearooms, restaurants in a setting of regal beech trees; the perfect place to rest after a hard day's pavement-pounding.

Excursions

There are a number of easy day trips from Brussels: **Waterloo** is closest, only 12½ miles (20 km.) south. Slightly further afield are **Antwerp,** 29 miles (46 km.) north, and **Ghent,** about 37 miles (60 km.) away. **Bruges** is 31 miles (49 km.) west of Ghent but is also highly recommended, and from there **Ostend** and the coastal resorts are easily accessible.

Antwerp

Antwerp is now a thriving and animated port. **Port tours** leave from the Steen, the castle on the right bank of the River Schelde. The town was the home of Peter Paul Rubens during his heyday.

The **Kathedraal,** well worth a visit for its **Rubens masterpieces** alone, also boasts a majestic open stonework **steeple** 400 feet (122 m.) high. **Groenplaats,** south of the cathedral and at one time its cemetery, is now a colourful square edged by open-air cafés, with a central statue of Rubens. And **Rubens' house** itself, at Rubensstraat 9–11, is an unexpectedly sumptuous affair—clear evidence of the painter's success.

For a fascinating glimpse into Antwerp's golden age—the 16th century—visit the **Plantin-Moretus Museum** (Vrijdagmarkt 22), where Christopher Plantin lived and set up his great printing press. The whole place presents a most informative history of books, printing and the evolution of handwriting. The omnipresent Rubens may be enjoyed at the **Koninklijk Museum voor Schone Kunsten,** which has a first-class collection of Flemish art. Antwerp also has marvellous **Zoological Gardens** and a couple of lovely parks, **Nachtegalen** and **Middelheim**—the latter with an open-air sculpture museum which includes pieces by Rodin and Henry Moore.

Ghent

Ghent should be appreciated for the first time from the middle of the **Sint-Michiels-brug** (St. Michael's Bridge), a splendid vantage-point from which to study the city. The magnificent Gothic and Renaissance **merchants' houses** lie on **Graslei** (Grass Quay) to the right and **Koornlei** (Corn Quay) to the left of the bridge —works of art in colour, form and detail. Also visible from the bridge, to the north, is the **Gravensteen,** the 9th- to 12th-century castle of the counts of Flanders, which has a dubious collection of sickeningly imaginative instruments of torture. The other castle, **Geraard de Duivelsteen,** in Bauwens square, dates from the 13th century and has an equally nasty reputation. Back towards St. Michael's Bridge is the 15th-century **Lakenhalle** (Drapers' Hall) with its great belfry, the architectural evidence of Ghent's ancient wealth. The multilingual "sight and sound" show in the huge hall sets the historical scene very well.

The **Museum voor Schone Kunsten** houses two of Hieronymus Bosch's best-known surreal paintings—*Saint Jérôme* and *The Bearing of the Cross*. Not to be missed is the **Museum van Oudheden,** housed in the medieval **Abbey of Bijloke.** It is a haven of tranquility, far removed from the bloody history of the torture chambers in the old castles.

Eating Out

When it comes to matters gastronomic the Belgians do nothing by halves—their reputation for sturdy appetites is nourished on the enormous portions and generous second helpings found in most restaurants; and quality is certainly not sacrified to quantity.

The stock caricature of the ruddy-cheeked Belgian munching stoically through an unvarying diet of mussels and chips is, of course, far from accurate—but fresh North Sea mussels steamed in a seasoned broth, and crisp, succulent *pommes frites* are delectable everyday fare. To make the most of the robust flavour of Brussels keep an eye open for such specialities as beer soup, delicious oysters from Zeeland, or *potjesvlees,* a cold veal, pork and rabbit pâté, to start your meal.

Main course delicacies include *anguille au vert*—baby eel with shredded herbs. *Waterzooi* is not to be missed—a fish stew with herbs, leeks and cream. A good variation on the theme is the Brussels version using chicken instead of fish. Beef casseroled in beer *(carbonnade)*; hare or rabbit served with prunes *(lièvre* or *lapin à la flamande)*; boiled goose *(oie à l'instar de Visé)* and a variety of powerful wine-soaked game dishes involving venison *(chevreuil)*, pheasant *(faisan)* or hare—all should be sampled, though the richness of Belgian food makes a strong stomach a useful acquisition.

The figure-conscious must be staunch indeed to by-pass Belgian **desserts**—waffles *(gaufres)* warm from the street stalls; apple pancake *(crêpe aux pommes)*; *tarte au sucre* (sugar tart) for the really sweet-toothed, or the famous *speculoos,* king- and queen-shaped gingerbreads.

Drinks

Brewing is an art-form for the Belgians, and there are a variety of beers to be savoured, preferably from the small-scale breweries which still thrive. Kriek, for instance, is flavoured with cherries during fermentation; and while most beers are of the lager type, the strong dark malt Trappiste is brewed around Antwerp.

Spirits and liqueurs are not sold in bars, so to sample Péguet, the local slightly sweet gin, you must visit a café labelled as a private club *(cercle privé)* and sign a membership form, or order it with a meal at a restaurant.

Shopping

Everything you ever needed is on display in this shop window of the world—at a price. The enormous international selection of goods and the cosmopolitan clientele make Brussels an expensive place to shop, and it's often hard to pick up authentic Brussels memorabilia when searching for mementos and presents.

The best value goods are Belgium's own products. The Belgians are masters of **lace** and **tapestry-making.** Much is machine-produced nowadays but a little detective work will often yield exquisite hand-made results. Try the Sablon antique dealers for tapestry. **Glassware, crystal** and **pewter** are all crafted in Belgium; fine **leather** goods are a speciality of Brussels itself; and of course for those who have the wherewithal the city still revels in its reputation as a centre for good **jewellery.**

All these products can be found in the chic boutiques of the Avenue Louise, as well as their more popular neighbours in the Marolles and the department stores of Rue Neuve and Boulevard Adolphe Max. But it is more rewarding for many people to pick up antique or second-hand versions, by browsing in the antique shops of the Sablon or haggling over prices in the flea markets of the Marolles. Indeed the markets are a joy not to be missed—flowers every day; the Sunday bird market in the Grand-Place; antiques and books at the weekend in the Place du Grand Sablon; the Midi market at the Gare du Midi on Sunday mornings.

No chocophile can pass by the chance to partake of Brussels' expensive but exquisite **pralines,** some of the finest and smoothest filled chocolates in the world. The arrays of mouth-watering **biscuits** such as spicy *speculoos* always go down exceedingly well—and extremely quickly—as presents. In fact, from a nation as conscious of the well-being of stomach and taste-buds as the Belgians, nothing could be more appropriate than a selection of their delicious comestibles for the folks back home.

Practical Information

Banking hours: Banks are generally open from 9.15 a.m. to 3.30 p.m., Monday to Friday. A few are open Saturday morning. Currency is the Belgian *franc (BF)* divided into 100 *centimes.* Coins: 50 c, 1, 5, 20 and 50 francs; notes: 50, 100, 500, 1000 and 5000 francs.

Language: Brussels is officially bilingual in Flemish and French, but about 80% of the native population are French-speakers. English is widely spoken so communication is unlikely to pose many problems.

Shopping hours: Stores are open from 9 a.m. to 6 p.m., six days a week, with late-night shopping on Fridays; smaller shops may close over lunchtime and stay open later in the evening. The post office at Gare du Midi (48a, avenue de Fonsny) is open 24 hours a day, every day of the year.

COLOGNE

West Germany

Introduction

Cologne, capital of the Rhineland, is one of the oldest and most distinguished cities in West Germany. It lies at the centre of a pious but never austere religious tradition where good Catholics take a secular, even pagan delight in the joys of the flesh. The great symbol of the Church's abiding authority is Cologne's gigantic, almost overpowering, twin-spired cathedral. Yet the town is the scene every year of Germany's most riotous, lusty, frolicking Carnival, when wives put away their wedding rings and the husbands are not home to complain.

Long a commercial and cultural centre, Cologne has witnessed the nation's growth from earliest Roman times through medieval prosperity to its present state of comfortable stability. It has been home to a number of famous people: in the 16th century Peter Paul Rubens, the painter of exuberantly fleshy nudes, grew up among the burgers'

stout wives. About 70 years later, in 1642, Maria de Medici, the wife of Henry IV of France, died here in exile; her heart is buried in the cathedral. The composer of *Orpheus in the Underworld*, Offenbach, was born here in 1819.

Cologne's site on the Rhine is of prime importance. The old city was founded on the left bank, the new industrial centre on the right (Deutzer) bank. It is the ideal starting place for a visit to the Rhine Valley, land of mists and towering rocks, terraced vineyards and avenues of poplars, Gothic churches and ruined castles, of every poetic image dear to the romantic side of the German character. But it's also coal barges, express trains and juggernaut lorries, cement works and power plants. Phoenix-like, Cologne arose after World War II from a rubble-strewn desert to the proud, businesslike city of today. For now, as in centuries past, Rhinelanders settle down to their romantic dreams only after a hard day's work.

A Brief History

1000–750 B.C. Celts settle on the west bank of the Rhine, Germanic tribes occupy the east.

1st century B.C.	In 72 B.C. the Germanic king Ariovistus crosses the Rhine with 15,000 troops and conquers part of Gaul. Gallic leaders call on the Romans for help and Caesar defeats Ariovistus in 58 B.C., driving the Germans back across the Rhine. Three years later the Gallic left bank is declared a Roman Protectorate. In 38 B.C., Augustus's general Agrippa brings a Germanic tribe, the Ubii, across to the left bank, and establishes the settlement of Oppidum Ubiorum.
1st–9th centuries A.D.	Julia Agrippina, wife and murderess of the Roman Emperor Claudius, renames her birthplace "Colonia Claudia Ara Agrippinensis", shortened later to Colonia. The Roman Rhineland suffers under invading barbarians, first the Alemanni who conquer Cologne, later the Burgundians, who are in turn defeated by the Huns. Turmoil continues with wars between the Alemanni and the Franks; the latter achieve supremacy under Clovis, who introduces Christianity. At the beginning of the 9th century, Charlemagne establishes a Christian European empire and builds his imperial palace on the edge of the Rhineland at Aachen. Cologne, already a bishop's see, becomes an archbishopric.
10th–11th centuries	The Rhineland becomes a major recruiting centre for the Crusades to rescue Jerusalem from the Infidel. At Easter, 1096, Peter the Hermit arrives in Cologne with thousands of French eager to fight for the cause. They influence the Rhinelanders to such an extent that they begin to massacre local Jewish communities.
12th–15th centuries	The medieval city blossoms into one of Germany's principal towns. The increased power of the church, represented by the cathedral begun in 1248, is matched by growing commercial strength. An independent city in 1475, and part of the Hanseatic League, Cologne grows fat on trade with Bruges and London and imposes its own system of weights and measures on other northern towns.
16th–18th centuries	Decline sets in with the collapse of the Hanseatic League and the growth of Lutherism. A bastion of the Catholic faith, Cologne resists the Reformation, and its Protestant craftsmen flee to other towns. The Thirty Years' War (1618–48) devastates the land, although

neutrality saves the city from destruction. The 18th century brings peace but also French domination.

19th century : In 1813 Napoleon is driven back across the Rhine into France, and the Congress of Vienna hands the Rhineland to Prussia. However, the area remains a hotbed of unrest until Wilhelm of Prussia defeats the French in 1870, taking Alsace and Lorraine.

20th century : After World War I, at the Versailles Peace Conference, Marshal Foch pushes for an independent Rhenish Republic under French supervision. Rhenish separatists, among them the Mayor of Cologne, Konrad Adenauer, stage a *coup d'état* on June 1, 1919. They declare a republic which lasts only a few hours, until Clemenceau, under Anglo-American pressure, sends orders to break it up. The effects of the Third Reich are longer-lasting. Hitler marshalls troops in the Rhineland in 1936, delivering a triumphant speech in Cologne cathedral. In May 1942 British bombs devastate the town. By 1945 the population has fallen from 800,000 to 40,000, but within 15 years the city is rebuilt.

COLOGNE

Sightseeing

For a taste of the Rhineland's mixture of the practical and the romantic, the serious and the humorous, there's nowhere better to begin than Cologne. And in Cologne the starting point is inevitably the **cathedral** (*Dom*).

After the devastating bombardments of World War II, it was one of the few buildings left standing, defiantly dominating the city. Today, amid Cologne's shining rebuilt prosperity, elevated on a terrace like a somewhat haughty dignitary, the cathedral occupies a position that has been sacred since Roman times. Around A.D. 50, it was the site of the Temple of Mercurius Augustus. The first Christian church was built there in the 4th century by Bishop Maternus.

Progressively expanded over the next few centuries, the church began to burst at its seams in the 13th century when thousands of pilgrims flocked to Cologne to view the shrine containing the relics of the Three Kings. In 1248 the church was replaced with a cathedral conceived on a gigantic Gothic plan. Work went on for 300 years and then halted for lack of funds, with the steeples still unbuilt. The church remained that way for another 300 years until, at the urging of the young German Romantics and nationalists, work was resumed and the steeples completed in 1880.

Those steeples are the first thing you see of the cathedral, the first thing you see of Cologne, in fact. They complete the largest façade—200 feet wide, 515 feet high (61 m. by 157 m.)—of any church in Christendom.

Inside, the true architectural glory of the cathedral is its **choir**, a magnificent example of 13th-century Gothic intensity, its slim, almost delicate lines forming a striking contrast to the massiveness of the whole edifice. Very impresive in their natural elegance, set on the pillars of the choir, are the statues of Christ and Mary flanked by the apostles, sculpted by Master Arnold, one of the building's original architects.

The cathedral's richest treasure, looking itself like a basilica, is the gold **Dreikönigenschrein** (Shrine of the Three Kings) behind the high altar. The bones of the Three Kings were brought by Friedrich Barbarossa's chancellor, Reinald von Dassel, from Milan in the 12th century. Nikolaus von Verdun was commissioned to design this masterpiece of the goldsmith's art. Begun in 1181, it took 40 years to complete. The solid gold figures include the kings and prophets of the Old Testament along with scenes of Christ's baptism and the adoration of the Kings.

Another highly prized work is Stephan Lochner's splendid 15th-century **Dombild**, a triptych to the right of the choir, celebrating the patron saints of Cologne—Ursula, Gereon and the Three Kings. On the left side of the choir is the fine 10th-century **Gerokreuz** (Gero Cross), named after Archbishop Gero who commissioned this movingly simple crucifixion. It is the earliest example of a Byzantine-style sculpture appearing in Western Europe. In the Sakramentskapelle is the beautiful **Milan Madonna**, sculpted around 1280, with the colour, crown and sceptre restored in the last century.

Appropriately enough, next door to this formidable Christian monument, in the **Römisch-Germanisches Museum**, is the delightfully pagan Roman tribute to Bacchanalian pleasure, the **Dionysos Mosaic**. One of the few nice things to have happened in Cologne

during World War II was the discovery of this marvellously well-preserved work in the course of digging an air-raid shelter. The museum in which it is now housed was built around the mosaic's original site, once the floor of a prosperous 3rd-century Roman wheat merchant's dining-room. Dionysos is the Greek name of the fun-loving god the Romans called Bacchus. You can see him leaning tipsily on an obliging satyr while around him other satyrs and nymphs cavort and make music.

Cologne's striking modern **cultural centre,** between the cathedral and the river, includes the Rhineland's most important gallery of historical art, the **Wallraf-Richartz-Museum.** The building itself is a triumph of imaginative lighting and display for an excellent collection of early Rhenish art and many fine examples of the great European painters—Lochner, Dürer, Cranach to name but a few.

The Wallraf-Richartz-Museum is not the only pole of attraction in Cologne's impressive cultural centre, which is skilfully integrated into the sloping terrain. The centre is also the home of the Cologne Philharmonic and **Museum**

124

Ludwig, devoted to 20th-century art. Lindt chocolate tycoon Peter Ludwig put this remarkable collection together, including the best of the modern masters—Picasso, Dali, Klee, Kandinsky and Max Ernst—and some great examples of 1960s pop art—like Claes Oldenburg's lusty *Giant Soft Swedish Light Switch.*

For just a hint of what the old town of Cologne used to look like, go back to the river, to the tiny **Altstadt** between the Gross St. Martin church and the Deutzer bridge. There, around the old Fischmarkt, along the Salzgasse and across the Eisenmarkt (Ironware Market), you can find miracles of survival and restoration of houses dating back to the 13th and 14th centuries. Now a thriving, renewed neighbourhood of restaurants, antique shops, art galleries and apartments with attractive gardens, the lively atmosphere helps you imagine what it was like in the good old days.

But Cologne also has a bouncing, bustling present attested by the gleaming, pedestrians-only commercial area along the Hohe Strasse south-west of the cathedral. Reflecting its taste for things French, the town offers plenty of outdoor cafés. Some of the most agreeable are around Am Hof where you can linger over a delicious pastry and coffee while contemplating the delightfully kitschy dwarfs and inquisitive tailoress of the Heinzelmännchenbrunnen (Heinzeldwarf's Well), sculpted in 1899.

To round off the church scene, you might like to look in on the **Antoniterkirche** (on the Schildergasse), the main church of the small Protestant community, and admire Ernst Barlach's 1927 sculpture *Der Trauernde Engel* (the Mourning Angel)—to which he has given the features of his fellow artist Käthe Kollwitz. The best of the city's Romanesque churches, indeed one of the most delicate in the Rhineland, is the **St. Aposteln** west of the Neumarkt on the Mittelstrasse. The apse is decorated with blind arcades and graceful galleries. But perhaps the most moving of Cologne's ecclesiastical edifices is the **Madonna in den Trümmern** (Madonna in the Ruins), the modern chapel built out of the rubble of the old Gothic St. Kolumba church on Brückenstrasse. World War II bombardments left standing only the stump of a tower and part of one outer wall. Amazingly, a statue of the Virgin Mary also emerged unscathed. Hence the name of the chapel, which Gottfried Böhm designed in the 1950s, artfully integrating modern simplicity with the Gothic remains. Here you'll get a true feeling of the city's history of pain and recovery.

On the western side of the Alter Markt is the proud old **Rathaus** or Town Hall. Its elegant Renaissance pillared loggia is as warm and inviting as the administrative extension of its modern Spanischer Bau is cold and forbidding. From the Rathaus, the Judengasse, once the main street of the medieval Jewish quarter, takes you to the **Gürzenich**, home of historic merriment. Cologne's most important secular Gothic building—and practically the only one to survive into this century—was designed as a dance hall for the city government and its honoured guests, including the occasional Habsburg or Hohenzollern. The original building, constructed in 1441, was damaged by fire in World War II. Rebuilt, it is still the most prestigious venue for Carnival balls, banquets and concerts, the perfect Gothic complement to the cathedral.

Carnival

The Carnival is seen at its craziest in Cologne. Traditionally, the festivities are announced at a meeting of all the town's various carnival clubs at 11 minutes past 11 on the 11th day of the 11th month—11 being the madman's lucky number. After this preliminary party, a mild warm-up, the revellers break up till the New Year when the round of balls and banquets and masked processions begins in not-too-much earnest. The long winter nights are often brightened by party-goers wandering around the streets in harlequin costumes and other inspired paraphernalia derived from the great Venetian revels of the 18th century.

Every trade and profession worthy of the name—cobblers and doctors, carpenters and lawyers, tailors and computer-salesmen—vie to put on the most ingenious and uproarious ball possible. The climax is the last weekend leading to Shrove Tuesday (Mardi Gras), before all good Catholics settle down to a sober Lenten existence of (relative) abstinence and seemly behaviour.

The tone is set on the Thursday with Weiberfastnacht (the Women's Carnival) when wives lord it over their husbands and their friends' husbands, dancing and playing with whom they choose, and nobody knows or worries who beneath the masks and costumes is married to whom. Friday and Saturday: more parties as the celebration continues with people strolling around town in the most outrageous outfits. Even if someone felt like blushing, you wouldn't be able to tell under all the clown make-up.

Sunday it's the kids' turn to parade through the streets. *Rosenmontag* (Rose Monday) brings the biggest procession of all, with hundreds of elaborate floats displaying papier-mâché masks of popular and unpopular political figures in invariably undignified postures.

On Tuesday, hung-over, everybody goes back to work. Or, on Wednesday.

Excursions

No visit to Cologne is complete without a trip along the Rhine. You could take a train south to Bonn, and return downstream by boat; or take a leisurely cruise upstream to Mainz, along the most scenic part of the river.

Bonn

Not many people take Bonn seriously as the capital of West Germany—least of all the

Germans themselves. This is as much a tribute to its quiet serenity as a complaint about its lack of dynamism. But Bonn does have a modest charm, rather a nice surprise for the seat of government of such a busy, purposeful, self-confident nation.

To get a feeling for the atmosphere in which the country conducts its official business, start at the complex of government buildings between the Rhine and Adenauerallee. The **Bundeshaus**, the parliament, offers multilingual guided tours when not in session. There's a fine view of the Siebengebirge (Seven Hills) across the river from the public restaurant on the 30th floor of the Abgeordneten-hochhaus (Deputies' Building).

You can change gears with a restful stroll at the other end of the Adenauerallee, around the old trees of the **Hofgarten**. This leads back to the university, housed in the elegant Baroque residence designed for the high-living elector of Cologne, Joseph Clemens, by Louis XIV's architect Robert de Cotte. It was in the elector's private chapel here that a bright 16-year-old schoolboy named Ludwig van Beethoven performed his first music.

Bonn's sunny Baroque style can be appreciated in the graceful **Rathaus** (Town Hall) with its balustraded outside staircase, very much the centre of the "quiet" city basking in its 18th-century dream. The shopping area, like Cologne's blocked off from traffic, keeps things in the subdued mode.

Beethoven was born in Bonn in 1770 and his birthplace, the **Beethovenhaus**, at Bonngasse 20, has been preserved as a museum, proudly claiming the largest and most valuable collection of Beethoven memorabilia. It includes one of the grand pianos he played towards the end of his life and the acoustical instruments he used to combat his increasing deafness.

The best of Bonn's museums is the **Rheinisches Landesmuseum**, outstanding for its Rhenish painters with some fine examples of the Cologne School. But the stars are undoubtedly the **Neanderthal Man** and **Cro-Magnon Couple**. Old Neanderthal, 50,000 years old in fact, was found by workmen in a quarry near Düsseldorf in 1856. His remains include the top of his skull and 16 other bones, enough for anthropologists to determine that he was 5 feet 4 inches tall and 60 years old when he died. The Cro-Magnon man and woman, dating back to 10,000 B.C., are displayed with carved bone figures buried with them in their grave.

Rhine Valley

The Rhine Valley that people dream about is the part betwen Koblenz and Mainz. This is where the mountains of the Hunsrück on the west and the Taunus and the Rheingau-Gebirge on the east come right down to the river forming a narrow valley of steeply terraced vineyards and pine forests guarded by castles and towering rocks, where myth and history mingle inextricably with the Nibelungs, medieval war and piracy, and romantic idylls.

The dreams begin just south of Koblenz, at **Stolzenfels**, high above the river. Friedrich Wilhelm IV of Prussia started rebuilding the 14th-century castle, sacked by the French in 1689, at the height of the German Romantic movement when the nation was lovingly reconstructing its past. His Koblenz architects gave it the full treatment—turrets and crenellated battlements, funny little arches, giddy external staircases leading nowhere in particular, half-hidden rose-windows under knobby min-

arets—all integrated into a fairy-tale "natural" setting of paths winding past gurgling brooks, of waterfalls among the pine trees, and shrubbery to break the fall of anyone accidentally cast into the dry moat.

Just before St. Goar, on the other side of the river, you will see Burg Thurnberg, better known as **Burg Maus**, coupled in popular imagination with **Burg Katz** (Cat) further south, directly opposite St. Goar. Katz was built at the end of the 14th century by Count Johann von Katzenelnbogen to snatch away the river-tolls that previously went to Maus. St. Goar itself has a splendid castle ruin, the **Burg Rheinfels**, built by an earlier—equally rapacious—Katzenelnbogen in 1245. Louis XIV's troops' rampage through the Rhineland left it unscathed, but in 1797 more French troops reduced it to the picturesque ruin you see today.

Across the river is the myth-laden rock of Lorelei, the siren that inspired Heinrich Heine's celebrated poem.

Rüdesheim is perhaps the best-known of the Rhineland's wine-villages. Certainly its **Drosselgasse** has the liveliest collection of taverns and wine-cellars of the region.

Here, in an atmosphere of perpetual festivity, you can try the Rheingau's famous Rieslings, the sparkling Sekt and the locally distilled brandies. You can sample one of the few good red wines of the Rhineland at **Assmannshausen**. People suffering from rheumatism or lumbago come here for the warm bromide of lithium waters at the Kurhaus.

On your way to Lorch, look back across the Rhine—the reconstructed castles of Rheinstein, Reichstein and Sooneck look much more romantic from a distance. **Lorch** itself has an attractive Gothic church, St. Martin.

Eating Out

After trekking through the city or sailing on the Rhine, you are sure to have developed a healthy appetite. You won't go hungry, as food in Germany is substantial.

Lunch is often the main meal of the day. Start with a thick soup: *Bohnensuppe* (bean), *Linsensuppe* (lentils) or *Kohlsuppe* (cabbage with sausage). In summer you may prefer one of the delicious cold fruit soups such as *Kirschensuppe*, made from cherries.

Pork comes in various forms, from local ham to spicy wurst sausages and milder frankfurters. Special pork dishes include *Himmel und Erde* (Heaven and Earth) with apples, blood sausage and leeks; and blood sausage with raw onions, a dish the Cologne residents laughingly call *Kölsche Kaviar*. Also taste *Halve Hahn*—not half a chicken, but a rye bread roll stuffed with hot mustard and Dutch cheese.

Sauerkraut is an acquired taste, but when prepared with juniper berries, caraway seeds and cloves in white wine, it deserves to be sampled at least once. And don't neglect sweet and sour red cabbage (*Rotkraut*) tossed with apples, raisins and white vinegar. *Reibekuchen* (potato pancakes) and *Kartoffelsalat* (potato salad) spiced with onions and bacon are truly mouth-watering.

The best wine is white from the Rheingau district between Wiesbaden and Rüdesheim,

where the vineyards face the sun. Other fruity labels come from the Rheinhessen region, the Rheinpfalz and the Mittelrhein. Don't worry about red and white rules. Drink what you want. But if you do like red with your steak then ask for Assmannshausen.

Shopping

The best souvenirs are always the ones which have a special association with the place they come from, so don't leave town without a bottle of **Eau de Cologne**.

If you collect **antiques**, you'll find the Altstadt (old town) a real haven. There's no knowing what you'll pick up: maybe a Biedermeier bookcase or a 19th-century romantic landscape painting.

Leather and **sportswear** are popular German goods, while **toys** such as model trains and scale models of Rhine Valley castles are designed with great ingenuity.

For **precision instruments**, best buys include binoculars, telescopes and cameras.

Old Meissen or modern Rosenthal **china** and German **linen** (especially the famous *Federbett*, duck- or goosedown quilts) are of top quality.

Practical Information

Banks: Open from 8.30 a.m. to 1 p.m., 2.30 to 4 p.m., Thursday until 5 p.m.

Currency: The *Deutsche Mark* (*DM*) is divided into 100 *Pfennig* (*Pf.*). Coins: 1, 2, 5, 10 and 50 Pf., DM 1, 2, 5, 10. Notes: 5, 10, 20, 50, 100, 500 and 1,000.

Post offices: Open from 8 a.m. to 6 p.m., Monday to Friday, and until noon on Saturday. Mail boxes are yellow with black post-horns.

Shops: Open from 9 a.m. to 6.30 p.m., Monday to Friday, and until 2 p.m. on Saturday (6 p.m. the first Saturday of the month).

COPENHAGEN

Denmark

Introduction

Centre of Danish government, administration and finance, Copenhagen is home to nearly one third of Denmark's five million people. It also lodges the oldest royal dynasty in Europe.

Broad highways carve through the 20th-century city. But, off them, Copenhagen still has a well-preserved old-town area of winding cobbled streets, stuccoed houses and curio shops. A quality of fairyland, of magic, pervades the city with its 17th-century green copper roofs and domes, royal legacy of Denmark's great builder-king, Christian IV.

A strong sense of fantasy and colour appears around any corner in Copenhagen. Postmen wear bright red jackets and ride yellow bikes. Chimney-sweeps wear black top-hats, into which they may tuck their lunchtime *smørrebrød* (sandwiches). Buses often drive merrily along with little red-and-white Danish flags fluttering each side of the driving cab.

"Wonderful, wonderful," sang Danny Kaye about Copenhagen. Most visitors would agree—a hundred times over.

COPENHAGEN

A Brief History

12th–14th centuries	In 1157 Valdemar I becomes king. At this time, Copenhagen is a little fishing village called Havn (harbour). But thanks to its position at the entrance to the Baltic, one of the main trading routes of medieval Europe, Havn quickly develops into an important trade centre. Statesman and warrior-hero Bishop Absalon builds a fortified castle on Havn's harbour island, Slotsholmen, in 1167, the year considered as founding date of today's city. In 1170, it changes its name to Køpmannæhafn ("merchants' harbour"). During his reign (1340–75), King Valdemar IV Atterdag leads Denmark into conflict with its Nordic neighbours. However his daughter Margrete marries Håkon VI, king of Norway and Sweden, and by the Treaty of Kalmar in 1397, the three Nordic countries are unified under her rule.
15th–17th centuries	The following 200 years are marked by internal strife, the Lutheran movement and constant wars against Sweden. Copenhagen is enlarged and becomes official capital under Christopher III of Bavaria. With the founding of its university in 1497 it also becomes the cultural centre of Denmark. The Reformation takes place in 1536 under Christian III who declares himself supreme authority of a State Church based on Lutheranism. During the first half of the 17th century, Christian IV enlarges Copenhagen and erects many fine buildings. In 1660 the town becomes a "free city"—all residents being granted the same privileges as the nobles.
17th–19th centuries	By the latter half of the 17th century, Denmark is forced to relinquish remaining Swedish possessions. During the 18th century, Copenhagen suffers a plague (1711/12) and two devastating fires (1728 and 1795). Serfdom in Denmark is abolished in 1788. Denmark gets involved in the European revolutionary wars without really wishing it. Copenhagen is attacked by the British in 1801 and again in 1807 when the Danes have to hand over the rest of their fleet to the British, only to be forced immediately afterwards to sign an alliance with Napoleon who is marching into Jutland. To pay off war debts, Denmark

has to hand over Norway to Sweden in 1814. 50 years later it loses the Schleswig and Holstein duchies to Bismarck's Prussia. In 1848 Frederik VII is forced to relinquish absolute rule to the National Liberal Party.

19th–20th centuries	Denmark stays neutral in World War I. In 1920, North Schleswig votes itself back again from Germany into Denmark. During World War II, Copenhagen escapes large-scale destruction. In 1949 the country enters NATO and in 1972 becomes a member of the EEC.

Sightseeing

No one visiting Copenhagen would wish to miss the statue of the **Little Mermaid** (*Den Lille Havfrue*), as well known and beloved as Hans Christian Andersen himself. In his fairy tale, the tragic sea-girl exchanged her voice for human legs in order to gain the love of an earthly prince, but mutely had to watch as he jilted her for a real princess. In desperation, she threw herself into the sea and turned to foam. Today she sits forever on a small clump of rocks,

looking wistfully out to sea.

Watching over the Little Mermaid is the 300-year old **Citadel** *(Kastellet)*, a cornerstone of Christian IV's defences of Copenhagen. The 300-year-old fort (built mostly between 1662 and 1725) is still used by the army—the church, prison and main guardhouse have resisted the assaults of time. It is a delightfully peaceful enclave in a modern city, and has a charming windmill (1847) as well as remains of the old ramparts.

The nearby **Gefion Fountain** is Copenhagen's most spectacular. Erected by the Carlsberg Foundation, it depicts the legend of the Nordic goddess Gefion, who turned her four sons into oxen and used them to plough the island of Zealand out of Sweden.

Amalienborg Palace, home of the royal family, is situated in a spacious and stately square off Bredgade. Actually, it is not a square but a cobbled octagon, on four sides of which stand identical mansion-like palaces. These were originally designed as noblemen's homes by court architect Nicolai Eigtved during a city expansion in the 1750's. After Christiansborg castle (formerly the royal residence), was destroyed by fire in 1794,

the royal family gradually bought up Amalienborg from the nobles and has lived there ever since. Today it's reckoned to be one of the finest Rococo ensembles in Europe. Its centrepiece is a unique copper **equestrian monument** to King Frederik V.

Outside, the ceremony of the changing of the guards is sometimes to be seen.

For a complete change of atmosphere you could visit the one-time seamen's quar-

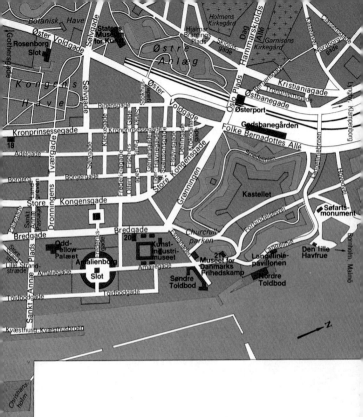

1 Louis Tussauds Voksmuseum
2 Koncertsal
3 Central Postbygningen
4 Ny Carlsberg Glyptotek
5 Universitetet
6 Domkirken
7 Rundetårn

8 Helligåndskirken
9 Sankt Nikolaj Kirke
10 Det Kongelige Teater
11 Charlottenborg
12 Teaterhistorisk Museum
13 Børsen
14 Holmens Kirke

15 Christians Kirke
16 Det Danske Filmmuseum
17 Vor Frelsers Kirke
18 Davids Samling
19 Marmorkirken
20 Sankt Ansgar Kirke
21 St. Alban's Church

COPENHAGEN

ter, lively **Nyhavn.** Hans Christian Andersen spent part of his life in this area. Though he would still recognize the façades and buildings, he would find quite a change: it is now a mixture of taverns, restaurants, discotheques and clubs on the immediate north side, and elsewhere of elegantly restored frontages, luxury apartments, restaurants and one superb hotel conversion of an 18th-century warehouse.

(From the Kongens Nytorv end of Nyhavn you can take a trip round Copenhagen's canals. Lasting about one hour, these trips provide an excellent view of many parts of the

city and of such fascinating harbours as Christianshavn.)

On Slotsholm Island, linked to the capital by several bridges, is the **Christiansborg Palace,** once the home of the royal family and now that of the Danish parliament.

This is the sixth castle or palace on the site since Bishop Absalon, founder of Copenhagen, built his fortress here in 1167, pillage, fire or rebuilding frenzy having taken their subsequent toll. The third castle became the permanent seat of king and government in 1417. The present edifice dates only from the early years of this century.

Christiansborg's chapel, the riding lodges and lovely restored **marble bridge,** which managed to survive two disastrous fires in 1794 and 1884, help to give the palace a more venerable aspect than its generally very recent origins might lead one to expect.

The palace houses three museums:

On a tour of the **Royal Reception Chambers** you can see a series of rooms in everything from imitation marble to the richly tapestried, gold and green room where monarchs are proclaimed from the balcony overlooking the Castle Square below.

In a vast building on the south-east side of Christiansborg is housed the **Royal Arsenal Museum** *(Tøjhusmuseet)* where you are greeted by attendants in three-cornered hats and knee-length red jackets. It's appropriate for a museum housing one of Europe's most important collections of military uniforms and historic equipment.

Across the royal riding grounds at the rear of Christiansborg, and in an elegant little terrace above the stables, is one of the world's most unusual theatre museums, the **Teaterhistorisk Museum.** It is unusual, for a start, because of the constant aroma of horses seeping up through the 200-year-old creaky floorboards, and it has always been thus. Already at the former Court Theatre's first production in 1767, the authentic country smell was remarked on.

The small auditorium and galleries of the former Court Theatre are packed with Danish and international theatre relics—memorabilia of Hans Christian Andersen, Anna Pavlova, Ibsen; playbills, costumes, prints and photographs of Danish theatre history.

Just off the Castle Square is the highly ornamented **Børsen**

(Stock Exchange), dating from the days of Christian IV. It has a green copper roof with a famous spire composed of four intricately intertwined dragons' tails.

The **Nationalmuseet** (National Museum) on Frederiksholm Kanal is the biggest museum in Scandinavia. It holds an uncountable number of exhibits in eight separate major collections, ranging from prehistoric to Middle Ages, town and manor culture, ethnographical, special and classical antiquity, coins and medals.

Rådhuspladsen (Town Hall Square) is the city's largest square from which 14 streets branch out in different directions. A hub of constant activity, it has several notable statues and, of course, the **Town Hall** itself. Built between 1892 and 1905, this building boasts, among other things, an impressive main hall and banqueting room, as well as a **world clock** designed by Jens Olsen.

One of the streets leading off Rådhuspladsen is **Strøget**, the capital's most famous pedestrian street with its numerous small bars, pavement cafés and excellent shops. It winds its way for three-quarters of a mile to the city's other main square, Kongens Nytorv, changing its name four times en route (Frederiksgade, Nygade, Vimmelskaftet and Amagertorv).

The famous **Tivoli Gardens** are just across the street from Rådhuspladsen. These gardens, the pride and joy of the people of Copenhagen, are unique in that they provide something for everyone. There are fountains, bands, orchestras, theatres, lakes, bridges, a pagoda, restaurants, flower beds, slot machines, and donkey rides; it is a place in which to enjoy yourself or simply relax.

Almost opposite Tivoli, down Axeltorv, is Copenhagen's famous **circus.** Established in 1887, it has been voted Continental Europe's best circus for four consecutive years.

The **Ny Carlsberg Glyptotek,** across Tietgensgade from Tivoli, was founded on the classical collection of Carl Jacobsen, Danish brewer and art connoisseur (1842–1914), and developed by his family. Today, under one elaborate roof, you can thus see one of the world's foremost exhibitions of Egyptian, Greek, Roman and Etruscan art, with enough statues and artefacts to equip 100 ancient temples.

In quite another vein, there are 25 Gauguins, three van Goghs and seven Rodin statues, as well as a complete set of Degas bronzes—73 delicate little statues that won the painter posthumous acclaim as a sculptor. A museum with two distinct sides to it, in fact.

Slightly off the main tourist route, but well worth a visit, is the **Rundetårn** (Round Tower), built in 1642 by Christian IV as an astronomical observatory. It has been one of the city's most beloved landmarks for 300 years, even if it only reaches the modest height of 118 feet (36 m.).

You can walk to the top, but not by steps—these would have been impractical for raising the heavy equipment needed there. Instead, a wide spiral sloping causeway winds its way round for almost 700 feet (209 m.) inside the tower. Not only did Czar Peter the Great ride up it on horseback in 1716—his empress followed in a coach-and-six.

Rosenborg Castle, on the other side of town, boasts exhibits which span Danish royal history over the past 300 years. Of special interest are Christian IV's tower room study, the Knight's Hall and the treasury which contains the **crown jewels.**

North of Copenhagen

At the **Frilandsmuseet** (Open-Air Folk Museum) at Sorgenfri, the 90-acre (36-ha.) site is scattered with forty farmhouses, cottages and workshops, all furnished in strictly authentic style.

Broadly, the buildings are divided into geographic groups laid out along country lanes, with old bridges and village pumps, the whole authentically landscaped.

Another popular excursion is the lovely drive to Helsingør, along the so-called Danish Riviera with its small fishing villages and bays. If it's seaside weather, you might be tempted to stop en route and join the bathers at **Bellevue Beach** near Klampenborg.

At **Helsingør** itself (better known as Elsinore), "Hamlet's castle" juts out dramatically towards Sweden. In fact, though the film was shot on this site, Hamlet himself never slept here, nor did he ever see a ghost within these walls.

The castle's real name is Kronborg, and it was built between 1574 and 1585 at the command of King Frederik II. Its purpose was to help extract tolls from ships entering the narrow Sound (and thus the Baltic) at this point.

Restored this century, the

moated brick castle stands today as Frederik's proudest memorial, now sparsely furnished but immensely impressive. It has the feel of solid strength and royal presence, permeating the elaborate little **chapel,** the long galleries and stone stairways, and above all the huge oak-beamed **Banqueting Hall.** At 205 feet by 36 (62 × 11 m.), it is the largest hall of its kind in northern Europe and one of the noblest rooms of the Danish Renaissance.

The interesting **Handels- og Søfartsmuseum** (Trade and Maritime Museum) in the castle's northern wing contains an exhibition of old navigation instruments as well as relics from early Danish settlements in Greenland and elsewhere.

In the rolling farmland of North Zealand lies **Fredensborg Slot.** Built between 1719 and 1722, it is a perfect example of Italian/Dutch Baroque, situated on a small hill, surrounded by grounds which were the delight of King Frederik V, who turned this hunting seat into a royal summer residence.

You can stroll around the beautiful, lakeside grounds any time, but the royal apartments and private garden are opened to visitors only when the royal family is absent.

Six miles (9 km.) away, near Hillerød, stands **Frederiksborg Slot,** one of the greatest Renaissance castles in northern Europe and the most monumental achievement of the "Great Builder", Christian IV.

In 1859 much of the interior of the castle was destroyed by

fire but was later restored by a Danish brewer, J. C. Jacobsen, and turned into a museum. Today, in more than 60 rooms, is a complete record of the Danish monarchy from Christian I down to the present queen.

Also of interest are the **Knights' Hall,** awesome in its dimensions, and the richly carved and ornamented **chapel** with an organ dating back to 1610, virtually unchanged. Remarkably, the chapel escaped almost untouched from the disastrous fire.

Eating Out

Smørrebrød

There are approximately 178 varieties of *smørrebrød,* those buttered slices of rye or white bread covered with one or a variety of delicacies: veal, beef tartare, liver paste, salmon, smoked eel, cod-roe, shrimps, herring, ham, roast beef, salad or cheese. This main layer is garnished with a variety of accessories carefully selected to enhance both taste and appearance.

Koldt bord

The cold buffet-style spread is known in Denmark as *koldt bord* ("cold table"), and resembles the Swedish *smörgåsbord.* For a fixed price, you start at one end of the table helping yourself to herring in various preparations, seafood, mayonnaise salads and other delicacies, and continue on to sample liver paste, ham and other cuts of meat. Despite its name, a *koldt bord* always includes a few hot items, such as meat balls, pork sausages, soup and fried potatoes. Several kinds of bread and salads are also provided.

En platte is a cold dish (smaller version of previous) made up of six to eight specialities, often eaten at lunchtime.

Fish

Herring is a great favourite, served pickled, marinated or fried, with a sherry, vinegar, curry or fennel dressing. The succulent red Greenland shrimps are keen competitors in the popularity stakes. Lobster is widely available (but not cheap), as are crab, salmon, cod and halibut. The little Øresund *rødspætte* (redspot plaice) is on every menu. A speciality in summer is *danske rejer,* the small pink shrimps from local waters, served piled high on white bread.

Meat

The commonest steaks are *fransk bøf*, filet steak served with herb butter and chips (French fries), and *engelsk bøf*, filet steak served with fried onions and potatoes. *Mørbradbøf*, or tenderloin of pork, is eaten with onions, gravy and boiled potatoes, and Danish meatballs *(frikadeller)*, a finely minced mixture of pork and veal, with potato salad. *Hakkebøf* is the crumbling Danish hamburger—and *pariserbøf* a slightly cooked, almost raw, hamburger.

Cheese

Danish Blue *(Danablu)*—rich, with a sharp flavour—is quite well known internationally. *Mycella*—similar but milder—is rarely found outside the country. *Fynbo* and *Samsø* are both mild, firm cheeses with a sweetish nutty flavour.

Desserts

Favourite desserts include: *æblekage* (stewed apples with vanilla, served with alternating layers of biscuit crumbs—and topped with whipped cream) and *bondepige med slør* (a mixture of ryebread crumbs, apple sauce, sugar—and whipped cream).

Shops, cafés and small bars abound on cheerful and informal Strøget.

Danish pastry

Oddly enough, Danish pastry is called Viennese pastry *(wienerbrød)* in Denmark. This distinctive light and flaky delight can be found in any *konditori*, and makes a scrumptious mid-morning or afternoon snack.

Drinks

The golden Danish lager comes in several types, from *lys pilsner* (light lager) at only 2 per cent alcohol, through the normal green-bottle *pilsner* to the stouts and special beers (like *elefantøl*) at 6–7 per cent or more.

All wine is imported and expensive in restaurants.

Akvavit is the fiery Danish *snaps*, made from potatoes, often with a distinct caraway taste, taken at mealtimes with the opening fish course, and often later with the cheese. Beware of over-indulging, or you'll need Gammel Dansk bitter for next morning's hangover.

After dinner you might like to try a glass of Denmark's famous cherry liqueur, Cherry Heering.

Shopping

There's value-added tax on all goods bought in Denmark. This tax will be refunded to visitors who make large purchases in shops displaying the red-and-white "Danish Tax-Free Shopping" sticker.

What to Buy

Amber necklaces. The local "gem" (actually fossil resin) found in the southern Baltic and on the North Sea coast, is probably cheaper here than back home, but starting prices still have a tendency to be rather high.

COPENHAGEN

Danish porcelain. The big names are Royal Copenhagen Porcelain and Bing & Grøndahl.

Furs are fantastic quality.

Glassware and household products in **stainless steel** are particularly good buys if you want top design matched with excellent craftsmanship.

Knitwear is Nordic-style, often highly patterned, warm and perhaps expensive.

Lamps are a lovingly designed product, as are **household textiles** and **hand-woven rugs.**

Silver is a Danish speciality, dominated by the name Georg Jensen. Silver in Denmark is quality-controlled and must be hallmarked.

Pipes are another indigenous craft.

Toys are simple and attractive, especially those in solid wood: trains, ships, etc.

Souvenirs are myriad: little mermaids, Copenhagen dolls in black lace caps and frilly skirts, ceramic blue figurines and animals. All kinds of trolls and Vikings also abound—naturally!

Practical Information

Banks: Open 9.30 a.m. to 4 p.m. Monday to Friday; 9.30 a.m. to 6 p.m. on Thursday. Money can also be changed at the Central Railway Station between 7 a.m. and 9 p.m. daily.

Clothing: It is a good idea to take a light raincoat when sightseeing as the weather can be fickle. Good walking shoes are also recommended.

Credit cards and traveller's cheques: Fairly widely accepted.

Currency: Danish *krone* (kr.) = 100 øre. Coins: 25, 50 øre; kr. 1, 5, 10. Notes: kr. 20, 50, 100, 500, 1,000.

Shops: Open 9–9.30 a.m. to 5.30 p.m. Monday to Thursday. Fridays 9.30 a.m. to 7 or 8 p.m, Saturdays 9.30 a.m. to 1 or 2 p.m.

Post offices: The main post office in Tietgensgade (just behind Tivoli) is open 9 a.m. to 7 p.m. Monday to Friday, and 9 a.m. to 1 p.m. on Saturday. You can usually purchase stamps as well when buying postcards. Postboxes are bright red.

DUBLIN

Eire

Introduction

Sightseers who prefer cities won't be disappointed in Dublin. The capital of Ireland is a very European city of low-profile buildings, many of them outstanding examples of 18th-century architecture.

Birthplace and inspiration of great authors, Dublin is pervaded by contrasting moods which can affect even the transient visitor: sweeping avenues and intimate side-streets, chic shopping and smokey pubs, distinguished museums and colleges along with sports galore. In this appealing melting pot of old and new, the traditional lace curtains still mask the windows of modern apartment blocks, and a policeman riding a bicycle reports to headquarters by lapel radio.

The name of Dublin comes from the Irish *Dubhlinn,* meaning "dark pool". But you'll also see a much older Gaelic name on buses and signs: *Baile Atha Cliath,* "the town of the hurdle ford", which explains why Dublin was originally settled centuries ago—as a place to ford the River Liffey near its exit to the sea. The river, a system of tranquil canals and the nearby Irish Sea all contribute to Dublin's special atmosphere. Seagulls frequent the centre of town; so do the ghosts of Vikings, Normans, Viceroys... and Leopold and Molly Bloom, late of Eccles Street.

A Brief History

Early times	The first settlers probably cross a land bridge from Scandinavia to Scotland, continuing across a narrow strait to Ireland. During the Neolithic period, the inhabitants turn to farming. They construct numerous tombs and temples, many of which survive. New settlers and new contacts with Europe bring Bronze Age weapons and skills. Celtic tribes arrive in the last years of the pre-Christian era, introducing their language and iron technology. Roman legions conquer Western Europe, stopping short at the Irish Sea.
5th–11th centuries	Celts stage raids on Roman Britain. St. Patrick makes converts to Christianity and establishes monasteries all over Ireland. In the 9th century, Viking raiders attack

coastal settlements and monasteries. Eventually they establish trading colonies—Dublin, Waterford and Limerick. Norse dominance comes to an end in 1014 with the decisive defeat of the Vikings at Clontarf.

| 12th–15th centuries | The Normans conquer, led by the Earl of Pembroke and in league with an Irish warrior-king, Dermot MacMurrough of Leinster. The crucial victory occurs in 1169 at Waterford. King Henry of England, overlord of the earl, asserts his sovereignty in 1171. Towns, abbey churches and castles are built. |

16th–17th centuries

Henry VIII is the first English monarch to call himself "King of Ireland". He attempts to introduce the Reformation into the country, but Catholicism is too firmly entrenched. Farmland is confiscated from Catholics and handed over to Protestant settlers. During the reign of Queen Elizabeth I, two major revolts are put down. Resistance is centred in Ulster. After 1654 Catholics are only permitted to hold land west of the River Shannon.

In 1690 William of Orange, a Protestant, defeats his Catholic father-in-law James II at the Battle of the Boyne. Although the rights of Catholics are guaranteed, the Catholic majority has little power or political influence.

18th–19th centuries

The Act of Union (1801) abolishes Ireland's parliament and establishes the United Kingdom of Great Britain and Ireland. Daniel O'Connell, an Irish patriot, calls for the repeal of the act, to no avail. The potato famine strikes Ireland mid-century. A million people die and another million emigrate.

20th century

Nationalist groups join forces to found the Sinn Fein movement in 1905. They go on to proclaim an Irish republic in the Easter Rising of 1916, but the insurrection is crushed and its leaders executed. Civil war breaks out and Ireland is partitioned in 1921. Six Protestant counties remain within the United Kingdom, while the others unite as the Irish Free State, a dominion of the British Empire. As proof of its independence, Ireland stays neutral in World War II. Sectarian violence continues in the post-war period, as the problem of Northern Ireland eludes solution.

Sightseeing

O'Connell Street to St. Stephen's Green

The main street of Dublin, **O'Connell Street** is worthy of a major capital, a lasting monument to the Wide Street Commissioners of the 18th century. It is 45 metres (150 ft.) across and as straight as the morals of Father Theobald Mathew, the 19th-century priest known as the Apostle of Temperance. You'll find him commemorated in one of the four monuments down the middle of the roadway. There used to be five. As an anti-British gesture in 1966, unidentified citizens removed the imposing Nelson Pillar erected in 1808. Many Dubliners admired the panache and technical skill of the demolition crew that blew it up in the middle of the night.

The best-known landmark of O'Connell Street, the **General Post Office,** has a significance far greater than its postal predominance. The GPO (as it is known) was the command post of the 1916 Easter Rising and badly damaged in the fighting. A plaque on the front of the building, in Irish and English, and a statue in the main hall mark the historic event.

At the south end of the street, facing O'Connell Bridge, stands the monument to Daniel O'Connell (1775–1847), "The Liberator", after whom the street and bridge are named.

From the three-arched bridge, almost as wide as it is long, you can look up and down the **River Liffey** and along the embankments. To the east, beyond the "skyscraper" headquarters of the Irish trade unions, rises the copper dome of the majestic 18th-century **Custom House.** Like many buildings along the Liffey, it was all but destroyed in the civil war fighting of 1921, but has been fully restored.

Some of the most interesting old buildings in Ireland, including disused churches, are now occupied by banks. But it may come as a surprise that the momentous white stone building facing College Green on the south side of the Liffey is the headquarters of the **Bank of Ireland** company. It was built in the 18th century for the parliament of Ireland, but when parliament was abolished (by the Act of Union of 1800), the bank moved in. The grand portico has 22 Ionic columns.

DUBLIN CENTRE

Behind the curved railings at the entrance to **Trinity College** are the statues of two famous alumni—the philosopher Edmund Burke and the playwright Oliver Goldsmith. Founded by Queen Elizabeth I in 1591, Trinity remains a timeless enclave of calm and scholarship in the middle of a bustling city. For centuries it was regarded as an exclusively Protestant institution; as recently as 1956, the Catholic church forbade its youth to attend Trinity "under pain of mortal sin". TCD, as it is generally called, is now integrated.

The campus is mostly a monument to the good taste of the 18th century, and visitors will enjoy roaming among the cobbled walks among trimmed lawns, fine old trees, statues and graceful stone buildings. But Trinity's greatest treasure may be found in the vaulted Long Room upstairs in the **Old Library.** Here the double-decker stacks hold thousands of books published before 1800, and priceless early manuscripts are displayed in glass cases. Long queues of students and tourists reverently wait for a look at the **Book of Kells.** This 340-page parchment manuscript, hand-written and illustrated by Irish monks in the 8th or 9th century, contains a Latin version of the New Testament. The beauty of the script, the decoration of initial letters and words, the abstract designs and above all the saintly portraits constitute the most wonderful survival from Ireland's Golden Age. The leaves of vellum on display are turned once a day to protect them from the light and to give visitors a chance to come back for more.

Some of Europe's finest Georgian houses face **Merrion Square,** once the proposed site for a Catholic cathedral, now a public park. The discreet brick houses have those special Dublin doorways, flanked by columns and topped by fanlights, and no two are alike. In a complex of formal buildings on the west side of the square stands Dublin's largest 18th-century mansion, the home of the Duke of Leinster. Today **Leinster House** is the seat of the Irish parliament, consisting of the Senate (*Seanad* in Irish) and the Chamber of Deputies (the *Dail*, pronounced doyle).

At the entrance to the **National Gallery** of Ireland is a statue of George Bernard Shaw, a Dubliner known locally as a benefactor of

The Old Library of Trinity College: a popular Dublin attraction.

the institution. The National Gallery displays some 2,000 works of art, but holds 6,000 more in reserve. Irish artists, reasonably enough, receive priority but important Dutch, English, Flemish, French, Italian and Spanish masters are also well represented. Among those on display: Fra Angelico, Rubens, Rembrandt, Canaletto, Gainsborough and Goya. Rounding out a prize collection of medieval religious art is the gallery's most recent acquisition, two glorious **frescoes** of the 11th or 12th century, delicately lifted from the walls of the Chapel of St.-Pierre-de-Campublic, in Beaucaire (near Avignon), France.

The main entrance to the **National Museum,** another important Dublin institution, is reached from Kildare

Street. The museum's collection of Irish antiquities contains all manner of surprises, from ancient skeletons and tools to exquisite gold ornaments of the Bronze Age. The most famous exhibits are the 8th-century **Ardagh Chalice,** the delicately worked **Tara Brooch** from the same era and the **Shrine of St. Patrick's Bell** (12th century). You can also examine ancient Ogham stones with inscriptions in what might seem a childish way of encoding Latin. And if you don't have time to make a tour of churchyards and far-off monasteries, you can admire replicas of the greatest carved stone crosses from the early centuries of Christian Ireland.

The south-east part of central Dublin is unusually well endowed with breathing space, thanks to a number of pleasant squares and parks. The biggest—possibly the biggest city square in Europe—is **St. Stephen's Green.** In the 18th century it was almost surrounded by elegant town houses, some of which survive; conservationists despair at the dwindling number. Inside the square is a perfectly delightful park with flower gardens and a man-made lake inhabited by waterfowl. The square contains many sculptures and monuments in varied style, including a memorial to the poet and playwright W.B. Yeats by Henry Moore. Nearby is a bust of Yeat's friend, Countess Constance Markievicz, the legendary defender of St. Stephen's Green during the 1916 insurrection and the first woman elected to the British House of Commons.

Another statue honours the man who paid for landscaping St. Stephen's Green in 1880. He was Lord Ardilaun, son of the founder of the Guinness Brewery. Some thirsty sightseers might be inspired to find a nearby pub and raise a toast to the stout-hearted benefactor.

Medieval Dublin

Dublin Castle was begun in the 13th century on a hill overlooking the original Viking settlement on the south bank of the Liffey. It was largely rebuilt in the 18th century, which explains why it no longer looks like a medieval castle. Over the centuries it served as seat of government, prison, courthouse, parliament and occasionally as fortress under siege—most recently in 1916. Many a visiting head of state has been fêted in the lavishly appointed State Apartments, once the residence of the British Viceroy.

Around the corner from the castle, Dublin's City Hall (formerly the Royal Exchange) was built in the late 18th century in neo-classical style. It contains ancient royal charters and the municipal regalia.

Dublin has not one but two noteworthy cathedrals. And though it is the capital of a predominantly Catholic country, both cathedrals belong to the Protestant Church of Ireland. The reason for two cathedrals is easily explained if you have the time to sift through 12th-century political and religious rivalries. In any case, **Christ Church** is the older of the two, dating from 1038. One unusual architectural touch is the covered pedestrian bridge over Winetavern Street, linking the church and its synod house. This was built in Victorian times but doesn't spoil the overall mood. Otherwise, Christ Church has Romanesque, Early English and neo-Gothic elements. The **crypt,** which extends under the whole church like a vast wine-cellar, is a remnant of the 12th century, when the cathedral was expanded by the Earl of Pembroke, whose remains

were buried here. However, the authenticity of the present Pembroke tomb—the statue of a recumbent cross-legged knight in armour in the southern aisle—is discounted.

A short walk south from Christ Church leads to Dublin's newer and larger cathedral, **St. Patrick's,** dedicated to the national saint. It is said that St. Patrick himself baptized 5th-century converts at a well on this site; a stone slab which covered the well is displayed in the north-west corner of the cathedral. This church was consecrated in 1192, but the present structure dates mostly from the 13th and 14th centuries. The cathedral is best known for its association with Jonathan Swift, the crusading satirist, who was appointed dean in 1713 and served until his death in 1745. Many Swiftian relics may be seen in a corner of the north transept, and a simple brass plate in the floor near the entrance marks his grave. Next to it is the tomb of the mysterious Stella, one of the two great loves of his life. Over the doorway to the robing room is his own bitter epitaph, in Latin: "...Savage indignation can no longer gnaw his heart. Go, traveller, and imitate, if you can, this earnest

and dedicated defender of liberty."

The talented choirboys of St. Patrick's Cathedral lift up their voices—and the spirits of the listeners—at services every day except Saturday. The Cathedral Choir School was founded in 1432. A joint choir from both cathedrals was first in the world to sing Handel's *Messiah* when the composer was in Dublin in 1742. A contemporary (1799) copy may be seen in Marsh's Library, next to St. Patrick's. This was Ireland's first public library, founded in 1701.

The North Bank

The most impressive building on the north bank of the Liffey is the domed home of the **Four Courts** (originally Chancery, Common Pleas, Exchequer and King's Bench). It's the work of James Gandon, the 18th-century English-born architect who also designed Dublin's Custom House. The

Among curiosities on view is a so-called Penitent's Pew in which sinners had to confess to the congregation. In the vaults, wood coffins and many a mummy can be seen in a remarkably healthy state of preservation. Some of them have been here for over 200 years, saved from normal deterioration, perhaps, by the dry air or its high methane content. It's all a bit spooky.

The last great official building designed by James Gandon, the **King's Inns,** is the headquarters of the Irish legal profession. It contains an important law library and a magnificent dining hall decorated with the portraits of judges.

On the north side of Parnell Square is Charlemont House, one of Dublin's best 18th-century mansions. Now the **Municipal Gallery of Modern Art,** it includes pieces from the superb collection of Sir Hugh Lane. He was drowned in the *Lusitania* disaster of 1915, provoking a long legal struggle over custody of his paintings. For 20 years pictures shuttled back and forth between Dublin and London. The latest agreement assures the Municipal Gallery three-fourths of the contested legacy, including works by Corot, Courbet, Manet, Monet and Rousseau.

courthouse was quite seriously damaged during the civil war in 1922. After lengthy reconstruction it was restored to its original use, and justice continues to be dispensed in the neo-classical Four Courts. Carrying on the tradition introduced by the British, Irish lawyers in action wear wigs and gowns.

St. Michan's Church, around the corner in Church Street, was founded in 1095 and rebuilt several times since.

Beyond the Centre

The **Phoenix Park** provides Dubliners with nearly three square miles of beautiful parkland on the western edge of the city. The most conspicuous monument, overshadowing flower gardens, forests and sports fields, is an immense obelisk commemorating the military victories of the Duke of Wellington. He happened to be born in Ireland but later quipped ungraciously that although a man may be born in a stable, that doesn't make him a horse.

Among the buildings discreetly planted in the park is the residence of the president of Ireland *(Aras an Uachtarain)*.

On the north-east side of the park, the Dublin **zoo** provides education and diversion. If you can't distinguish an ostrich from an emu, the informative signs will remove all doubts. The zoo is noted for successfully breeding lion cubs in captivity.

In Kilmainham, a half-mile south of the park on the South Circular Road, a stone towergate in a style sometimes reviled as "gingerbread gothic" guards the grounds of the **Royal Hospital.** The building within, Dublin's principal 17th-century monument, was a home for army pensioners. Now it houses an exhibition centre.

An ugly, forbidding structure, **Kilmainham Jail** has been painstakingly restored as if it were a work of art. But its relevance is historic not aesthetic. The prisoners who lived and died within its walls include many heroes of Irish nationalism. Guided tours are organized every Sunday afternoon. The central cellblock now features exhibitions from Irish revolutionary history.

Jails are unlikely tourist attractions, and so are factories. But many a pilgrim makes his way to the biggest industrial enterprise in Dublin, the **Guinness Brewery** at St. James's Gate. The firm has been on this site since 1759 and its dark, full-bodied stout is known far and wide. Visitors are shown a film about the manufacturing process and invited to sample the finished product so much a part of Irish life. There's also an art gallery on the premises, featuring changing exhibitions of modern art.

In the Ballsbridge district of south-east Dublin are the spacious grounds of the **Royal Dublin Society** (RDS). A green and golden privet hedge surrounds the fields on which one of the world's great horse shows is held every August. The RDS complex is also the site of agricultural and industrial exhibitions as well as conferences and concerts.

This area of parks and large residences contains many foreign embassies, especially in Ailesbury Road. Around the corner in Shrewsbury Road is the **Chester Beatty Library and Gallery of Oriental Art.** The collection is known for its priceless manuscripts and miniatures from the East: jade books from the Chinese imperial court, early Arabic tomes on geography and astronomy and a sampling of Korans. The collector and donor was Sir Alfred Chester Beatty (1875–1968), an American who retired in Ireland.

Eating Out

Like most Anglo-Saxons, the Irish prefer "honest" meat and potatoes heaped high on their plates. Not for them the esoteric sauces and spices of European cuisines. Following is a selection of specialities.

Irish soups are usually thick and hearty: vegetables and barley and meat stock and a dab of cream, for instance. Look for potato soup made of potatoes, onions and carrot.

Fish fresh from the Atlantic or the Irish Sea or the island's streams is sensationally good. Keep an eye out for these great Irish delights: fresh salmon (poached or grilled), smoked salmon, sole, trout from sea or stream. Dublin Bay prawns are a famous natural resource, as are Galway oysters (often washed down with a bottle of stout). With luck you'll be offered local mussels or lobster, though the bulk of the catch is exported to appreciative clients on the Continent.

Meat of the highest quality is the centre-piece of Irish cuisine. The beef is excellent but there is little veal. You'll have a choice of sumptuous steaks (T-bone, sirloin or filet mignon) or roast beef. Lamb appears in tender chops or roast or as the main ingredient in Irish stew, a filling casserole with potatoes, carrots, onions, parsley and thyme. Irish pork products—bacon, sausages, chops, Limerick ham—are also famous. Dublin Coddle is a stew of bacon, sausages, onions, potatoes and parsley, a favourite Saturday night supper in the capital.

Vegetables as basic as potatoes and cabbage play a big role in Irish cooking. Potatoes have been a mainstay of the Irish diet since the 17th century. Mushrooms, which thrive in the cool and humid atmosphere, are Ireland's biggest horticultural export.

Desserts are often similar to English "puddings"—trifles, gateaux and generally very sweet sweets, often fruity, with a scrumptious topping of thick sweet cream.

Drinks

The Irish drink nearly 500 million pints of beer a year, mostly a rich creamy dark-brown version, stout. Irish lagers and ales, much less filling, are also worth trying. A unique Irish drink, Black Velvet, combines stout and champagne; it is said to be helpful in the event of a hangover.

Pot-stilled Irish whiskey is matured in wooden casks for at least seven years. It's drunk neat or with a little water. Never with ice. Irish coffee, served in a stemmed glass, consists of hot coffee laced with whiskey and sugar with a

tablespoonful of thick cream floating on top. Two Irish liqueurs merit a try: Irish Mist—honey and herbs in a whiskey base—tingles the palate, and Irish Cream Liqueur contains whiskey, chocolate and cream, like a leprechaun's milkshake.

Shopping

Friendly, low-keyed sales personnel help make shopping in Ireland such a pleasure. Shopkeepers and assistants are full of informed advice, and so sincere they're likely to advertise a competitor if they think he's selling something better or cheaper.

The most appealing products here are made by Irish craftsmen in traditional or imaginative new styles. Some ideas for shoppers, in alphabetical order:

Aran sweaters. The elaborate stitches in this fisherman's sweater, knitted of undyed wool, can easily be recognized. Demand so far exceeds the supply that they are made in mainland factories as well as in the cottages of the islands of their origin. Be sure to examine the label to find out whether the Aran sweater, scarf or cap is hand-knit.

Connemara marble, rich green in colour, made into book ends, bracelets and brooches.

Crosses. Especially reproductions of ancient Christian crosses, and St. Brigid crosses of straw.

Dolls, dressed in traditional regional costumes.

Enamel dishes, plaques and pendants by local craftsmen.

Fishing flies from Donegal and Tipperary.

Glassware. Waterford crystal, world renowned until the industry succumbed to 19th-century economic pressures, is again a going concern.

Jewellery. Ancient Celtic designs and illustrations from the Book of Kells inspire some of today's goldsmiths and silversmiths.

Kinsale smocks. Stylish cotton wind-cheaters for sailors. Not to be confused with Kinsale cloaks, traditional local dress now revived as chic evening-wear.

Lace. Convents in Limerick and County Monaghan have kept this industry alive.

Linen. Weaving goes on in Northern Ireland but the finished product—from handkerchiefs to table sets—is sold everywhere.

Peat. The turf of Ireland is now compressed and sculpted into reproductions of ancient religious and folklore symbols.

Pottery. Traditional and modern designs in tableware and ovenware.

Records. Individuals and groups sing or play traditional tunes.

Rushwork. In this land of thatched cottages, the makers of woven baskets and similar wickerwork are still in business.

Smoked salmon. The souvenir you can eat is specially packed for travelling, on sale at the airport. So are Irish sausages, and butter, if it comes to that.

Tweed. Handwoven Irish fabrics come in a considerable variety of colours and weights, fit for winter overcoats or light shawls or drapes.

Whimsical souvenirs. Leprechauns in all sizes, "worry stones" of marble, Irish coffee glasses and shillelaghs (cudgels).

Practical Information

Banks and currency exchange: General banking hours are 10 a.m. to 12.30 p.m. and 1.30 to 3 p.m., Monday through Friday. On Thursday, Dublin banks stay open until 5 p.m. The bank at Dublin Airport is open every day except Christmas from 6.45 a.m. to 10.30 p.m. (summer) and 7.30 a.m. to 9.30 p.m. (winter).

Clothing: A raincoat or umbrella always comes in handy. Heavy clothing is essential in winter, but even in summer evenings can be nippy, so pack a sweater or coat.

Currency: The Irish pound (£) is divided into 100 pence. Irish banknotes are issued in 1, 5, 10, 20, 50 and 100 pound denominations. Coins come in 1 p, 2 p, 5 p, 10 p, 20 p and 50 p pieces.

Post offices: Most branches operate weekdays from 9 a.m. to 5.30 p.m. but the General Post Office keeps longer hours—until 8 p.m. six days a week (6.30 p.m. on Sundays).

Businesses. Shops normally open from 9 a.m. to 5.30 p.m. Monday through Saturday, and pubs from 10.30 a.m. to 11.30 p.m. (11 in winter).

EDINBURGH

Scotland

Introduction

"Elegant", "civilized" and "dignified" are the adjectives most frequently used to describe the capital of Scotland, Edinburgh. As you visit the city—most of the sights are within walking distance of each other—you may well add "surprising" to that list of adjectives. You'll be astonished by an easy-going atmosphere and the graceful architecture, more usually associated with a southern European city. From the castle above the city you'll look down on one of Europe's finest urban panoramas. Impressive buildings set in green and manicured parks, broad and stately streets, ancient steeples and towers all proclaim that Edinburgh has undeniable individuality and style.

The scene of so many dramatic historical events, Edinburgh is today the setting for the drama, liveliness and excitement of a three-week international festival held at the end of summer. It's one of the great arts festivals of Europe. Edinburgh is very much the cultural capital of this nation of some 5 million people that has made such an impact on

the world. Scotsmen have ranged far and wide as soldiers, scholars and priests, as explorers, poets and engineers.

And in turn, the romance of Scotland and the reputation of the Scots have drawn people here from all over the Anglo-Saxon world—to claim de-

scent from clansmen of old and to share in national pride. Whether your name is Scottish or not, you'll find that the generosity and lively humour of this immensely talented and practical people will dispel from your mind forever the image of the dour and tight-fisted Scot.

Edinburgh's proud castle is the inescapable feature of city skyline.

A Brief History

Early times	The Picts, a Celtic tribe, manage to hold off the Roman legions, who penetrate no further than Hadrian's Wall. Scots, originally from Ireland, form a kingdom in the 6th century. In A.D. 563 St. Columba establishes himself on Iona and spreads Christianity. Scotland suffers Viking raids during the 8th and 9th centuries.
11th–14th centuries	Scottish kings extend the country's frontiers south to the present-day border in the 11th century. Defeat at the battle of Largs in 1263 forces the Norsemen out of the Western Isles. The death of King Alexander in 1286 touches off a civil war. Edward I of England invades and occupies Scotland, crushing a revolt by William Wallace. Robert Bruce eventually ousts the English after defeating Edward II at Bannockburn in 1314.
15th–17th centuries	Scotland takes Orkney and Shetland from Norway in 1472. The Scots suffer their worst military disaster at Flodden in 1513 when James IV attacks England. In 1561 Catholic Mary Queen of Scots claims the throne of Scotland, only to be caught up in the turbulence of the Reformation. Forced to abdicate, she flees to England where she is imprisoned by Elizabeth I and finally beheaded. Mary's son, James VI, becomes James I of England when Elizabeth dies in 1603. The 17th century is marked by political and religious struggles. In 1688 Presbyterianism becomes the state religion.
18th–20th centuries	The United Kingdom comes into being in 1707 with the Act of Union between Scotland and England. During the first half of the 18th century, Jacobites rise four times in the attempt to put a Stuart back on the throne, now occupied by the House of Hanover. In 1745, the Young Pretender, Bonnie Prince Charlie, invades England but is eventually beaten and sent into exile. England forces reprisals on Highlanders, evicting small farmers in favour of big estate owners. In the south, Edinburgh develops as a cultural centre. Scottish scientists, explorers and literary figures gain international renown during the 18th and 19th centuries. In the 1970s petroleum is found in Scottish waters, bringing new prosperity.

Sightseeing

Edinburgh Castle

Heavy with history, Scotland's most popular tourist attraction stands on an extinct volcano, high above the city. No one knows how long ago Edinburgh's history began on this great rock, but a stone fortification was definitely erected late in the 7th century and the first proper castle built in the 11th century.

Two Royal Scots guards,

bayonets fixed on their unloaded rifles, are posted for your camera at the first gate leading up the cobblestoned rampways to the castle. The impressive black naval cannon poking through the ramparts have never been fired, but you'll see the canon which booms out over the city every weekday to mark 1 p.m. Why isn't it fired at noon? "Remember where you are," quips the guide. "One cannon shot at one o'clock is much cheaper than 12 at noon."

Tiny **St Margaret's Chapel** with its plain whitewashed interior is the oldest building in Edinburgh and the oldest church in use in Scotland. Built by the devout Queen Margaret in about 1076, it survived assaults over the centuries that destroyed the other structures on Castle Rock. The simply restored Norman chapel is kept decorated with flowers each week by Scotswomen named Margaret.

On the promontory commanding one of Castle Rock's many grand views over Edingburgh stands **Mons Meg,** a stout cannon forged in the 15th century, probably in Flanders. The five-ton monster ingloriously blew up 200 years later while firing a salute to the Duke of York.

Close by is an oddity, the world's most spectacular canine graveyard. In a niche overlooking the city you'll find the Cemetery for Soldiers' Dogs with tombs of regimental mascots.

In the Palace Yard is the **Great Hall,** built in 1502, which claims the finest hammer-beam ceiling in Britain. The oak timbers are joined without a single nail, screw or bolt. Scotland's parliament met here for a century. Among the arms on display is a hefty 900-year-old claymore (from the Gaelic word for broadsword), labelled only with "Do Not Touch". The adjacent military museum exhibits a vast array of regimental paraphernalia.

Queen Mary's Rooms in the royal apartments include a

Careful restoration has preserved the charm of the Royal Mile.

very small chamber where she gave birth to James VI (later James I of England) in 1566.

The castle's greatest treasure, the crown, sceptre and sword of Scotland, are displayed in the **Crown Room.** At times more than 10,000 viewers a day file through here to see the oldest royal regalia in Europe. The gold and pearl crown has been altered since it was first used for the coronation of Robert Bruce in 1306. Charles II wore it for the last time in 1651. Popes Alexander VI and Julius II gave the sword and sceptre to James IV. In cases on the wall hang a huge necklace and other pieces of dazzling jewellery.

Note: Edinburgh Castle's entrance lies just beyond the **Esplanade,** formerly a site for the execution of witches, later a parade ground, now a modern parking lot where the celebrated Military Tattoo is performed during the annual Edinburgh Festival.

On Castlehill the **Camera Obscura** atop the Outlook Tower offers a fascinating 25 minutes—in clear weather. After climbing the 98 steps to a darkened octagonal chamber, you'll enjoy living panoramas of Edinburgh projected onto a circular table-screen by a periscope-like device. The accompanying commentary is masterly.

Entrance is free to the castle's outer precincts, including St Margaret's Chapel. But for a token charge you can join a group being escorted by one of the witty and lore-loving palace guides, a great bargain.

The Royal Mile

It's all downhill along the high ridge from Edinburgh Castle to the royal palace, Holyroodhouse. The Old Town's famous thoroughfare, its cobbles now smoothed, is actually about 1¼ miles (2 km.) long—the Scottish mile was longer than the English. Edinburghers of this area of high tenements and narrow closes (entryways) seem to take delight in recounting how the residents used to toss their slops and refuse from windows after a perfunctory shout of "Gardyloo!"—the local equivalent of *gare de l'eau.* That meant centuries of rampant disease and a decidedly unpleasant reputation for a city so graced with intel-

Shoppers and sightseers endlessly throng broad, stately Princes St.

lectual genius. Today, odourless, tidy and lined by historic buildings, the Royal Mile assumes five names as it descends: Castlehill, Lawnmarket, High Street, Canongate and Abbey Strand just before the palace.

Food and cloth merchants no longer hawk from stalls in the **Lawnmarket.** In James Court here (named after its builder, James Brownhill), Samuel Johnson once visited his biographer, James Boswell. Brodie's Close recalls one of Edinburgh's favourite stories. Deacon Brodie was a respected city official and carpenter by day, a burglar by night (having taken wax impressions of his clients' house keys). Finally arrested and condemned to death, Brodie thought he could escape death by wearing a steel collar concealed beneath his shirt. He was wrong. The city gallows, which he himself had designed, worked. Brodie's double life inspired R. L. Stevenson's *Dr. Jekyll and Mr. Hyde*.

It's a brief detour down George IV Bridge to the head-high statuette of **Greyfriars Bobby.** This Skye terrier waited by his master's grave in nearby Greyfriars Churchyard for 14 years until dying of old age in 1872. Admiring

the dog's fidelity, authorities made Bobby a freeman of the city—meaning he had the vote long before women, they'll tell you.

Back along the Royal Mile, **St Giles,** the High Kirk of Scotland, dominates Parliament Square. Its famous tower spire was built in 1495 as a replica of the Scottish crown. The oldest elements of St Giles are the four huge 12th-century pillars supporting the spire, but there was probably a church on the site since 854. John Knox preached here and is thought to be buried in the rear graveyard. St Giles' soaring Norman interior with splendid stained glass is spectacular, filled with memorials recalling great moments of Scottish history. Most beautiful is the vaulted **Thistle Chapel,** ornately carved of Scottish oak. You'll see a stall for the queen and a princely seat for each of the 16 Knights of the Thistle, Scotland's oldest order of chivalry.

Farther down the Royal Mile are the popular Edinburgh Wax Museum, the Museum of Childhood with toys from yesteryear and Huntly House, the principal city museum. From carefully restored White Horse Close,

17th-century stage coaches used to trot off towards London.

The celebrated royal palace of **Holyroodhouse** began life about 1500 as a mere guest residence for the adjacent, now-ruined, abbey. Much expanded and rebuilt in the 17th century, it has often housed visiting monarchs. During the summer, Holyroodhouse is closed to the public for the week or so that the Royal Family is in residence.

In the long Picture Gallery, snide comments abound as guides shepherd groups past 111 portraits purportedly of Scottish kings, dashed off between 1684 and 1686 by Jacob de Wet, a Dutchman who had imagination, brushes and paint.

Upstairs in King James' Tower, connected by an inner stairway, are the apartments of Darnley and Mary Queen of Scots. A plaque marks the spot where the hapless Rizzio, Mary's secretary, was stabbed 56 times with a dagger. You'll hear all about it.

The New Town

Until late in the 18th century all of Edinburgh was confined to the crowded, unhealthy Old Town along the ridge from the Castle. The population, about 25,000 in 1700, had nearly tripled by 1767 when James Craig won a planning competition for an extension. With significant help from the noted Robert Adam, the resulting New Town has become the most complete complex of Georgian architecture.

A fetid stretch of water called Nor' Loch was drained and made into **Princes Street Gardens,** the city's attractive green centrepiece. Rising from the gardens is the landmark spire of the Scott Monument, which has a statue of Sir Walter with his dog, statuettes of Scott's literary characters and 287 steps to the top. For climbing them you get a certificate and an excellent panorama. The celebrated **floral clock,** with some 24,000 plants, also adorns Princes Street Gardens.

A sloping road known as the Mound (formed from refuse during construction of the New Town) passes through the gardens. Here you will find the **National Gallery of Scotland,** a distinguished small collection of the great painters. Look for Van Dyck's *The Lomellini Family* with its five pouting members, Rubens' dramatically gory *The Feast of Herod,* Velásquez's striking *Old Woman Cooking*

Eggs and four Rembrandt portraits. The English school is represented by Turner, Gainsborough and Reynolds, and you'll see numerous paintings by the city's own Henry Raeburn.

Past Edinburgh's main thoroughfare, ever-busy Princes Street (the apostrophe was dropped long ago), spreads the neo-classical New Town. Its masterpiece is **Charlotte Square,** "the noblest square in Europe". The 11 symmetri-cally façaded houses forming the square's north side are considered the finest accomplishment of Robert Adam, Scotland's esteemed 18th-century architect. **No 7 Charlotte Square** has been converted by the National Trust for Scotland into an authentic Georgian show house. In the dining room you'll see an enviable table setting for eight of Wedgwood and Sheffield, and in the bedchamber a marvellous old medicine chest, a ca-

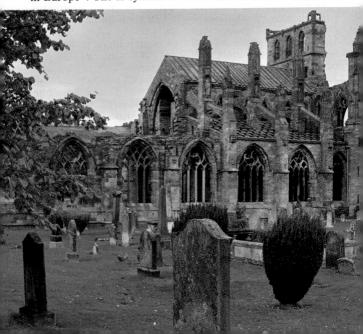

nopied four-poster and an early 19th-century water closet called "the receiver".

The **Scottish National Gallery of Modern Art** occupies premises in Belford Road. The collection is ambitious, with an emphasis on Scottish and British work.

Along Inverleith Row extend the 75 acres of the much-admired **Royal Botanic Gardens** with perhaps the world's largest rhododendron collection, cavernous plant houses and a remarkable rock garden containing hundreds of meticulously cultivated specimens.

A colony of some 200 parading penguins is the main attraction at Edinburgh's famous **zoo,** set in rolling parkland in the western suburb of Corstorphine.

Excursions

Hopetown House, the finest Adam mansion in Scotland, lies 10 miles (16 km.) west of Edinburgh. Deer and the rare four-horned St. Kilda sheep roam the grounds of this neo-classical house set in 100 acres (40 ha.) of parkland. The ruins of the great fortified palace where Mary Queen of Scots was born stand nearby in Linlithgow, overlooking the loch.

Picturesque landscapes unfold east of Edinburgh in the resort area of East Lothian, with its pretty villages and romantic ruined castles. Further south, four great monasteries founded in the 12th century lie in ruin. The battered shells of the **abbeys** of Melrose, Dryburgh, Kelso and Jedburgh bear witness to a violent past. The monks used to export cloth to the Continent, and weaving is still a major industry in the border area.

EDINBURGH

Eating Out

When the Auld Alliance linked Scotland to France five centuries ago, Scotsmen began to take a serious interest in food. Since that time porridge, kippers, smoked haddock, smoked salmon, shortbread and marmalade have been exported worldwide to the further glory of Scotland.

The secret of Scottish cooking lies in the quality of the ingredients used. Aberdeen Angus cattle provide prime beef. From the icy waters of the North Sea and north Atlantic come some of the world's finest seafood. Scotland is also the land of game: venison, pheasant, partridge.

The Scottish Tourist Board has launched a campaign to revive some of Scotland's traditional specialities, including cock-a-leekie soup, an Edinburgh favourite made with chicken, leeks and prunes, and Fife broth, a rich soup of pork ribs, barley and potatoes.

For the next course, how about *stoved howtowdie wi' drappit eggs,* young chicken stewed with spinach and served with poached eggs. Kingdom of Fife pie contains rabbit and bacon, while the pastry of *Forfar bridies* encloses a rich steak filling.

That king of fish, salmon, is poached and served with a delicate wine sauce in a dish called Tweed kettle.

Perhaps one of the most intriguing Scottish preparations is haggis. Burns' "great chieftain of the pudding race" comprises sheep's innards, oatmeal, suet, onion and seasoning stuffed into a sheep's stomach bag and boiled. Eat it with *chappit tatties and bashed neeps:* mashed potatoes and turnips.

Drinks

Nobody outside Scotland has been able to duplicate Scotch whisky, however hard they try. The Scots claim it is the pure water, the aroma of peat and the highland air that makes Scotch what it is.

There are two types— straight malt, distilled from malted barley, and grain whisky distilled from malted barley and grain. Most whiskies are blended from both types. You may offend your Scottish host if you drink his malt with anything other than a little plain water.

The other great Scottish drink is beer. Ask for a pint of heavy. You can drink it as a chaser with your whisky, in which case you ask for a "half and half".

Shopping

Woollens are among Scotland's finest products. Tweed is woollen cloth unrivalled for warmth and durability, especially Harris Tweed from the Outer Hebrides. Shops selling tartans will endeavour to find some clan affiliation for you, however unscottish your name sounds. Shetland sweaters, cashmere and **sheepskins** have a deserved reputation for quality.

Bagpipes will proclaim unmistakably that you've been to Scotland, especially if you learn how to play them.

EDINBURGH

The Scottish Craft Centre in Canongate, a non-profit-making enterprise, sells the work of local artisans. The variety of **hand-crafted goods** is astounding—textiles, pottery, silverware, metal, wood and leather work, tapestry, calligraphy.

Few visitors can resist the array of Scottish **edibles:** cakes, shortbread, marmalade, fudge, and other sweets.

Scotland's most famous product, **Scotch,** is quite likely to be no cheaper here than anywhere else, and probably somewhat more expensive. But you will be able to purchase some rare whiskies and fine malts that would otherwise never leave the country.

Practical Information

Banks: Open from 9.30 a.m. to 12.30 p.m. and from 1.30 to 3.30 p.m., Monday to Friday, from 4.30 to 6 p.m. Thursdays, and during the lunch hour Fridays.

Clothing: For excursions take windproof and waterproof clothing and stout shoes or rubber boots. Be prepared for changeable weather. Men should wear jackets and ties in the smarter establishments in the evening.

Currency and credit cards: The pound sterling equals 100 pence. Coins: 1, 2, 5, 10, 20, 50 p; £1, 2. Banknotes: £5, 10, 20, 50, 100. Scottish and English banknotes are interchangeable; some Scottish banks issue their own notes. Major banks change foreign money. International credit cards are widely accepted.

Post offices: Open from 9 a.m. to 5.30 p.m. weekdays, from 9 a.m. to 12.30 p.m. Saturdays.

Pubs: Generally open from 11 a.m. to 11 p.m.

Shops: Open weekdays (often including Saturday) from 9 a.m. to 5.30 p.m.

Tipping: Service charges are generally included in restaurant bills. Filling station attendants and barmen do not expect tips.

FLORENCE

Italy

Introduction

Florence is one of history's phenomena. Few nations, let alone cities, can boast such an overpowering array of talent—literary, artistic, political—concentrated over so short a period of time. The names of some of Florence's greatest sons—Dante, Boccaccio, Giotto, Donatello, Botticelli, Leonardo da Vinci, Michelangelo, Cellini, Machiavelli—are known the world over. Not a bad achievement for a city whose great period spanned less than 300 years.

At every turn of this amazing city, historic churches and museums unfold for you all the treasures of the flowering of the Renaissance. And in the narrow streets loom the stony masses of the *palazzi*—from medieval fortress dwellings and Renaissance mansions to ornate 17th-century buildings—with names like Strozzi, Pazzi, Salviati, Medici, straight out of history.

Florence is much more than a museum of stone, marble and bronze. Its historic palaces, its great churches, its innumerable works of art are not dry-as-dust relics. They're very much lived-in, worked-in, prayed-in and prized by today's Florentines.

Only an hour's drive from Florence lie the marvels of Pisa, where the 800-year-old Leaning Tower, delicate as carved ivory, continues to defy gravity alongside the exquisite marbel cathedral and baptistery.

It's hard to believe today, but Pisa was once the River Arno's estuary (now at Marina di Pisa, 6½ miles away). A flourishing seaport colonized by the Greeks, settled by the Etruscans, then the Romans, it had become a rich, powerful naval republic by the 12th century, battling the Saracens throughout the Mediterranean and building fine churches to celebrate its victories. But with the silting up of the Arno, Leghorn (Livorno) supplanted Pisa as a port and the burgeoning Republic of Florence soon dominated both.

Earlier, the city of Lucca surpassed even Florence and Pisa in prestige. Its arms still proudly bear the one word "Liberty". Its ancient walls enclose a plethora of marble churches, chapels and palaces.

At different epochs, the names of each of these great Tuscan cities—Florence, Pisa, Lucca—spelt power and wealth. They will open for you a window onto a golden era of European civilization.

A Brief History

Early times	Florence and Pisa are founded by the Etruscans.

1st century
B.C.– 4th
century A.D.

Florence, Pisa and Lucca develop as Roman military and trading towns.

5th–13th
centuries

With the fall of the Roman Empire, the Tuscan towns fall into chaos, invaded in turn by Goths and Lombards.

In the late 11th century Florence prospers under the rule of Countess Matilda; guilds of merchants develop. Pisa becomes a great commercial and seafaring city. Lucca prospers as the foremost city in Tuscany and remains a free commune for 700 years from 1119.

In 1138, Florence becomes a self-governing republic. Florence and Pisa feud with other north Italian cities for supremacy. Pisa is decisively defeated by Genoa in 1284.

14th–18th
centuries

The Black Death (1347–1348) ravages Tuscany and kills half the population of Florence. Florentine merchants and bankers make the city the leading commercial and financial centre of Europe.

In 1406 Pisa falls under Florentine sway, but Lucca remains independent after a hard-fought war with Florence. The Renaissance in art and architecture unfolds in Florence; the Medicis dominate the city for 60 golden years (1434–1494). They continue to rule until 1737 when the Habsburgs take over.

19th century

English poets Byron, Shelley and the Brownings revive interest in the artistic riches of Tuscany. In 1860 Florence and Lucca are incorporated in the new Kingdom of Italy, and Florence serves briefly as capital from 1865 until nationalist forces enter Rome in 1870.

20th century

During World War II, the retreating German forces blow up all bridges across the Arno in Florence except the Ponte Vecchio. In 1966 the Arno bursts its banks, flooding Florence and damaging paintings, frescoes and old books.

Sightseeing

Florence

Florence is a city to be savoured, its finest monuments and works of art to be lingered over. The city can be divided into six geographical areas to facilitate sightseeing. Each district can be covered on foot (cars, anyway, are banned from the historic centre).

From the Duomo to the Uffizi

A good place to start your tour is in the twin squares around the **Duomo** (Cathedral), undoubtedly Florence's religious hub for tourists. Officially known as Santa Maria del Fiore (Our Lady of the Flower), the green, white and pink marble-faced Duomo was intended by city-proud Florentines as a cathedral to end all cathedrals (it can hold over 20,000 people!).

The cathedral itself, flanked by its free-standing **Campanile** (bell tower) was designed by the great architect Arnolfo di Cambio in the 13th century, and the mighty **cupola** is a contribution from the Renaissance. First and unquestionably greatest of his talented peers, the architect Filippo Brunelleschi (1377–1446) had marvelled at the dome on Rome's Pantheon, rebuilt for Emperor Hadrian about A.D. 125. No one had subsequently achieved such an engineering feat. The cupola's 138-foot (42-metre) diameter surpasses the domes of the Pantheon, St. Peter's in Rome, and St. Paul's in London.

Il Battistero (Baptistery), a precious gem of Romanesque architecture, was built in the early 12th century on the site of a Roman temple of Mars. Salvaged Roman columns were used in its construction. The Baptistery's tourist popularity rests on its three sets of bronze doors: those on the south side are by a 14th-century artist, Andrea Pisano; those on the east side, made by Ghiberti, were called the **Doors of Paradise** by an admiring Michelangelo.

If the Piazza del Duomo is Florence's religious heart, then the civic heart lies in the **Piazza della Signoria,** dominated by the fortress walls of the **Palazzo Vecchio** or Palazzo della Signoria. Designed by Arnolfo di Cambio, the Duomo's architect, this future seat of the city's government (it's still Florence's city hall) was completed in 1314.

Flanking the square, the **Loggia della Signoria,** or Loggia dei Lanzi, shelters celebrated statuary, including Cellini's fine bronze *Perseus*; two Giambologna works *(Rape of the Sabines* and *Hercules and the Centaur)* and some Roman statues.

Michelangelo's *David* outside the *palazzo* was moved to the Accademia in 1873 and replaced by a copy.

Highlights of the Palazzo Vecchio include the massive first-floor **Salone dei Cinquecento.** Built in 1496 for Savonarola's short-lived republican Council of 500, it was turned into a grand throne-room by Cosimo I, adorned with giant Vasari frescoes of Florentine victories and Michelangelo's *Victory* statue in a niche. Three centuries later, the first Italian national parliament sat here.

On the second floor are the apartments of Eleonora of Toledo (Cosimo I's wife), a riot of gilt, painted ceilings and rich furnishings. Visit the nearby 15th-century **Sala dei Gigli** (Hall of the Lilies), all blues and golds, lavishly decorated with Florentine heraldry, fine gilt-panelled ceiling, bright Ghirlandaio frescoes and doors superbly inlaid with figures of Dante and Petrarch.

Don't miss the splendid **Guardaroba,** a cupboard-lined room whose panels were painted in the 1570s with 53 maps of Tuscany and the four continents by two learned and artistic Dominican friars. Medici treasures were once stored here.

Climb up to the gallery below the battlements and, a little higher, to the top of the tower 300 feet (90 metres) above the ground, for one of the most sensational **panoramas** in all Florence. See also the cell where Savonarola was locked up awaiting his execution in the piazza below.

To the *palazzo's* right, the **Uffizi Museum** stretches in a long U-shape right up to the Arno. Built as headquarters for government offices (hence the name), it's now one of the world's most famous art museums.

Paintings, in chronological order, cover the cream of Italian and European art from the 13th to the 18th century. Start with the altarpieces of those early Tuscan "greats", Cimabue and Giotto. Enjoy Fra Angelico's *Coronation of the Virgin,* full of light and music; and Paolo Uccello's *Battle of San Romano,* an astounding exercise in perspective and volume.

Best loved and most re-produced among Renaissance paintings are Botticelli's haunting *Primavera* (spring) and the renowned *Birth of Venus*. Outstanding among the 15th-century Flemish paintings is Hugo van der Goes' huge *Adoration of the Shepherds* triptych.

One room belongs to Leonardo da Vinci. See the *Baptism of Christ,* painted with his great teacher, Verrocchio. The exquisite *Annunciation,* painted around the same time, is entirely Leonardo's work.

Among German master-pieces in the Uffizi, don't miss Dürer's *Portrait of His Father* and *Adoration of the Magi;* and Cranach's life-like little portraits of *Luther,* his renegade-nun wife and a solidly Germanic *Adam and Eve.*

There is only one work by the great Michelangelo in the Uffizi: a round panel, the *Holy Family,* firmly but humanly treated, his earliest known painting (1503).

Equally notable are Raphael's placid, maternal *Madonna of the Goldfinch* and Titian's voluptuous *Venus of Urbino.*

Not to be missed is Rubens' *Portrait of his Wife.* She is so glowingly alive it's sad to think she died a year after it was painted.

From San Lorenzo to San Marco

With its rough, unfaced stone façade, **San Lorenzo** looks for all the world like a Tuscan barn. Florence's first entirely Renaissance church and one of Filippo Brunelleschi's earliest architectural triumphs, the building was begun in 1419 on the site of a 4th-century church.

The Medici are buried here in force. Cosimo the Elder himself is in the crypt, his father and mother in the Old Sacristy; Cosimo's two sons Piero the Gouty and Giovanni lie here, too, in a sumptuous bronze and porphyry tomb by Verrocchio.

The adjacent **New Sacristy** *(Sagrestia Nuova)* is an amazing one-man show by Michelangelo, who designed the interior and most of the sculptures; it took him more than 14 years. Two undistinguished Medicis are immortalized by Michelangelo in two of the most famous funeral monuments of all time, their elegantly curved sarcophagi surmounted by splendid figures symbolizing *Night* and *Day, Dawn* and *Dusk.*

The old monastery and museum of **San Marco** offer one of Florence's most evocative attractions.

Fra Angelico (1387–1455) lived here as a monk, and most of his finest paintings and frescoes can be seen in this museum. Off the graceful, columned cloister you'll find Angelico's luminous paintings; and, in the small refectory, a vivid Ghirlandaio mural of the *Last Supper*.

Upstairs, visit the simple monks' cells, each one frescoed for religious inspiration by Fra Angelico and his pupils. His famous *Annunciation* fresco is located in cell no. 3. At one end of the row of cells see the suite reserved for Cosimo de' Medici's meditations and, at the opposite end, that of the monastery's fiery prior and enemy of the Medici, Girolamo Savonarola.

Set in the most Renaissance of Florence's squares, the church of **Santissima Annunziata** deserves to be savoured in the context of its surroundings. Giambologna's bronze equestrian statue of Grand Duke Ferdinando I (1608) and the two 17th-century fountains add to the unity of the square and the feeling of spaciousness.

The graceful Campanile was designed by that many-sided genius, Giotto.

The **Galleria dell'Accademia** is second in importance only to the Uffizi. It boasts seven major Michelangelo sculptures, including the original *David*.

Mercato Nuovo to Santa Maria Novella

The main attraction of **Mercato Nuovo** (the Straw Market) are the stalls selling leather goods and straw baskets. But don't overlook the 17th-century bronze statue of a boar, known as *Il Porcellino* (the piglet). Tradition has it that if you stroke his nose and throw a coin into the fountain, you will be sure to return to Florence. In the centre of the market is a marble circle, the Batticulo (buttock smacker), where, in the 16th century, welchers and swindlers were soundly beaten.

The 15th-century **Palazzo Strozzi,** one of the most beautiful private residences in the whole of Florence, is nearby on Via de' Tornabuoni.

One of Florence's greatest monastic churches, **Santa Maria Novella** was designed by Dominican architects in the mid-13th century. An unlikely setting for the beginning and end of Boccaccio's *Decameron!* Walk through the mystic gloom of the nave to a cluster of richly frescoed family chapels around the altar. The chancel behind the altar features *Scenes from the Lives of the Virgin and St. John* **frescoes** by Ghirlandaio and his pupils.

Most striking of all is Masaccio's *Trinity* (c. 1427) on the wall of the left aisle. Amazing for its uncanny spatial depth, the fresco sets the crucifixion, with kneeling husband-and-wife donors, in a purely Renaissance architectural setting.

To the left of the church the great 14th-century **cloister** with its three giant cypresses is a haven of tranquillity after the noisy piazza.

From the Bargello to Santa Croce

The forbidding fortress of the **Bargello** in Via del Proconsolo contains the National Museum and represents for sculpture what the Uffizi is to painting. Florence's first city hall and one of its earliest public buildings, it served as the seat of magistrates *(podestà)* responsible for law and order and later housed the Captain of Justice *(bargello),* 16th-century equivalent of a police commissioner.

Men were imprisoned, tortured and executed here. Its outer walls were decorated with life-like effigies of traitors and criminals hung by the neck or by one foot.

Just off the courtyard lies the Hall of Michelangelo and 16th-century Florentine sculptors. Michelangelo was 21 when he finished his early masterpiece *The Drunken Bacchus*. He sculpted the marble *Virgin and Child (Pitti Tondo)* eight years later, while working on his famous *David*.

The **Great Hall** contains the spirit of Early Renaissance Florence. Donatello's sturdily human *St. George* (1416), embedded in a huge expanse of blank wall, dominates the high-vaulted room. It's generally held to be the first great sculptural breakthrough of the Renaissance.

With its vast expanse of open piazza, **Santa Croce** became one of the city's social and political hubs.

Within the church are buried some of the most illustrious figures in Italian history. Biographer Vasari designed Michelangelo's tomb (first on the right-hand wall). Smuggled out of Rome in a packing-case, his body was given the finest funeral in Florentine memory.

The next tomb, Dante's, has no body, much to the Florentine's dismay. His real grave is in Ravenna where he died. Further along you'll spot Machiavelli's (1469–1527) tomb.

Opposite Michelangelo is the Pisan genius Galileo (1564–1642) who perfected the earliest astronomical telescope. On the same side lies Lorenzo Ghiberti, creator of the Baptistery doors.

Immediately to the right of the altar in the **Bardi Chapel,** you'll find Giotto's finest, most moving paintings: scenes from the life and death of St. Francis, done around 1320.

The Santa Croce museum contains frescoes and statues removed from the church, but its proudest treasure is Cimabue's massive 13th-century **painted cross,** almost destroyed in the 1966 flood.

Pitti Palace to Santa Maria del Carmine

Cross over the Arno on the oldest bridge in Florence, **Ponte Vecchio,** the only one spared in the last war. The present construction, complete with overhanging boutiques, dates back to 1345. Vasari built the covered passageway above the shops so that Grand Duke Cosimo de' Medici could go from the Pitti to the Uffizi without getting wet.

From the double terrace in

the middle, admire the elegant, softly curved arches of **Ponte Santa Trinità.** Destroyed in 1944, the bridge was carefully reconstructed, exactly as Ammannati had built it in the 16th century.

Official Medici and grandducal residence since 1549, royal palace of united Italy from 1865 to 1871, the **Pitti Palace** comprises museums and galleries, plus some ten acres of ornate Italian gardens.

In the sumptuous **Galleria Palatina,** you'll feel more like a collector's guest than a tourist. Priceless paintings hang four-high against a lavish gilt, stuccoed and frescoed décor.

There are splendid works here by Botticelli, Raphael, Titian, Rubens, Velazquez and Murillo. In the 16 sumptuously decorated rooms of the **Museo degli Argenti** (Silverware Museum), admire some of the Medicis' most cherished jewels, cameos, gold, silver, crystal and ivory objects, furniture and porcelain.

The **Giardino di Boboli** is an Italian pleasure-garden of cypress- and hedge-lined alleys and arbours filled with unusual statuary, lodges, grottoes and fountains.

Mecca of artistic pilgrimage, the unpretentious church of **Santa Maria del Carmine** shelters some of the most momentous **frescoes** ever painted. Commissioned by the Brancacci family, Masaccio and his teacher Masolino worked from 1423 to 1427 on fresco decorations for their chapel here. Masaccio's *Tribute Money* and the *Expulsion of Adam and Eve from the Garden of Eden* lift painting to a completely new plane. His feeling for light and space, his dramatically stage-set figures, the concreteness of their forms are little short of an inspired miracle. Nothing of the kind had been painted before; the Renaissance had come to stay. Masaccio died at 27 before completing his commission.

Piazzale Michelangelo

For a panoramic view over the city, drive up to the **Piazzale Michelangelo** (yet another *David* statue!) and to the church of **San Miniato** nearby.

St. Miniato, an early Christian martyred in the 3rd century A.D., is said to have carried his severed head up here from Florence and set it down where the church was later built.

Rebuilt in the early 11th century, it's a remarkable example of Florentine-style Romanesque architecture.

Pisa

The irony is that fame came to this city straddling the River Arno because of an engineering error. For centuries, visitors have flocked to Pisa to see its architectural oddity, the **Leaning Tower** (*Torre Pendente*).

When Bonnano Pisano and Tedescho bent over their drawing boards around 1172 and designed the cylindrical campanile, or bell tower, they planned a ground floor, six stories of open loggia and then the bell chamber. But by the time they got to the third cornice, it became obvious that the foundations were inadequate. Work was abandoned. A century later, Giovanni di Simone resumed, lightening the weight on the leaning side and modifying the inclination. By 1350 the bell chamber with seven bells had been added—though, nowadays, to avoid vibration, they are never tolled. About 250 years later, Galileo, Pisa's leading luminary, is supposed to have used the tower to demonstrate the principles of gravity.

Approximately 180 feet (60 metres) high, the white marble tower leans about 14 feet (4.3 metres) to one side. And, yes, it is still falling—at a rate of 0.8 millimetre every year. To this day countless experts and amateurs continue proposing solutions to "save" the famous curiosity.

The Leaning Tower is one of a trio of architectural jewels, standing together on a green sward in the centre of Pisa. Next to it is the **Cathedral** (*Duomo*), a beautiful and unusual building, composed of different shades of marble and harmoniously blending classical, paleo-Christian, Byzantine and Arabic motifs in its Romanesque architecture. You'll see beautiful mosaics over the main altar, and each transept altar has a painting by Andrea del Sarto, halfway along the nave.

The other noteworthy building on the Piazza del Duomo (it's also called the Piazza of the Miracles), is the circular **Baptistery** (*Battistero*). Begun in 1152 by Diotisalvi, it has a light and airy interior, famous for the echo.

A door through the piazza's north wall leads to the **Campo Santo,** a cemetery still used today for very important people. Legend says the soil came from Mount Calvary and was blessed by the Lord.

Once Pisa was a totally walled city; now only parts of the fortifications remain. The

the Arno's banks, you'll find half a dozen varying in decoration and style. Across the river the **Museo Nazionale** displays Pisan artists work and a fascinating collection of printed matter.

Lucca

The walls of Lucca encircle the city for 4 kilometres (2½ miles), preserving within them a medieval core of old houses and palaces and more than 70 churches. The abundance of marble from the quarries at nearby Carrara encouraged the development of an individual style, found in Pisa as well as in Lucca, where Romanesque architecture has been embellished by delicate loggias and fine sculpture.

Begin your tour at the **Cathedral of San Martino,** founded in the 6th century and rebuilt 500 years later in black and white marble, with three rows of loggia above the triple-arched portico. A venerated relic in the cathedral is a cedar crucifix, known as the *Volto Santo* ("Holy Face"), said to have been sculpted by Nicodemus before Christ was laid in the tomb.

Alongside the Archbishop's Palace, behind the cathedral, you'll find the chapel of **Santa Maria della Rosa,** a gem of

Pisa's tower permitted Galileo to test the principles of gravity.

city is full of interesting churches. Walking from the Duomo down Via Roma and along Via Crispi to Piazza Vittorio Emanuele II and back along the Corso Italia to

Gothic-Romanesque architecture.

The main square, Piazza Napoleone, is dominated by the **Palazzo della Prefettura** (formerly the palace of the grand dukes), which includes the **Pinacoteca** picture gallery, with works by Tintoretto, Giordano and Fra Bartolomeo.

Take the road north from the Piazza Napoleone for the church of **San Michele in Foro,** topped by a statue of the Archangel Michael, built on the site of the old Roman forum. The arches of the graceful fourfold loggia surmounting the arcaded entrance echo the style of the cathedral.

The beautiful **Via Fillungo,** noted for its jewellers' and antique shops, leads past ancient towers of Lucca's noble families to the Piazza del Mercato, once a Roman **amphitheatre.** Nearby you should visit the basilica of **San Frediano,** founded by the Irish bishop Frigidian in the 6th century. Within this rather austere building is kept the embalmed body of St. Zita, patron saint of housemaids!

No visit to Lucca would be complete without a walk on the **ramparts** for a magnificent view over the city's churches, towers and belfries.

Eating Out

For starters look out for local specialities such as *prosciutto crudo con fichi* (raw ham with fresh figs) or *crostini, fettunta* (toasted country bread rubbed with garlic and sprinkled with olive oil).

For pasta, try *pappardelle* (broad noodles, served in season with hare sauce), *paglia e fieno* ("straw and hay"—mixed white and green pasta), or *ravioli con panna* (ravioli in fresh cream sauce).

The famous *bistecca alla fiorentina,* a mammoth charcoal-grilled T-bone steak, served with lemon, is a must at least once.

Try also *arista* (roast loin of pork), *trippe alla fiorentina* (tripe cooked with ham, tomato and parmesan), *fritto misto* (deep-fried mixed meats and vegetables) and all kinds of liver *alla fiorentina,* sautéed and flavoured with sage or rosemary.

Chicken *(pollo)* crops up regularly in Tuscan cooking, and you'll probably taste it either *alla cacciatora* (with tomatoes and vegetables), *alla diavola* (charcoal-grilled), *arrosto* (roast) or as *petti di pollo saltati* or *fritti* (chicken breasts sautéed or fried).

For an unusual fish dish try

the tasty Livornese *cacciucco* (red mullet or other fish cooked in tomatoes, onion, garlic and red wine, served on garlic-flavoured croutons).

In Italy vegetables *(contorno)* are usually served and charged for apart. Sample *carciofini fritti* (crisply fried artichokes) or, in autumn, a plateful of grilled mushrooms *(funghi)*. Try also *fagiolini* or *fagioli all'uccelletto* (boiled green or butter-beans sautéed with tomato and sage) or just settle for an *insalata mista* (mixed salad).

For a satisfying dessert, have a slice of *zuccotto,* a large liqueur-soaked, chilled sponge and chocolate cake. For a delightful treat on a warm summer's evening, you can't improve on a cool, juicy slice of watermelon *(anguria* or *cocomero)*. Ice-cream *(gelato)* is also a must in Florence.

The local wine, Chianti, is red and light and can be drunk with almost anything. Among the few Tuscan white wines are the excellent dry Vernaccia di San Gimignano, Montecarlo and the mellower Bianco dell'Elba.

Tuscans often like to end their meal with a small glass of Vinsanto ("holy wine"), a deep amber-coloured sweet wine.

Shopping

Window shopping is a delight in Florence. Fashion boutiques catch the eye along smart expensive Via de' Tornabuoni; jewellery, silverware, chinaware and leather shops outdo each other in lavish displays.

Leather. The best buys are gloves, belts, purses, wallets and boxes of all shapes and sizes.

Gold and silver. Creative gold jewellery is expensive, but simpler items like gold or silver charms are quite reasonable. Look for pill-boxes, napkin rings, photo frames, cruet sets, sugar bowls and candlesticks.

Ceramics and glassware. High-quality but expensive table china, ceramic ornaments and innumerable statuettes exist for every taste.

Inlays and mosaics. A Florentine speciality. Larger items like tables are expensive; small "pictures" of birds, flowers, landscapes are comparatively cheap. The colourful, delicate glass mosaic brooches, pendants, bracelets and rings, made at home by Florentine women, are best value-for-money trinkets.

Food and drink. The sweet-toothed should take home

Italian candied chestnuts; nutty *torrone* (nougat); biscuits from Siena or the famous Sienese *panforte,* a rich, chewy mixture of nuts and spiced candied fruits. And don't leave without one of those quaint aromatic monastery liqueurs or a genuine *fiasco* of Chianti to help you remember it all by.

Fashion. Florentine designers share the limelight with Paris, Rome and London. Exclusive dress or coat models are pricey but still far cheaper than they would be at home. There's always a marvellous selection of smaller designer items like scarves and belts.

Straw-work. In the Mercato Nuovo or Straw Market, stalls offer attractive straw bags, sunhats, semi-precious stone trinkets, glass-mosaic jewellery, reproduction Davids and typical Florentine gilt-patterned wooden articles.

Practical Information

Banks: Open Monday to Friday, from 8.20 a.m. to 1.20 p.m.

Clothing: Summerweight clothes from May to September, with a light jacket or wrap useful in the evening. Slacks are acceptable for women, but bare shoulders, miniskirts and shorts are frowned on in churches.

Currency: Italian *lira* (plural *lire*) abbreviated to *L.* or *Lit.* Coins: L. 5, 10, 20, 50, 100, 200 and 500. Banknotes: L. 1,000, 2,000, 5,000, 10,000, 50,000 and 100,000.

Shops: Shops and department stores open from 8.30 or 9 a.m. until 1 p.m. and from 4 to 8 p.m.

FRANKFURT

West Germany

Introduction

The business of Frankfurt is, overwhelmingly, business. For this is one of the world's great financial centres and Germany's largest inland port, where trade has been a way of life for at least a thousand years.

Having invested heavily in the future—the post-war skyline is unmistakably modern —Frankfurt has also been rediscovering its past. Historic buildings and old quarters still exist, the Opera House has recently been restored to its 19th-century glory, and the numerous museums are superb. But balancing the demands of the future with those of the past requires subtlety and foresight: setting the value of ever-higher skyscrapers against that of medieval buildings, and the need for a larger airport against the conservation of the "green belt".

With a prime position at the heart of Germany, Frankfurt has been at the crossroads of Continental trade since time immemorial. Bronze Age amber merchants passed through here on their way south from the Baltic, taking advantage of the natural ford across the great River Main. The Romans chose this site for a hill fortress, and the Carolingians established Frankfurt as an urban centre and gave it its name. Even when the city's political fortunes were waning, there were other fortunes to be made—from passing traffic (the first customs house was recorded in the 11th century) and then from annual trade fairs. To this day the trade fairs attract visitors year-round from all over the globe; particularly well attended is the Book Fair, held each October at the Messegelände.

Frankfurt has long since outgrown its early boundaries: the ancient city was originally guarded by ramparts arching in a semi-circle to the north of the Main, but no more than a small segment of the 12th-century wall still stands. The later medieval ramparts were also largely obliterated. Inevitably, Sachsenhausen, named for the 6th-century Saxon refugees who settled across the Main on the south bank, has come within the city's boundaries, as have the more far-flung suburbs of Höchst, Bergen-Enkheim and Seckbach, to make up a prosperous conurbation of 3 million inhabitants.

The city makes a good base for some enjoyable excursions into the superlative countryside along the Rhine (not to mention a river cruise) but also to some world-famous towns. Mainz, birthplace of Johann Gutenberg, who spread the good word with his magic printing press, is the trading centre for the wines of the Rhineland. Wiesbaden enjoyed its golden era in the 18th and 19th centuries as a fashionable spa resort, where royalty mingled with the captains of industry in the casino and Kurhaus and along the elegant Wilhelmstrasse. And Heidelberg, the university town dating back to 1386, is renowned for the verve of its students. The scholars here have always drunk a lot, duelled a little and, when necessary, done an amazing amount of academic work. It has been a poet's delight, a cradle of the German Romantic movement. Situated at the western end of the lovely Neckar valley, the old capital of the Palatinate has survived its strife-ridden history to offer visitors a haven of pure pleasure.

A Brief History

1500 B.C. –A.D. 100	A ford across the River Main becomes an ancient port of call for Bronze Age merchants from Jutland, who travel along regular trade routes to bring amber to the Adriatic and Mycaenae. In the 1st century A.D., the Romans under Domitian establish a military outpost opposite the fine natural crossing, but the settlement does not outlast the Roman occupation and even its name is forgotten.
5th–10th centuries	The lands along the Rhine form part of the Frankish kingdom during the reign of the Merovingian King Chlodwig (481–541). The old dynasty is overthrown in the 8th century and Charlemagne conducts a campaign in northern Germany to force the Saxons to submit. He sets up court in Frankfurt and settles some of the exiled Saxons along the south bank of the Main. Charlemagne's grandsons carve up the Carolingian empire in 843, and Ludwig "the German" takes Frankfurt for the

capital of his new, German-speaking kingdom in the east. With the death of Ludwig the Child in the 10th century, Frankfurt disappears from the political scene.

11th–15th centuries

Increasing communications and trade across Europe are reflected in Frankfurt's growth as a commercial centre. The charter for an annual summer fair is awarded to the city in 1240, and another in 1330. The Golden Bull of 1356 legally confirms Frankfurt as the seat of the election of German emperors by appointed electors, a tradition begun by Friedrich Barbarossa, who was crowned in the Dom. In 1372 Frankfurt is declared a free and imperial city with independent status, and builds new fortifications to defend its liberty.

16th–18th centuries

Coronation of the Holy Roman Emperors is held in the Dom from 1562. In 1595, the stock exchange opens for trading. Frankfurt falls into French hands briefly in 1792. That same year the last emperor is crowned in the city. Despite its wavering political fortunes, Frankfurt's financial affairs remain healthy and the Rothschilds open their first bank here at the end of the century.

19th century

The formation of the Confederation of the Rhine in 1806 marks the end of Frankfurt's political autonomy. Awarded to the Prince of Dalberg, it is established as the capital of a new "grand duchy". The ramparts around the outer perimeter are demolished and elegant promenades laid out. The Congress of Vienna in 1815 once again declares Frankfurt a Freie Stadt, and it becomes the capital of the reconstituted German Confederation. Nationalists gathering in Frankfurt in 1848 demand an all-Germany National Assembly which meets during this year—its only session. Free status is lost for good in 1866, during the Prussian campaign for unification and political domination. The treaty ending the Franco-Prussian War is signed at Frankfurt in 1871.

20th century

Little of the old city remains standing after the Allied bombing raids of 1943–44. Frankfurt embarks on a post-war programme of modern development instead of reconstruction.

Sightseeing

The heart of Frankfurt lies in the **Altstadt**, the Old City. Before it was razed in the bombings of 1944, this ancient quarter was one of the finest medieval towns in Germany. Since the war, some of the original buildings have been reconstructed; and recent archaeological excavations have revealed evidence of Roman and Carolingian settlements.

At the centre of the Altstadt, lying close to the Mainkai, the **Römerberg** is a pleasant square (now a pedestrian area) with many historical associations. The fountain in the middle, with its graceful statue of Justitia (1543), was untouched by the bombing. The **Römer**, one-time city hall, dominates the square. Its distinctive gabled façade comprises three buildings—from left to right, Alt Limpurg (1495), Römer (1405) and Löwenstein. Inside, the magnificent **Kaisersaal** provided a worthy setting for the imperial coronation banquets held here from 1562.

Across the square, **Nikolaikirche** (St. Nicholas' Church), built of local sandstone, was once the chapel of the city hall, although it pre-dates the Römer by three centuries. A carillon of 40 bells rings morning, noon and early evening.

Behind the Römer, the Historisches Museum incorporates the **Saalhofkapelle**, the oldest surviving building (1175) in the town centre and all that remains of the once-great palace of the Emperor Friedrich Barbarossa.

Paulskirche (St. Paul's Church), built between 1787 and 1833, looms nearby. This massive church, readily identified by its neo-classical dome, was never actually consecrated, but served instead as the seat of the first German National Assembly.

The **Dom**, or Cathedral of St. Bartholomew, dates from the 13th to 15th centuries, but archaeological evidence points to the existence of a Carolingian church from 852 under its foundations. A parish church rather than a bishop's seat, the Dom has had its moments of glory; here, between 1562 and 1792, the German emperors received their crowns. The building's proportions—its eccentrically short nave and over-sized transept—were intended to facilitate great state occasions by providing more space for the attendant hordes of courtiers and clerics. The Gothic sandstone tower, with its 383

202

steps, offers a commanding view of the countryside; unfortunately it is not usually open to the public.

Beyond the Dom, the 13th-century Dominican and Carmelite foundations, with their convents and churches largely restored, house some beautiful frescoes; the Carmelite refectory is now a museum (*Museum für Kunsthandwerk*), boasting a fine collection of artefacts, textiles, ceramics, furniture and sculpture.

Frankfurt also has a prominent place on the literary map: Germany's greatest poet, Goethe, was born within the ancient walls in 1749. His family house, **Goethehaus**, in the Grosser Hirschgraben has been beautifully restored and furnished authentically. Here and in the adjoining **Goethe-museum**, you can take a step back in time to witness how Goethe lived and follow his progress as a writer.

Beyond the bounds of the Altstadt, Frankfurt's *alter ego* takes over. The so-called **Neustadt** (New Town) in fact dates from the 17th century, but it continues to be the hub of commercial activities ranging from a stock exchange to department stores and international banking.

The focal point of this bus-tling quarter is the square, An der Hauptwache, dominated by the fine Baroque **Hauptwache**. Built in 1730, this once served as the central guardhouse for the municipal police; it was destroyed in World War II and reconstructed, then dismantled while the under- and above-ground public transport system was being laid, and finally restored to its original site to become a popular café.

Across the square, in the Protestant **Katharinenkirche** (St. Catherine's Church), Goethe was baptized and confirmed. The **Rossmarkt**, traditionally the city's horse-market, was also the place of execution where Faust's Marguerite—Margaretha Brandt—was put to death.

Somewhat incongruously, the ancient **Eschenheimer Turm** presides over the glittering financial district. Standing 154 feet (47 m.) high, this round, five-spired gate to the ancient city symbolizes Frankfurt's former glory as an influential and privileged free state. Now, the tower is dwarfed by glass and steel structures, which import a sense of new power, but perhaps not the same feeling of permanence. The **Post Office Communications Centre**, built

1951–55, does at least acknowledge its antecedents: features of the 18th-century palace of the Prince of Thurn and Taxis, one-time Minister of the Imperial Post, have been incorporated into the modern façade. The **Börse**, an Italianate Renaissance building of 1879, is now the Federal Republic's largest stock exchange, with 4,500 listed stocks and an annual turnover of some 94 billion marks. Drop in at the visitor's gallery to watch the frenetic trading on the floor.

A source of pride to the people of Frankfurt is the recently renovated **Alte Oper**

(Old Opera House). After World War II, all that remained of this superb building were the walls: it was a bombed-out shell. Now restored to all its former opulence, it stages musical productions from classical opera to rock music.

The parks and gardens of Frankfurt offer unmitigated delight. It is possible to walk the boundaries of the entire city centre by following its "green belt" and riverside promenades, including the "Mediterranean" Nizza. Further from the centre, the **Bethmannspark** to the north-east and the **Rothschildpark** on the north-west corner of the old ramparts are oases of calm.

More of Frankfurt's flora and fauna can be glimpsed at the botanical and zoological gardens. The **zoo,** founded in 1858, is renowned for its success in breeding animals in captivity. Its policy is the recreation of natural habitats —landscaped enclosures, an extensive aviary, a house for nocturnal animals and a reptile house specially designed for safe observation. On the other side of the city, the famous **Palmengarten** includes one of the finest collections of tropical plants in the world, housed in vast conservatories.

Sachsenhausen, on the south bank of the Main, has escaped lightly from both destruction and reconstruction. This ancient quarter captures a little more of the atmosphere of life in bygone times, although it, too, has been built up considerably. Now a residential suburb of Frankfurt, Sachsenhausen was once a village presided over by the powerful Order of Teutonic Knights who arrived here in 1221. Their surviving house, the Deutschordenshaus (1705), now contains a fine collection of Roman artefacts.

Climb aboard the cheerfully painted old-time tram, the Äppelwoi Express, for a light-hearted tour of old Frankfurt and Sachsenhausen. From its departure point at the Ostbahnhof, it clangs past the zoo, across the Main to applewine country, then back up to the Opera House and round the Römerberg —all to jolly music, a jug of applewine and a pretzel.

Museums

In Frankfurt there is a museum to suit every taste. Curiously, no fewer than seven are concentrated in Sachsenhausen, close to the river. Most outstanding is the **Städelsches Kunstinstitut**, housing the city's own art collection. Old masters from the German, French, Italian, Dutch and Spanish schools hang here, plus an important collection of European drawings and over 65,000 engravings. Works by Rodin are included among the sculptures.

The **Liebieghaus**, once home to the Baron von Liebieg, is now a museum of sculpture, the Museum Alter Plastik, with specialist collections from the ancient and classical worlds, medieval Europe and the Far East.

Even the Post Office has its museum, the **Bundespostmuseum**, which chronicles the development of national and international communications. The film and architecture museums opened in the summer of 1984.

The **Museum für Völkerkunde**, or Ethnology Museum, transports its visitors to the most exotic corners of the earth. The exquisite **Museum für Kunsthandwerk** houses a fine collection of 18th-century furniture, porcelain and silver.

Across the river, the museums are no less varied or excellent. In the **Historische Garten** you'll see the excavated remains of Frankfurt's Roman outpost and the Carolingian imperial palace, set in the unusual surroundings of a sunken garden.

The Johann Wolfgang Goethe Universität's **Senckenberg Museum** makes a significant contribution to the study of natural history and is outstanding for its zoological material, which includes a skeleton of a diplodocus—the only one of its kind in Europe, imported from the United States. But perhaps the most unusual museum is the **Museum für Vor- und Frühgeschichte**, which concentrates on local prehistoric and ancient cultures. It is located in a small moated castle set in the lovely Adolf von Holzhausen Park on the outskirts of Frankfurt.

Environs of Frankfurt

Public transport in and around the city is excellent. A convenient bus ride to the **Stadtwald** (City Forest) southwest of Frankfurt reveals another side to the German character—a passion for forests. The Stadtwald had its origins as the first tree farm in Europe, where acorns planted in the 16th century grew to be the oak heart of what is now, at more than 3,000 acres (1,214 hectares), the largest municipal woodland in Germany. To appreciate the glories of the Stadtwald requires no more than a leisurely meander down one of the beautifully laid-out nature trails. For the more energetic, there are numerous well-planned bridlepaths or the outstanding facilities at the sports stadium, which include three pools, an ice rink and tennis courts.

Day excursions along the Main make pleasant sightseeing. Or, an old-fashioned steam train plies the river banks on an hour-long tour. You can use one of a number of ferry services to explore territory further afield. But nothing can match the elegance of a river cruise, and the scenery along the Rhine Valley is unrivalled. Steamship berths can be reserved for three-day journeys or longer.

All three of Frankfurt's medieval suburbs can be easily reached by train, underground (subway) or tram. While each is worth a visit, Höchst has some unique features that reward even a flying visit. This town is fortunate to have escaped wartime damage: the centre and its buildings are authentic. The **Justinuskirche** (St. Justine's Church) dates back to 834; other structures still standing are in the arching Romanesque style of the 11th and 12th centuries and the more elaborate Gothic. Remains of the ancient city walls and castle with its round tower of 1360 impart a sense of what it was like to live within the protecting circle of a walled city.

The setting of the **Bolongaro Palace** in its own parkland is inexpressibly serene. Its almost staid Baroque features seem appropriate to the German countryside, although its building was commissioned by an Italian snuff manufacturing family. Beauty of another kind can be found at the **Dalberg Haus**, site of the town's famous porcelain works, which now houses a priceless collection.

Frankfurt also has the **Taunus Mountains** on its doorstep. Many lovely resort towns here have been visited for centuries by the crowned heads of Europe, often to take the waters at the numerous spas. Most famous of these is **Bad Homburg** (which gave its name to the Homburg hat), only 12 miles (19 km.) from the city. The Romans were acquainted with the curative properties of the waters, as were Czar Nicholas II and Edward VII; the **Thai Temple** recalls the visits of King Chulalongkorn. After you have been refreshed by the sparkling mineral waters of the **Elisabethbrunnen**, you will be ready to tour the ancestral seat of the princes of Hessen-Homburg, a 17th-century castle, and its magnificent state apartments. The **Weisse Turm**, or White Tower, is all that remains of the original 12th-century fortifications. Bad Homburg's renown extends to its casino, which pre-dates the more famous institution at Monte Carlo by a quarter of a century, having opened its doors to the world's wealthy in 1840.

Excursions

Rüdesheim
This is the heart of the Rheingau, Germany's premier wine-growing region, where the hills that rise sharply from the banks of the Rhine are dotted with romantic medieval ruins and wild flowers. Wine connoisseurs and oenologists hold Rüdesheim and the surrounding vineyards in the highest esteem, particularly for the effect that *Botrytis cin-*

era—otherwise known as the "noble rot"—has on the flavour of the wine. More than half the wine produced is drunk locally, much of it in wine taverns along the Drosselgasse. Here in an atmosphere of perpetual festivity, you can try the Rheingau's famous Rieslings, the sparkling Sekt and the locally distilled brandies.

Find out how it's all done in the national wine museum in the **Brömserburg** castle. World War II bombardments destroyed most of the original Gothic and Renaissance timber-framed houses, but the reconstructions are quite faithful replicas. The best surviving authentic example of the town's architecture is the 15th- and 16th-century **Brömserhof**, richly decorated with hunting scenes and coats of arms of the local nobility.

The hills above Rüdesheim afford spectacular views of the Rhine. There is a spa at Presberg, about 1,400 feet (427 m.) above sea level, where people come to take the waters. A chair-lift runs down from Jagdschloss Niederwald to Assmannshausen, a small town with a reputation for producing an excellent red wine in a district otherwise known for its whites.

Mainz

Mainz begins at its cathedral, the **Dom**, whose harmony seems the best possible expression of the city's enduring spirit. On the east it's an austerely simple construction of the 12th century, on the west a more ornate synthesis of Romanesque, Gothic and Baroque.

The cathedral's lasting treasures are its 29 monumental **tombstones** honouring archbishops of Mainz. Enter by the 13th-century Markportal, with its thousand-year-old bronze doors named after archbishop Willigis.

North of the cathedral on the lively market square is a magnificent Renaissance fountain, the **Marktbrunnen** (1526), the oldest of its kind in Germany. It commemorated the victory of Emperor Karl V over the French at Pavia.

The **Gutenberg Museum** is on the Liebfrauenplatz, east of the cathedral, a neatly designed modern building adjoining and incorporating the fine old 17th-century inn, Zum Römischen Kaiser. Since 1962 it has been the World Museum of the Art of Printing. It presents a fascinating history of man's efforts to communicate with each other in writing, from the most primitive stone and papyrus to today's sophisticated technology of mass-communication.

Wiesbaden

The **Wilhelmstrasse** has adapted to the modern world with chic boutiques and the most elegant of Hesse's gentry. At the southern end is the **Städtisches Museum** (Municipal Museum) with German artists well represented.

Beyond the theatre is the **Brunnenkolonnade** (Colonnade of Springs) and **Kurhaus**, if you feel like taking the waters or trying your hand at roulette or baccarat in the casino. East of the Kurhaus is the beautiful **Kurpark**, which takes you into another dream world with its open-air concerts, delightful beds of flowers and shrubs, beyond which, a walk of about half an hour, is the lovely, restful Rambach Valley.

Heidelberg

Americans have long had a special affinity for Heidelberg. It is said that this is why it was not bombed in 1945. It had already been singled out as headquarters for the U.S. Army at the end of the war.

The **castle** was ravaged by the troops of Louis XIV in 1689 and 1693. Yet, visiting these remains from the 14th and 17th centuries certainly proves to be more of an adventure than a tour of a perfectly preserved castle. The terrace and various lookout points, especially the **Rondell** on the west side, command an enchanting view of the castle gardens, the old city and the wooded slopes of the Neckar valley.

The styles span 500 years of architecture. In the north-east corner you can compare the Italian Renaissance style of the **Gläserner Saalbau** (Hall of Mirrors), 1549, and the later German Renaissance **Ottheinrichsbau**. The statuary in the niches of the early 17th-century **Friedrichsbau**'s façade represent the various members of the Wittelsbach family who provided the Electors Palatine—the originals can be seen in the castle museum.

Heidelberg's city centre retains some of its 17th-century atmosphere around the Marktplatz, thanks in large part to the exclusion of car traffic. The Heiliggeistkirche (Church of the Holy Ghost) on the square is notable mainly for the little shops and stalls that still cling to its walls. Opposite, at Hauptstrasse 178, is the fine Renaissance house **Zum Ritter**, built

in 1592. The town's taverns are as lively as ever, for students from 18 to 88.

The **Kurpfälzische Museum** (Palatinate Museum) has some admirable 15th-century art from the Rhineland and southern Germany; its prize piece—Tilman Riemenschneider's wooden sculpture of the **Zwölfbotenaltar** (Altar of the Twelve Apostles).

The **university** has always been known for a mixture of earnest scholarship and good fun. Its great scholars have included sociologist Max Weber, physiologist Hermann von Helmholtz, physicist Robert Kirchhoff and his more famous colleague Robert Bunsen (1811–99), known for the burner used in all laboratory experiments, forerunner of the modern gas stove.

For a tranquil moment away from the town's bustle, walk along the right bank of the River Neckar. Take the

Philosophenweg (Philosopher's Path) through a garden and uphill to the Heiligenberg. You'll pass another garden dedicated to poet Friedrich Hölderlin and easily understand, as you look around the peaceful valley, why Heidelberg attracted the German Romantics.

All That Jazz

Unpredictably, perhaps, Frankfurt is the capital of the German jazz scene and one of the most important jazz centres in Europe. No matter what the time of year, you can be assured of hearing jazz, whether at a fixed engagement (Sunday mornings at the Museum of History), jam sessions at a jazz club, or extemporaneous performances underground at the U-Bahn station. There are open-air concerts all summer.

The Jazzkneipe in the Berlinerstrasse offers swing; Der Jazzkeller specializes in modern and free jazz; and Jazz Life Podium is more likely to appeal to aficionados of Dixieland. The Palmen Garten and Höchst Castle are just two of the more unusual venues. Those fortunate enough to have business in Frankfurt in the autumn can take in the annual German Jazz Festival, which has been a local institution since 1951.

Eating Out

Frankfurt is bound to satisfy gourmet and gourmand alike. Its wine and food district is called the Fressgasse, a local phrase roughly translated as the "eating trough"—and reflecting the abundant delicatessens, wine shops and restaurants to be found here. Locals are deeply attached to traditional, wholesome food, and the city abounds in wine and beer restaurants where, above all, the famed frankfurter is esteemed. A variety of regional sausages should be sampled along with domestic beers. Other favourites include game, particularly venison and boar, and *Rippchen mit Sauerkraut* (smoked pork chops with sour cabbage).

Sachsenhausen has its own distinctive cuisine. Its *Äppelwoi* (dialect for *Apfelwein*) or dry cider is decidedly idiosyncratic, but the palate quickly becomes accustomed. The earthy taverns where this drink is sold owe nothing to the tourist trade (although visitors are made to feel welcome). These offer as an accompaniment *Handkäs mit Musik*, a ripe cheese with "music"—in this case provided by a raw onion salad.

Shopping

Prosperous, sophisticated Frankfurt offers its international visitors an extensive choice when it comes to shopping. The Zeil, a broad avenue lined by department stores, was redesigned in 1983 and made into a pedestrian precinct.

For those who prefer to hunt for their treasures, boutiques abound in the pedestrian zone leading to the Eschenheimer Turm. Shops specializing in **shoes** and **leather goods** can be found around the Rossmarkt, while the **furriers** are concentrated in the area to the west.

Those in search of **luxury** head towards the Opera House and the district known for its designer boutiques, jewellers and *parfumeries*. **Book-lovers** would do well to explore the area around the Goethehaus and Hauptwache or, for second-hand and rare books, around the Römer and Dom.

Bargains are to be found in the street markets, which offer a shopping ambiance a little more off the beaten track. The famous Sachsenhausen flea market is held every Saturday in its grounds along the River Main.

Practical Information

Banks: Open weekdays from 9 a.m. to 1 p.m., and from 2.30 to 4 p.m., until 6.30 p.m. on Thursday.

Currency: Germany's monetary unit is the *Deutsche Mark (DM)*. The mark is divided into 100 *Pfennig (Pf)*. Coins: 1, 2, 5, 10 and 50 Pf. and DM 1, 2, 5 and 10. Notes: DM 5, 10, 20, 50, 100, 500 and 1,000.

Shops: Open weekdays from 9 a.m. to 6.30 p.m., Saturdays from 9 a.m. to 2 p.m. On the first Saturday of every month, shops stay open until 6 p.m.

GENEVA

Switzerland

Introduction

Geneva's setting is superb: a city of old-fashioned elegance, it stands astride the narrow tip of one of the largest lakes in Europe. The rugged Jura mountains shelter it from the north; and to the south rise the glittering snowcapped Alps, dominated by Mont Blanc.

The largest town in French-speaking Switzerland, Geneva offers good theatre, music and art; excellent shopping; windsurfing, sailing and skating; and easy access to some of the best skiing anywhere.

The Lake of Geneva (its correct name is Lac Léman) curves in a crescent for 45 miles (70 km.), overlooked by forested hills, vineyards and small towns, each huddled round its castle. The principal port on this international lake (you can sail over to France for lunch!) is Lausanne, capital of Vaud canton and world headquarters of the International Olympic Committee.

Set in parkland along the lake shores between Geneva and the riviera round Montreux, you'll find some of the world's most expensive real estate, eagerly sought after by exiled royalty, industrial millionaires and film stars.

Like them, you may never want to leave this well-ordered world of scenic grandeur, where good hospitality, food and drink are served up with inimitable Swiss flair.

A Brief History

5000–2000 B.C.	A lake city, built on piles, develops at the present site of Geneva; buildings spread later to a nearby hill (now the old town).
1st century B.C.–4th century A.D.	By Roman times, Geneva is a walled town inhabited by the Allobroges tribe, with temples, aqueducts and a port. In 58 B.C., Julius Caesar blocks the Helvetians at Geneva when they try to migrate to Gaul.
5th–15th centuries	After the collapse of the Roman Empire, the Burgundians move into western Switzerland, as far as the Sarine River, today's linguistic frontier.
	By the middle of the 13th century, the House of Savoy and the Habsburgs predominate. Prince-bishops of Geneva and counts of Savoy feud over the city.

16th century	Geneva supports the Reformation and in 1535 adopts the Protestant faith. The following year the Bernese rescue Geneva from a Savoyard attack, occupy Lausanne and capture the castle of Chillon. Geneva becomes a refuge for persecuted Protestants; the French Reformation leader Calvin is virtual ruler of the city until his death in 1564.
17th century	On the night of December 12, 1602, the Savoyards try to scale the walls of Geneva (the *"Escalade"*), but are repelled.
18th century	Clockmaking prospers, with the aid of Huguenot refugees. The French annex Geneva in 1798.
19th century	After the fall of Napoleon, the city joins the Swiss Confederation in 1815.
20th century	Switzerland remains neutral in the two world wars and Geneva in 1947 becomes the European headquarters of the United Nations.

Sightseeing

Geneva's special attraction lies in its esplanaded **waterfront,** enclosing the end of the lake and the banks of the Rhone. The long and busy Mont-Blanc bridge connects the two halves of the city. From one side of the bridge you can see the city's tallest monument, a feathery jet of water, the **Jet d'Eau,** pumped straight up from the harbour to the height of a 40-storey building, and the colourful spinnakers of the yachts racing down the lake. From the other side you can watch the River Rhone surging out of the lake to resume its rush towards the Mediterranean.

Cross the main shopping streets on the left bank and climb up to the highest point of the **old town,** a place of worship since pagan days. The present **Cathédrale St-Pierre** (St. Peter's Cathedral) was begun in the 12th century in Romanesque style but evolved into Gothic innovation. In the 18th century the façade was remodelled, and classical columns, still controversial, were tacked on.

It was a Catholic church until 1535, when the Reformation swept out the priests. The Protestant Jean Calvin preached in St-Pierre for more than 20 years.

Under the flowered arcades of the **Arsenal,** ancient cannon are deployed against a background of modern mosaics depicting medieval Geneva.

Across the street from the Arsenal, the **Hôtel de Ville** (Town Hall) has an elegant Renaissance courtyard, with a ramp instead of a staircase leading to the upper floors. It was here that the first of the Geneva conventions on the humane treatment of wounded and prisoners-of-war was concluded in 1864.

Below the ramparts of the old town lies the Place Neuve, faced by three classical buildings: the **Grand Théâtre,** for opera and ballet, the Conservatoire de Musique, and the **Musée Rath,** which presents temporary art exhibitions.

In the park opposite, an imposing **Reformation Monument** portrays Calvin and his associates.

The international quarter of Geneva lies on the right bank, beyond Quai Wilson, named for the American president who made Geneva the headquarters of the League of Nations after World War I.

In the 60 years since then, countless new international organizations and agencies have set up shop here, among them the World Health Organization, the International Telecommunications Union and the International Labour Office (ILO).

The **Palais des Nations** was the headquarters of the League of Nations. After World War II, the new United Nations took over the building for its European headquarters. The U.N. runs guided tours of the numerous conference halls and committee chambers.

Geneva is justly proud of its spacious parks on both banks, with their fountains, sculptures, bandstands and cafés.

The city's many museums are equally prized. The **Musée d'Art et d'Histoire** covers a wide range from pre-history to modern art. The **Musée Ariana,** a marble-columned palace surrounded by parkland, unfolds the art of ceramics from medieval Spanish pottery to modern porcelain. The four floors of the **Petit-Palais** are packed with Impressionist and post-Impressionist works, including some of Renoir and Picasso.

Along the Lake

You can take an excursion boat along Lake Geneva, sweeping past sunny vine-

yards, patrician houses, old stone villages and geranium-decked piers. Or you can drive round the Swiss shore of the lake to the Vaud Riviera at Montreux.

Coppet, a town of thick-walled stone houses, recalls the French writer Mme de Staël, whose banker father bought the **château** in 1784.

Nyon is dominated by a fairy-tale castle, seized by Bernese troops from the Savoyards in the 16th century. The town was once a Roman outpost and three Corinthian columns discovered here have been installed in a neat park above the port.

The imposing square castle in **Morges** (which now houses a Military Museum) was built in the 13th century by Prince Louis of Savoy, who founded the town as a power base to rival the prince-bishop of Lausanne.

Lausanne is a prosperous business, administrative and university centre, with a population of 135,000, situated on a steep hillside that sweeps down to the lake. Its mile-long lake-front, with parks and gardens, is the liveliest, loveliest place in town when the weather's fair.

From this part of the city, called **Ouchy** (pronounced oo-shee), a rack-railway makes the ascent in six minutes to the centre at Place St-François. This hectic conglomeration of banks, shops and trolleybus stops used to be the site of a Franciscan monastery. On an island of peace in the middle is the 13th-century **church of St. François.** One of Lausanne's smartest shopping streets, the cobbled **Rue du Bourg,** wanders steeply upwards from it.

Lausanne's Gothic **cathedral** stands on the city's heights; it was consecrated in 1275 by Pope Gregory X. A superb **rose window** has survived the anger of the Reformation, when most of the stained-glass windows were shattered.

Covered steps lead down from the cathedral to **Place de la Palud,** Lausanne's market-place since medieval times, overlooked by the 17th-century **Hôtel de Ville** (Town Hall), with its arches, clock tower and fierce gargoyles.

Down by the lake at **Vidy,** you can visit the original Roman settlement of Lousonna, its stone foundations laid bare by recent excavations.

From the outskirts of Lausanne to the eastern end of the lake, the **Vaud Riviera** sprawls in the sun, a land of sophisticated resorts and wine-growing villages.

Wine and milk chocolate keep the lakeside town of **Vevey** afloat. The curved glass structure in United Nations style is the world headquarters of Nestlé, the multinational food company. A gigantic wine festival is held in Vevey once every 25 years.

By the time you reach **Montreux,** the lake has narrowed and steep mountains shelter the town from north-east winds. A three-mile lakeside promenade exploits this unique hothouse atmosphere: all kinds of flowers and even palm trees thrive here. This is a full-time tourist resort, where something is always happening—an international conference, TV awards, an impressive art exhibition or a jazz festival.

Jutting into the lake beyond Montreux, the **Château de Chillon** is a moody feudal fortress which has known battles and torture, feasts and romance. Once a Roman strongpoint, later fought over by the counts of Savoy and the Bernese, the castle was made famous by Lord Byron, who told the story of the imprisoned prior Bonivard in his poem "The Prisoner of Chillon". Visitors to the castle are shown the pillar where Bonivard was chained by the Savoyards and the channels his footsteps wore into the stone floor.

Eating Out

You must try some of the Swiss specialities, many of them based on cheese.

Fondue is filling and fun to eat. The celebrants sit around a bubbling cauldron stirring chunks of bread, speared on long forks, in a mixture of cheeses diluted with white wine and a dash of cherry-based brandy.

Fondue bourguignonne. The scene is the same but the pot is filled with boiling oil, and the diners dip in pieces of steak.

Fondue chinoise, the "Chinese" version. Impale a paper-thin slice of meat on a long fork and immerse it in a boiling pot of broth.

Raclette. Melted cheese is scraped onto boiled potatoes and eaten with pickled onions and gherkins.

Swiss lakes provide a good variety of fish: trout, perch, pike, or *omble chevalier* (char).

For the meat course, many restaurants feature hare, venison and game birds in season, often in heavy red-wine sauce. For a local dish, try the *saucis-*

son vaudois, a spicy smoked sausage.

Local cheeses are mild and creamy: the *Vacherin,* an unctuous runny treat that comes in a round wooden box; the *Tomme vaudoise,* sometimes flavoured with caraway seeds; and the *Reblochon,* soft and delicious.

White wine from the canton of Vaud is classified as Dorin; it can be light and lively or somewhat flinty. The best red wines, Salvagnin and Pinot Noir, are mellow and fragrant.

In the canton of Geneva, the white Perlan wines are mild and fruity; the reds are labelled Gamay.

Shopping

Geneva and the lakeside towns have inviting shops and high-quality merchandise. Some of the best buys:

Cheeses from all over Switzerland, with attractive tile-and-wood cheese boards.

Embroidered handiwork: tablecloths, aprons, handkerchiefs.

Knives: The Swiss Army pocket knife comes in many sizes and prices; the big ones include magnifying glass, corkscrew and scissors.

Watches at all prices; even the cheapest are masterpieces of Swiss design and precision.

Practical Information

Banks: Open 8.30 a.m. to 12.30 p.m. and 1.30 to 4.30 or 5.30 p.m., Monday to Friday.

Climate: Cold and often foggy in winter, clear and cool in spring and autumn; and warm in midsummer.

Clothing: Wear warm clothing with an overcoat in winter, early spring and late autumn; and light clothing in summer, with a raincoat or umbrella handy.

Currency: The Swiss *franc* (in German *Franken),* abbreviated *Fr.,* is divided into 100 *centimes* (in German *Rappen).* Coins: 5, 10, 20, 50 centimes, Fr. 1, 2, 5. Banknotes: Fr. 10, 20, 50, 100, 500, 1,000.

HAMBURG

West Germany

Introduction

For sea-weary sailors and thrill-seeking tourists, Hamburg is renowned as one of the raunchiest ports on earth. Yet by the prestige of its centuries-old commercial pre-eminence, the city is also known to Germans for its great dignity and matchless civic pride. That pride can be seen in the silhouette of church steeples and town hall, restored after World War II bombardment as a counterpart to the skyscrapers of its new prosperity.

Independent-minded and efficient, but also lively and elegant, the people, like their town, are much more meaty and infinitely less bland than the famous piece of fast-food named after them. Their own hamburger, by the way, is typically extremely spicy. Attracting in the past great composers such as Brahms and Mendelssohn, and writers Heine, Klopstock and Lessing, the city today enjoys a vigorous cultural life.

The University, founded only in 1919, is already one of the most distinguished in the country, and Hamburg is the headquarters of West Germany's news agency (wire-service) DPA and principal magazine publishers. Horse-lovers admire the town's great show-jumping competitions and soccer fans respect Hamburg SV.

But the city's greatness is founded above all on its rôle as a major international trading port—even though it's situated 70 miles (110 km.) from the North Sea, on the right bank of the Elbe estuary as it meets the River Alster. Over 18,000 ships from 90 countries serve the port each year, accounting for 20 per cent of West Germany's imports and also serving as the shipping link for much *East* German trade with the West. You'll see perhaps a fraction of the 40 miles (64 km.) of quays around the 62 dock basins.

All that vital shipping activity, in addition to its chemical, electrical, machine-tool and rubber industries, has endowed Hamburg with the special status of a city-state or *Land*. It's governed within the West German federal system by a Senate that dates back to the proud old days of the Hanseatic League, when Hamburg ruled Germany's sea-going trade with Lübeck and Bremen.

But besides the wealth and prestige, the port also brings in sailors looking for rough-

and-tumble revelry on the world-famous Reeperbahn of the St. Pauli red-light district, with its aptly named street of prostitutes, *Grosse Freiheit* —"Great Freedom".

More elegant ladies—and gentlemen—can be seen shopping in the extremely chic boutiques around the Binnenalster lake. There's something here for everyone.

A Brief History

9th century	Emperor Charlemagne builds Hammaburg fortress to resist barbarian attacks from the north and east. In the Middle Ages, it becomes a bastion for the Catholic Church on its missions to northern Europe, and for international trade—Arabs appear there in 1150.
13th–17th centuries	Hamburg is co-founder with Lübeck of the Hanseatic League, to manage trade monopoly with Scandinavia and Russia. The League is dissolved at the end of the 17th century, following its decline due to the discovery of America, but formal links are maintained with Lübeck and Bremen.
	In 1558, with the creation of the Stock Exchange, the city takes on a new rôle as entrepôt for international trade in face of Spanish, Portuguese and British domination of the seas. It becomes a cosmopolitan home for English clothiers thrown out of Antwerp, Dutch Protestants fleeing the Spanish and Jews fleeing from Portugal. In 1618 Hamburg is recognized by the German Empire as an independent free city-state.
18th–19th centuries	Hamburg flourishes as an intellectual centre around writers Klopstock and Lessing. The city suffers from a British blockade during the Napoleonic Wars. In 1806 it is occupied by the French after the Battle of Lübeck, and is incorporated into the French Empire from 1810 to 1814. A major city fire in 1842 leads to large-scale reconstruction and urban development. Industrial growth burgeons with the advent of steam-ships, to expand the port.
20th century	By 1913 the Hamburg–Amerika has become the world's largest shipping line. Despite conservative business traditions, the city is in the forefront of social reform

and ripe for an albeit short-lived Socialist Republic in the 1918–1919 revolution. The city's progressive elements are crushed by Hitler. Heavy World War II bombardment from 1943 to 45 destroys 90 per cent of its naval installations and 300,000 houses, and kills 50,000 inhabitants. Participation in West Germany's post-war economic recovery is spectacular, the city taking the 1962 flood disaster in its stride.

Sightseeing

The distinctive feature of Hamburg, as a city attached essentially to the water, is its two lakes, the Aussenalster and Binnenalster, fed by the River Alster and separated by the Kennedy and Lombard bridges. It's a good idea to start your tour at the **Aussenalster** for a superb overall **view** of the town's silhouette of church steeples and Rathaus (Town Hall) belfry.

This handsome stretch of water offers the boat-buffs of Hamburg plenty of opportunities for sailing and canoeing. You might like to take one of the boat tours for a leisurely look at the city from the water.

Or else wander through the pretty parkland on the west bank of the Aussenalster to the smart modern neighbourhood of **Pöseldorf,** favoured by artists and the town's trendier residents for its galleries, boutiques and colourful painted façades epitomizing Hamburg's bouncing post-war prosperity.

The **Binnenalster** is just as chic. There, on the south bank's Jungfernstieg, the great attraction is the time-honoured elegance of coffee and pastries at the **Alsterpavillon** jutting out over the lake.

At the northern end of shop-lined Ballindamm, on the Glockengiesserwall, is the city's major art museum, the **Kunsthalle.** Its fine collection ranges from the Middle Ages to the 20th century. Look out for the famous 14th-century altar paintings of the Grabow Altar by Meister Bertram, depicting *The Salvation.* Another 14th-century work will be of particular interest to British visitors, Meister Francke's portrait of Thomas Becket, Archbishop of Canterbury. The Dutch masters are well represented, but the later highlights are undoubtedly the 19th-century German

Romantics—the mysterious landscapes of Caspar David Friedrich and equally ethereal Philipp Otto Runge. For the more troublesome 20th century, there's the anguish of Norwegian Edvard Munch, the disturbing interrogations of Max Lieberman, Lovis Corinth and Emil Nolde, and the "Blue Rider" experiments of Paul Klee and Franz Marc.

In the **Altstadt** (Old Town) district south-east of the Binnenalster, Hamburg's civic pride is proclaimed by the soaring belfry of the neo-Renaissance **Rathaus** (Town Hall), hoisted up on 4,000 stilts at the end of the 19th century. Note, before you go into the wine-cellars, the nice 16th-century statue of good old Bacchus on the **Ratswein-keller.**

East of the Hauptbahnhof (Main Railway Station), the **Museum für Kunst und Gewerbe** (Decorative Arts Museum) has a splendid collection of furniture, silverware and porcelain. This includes work of the Jugendstil, or Art Nouveau, period, from both Germany and the Nether-

You'll never forget the palatial opulence of Hamburg's Rathaus.

lands, and also some exquisite Japanese porcelain. Notice, too, the fascinating display of North German clocks.

A revered monument of the Altstadt has always been the 14th-century **St. Jakobi-kirche,** badly damaged in World War II bombing, but tastefully rebuilt in 1959. The medieval altars survived—note especially the Cooper's Trip-tych. The famous 1693 organ has been lovingly restored.

But south-west of the Binnenalster, in the **Neustadt** (New Town—some of it 18th century, but "new" in Ham-burg is a relative term), the town's greatest architectural symbol has remained the **St. Michaeliskirche,** with its dome-topped steeple. The 433-ft. (132-m.) tower beside it is popularly known as the "Mi-chel" and you can take an elevator to the top for a grand view of the city's vast harbour. The church itself, completed in 1762, is a rare example of North German Baroque and generally considered by art-historians to be a masterpiece of the genre. Built for Lutherans, it is less ornate than its Catholic counter-parts, but nonetheless light, airy and comfortable.

Be sure to see, near the church of St. Michaelis, the **Krameramtswohnungen** (at Krayenkamp 10), quaint wood and brick houses built in 1670 for poor widows and today converted into galleries and artists' studios.

The **port** is well worth a separate visit. Stretching some 10 miles (16 km.) on both sides of the River Elbe, it devotes 38 of its 62 docks to ocean-going vessels—650 of which leave the port each month bound for the Americas, Asia, Africa and Australia, as well as other parts of Europe. Tours of the impressive port facilities are organized from the St. Pauli Landungsbrücken.

If you're in port early on Sunday morning, try to make it, to the bustling **St. Pauli Fischmarkt** on the bank of the Elbe. It closes at 10 a.m., to the chimes of the St. Pauli church bells. The colourful market sells not only fish—in-cluding the local delicacy, eel—but also vegetables, fruit and flowers and even geese and goats. The high spot of the market-day is the wonder-fully boisterous eel-auction. Be careful you don't wave to a friend during bidding or you may find you are the unwitting buyer of a few kilos of slither-ing eel.

The city's exuberant history is well displayed at the

Museum für Hamburgische Geschichte. This shows not only the town's pious beginnings, with models of the first church missionary buildings of Hammaburg—together with models of the town in its proud Hanseatic heyday—but also (in Room 107), mounted on skewers, the skulls of two beheaded pirates. Hamburg's more respectable shipping history is recounted with port and ship models dating back to the Middle Ages, and a beautiful reconstruction of the interior of an ocean-going steamship from the early 1900s. The museum boasts Europe's biggest miniature model railway—5,900 ft. (1,800 m.) of tracks with 50 engines pulling 315 wagons.

If trees and flowers are more to your taste, make for the city's celebrated public park, **Planten un Blomen.** Wander around the richly endowed experimental botanical garden and you'll be amazed by some of the tropical specimens growing at this northern latitude. If you're suffering from "sightseeing feet", take the mini-train tour. The gardens are lit up at night, with organ-music playing by prettily illuminated fountains.

The Congress Centre is dominated by the 890-ft. (271.5-m.) telegraph tower officially named the **Heinrich-Herz-Fernmeldeturm,** but more popularly known as the **Tele-Michel,** by association with the church tower. There's a revolving restaurant 433 ft. (132 m.) up. The people of Hamburg are not shrinking violets when it comes to offering great views of their city.

Last, but not least, the **Reeperbahn.** It is pronounced "raper-barn", but in fact it's named after the rope-makers who used to inhabit this once respectable neighbourhood of St. Pauli. The now world-famous red-light district is handily close for sailors to lurch in from the harbour. On the **Grosse Freiheitstrasse,** which got its name for *religious* tolerance in the 19th century, the girls move about on the street. It's on the **Herbertstrasse** (tucked away behind a wall to keep children out) that the shop-windows are dressed with live, undressed girls.

Eating Out

If you have time for a meal, try the great local delicacy, *Aalsuppe* (eel-soup). This deliciously pungent concoction varies from restaurant to restaurant, but a typical version will accompany the small slices of fresh eel with leeks, carrots, little dumplings, dried apricots, prunes and apples, spiced with sage, thyme and coriander, the whole given a "sweet-and-sour" flavour with a base of ham-broth in vinegar and sugar. You thought you were in for a simple soup?

Less ambitious is the other Hamburg speciality, *Labskaus*—minced meat and fish with fried eggs.

By all means, sample the great white German Rhine and Mosel wines, but don't overlook the equally respectable local beers and schnapps. *Prost* and *Guten Appetit!*

Shopping

Prosperous Hamburg rivals Munich, Düsseldorf and West Berlin for the elegance of its shops. The best boutiques are situated around the Binnenalster—on the Ballindamm, the Neue Jungfernstieg and the delightful Colonnaden. Big department stores can be found west of the Hauptbahnhof (main railway station) in the pedestrian zone of Spitalerstrasse and Mönckebergstrasse. All the major French and Italian couturiers are represented.

You can find some excellent buys in German **porcelain, cutlery, cameras, binoculars** and **telescopes,** and superb **bed** or **table linen.**

Practical Information

Banks: Open weekdays from 9 a.m. to 1 p.m., and from 2.30 to 4 p.m. Thursdays late closing, 6.30 p.m. The exchange at the main railway station is open every day from 6.30 a.m. to 11 p.m.

Currency: Germany's monetary unit is the *Deutsche Mark (DM)*. The mark is divided into 100 *Pfennig (Pf.)*. Coins: 1, 2, 5, 10 and 50 Pf. and DM 1, 2, 5 and 10. Notes: DM 5, 10, 20, 50, 100, 500 and 1,000.

Shops: Open weekdays from 9 a.m. to 6.30 p.m., Saturdays from 9 a.m. to 2 p.m. On the first Saturday of every month, shops stay open until 6 p.m.

HELSINKI

Finland

Introduction

Helsinki calls itself the "Daughter of the Baltic", and rightly so, for the large northern sea provides the lifeblood of Finland's capital. The city grew up around its harbour, gradually expanding into today's metropolis, with its innovative architecture and visionary satellite towns.

Half a million people live in Helsinki, the indisputable centre of Finnish commerce and cultural life. But in spite of its size and sophistication, the city preserves many of the customs and all of the charm of a small 19th-century seaport. Finns love nature and treat it with a care that verges on reverence. For a large city in an industrialized nation, Helsinki boasts a remarkable lot of greenery and space.

Only in 1812 did Helsinki become the capital of the Russian Grand Duchy of Finland, an event that triggered an unprecedented building boom. The structures centering on Senate Square are typical of the early 19th-century construction.

The harsh winter climate,

Statue in central Helsinki honours Mannerheim, leader of resistance to the Soviet army in Winter War.

with up to 19 hours of darkness daily in December, is said to have encouraged the development of the Finns' aesthetic sensitivity: all around you, in Helsinki's architecture, in the handicrafts and the decorative arts, you'll see manifestations of the Finnish sense of design and creativity. This, combined with their legendary *sisu*—courage, tenacity and endurance in the face of adversity—sets the Finns apart from their neighbours in more clement latitudes.

A Brief History

12th century   In the early 12th century Sweden's King Erik IX seeks to establish trade routes across Finland to the Russian city-state of Novgorod, thereby beginning Christianization of Finland—and introducing Swedish rule.

13th–16th centuries   A provincial governor is appointed by the Swedish king, but throughout the Middle Ages Finland retains a semi-independence. Lutheranism is introduced. The tiny port of Helsinki, first called by its Swedish name Helsingfors, is founded in 1550 by a decree of King Gustav I Vasa of Sweden.

17th–18th centuries   Finland in the 17th century becomes an integral part of Sweden. The national assembly normally convenes in Turku until King Gustav II Adolf orders it in 1616 to meet for the first time in Helsinki. The original site of Helsinki is abandoned in 1640, but even in its new situation a few miles away the town is beset with troubles (fire, famine). During the Great Northern War between Sweden and Russia (1700–1721), Helsinki's population is decimated by epidemic and then fire lit by the retreating Swedes. After another conflict between Russians and Swedes in 1741–43, the latter—backed by their French allies—decide in 1748 to build a great sea fortress (Suomenlinna) near Helsinki bringing a new era of progress to the town.

19th century   In the short war between Russia and Sweden in 1808, the Russians occupy Helsinki, but find two-thirds of the town razed. The 1809 treaty incorporates Finland into Russia with Czar Alexander I as Grand Duke. In 1812 he proclaims Helsinki capital of the new Grand Duchy. In

1819 the Senate is transferred from Turku to Helsinki, followed by the university in 1827. Finnish is recognized as official language in 1863. In late 19th century, Czar Nicholas II launches a campaign of Russification.

20th century A general strike at the beginning of the 20th century forces the czarist government to concede reforms. During World War I and the turmoil of the Russian Revolution, the Finns declare their independence on December 6, 1917. Civil War (1917–19) breaks out between the revolutionary-led Reds and the conservative Whites. In 1919 a republican form of government is established. In 1939 Russians attack Finland that, under General Mannerheim, puts up incredible resistance during the Winter War until finally beaten in spring 1940. During World War II Finland allies itself with Germany. Under armistice terms in 1944, Finland pursues a policy of absolute neutrality.

Sightseeing

Most of the sights a visitor should see are concentrated in the compact and eminently walkable centre of Helsinki.

Market Square

The open-air market, held year-round, weekdays and Saturdays, on **Kauppatori** (Market Square), is at its best early in the morning when stalls are well stocked with fruit and vegetables. Freshly caught fish is sold from boats anchored in Kolera-allas (Cholera Basin), so-called because an epidemic of the disease broke out here at the turn of the century.

Stand for a moment amid the flower-sellers around the **Havis Amanda fountain,** the symbol of Helsinki, and admire the charming sea nymph by Ville Vallgren that scandalized townspeople when it was placed in the square in 1908.

Helsinki's handsome, neoclassical **Town Hall** (*Kaupungintalo*), facing the market between Katariinankatu and Sofiankatu, dates from 1833 and was designed as a hotel by German-born Carl Ludvig Engel, the architect responsible for much of central Helsinki.

Solemn state occasions take place in Helsinki's neo-classic cathedral.

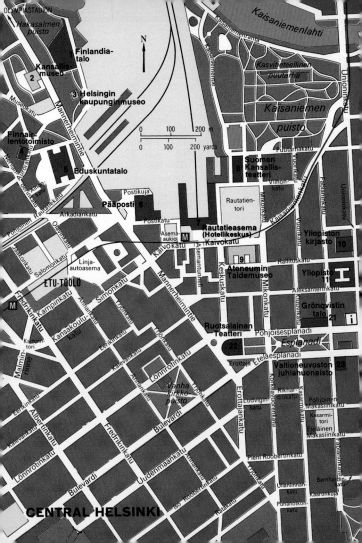

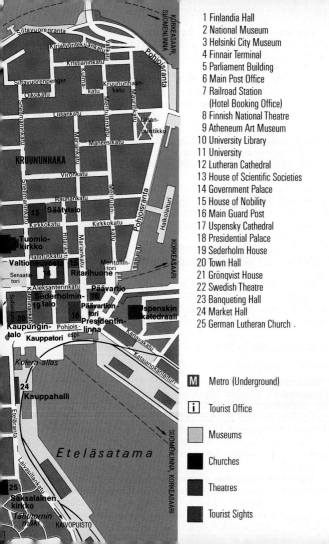

1 Finlandia Hall
2 National Museum
3 Helsinki City Museum
4 Finnair Terminal
5 Parliament Building
6 Main Post Office
7 Railroad Station
  (Hotel Booking Office)
8 Finnish National Theatre
9 Atheneum Art Museum
10 University Library
11 University
12 Lutheran Cathedral
13 House of Scientific Societies
14 Government Palace
15 House of Nobility
16 Main Guard Post
17 Uspensky Cathedral
18 Presidential Palace
19 Sederholm House
20 Town Hall
21 Grönqvist House
22 Swedish Theatre
23 Banqueting Hall
24 Market Hall
25 German Lutheran Church

M Metro (Underground)

i Tourist Office

Museums

Churches

Theatres

Tourist Sights

The main hall is now the place for municipal council meetings, as well as occasional banquets and galas.

Two blocks east of the Town Hall, at the corner of Mariankatu, you'll see the dignified **Presidential Palace** *(Presidentinlinna)*, where a stoical sentry usually stands guard. Only nominally a residence, the palace is used on state occasions.

The building dates from 1814 and was originally the home of a wealthy merchant. It was remodelled by Engel into a palace in 1843. Not until 12 years later did a czar, Nicholas I, actually stay there.

Esplanadi (or "Espa", as it is popularly called) is an elegant shopping boulevard that runs from Market Square to the beginning of Mannerheimintie, the city's main artery.

Neo-classical Sights

Senaatintori (Senate Square) lies at the heart of the Helsinki town plan devised by Albrekt Ehrenström between 1812 and 1825, a masterpiece of city design, impressive but not overwhelming.

The most imposing of Senaatintori monuments, the **Lutheran Cathedral** *(Tuomio-* *kirkko)*, was intended by architect Engel to be uncompromisingly neo-classical, with one great dome. But on his death in 1840, another Prussian émigré, Ernst Lohrmann, took over the project. Fearing that a single cupola might not be sufficiently monumental, he added four smaller domes spangled with gilded stars, and lined the roof with copies of statues by Bertel Thorvaldsen in Copenhagen's Church of Our Lady. The result is striking, but not at all what Engel envisaged.

In deference to both classical and Lutheran traditions, the interior is relatively simple and severe. There are statues of Martin Luther, Mikael Agricola (the great reformer who translated the New Testament into Finnish) and Philip Melanchthon, Luther's assistant and the interpreter of his teachings.

Mannerheimintie and Neighbourhood

Mannerheimintie, the longest street in Helsinki, begins at the western end of Esplanadi and runs north-west for 3 majestic miles.

The political life of Finland centres around the grey granite **Parliament Building** *(Edus-* *kuntatalo)*. This solemn structure was completed in 1931. The one-chamber Parliament of 200 members (over 25 per cent of them women) meets in a domed chamber decorated with sculpture by Wäinö Aaltonen.

From the Parliament Building, a short detour leads to **Töölö,** the residential district that lies to the west of Mannerheimintie, with the famous **Rock Church** *(Temppeliaukion kirkko),* a spectacular example of modern Finnish ecclesiastical architecture designed by two brothers, Timo and Tuomo Suomalainen. They took as their starting point a rocky outcrop that rises some 40 feet (12 metres) above street level. The result is an ingenious modern version of the rotunda, with interior walls blasted from bedrock and spanned by a huge dome covered with copper wire. The plan was conceived from the inside out to achieve the maximum interior effect.

The **National Museum** *(Kansallismuseo),* a local landmark, stands in its own little park. This exuberant example of the National Romantic style was designed in 1902 by three distinguished architects: Armas Lindgren, Herman Gesellius and Eliel Saarinen. To express the na-

tional spirit, they incorporated features from historic Finnish buildings: the tower is reminiscent of the cathedral in Turku, the wall along Mannerheimintie resembles the ramparts of Vyborg Castle and there is a turret modelled after those of Olavinlinna, the famous fortress at Savonlinna. Native building materials were used throughout.

Visitors to the museum first have to go by a rather mournful stone bear, who stands guard outside the main entrance. You then pass through an ornamental bronze door into the entrance hall, decorated with frescoes by Akseli Gallen-Kallela illustrating the *Kalevala,* Finland's national epic. The work was designed for the Paris World Fair in 1900 and later repainted in Helsinki.

Across from the National Museum, the **Helsinki City Museum** *(Helsingin kaupunginmuseo)* occupies a lovely neo-classical mansion by Lohrmann, Villa Hakasalmi. The exhibits trace Helsinki's history from its founding to the present day.

Next to Villa Hakasalmi rises that famed marble edifice, **Finlandia Hall** *(Finlandia-talo),* one of Europe's finest congress centres, incorporating a concert hall and restaurant. The complex comprises a main building (1971) and congress wing (1975), both designed by Alvar Aalto, whose bust is displayed in the grand foyer. Completed shortly before the architect's death in 1976, Finlandia Hall is not only Aalto's last major work, but also his masterpiece.

At the end of Hesperia Park that turns west along Hesperiankatu lies **Hietaniemi Cemetery** (*Hietaniemen hautausmaa*), established 150 years ago. Many of the great men of Finland are buried in the beautifully landscaped grounds, not least among them Carl Ludvig Engel. The grave of the Finnish Unknown Soldier is here, not far from that of his commander-

Child romps near the likeness of Sibelius, Finland's great composer.

in-chief, Carl Gustav Mannerheim. The marshal was laid to rest alongside more than 3,000 of his troops, fallen in battle during the Winter War. At Christmas lighted candles are placed on the graves in a moving gesture of tribute.

From the cemetery, it is a pleasant walk north along the water to **Sibelius Park** *(Sibeliuksen puisto)* a park laid out in honour of the composer Jean Sibelius. The lovely and largely natural grounds, broken up by rocky outcrops and shaded by old birch trees, preserve the kind of rugged Finnish beauty that inspired Sibelius in his work. To one side of the park stands a massive sculpture, the **Sibelius Monument,** created by Eila Hiltunen and dedicated to the musical vision of Sibelius. The work, unveiled in 1967 on the tenth anniversary of the composer's death, took six years to complete. Next to it is a relief of Sibelius, showing him as he looked at the height of his powers.

Helsinki's **Olympic Stadium** is situated to the east of Sibelius Park in another setting of greenery. It was constructed for the 1940 Olympic Games, which were cancelled when war broke out. Finland eventually hosted the games in 1952, a proud event that demonstrated the nation's remarkable post-war recovery to the world.

South-East Helsinki and Suomenlinna

Kaivopuisto (Spa Park) which gives its name to the surrounding district, remains one of the most gracious of the city's green spaces, with delightful footpaths and splendid sea views.

The park was once part of a lively health resort developed in the 1830's and at the height of popularity in the middle decades of the 19th century, when the Russian nobility came by steamer from St. Petersburg just to take the waters. A tree-lined avenue leads to the former main spa building, originally designed by Engel in 1838, but much remodelled. The elegant setting created for the baths now lends its charm to a popular restaurant.

Suomenlinna (Fortress of Finland), once known as the "Gibraltar of the North", is now no more than a recreational adjunct to Helsinki. But for nearly a century, the island group with its great fortress was an important community. The fortress, begun by the Swedes in 1748, was called Sveaborg (Fortress of Sweden), and was built in an attempt to contain Russian expansion into the Baltic, an objective enthusiastically endorsed by France. In fact, the French underwrote the cost of construction and undertook the building of the fleet that was based here.

The five main islands of Suomenlinna are inter-connected, so it is easy to stroll about. The ramparts make a popular promenade, and the old fortifications with their decorative cannon and attractive gardens can take some time to explore.

Other Major Sights

In 1951 a variety of citizens' groups founded the garden city of **Tapiola,** one of four centres of habitation within **Espoo,** a development considered worldwide a model of urban design. Tapiola occupies a vast site a few miles outside Helsinki, spacious enough for 16,000 residents from all walks of life. Visionary planners like Alvar Aalto have provided a wide range of housing, from moderately priced multi-storey condominium complexes to expensive single-family bungalows.

Many of the innovations carried out at Tapiola have their origins in the work of Eliel Saarinen, Armas Lindgren and Herman Gesellius—the architects most responsible for creating the National Romantic style. There is no better illustration of their collective ingenuity than **Hvitträsk,** a fieldstone castle on Lake Vitträsk in Espoo. They designed the fanciful structure at the turn of the century to serve as a common studio and individual living quarters. Recent restoration has returned Hvitträsk to its original state.

The composer Jean Sibelius lived in a rural setting at **Ainola,** the house where he wrote five of his seven symphonies. "Here at Ainola the silence speaks", Sibelius said. The house is situated 24 miles (39 km.) north of Helsinki in the small town of Järvenpää. It was designed by Lars Sonck and named after the composer's wife Aino, who lived in the house from its completion in 1904 until her death in 1969 at the age of 97.

Only the ground floor is open to the public. The drawing room is dominated by the Steinway grand piano friends presented to Sibelius on his 50th birthday, and the walls are hung with paintings and mementoes.

Eating Out

In the strawberry season, Finns find many uses for the fresh fruit.

Ferocious Vikings with appetites to match, hard-riding (and drinking) Cossacks, Lapp reindeer herdsmen, French army officers and Russian and Swedish aristocrats have all added a pinch of pepper to Finland's culinary pot. As you might expect, the result is delicious.

Fish

Like other Scandinavians, the Finns do wonderful things with Baltic herring *(silakka)*, available all the year round. Salted or marinated, it makes a popular first course, always accompanied by boiled potatoes and often by a schnapps. A larger variety of herring *(silli)* is also widely served.

Meat Dishes

For local flavour, try reindeer meat *(poro, poronliha)* served in cream sauce *(poronkäristys)*, cold smoked reindeer *(savustettua poronlihaa)* or reindeer tongue *(poronkieli)*.

Game appears on menus in season: duck *(sorsa)*, pheasant

(fasaani), white ptarmigan *(riekko)*, hare *(jänis)*, bear *(karhu)*, elk *(hirvi, hirvipaisti)*.

Smörgåsbord *(Voileipäpöytä)*
Finland has its own version of that Scandinavian invention, the *smörgåsbord*. Here, as in other Nordic countries, you choose freely from a buffet table laden with dozens of dishes.

Cheese
Finnish cheeses *(juusto)* such as cheddar *(juhla)*, and the blue-veined Roquefort-type *(aura)* compare favourably with the best of other countries.

Snacks
Try to sample *kalakukko*—a thick loaf of rye bread baked with a filling of fish (usually *muikku* or perch) and pork, served sliced and spread with butter. Another portable snack called *karjalanpiirakka*, a thin shell of rye dough stuffed with rice or potato, is also good.

Desserts
Finns are fond of cakes and pastries, but these are mostly eaten as a snack with coffee, rather than after a meal. The most popular desserts, available only during the summer months, are wild berries made sweet by the midnight sun: *lakka* (Arctic cloudberries—a sort of yellow raspberry with a delicate flavour), *karpalo* (cranberries) and *pihlajanmarja* (rowanberries).

Drinks
Coffee *(kahvi)* is so much in evidence in Finland that it must be considered the national drink. You will be offered countless cups—at breakfast, after lunch, in the afternoon, at dinner, even late at night, generally with pastries, cookies or cakes.

Domestic wine made from berries and fruits is little more than a curiosity, but you may want to sample Elysée, a sparkling white wine made from currants. On the other hand, domestic liqueurs distilled from wild berries are widely appreciated. Ask for Lakka (yellow cloudberry liqueur), Polar (red cranberry), Mesimarja (red Arctic bramble) or Vaapukka (red raspberry).

Vodka, the most popular strong drink in Finland, is served either as a schnapps *(snapsi)* or mixed with juices, for instance lingonberry *(puolukkamehu)* or orange *(appelsiinimehu)*. An interesting aperitif, Vodka Polar, combines vodka with Polar liqueur.

Shopping

Finnish goods have been world-famous for fine design since the 1950's when talents like Tapio Wirkkala and Timo Sarpaneva reaped awards in international exhibitions. The hallmarks of the style they created are simplicity, utility and functional beauty. Finnish designers make good use of the country's natural resources, working with wood, clay, textiles, and native semi-precious stones to produce objects of great beauty. If actual bargains are rarely met with, quality is uniformly high.

Many internationally known Finnish firms have shops on one or both sides of the Esplanadi. Finland's oldest and largest department store, Stockmann's, lures shoppers to Aleksanterinkatu, the parallel street.

Best Buys

Boots are well-made, elegant (warm, too) and less expensive than in many other countries.

Candles come in a wide range of colours and sizes.

Clothing, and, in particular, sportswear and leisurewear designed by the internationally known Marimekko, Vuokko and others, is distinguished for bright colour,

high quality and practicality. Both workmanship and design are of a high calibre for fur coats and hats of native mink and blue fox.

Glassware and ceramics figure among Finland's most popular exports. Make your selection from the wide range of bowls, tumblers and tableware, all designed by distinguished craftsmen with international reputations.

Souvenirs include objects made of wood, *puukko* hunting knives and reindeer skins and antlers. Lapp crafts are popular too. Look for carvings made from reindeer bones, for felt items and for dolls.

Textiles for home decoration range from brightly patterned tablecloths and napkins to wall rugs, hangings, curtains, carpets and cushions.

Practical Information

Banks and currency exchange: Generally open 9.15 a.m. to 4.15 p.m., Monday to Friday. The currency-exchange office at Helsinki railway station is open 11 or 11.30 a.m. to 6 p.m. daily. A bank at the Olympia boat terminal *(Olympiaterminaali)* is open 9 a.m. to noon and 3 to 6 p.m. daily.

Credit cards and traveller's cheques: Major credit cards are accepted in bigger restaurants. Internationally recognized traveller's cheques are easily cashed, although you may need your passport for identification.

Currency: Finnish *mark (mk.)* = 100 *penni*. Coins: 5, 10 20 and 50 p, 1, 5 and 10 mk. Banknotes: 5, 10, 50, 100 and 500 mk.

Post office: Open from 9 a.m. to 5 p.m., Monday to Friday. Mailboxes are painted yellow with the traditional posthorn in black. You can also buy stamps at stationery shops, hotels (a small extra charge is sometimes made), railway stations and from yellow stamp machines.

Shops: Usually open 9 a.m. to 5 p.m., Monday to Friday, on Saturdays until 2 p.m. Department stores remain open until 7 or 8 p.m. Mondays and Fridays, on Saturdays until 3 or 4 p.m.

INNSBRUCK

Austria

Introduction

The Tyrolean capital of Innsbruck nestles in the valley of the River Inn, with the Karwendel mountains to the north and the domed Patscherkofel to the south. It is the former home of dukes and princes which still retains the power to captivate through an authentic charm, and a sense of quiet majesty.

This town of 122,000 people plays host to visitors all the year round. In summer it is a departure point for tours of the surrounding countryside, with its forests of larch and pine, brilliant green meadows and clear blue lakes, while in winter the city teems with skiers attracted by the world-class skiing combined with the amenities of a large town.

The temptations of the Old Town are many and should not be resisted. Offering sights like the Goldenes Dachl, the loggia of Emperor Maximilian's residence, with its gilded copper shingles, and the monumental tomb of the same Maximilian which, confusingly, does not house his remains, Innsbruck is a splendid place for strolling and looking.

The Tyroleans have been in the business of tourism for a long time. By the 15th century a brisk traffic of Catholic pilgrims, German students and journeymen artisans was making its way north and south through the region, so if you find people more efficient than Austria's easy-going national reputation might have led you to expect, it's because they've been in the business a few centuries longer than anyone else.

A Brief History

8th century B.C.–6th century A.D.	Tyrol's alpine passes become thoroughfares for transporting Greek and Etruscan goods to the eastern Alps and northern Europe. In A.D. 50, Emperor Claudius incorporates the Tyrol into the Roman province of Rhaetia. In the 4th century, a major military base is established at Wilten, today a suburb of Innsbruck. In 550 the Franks take over.
9th–16th centuries	The region falls into the hands of Lombards, Slavs and Bavarians. Charlemagne incorporates the Tyrol into his empire in 788.

During the Middle Ages, traders settle at the site of present-day Innsbruck. In 1239 Innsbruck is awarded official status of a town with its own rights and privileges.

During the first half of the 14th century the Tyrol becomes a focus for dynastic struggles between the Habsburgs and the Bavarian Wittlesbachs. In 1363, the Habsburgs take control. A time of prosperity ensues. In 1420 Friedrich IV establishes his residence in Innsbruck, which becomes the capital of the Tyrol.

Maximilian rules as Archduke of Tyrol from 1490 to 1519.

17th–20th centuries

The Tyrol knows more prosperity under the reign of Maria Theresa (1740–80).

Innsbruck becomes a battlefield in the War of Liberation, fought under resistance hero Andreas Hofer, after Napoleon gives Innsbruck to the Kingdom of Bavaria. The Tyrol is returned to Austria by the Congress of Vienna in 1815.

The Tyroleans fight with great patriotism in World War I. In 1918 Italian aircraft bomb Innsbruck.

Austria is annexed by Germany in 1938, and Innsbruck is damaged in air raids during World War II. In 1945 the town is occupied by American troops, and later becomes the headquarters of the French zone of occupation. The French depart in 1955.

In the latter half of the 20th century, the Tyrol prospers as a haven for winter sports enthusiasts and summer tourists.

Sightseeing

Stand on the broadest part of the elegant **Maria-Theresien-Strasse**—which opens into a market square—and you'll see to the north the positively magic **panorama** of the old town's 15th- and 16th-century houses, town hall tower and cathedral domes set against the deep green fir and pine forest of the Karwendel foothills.

This broad thoroughfare, now the town's main shopping street, was built in the 13th century. It was later named after Empress Maria Theresa, who erected the **Triumph-pforte** (Triumphal Arch) at

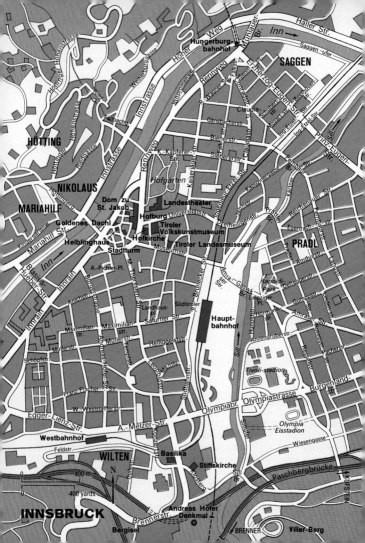

the southern end in 1765 to celebrate the wedding of her son, the future Emperor Leopold II.

More truly triumphant, the **Annasäule** (St. Anne's Column) in the middle of the old marketplace celebrates a famous Tyrolean victory over the Bavarians on St. Anne's Day (July 26) in 1703.

Altstadt *(Old Town)*
Maria-Theresien-Strasse leads to Herzog-Friedrich-Strasse, which penetrates the very heart of old Innsbruck, the Altstadt. Now a pedestrian zone, it is bounded by the River Inn on the north-west; Marktgraben and Burggraben on the south trace what was once the town's semi-circular medieval protective moat.

Directly opposite the **Katzunghaus** (No. 16), with some fine 18th-century reliefs on its gable, is the **tower** *(Stadtturm)* of the Old Town Hall *(Altes Rathaus)*.

The most decorative of the residences, **Helblinghaus**, stands at the corner of Herzog-Friedrich-Strasse as it turns west. Pink, turquoise and ivory stucco cherubim, acanthus wreaths and merry masks ornament the dazzling Rococo façade.

The house provides a fitting frame for Innsbruck's grandest monument, the **Goldenes Dachl**, a loggia built onto what was then Emperor Maximilian I's Innsbruck residence *(Neuer Hof)*. Literally "little golden roof", the loggia—a royal box from which to view tournaments—was commissioned at the end of the 15th century to celebrate Maximilian's second marriage to Bianca Maria Sforza, daughter of the Duke of Milan.

In addition to the brilliance of some 2,700 gilded copper shingles on the roof, the loggia is notable for the relief panels on the second-storey box, sculpted by Nikolaus Türing. At the first-floor level are coats-of-arms of territories which Maximilian possessed or merely dreamed of possessing.

Just east of the Goldenes Dachl, the narrow Pfarrgasse leads to the cathedral, **Dom zu St. Jakob**, built in 1722 to replace a Gothic edifice devastated by earthquake. Designed by Johann Jakob Herkommer, the late Baroque exterior is a masterpiece of restraint in an age not known for architectural austerity. The cathedral's most prized art work is the Lucas Cranach *Mariahilf* (Madonna with Child) over the high altar.

Hofburg and Hofkirche

Facing away from the old town, the bright yellow and white **Hofburg** at the north end of Burggraben is Maria Theresa's Baroque unification of the once sprawling Gothic ducal residence, completed long after the Habsburg dukes had deserted the Tyrol for Vienna. The best view of the palace is from the **Leopolds-brunnen**, a fountain erected for Archduke Leopold V.

South of the palace stands the **Hofkirche** (Court Church), a "must" for the magnificent, monumental **tomb** of Maximilian—minus his remains. A combination of demands for more taxes and too many personal bills left unpaid, turned local people against Maximilian, upon which he reneged on his plan to be buried in Innsbruck. His remains lie at Wiener Neustadt just outside Vienna. Of the planned 40 larger-than-life-size statues, 28 now-blackened bronzes stand perpetual watch over the wrought-iron cage protecting Maximilian's white marble cenotaph.

Archduke Ferdinand II and his commoner-wife Philippine Welser lie buried in the splendid **Silberne Kapelle**, which takes its name from the silver Madonna on the altar.

Museums

Next door to the Hofkirche in Universitätsstrasse, the **Tiroler Volkskunstmuseum** (Museum of Popular Arts) offers wonderfully rich—and often very moving—insights into the everyday life of old Tyrol.

Innsbruck's fine arts collection is housed in the **Tiroler Landesmuseum** or Ferdinandeum (Museumstrasse 15). The museum has some exquisite Romanesque and Gothic sculptures salvaged from churches redecorated in the Baroque style, plus works by Tyrolean artists.

Wilten and Bergisel

On the southern outskirts of Innsbruck, Wilten, site of the ancient Roman camp of Veldidena, possesses two noteworthy churches. The 17th-century **Stiftskirche St. Laurentius** is a work of the Gumpp family, Christoph, Johann Martin and Georg Anton. Complementing an attractively warm ochre-and-red exterior are the rich black-and-gold altars inside, beneath a white stucco, vaulted ceiling.

Across Leopoldstrasse stands **Basilika Wilten**, the triumphant jewel of Tyrolean Rococo—gleaming yellow without, a blaze of colour within.

Schloss Ambras

Solid enough fortress in the Middle Ages, Ambras (south-east of town) was turned into a palace *(Lustschloss)* by Ferdinand II for his wife Philippine in the 16th century. One of the highlights of a visit is the beautiful **armoury** collection.

A great curiosity is the **Kunst- und Wunderkammer** (Chamber of Art and Wonders), which dates from a time when Renaissance princes delighted in collecting weird and grotesque objects, paintings and sculptures. Don't miss the portrait of gruesome Gregor Baci, a 16th-century dwarf who went about with a lance through his head.

Eating Out

The Tyrol is a simple, peasant place that serves simple peasant food.

Soups are a regular feature of the meal. The choice includes *Bohnensuppe* (bean soup), often with pieces of sausage or bacon, and *Knödelsuppe* (dumpling soup), a chicken or beef broth with dumplings of flour, breadcrumbs, onions, bacon, parsley and garlic.

The king of hors d'oeuvres is *Tiroler Bauernspeck:* piquant, home-cured bacon

served raw, aged to a dark, Burgundy red and cut to an almost transparent thinness.

Perhaps the most popular local speciality is *Tiroler Gröstl,* a hearty dish of beef or pork sautéed with potatoes, chives, cumin and other herbs. The variation known as *Herrngröstl* includes a fried egg.

The variations of cherries, strawberries, hazelnuts, walnuts and apple in cakes *(Kuchen)* or pies and tarts *(Torten)* are endless. The best-known chocolate cake is Viennese *Sachertorte,* with a layer of apricot jam.

Hot desserts are popular, too. Try also the Hungarian-style *Palatschinken,* wafer-thin pancakes filled with jam or nuts, and *Apfelstrudel,* thinly sliced apples with raisins and cinnamon rolled in an almost transparent flaky pastry.

The wine served in Tyrol is most often white, which Austrians drink quite happily with meat and fish alike. Local beers are good, especially Zillertaler, and the regional schnapps and liqueurs made from apricots, cherries, gentian and rowanberry *(Vogelbeere)* are heart-warming delights.

Shopping

Like folklore, Tyrolean **craftwork** is not always easy to find in its authentic form, but genuine pieces are available.

As for **clothing,** you might like to buy *Lederhosen*—leather shorts that last forever. The sturdy woollen *Loden* coats and jackets are now made in a range of bright colours, as well as traditional olive and grey. Long woollen socks are a real find in this land of outdoorsmen, all marvellously resistant to the cold and the wet.

Sports shops are, of course, stocked with the best **skiing** and **mountain-climbing equipment**.

Practical Information

Banks: Banks are open from Monday to Friday 7.45 a.m. to 12.30 p.m., and 2.30 to 4 p.m. On Thursday they stay open until 5.30 p.m.

Currency: The *Schilling,* abbreviated *S, ÖS,* or *Sch.,* is divided into 100 *Groschen* (abbreviated *g*). There are coins of 1, 5, 10 and 20 S, and 10 and 50 g. Banknotes come in denominations of 20, 50, 100, 500 and 1,000 S.

Shops: Most shops are open from 8.30 a.m. to 6 p.m., although smaller establishments close for a few hours at lunch time. On Saturdays shops close at noon.

LISBON

Portugal

Introduction

Although the Atlantic is only a few miles down the estuary, Lisbon looks and feels part of the Mediterranean. Palm trees and bird-of-paradise flowers flourish in the mild winters, and there's always time enough for coffee or a glass of wine in an outdoor café, or an admiring look at the city itself. Lisbon has nearly two dozen vantage points—not seven hills as legend claims—and each gives a new perspective over the tile roofs and the magnificent harbour.

The people of Portugal's capital city show a keen eye for beauty: colourful flower pots decorate balconies, intricate mosaic work lines pavements and hand-painted tiles cover the walls. Roaming the steep, narrow streets you'll find evidence, mostly circumstantial, of Lisbon's distant past. Most of the ancient monuments succumbed to war or earthquake, but you'll notice the Phoenician profile of the modern fishing boats, the Moorish flair with the art of tile, the sad, dark eyes of the people, and their timeless lament, the music of the *fado*.

Don't expect to be shown the world's grandest plaza or tallest cathedral in this low-profile metropolis of nearly a million inhabitants. The modest Lisboans steer clear of superlatives, aiming instead for the happy medium. They dress in conservative colours and styles and never boast about their city or themselves.

Lisbon spares your budget: the shopping, at smart boutiques or in the bustle of street markets, need not be expensive. Handicrafts are usually the best bet. Bargain prices also add to the allure of most food and wine.

Out of town, an easy commuter run passes fishermen's villages on the way to the famous beach resort of Estoril. Inland tours go to one of Europe's prettiest towns, Sintra, and the Versailles-style palace at Queluz. Across the river from Lisbon are castles, vineyards, windmills and beaches. Farther afield, excursions go north to Portugal's most picturesque fishing port, Nazaré, and the pilgrims' sanctuary at Fátima. Wherever you roam, you'll be glad to come back to the drama of Lisbon's waterfront, to the golden reflections on the wide Tagus River as it flows to the sea. From here the daring explorers of the 15th and 16th centuries sailed to find and found the farthest-flung empire of the age.

IGREJA DA MADRE DE DEUS,
MUSEU DA CIDADE

LISBON

Rio Tejo

A Brief History

Early times	A Phoenician trading station is established on the site of Lisbon in 800 B.C. The Romans oust the Carthaginians in the 3rd century B.C., founding the city of Lisbon. In the 5th and 6th centuries A.D., Vandals and Visigoths fill the vacuum after Rome's decline.
8th–15th centuries	Moors from North Africa rule Lisbon; Christians fight back intermittently for four centuries. Crusaders capture Lisbon in 1147 after a four-month siege. In 1497 Vasco da Gama sails from Lisbon for East Africa and India.
18th–19th centuries	An earthquake devastates the city in 1755, touching off fires and a severe tidal wave. Napoleon rules Portugal from 1807–11.
20th century	The Portuguese monarchy falls, as a republican uprising deposes Manuel II in 1910. Antonio de Oliveira Salazar heads the government from 1932–68. The armed forces overthrow the dictatorship in 1974; Portugal begins withdrawal from its African possessions and the transition to democracy begins.

Sightseeing

The **bridge** across the Tagus, called Europe's longest suspension bridge, dates from 1966. Before that only ferryboats linked Lisbon to the rest of Portugal beyond. Looming over the bridge's toll booths, facing the city, a statue of **Christ the King** stands more than 27 metres (90 ft.) high. A viewing terrace here provides a 360-degree panorama of the whole estuary, Lisbon, and much of Portugal to the south.

On the north bank, **Belém** is the place from which the great Portuguese discoveries were launched. A modern **Monument to the Discoveries** juts from the river bank like a caravel cresting a wave, with a statue of Prince Henry the Navigator in the prow. The historic **Belém Tower,** in its own waterfront park, is graceful and imaginative but smaller than you may have thought. You can cross the moat that surrounds it and enter a 16th-century world, the most handsome aspect being the side facing the river, with a lovely loggia.

The riches that Portuguese ships brought back from the East paid for Lisbon's biggest and most admirable religious monument, the **Jerónimos Monastery.** The convent wing was shattered in the earthquake of 1755, but the church and cloister built by King Manuel I still survive as moving testaments to 16th-century faith and taste. The main **portal** of the church is a marvel of intricate stonework. Though it's usually quite dark inside the church, you'll probably be able to discern several royal **tombs,** set atop pompous sculpted elephants. Near the west door are the modern tombs of two giants of Portugal's golden age, the explorer Vasco da Gama and the national poet, Luís de Camões.

A few streets closer to the centre of town, the **National Coach Museum** is housed, aptly, in the former riding school of the Belém Royal Palace. Two great halls display dozens of horse-drawn carriages for city or ceremonial or cross-country travel during four centuries of European history. The most extravagant of the exhibits are three gilt carriages used by the Portuguese embassy in Rome in the early 18th century to impress Pope Clement XI. In this museum, called the world's greatest collection of coaches, nothing has been overlooked—not even regal riding accessories from stirrups to coach horns.

Central Lisbon

Stately pink arcades line three sides of the vast **Praça do Comércio** (Commerce Square); the fourth is open to the harbour, with Venetian-style stairs leading right into the Tagus. A triumphal arch connects the government buildings on the north side of the square. Through the arch you can see the length of Rua Augusta, the main street of this rigidly rectangular 18th-century district, called the **Baixa** (lowland). It's full of banks, shops, small restaurants and tea shops.

The top end of Rua Augusta runs into Lisbon's main square, the **Rossio.** In olden days it was the scene of witch burnings and bullfights, and it's still the very centre of activity—the place to meet friends, drink coffee, buy flowers from the quaintly costumed vendors, and listen to the gushing fountains and the incomprehensible calls of the newsboys. The Rossio suburban railway station looks at first glance like a vision of a Moorish palace. Actually, it's a romantic effort of the late 19th century; the style is called neo-Manueline.

A fairly straightforward obelisk marks the Praça dos Restauradores, commemorating the overthrow of Spanish rule in 1640. Opposite the splendid palace on the west side of the square, the Palácio Foch, is Lisbon's main post office.

From here the **Avenida da Liberdade** (Liberty Avenue), often likened to the Champs-Elysées in Paris, heads uphill for about a mile. Lisbon's central boulevard is wide enough for 12 lanes of traffic and a couple of parkways enlivened by palm trees, duck ponds and mosaic pavements. The avenue ends at a big traffic circle (roundabout), beyond which lies a formal park of mani-

cured lawns and shrubs, named after England's King Edward VII.

Lisbon's most original botanical triumph occupies the north-west corner of this park. Called the **Estufa Fria** ("cold greenhouse"), it's a tropical rain-forest protected by a simple system of slatted roofs and walls to moderate the extremes of weather. Amid moody pools and waterfalls, bananas grow big enough to eat (but too high to grab).

Old Lisbon

The highest and best of all the belvederes in hilly Lisbon belongs to the ancient **Castelo de São Jorge** (St. George's Castle). The natural strategic value of this promontory just above the centre of the city prompted the Romans to build the first defensive walls here about two thousand years ago. Earthquakes and wear-and-tear over recent centuries left little intact, but a serious restoration programme has given new life to the old ruins. The citadel and palace, ramparts and towers again tell their tale, long and sometimes sad.

Lisbon's **Sé** (Cathedral) was begun as a fortress-church in the 12th century. Its towers, and walls with firing slits, still suggest a beleaguered citadel. Just a few steps down the hill is a church honouring the city's most revered native son, St. Anthony of Padua (1195–1231)—preacher, theologian, patron of the poor and defender of human rights.

Between here and the waterfront, one last old building

Shady lookout point surveys the ancient tile roofs of Lisbon.

LISBON

ought to be glimpsed. The **Casa dos Bicos** (House of Facets), built in the early 16th century, is faced with stones shaped like pyramids.

Alfama

This is the most fascinating part of Lisbon, a labyrinth of crooked streets, stairways and alleys that go nowhere deviously but charmingly. Alfama is a chaos of tilting houses with mismatched windows, fish stalls and bars, laundry dripping onto the street, and the feeling that nothing has changed since the Middle Ages. It can be explored only on foot: most streets are too narrow for anything but a donkey cart.

Here are a few of Alfama's highlights: **St. Michael's Church,** built in the 12th century, restored in the 18th, with a splendid ceiling of Brazilian jacaranda wood; **Beco da Cordosa,** an alley with blind-alley offshoots, the very essence of

the higgledy-piggledy delights of Alfama; the octagonal, 13th-century **St. Stephen's Church; Rua de São Pedro,** the boisterous main shopping street, with shrieking fishwives and an ever-changing obstacle course of chickens, dogs and children.

Bairro Alto

Like Alfama, the Bairro Alto ("high neighbourhood") is a hilly section of evocative old houses with wrought-iron balconies occupied by bird cages and flower pots. At night the district's restaurants, *fado* nightclubs and disco bars come alive. The most unusual of the local churches, the **Carmelite Church,** was built in the 14th century. As you stand on the grass inside the shell of what was one of Lisbon's great churches of the age, look up through the arches into the blue sky and imagine the scene on that All Saints' Day in 1755 when the earthquake rocked the pillars and the roof fell in on a full congregation.

The Bairro Alto is linked to the centre of town by a funicu-

Cobblestone paths lead through the medieval labyrinth of Alfama.

lar and a curious free-standing **lift,** inaugurated in 1901 and originally powered by steam.

The longer, slower way downhill meanders through the district called the **Chiado.** For centuries these zigzagging streets have been known for Lisbon's most elegant shopping—silverware, leather, fashions, books—and fine pastry and tea shops. But in 1988 the area was devastated by a fire, called the city's worst disaster since 1755. Two of Europe's oldest department stores were wiped out.

In city of hills, Edward VII park goes downhill towards the river.

Excursions

"Portuguese Riviera"

Central attraction of the sunny coast west of Lisbon, **Estoril** is a fashionable resort with a big reputation. A formal park with ranks of palms, disciplined shrubs, flower beds and ponds fronts the town's most imposing building, the **casino**—a one-stop amusement centre. Elsewhere, Estoril is as discreet as a big winner ought to be. Victorian villas and some sleek modern mansions are tucked away behind green curtains of palms, eucalyptus trees, pines and vines. Since the turn of the century many an ex-monarch, suddenly unemployed, has gravitated to Estoril or neighbouring Cascais to enjoy stylish exile.

While Estoril is cosmopolitan and sybaritic, **Cascais** lives a dramatic double life. In the "town of fishermen and kings" simple men of the sea coexist with the lords of local villas and camera-slung tourists. You can watch the fishing catch unloaded on the beach from blue, yellow or red boats and then put up for sale in the modern auction building. You may not understand the auctioneer's chant, but you'll like the looks of the lobster, shrimp, hake, sardines and squid he's selling. You can sample the seafood at any of the dozen or so restaurants within walking distance of the shore.

Queluz and Sintra

From the highway, the 18th-century pink **palace** of **Queluz** seems rather unprepossessing. But the Portuguese abandoned their customary modesty on the inside of this sprawling monument, 14 kilometres (9 mi.) west of Lisbon. The most lavish hall of all, the throne room, has overpowering chandeliers and walls and ceilings burdened with gilt. Outside, the **gardens** of Queluz go on and on, with clipped hedges in geometric array and bushes trimmed into inventive shapes. One original attraction is an "artificial" river. Enclosed between restraining walls covered in precious painted tiles, a real stream was diverted to pass through the palace grounds and dammed whenever the royals felt like a boat ride.

Sintra, a town 25 kilometres (15 mi.) north-west of Lisbon, is the kind of place you visit for a day and yearn to return to forever. Up and down forested hillsides are palaces and stately homes and lovely vistas. Even the local jail is housed in a castle.

The **Royal Palace,** in the centre of town, was the summer home of Portuguese kings starting in the 14th century. Every room has a story to tell, so you won't want to miss the details—like the paths worn in one brick floor by the pacing of an imprisoned deposed king.

Sintra's oldest monument, the **Moorish Castle,** overlooking the town, was probably built in the 8th or 9th century. On a slightly higher hilltop stands the **Pena Palace,** a tremendous Victorian folly in a park of flowering trees and vines. This Disneyesque cocktail of Gothic, Renaissance, Moorish and Manueline architecture was designed in the 19th century as a love nest for Queen Maria II and her romantic husband, Ferdinand of Saxe-Coburg-Gotha.

Arrábida Peninsula

Across the suspension bridge from Lisbon and some 30 kilometres (19 mi.) to the south, the golden sand of the beach at **Sesimbra** is shared by vacationers and professional fishermen. In the Middle Ages, when the threat of invasions made seaside living too chancy, the town was situated on the hilltop overlooking the beach. Those **castle walls** you see are genuine, though recently restored. Planted on the hillside are three squat white **windmills**—a reminder that Portugal has vastly more windmills than Holland.

The district capital of the Arrábida peninsula, **Setúbal,** is the nation's third largest fishing port as well as a market town and resort centre. Look for the Church of Jesus, built about 1490 by the French architect Boytac, who later created Lisbon's Jerónimos Monastery. The 16th-century fort overlooking Setúbal is now a government-sponsored inn.

Between Lisbon and Setúbal the landscape is a pleasing mixture of olive and citrus groves, with cows and donkeys sunbathing along the way, and farther south, vineyards. The grapes of the Setúbal region are transformed into a highly regarded muscatel, so don't leave without tasting it.

Excursions North

In **Fátima,** a hill town about 135 kilometres (83 mi.) north of Lisbon, the church faces a square said to be twice as big as St. Peter's in Rome. Many thousands congregate here on pilgrimage days (the 13th of every month), but even on an ordinary weekday, crowds of believers, some in wheelchairs, some kneeling in penitence, come to the shrine. The focus of faith is the spot where, in 1917, three young shepherds saw a series of miraculous visions, climaxed by a solar phenomenon witnessed by many townsfolk.

But the biggest church in Portugal is at **Alcobaça.** Inside you can see the **tombs** of King Pedro I and his beloved, Inês de Castro. The tombs are decorated with medieval stone-carvings illustrating the drama of this romantic couple: Inês was murdered for political reasons in 1355; later, when Pedro became king, he exhumed her body and crowned his true love queen.

And so to the coast, and **Nazaré,** the fishing village you've seen in pictures. The fishermen don black stocking-caps and plaid trousers, the women wear seven petticoats and oxen sometimes pull the fishing boats ashore. From a cliff at the north end of Nazaré you survey the hilly green countryside, the neatly packed town, and mile after mile of **beach** open to the full force of the Atlantic. Tourism is big business nowadays, but the fishing and folklore seem unaffected.

Eating Out

Meat-lovers can find delicious pork and lamb dishes and even a presentable steak, but it's the freshly caught seafood that adds an exclamation point to the Portuguese menu. The best advertisement for seafood is in the window of a restaurant—a refrigerated display case full of prawns and crabs, oysters and mussels, sea bass and sole.

Some typical dishes:

Ameijoas na cataplana: steamed mussels with ham, sausages, white wine, tomato, onion and herbs.

Açorda de marisco: a spicy, garlic-scented bread soup full of seafood bits; raw eggs are folded into the mixture at the table.

Bacalhau à Gomes de Sá: chunks of dried cod baked with potatoes, onion, parsley and olives, garnished with grated hard-boiled egg.

On the meat side, look for *cabrito assado,* baked kid served with both potato and rice, and *espetada mista,* chunks of beef, lamb and pork on a spit. Chicken *(frango* or *galinha)* is popular stewed, fried, roast or barbecued to a tasty crispness.

Meals often begin with a hearty soup, but try to save

some room for dessert—a very sweet pudding, a fresh fruit salad, or Portuguese cheese.

Always potable, Portugal's table wines are often admirable. Choose from *tinto* (red), *branco* (white) or *vinho verde* ("green wine")—a semi-sparkling young white.

Nightlife

A century ago, "respectable" people were reluctant to be seen in a *fado* club, but nowadays there's no danger at all—physically, morally or even financially. You can have a rousing night out at one of the *fado* houses in the atmospheric Alfama or Bairro Alto districts. The *fado* (meaning fate), a song of longing and lament, is as inescapably Portuguese as the samba is Brazilian or the waltz Viennese. Guitars accompany a woman in black who wails out her song of tragedy and despair. The *fado* is never danced, but sometimes regional fishermen's and shepherd's dances enliven the show.

In Lisbon you can also find conventional nightclubs with extravagant floor-shows and dark, cosy *boîtes,* discotheques, jazz clubs and bars for all tastes.

For entertainment and gambling, the Estoril casino is open from 3 p.m. to 3 a.m. every day of the year, except Good Friday and Christmas Eve. If you need a refresher course in the rules of roulette, "French Bank", baccarat, craps or blackjack, illustrated instruction leaflets in English and Portugese are provided.

Shopping

In chic boutiques, in "commercial centres" (modern shopping complexes open till late at night) or the flea market at Campo de Santa Clara (Tuesdays and Saturdays only), shopping is old-fashioned fun in Lisbon. Antiques, from old gold to used cowbells, will interest the knowledgeable browser, but most visitors concentrate on handicrafts:

Embroidery. Thousands of women on the island of Madeira produce delicate needlework. Lisbon shops also stock hand embroidery from the Azores and various mainland villages.

Filigree. Invading Moors brought this speciality to Portugal in the 8th century. Look for caravel designs of gold or silver wire, or lace-like brooches in the form of flowers or butterflies.

Knitwear. Hand-knit pullovers in sophisticated designs or rugged fishermen's sweaters.

Madeira or **port.** Sunny bottled souvenirs for before or after dinner. Even in Portugal, though, really good port can be expensive.

Pottery. Fine workmanship and cheerful colours distinguish Portuguese porcelain.

Roosters. Everywhere you'll see brightly hand-painted statuettes of ceramic or wood, honouring a legendary rooster which arose from a judge's dinner plate to crow the innocence of an unjustly condemned man.

Rugs. The Alentejo village of Arraiolos has a three-century-old rug industry noted for its spirited colours.

Shawls. If the sweeping black model affected by *fado* singers is too severe, consider the selection of gaily coloured scarves.

Tiles. Hand-painted *azulejos* have been adorning Portuguese walls for centuries. Some places will paint tiles to order.

Wickerwork. Choose from pretty baskets, sturdy furniture, ship's models and animal figures.

Practical Information

Banks: Open 8.30 to 11.45 a.m. and 1 to 2.30 or 2.45 p.m. Mondays to Fridays. Among special facilities for tourists is a bank in the Praça dos Restauradores, open from 6. p.m. to 11 p.m.

Credit cards and traveller's cheques: Accepted in major hotels, restaurants and tourist-oriented enterprises.

Currency: The Portuguese *escudo* (abbreviated *esc.*) is divided into 100 *centavos*. The most common coins are 50 centavos, 1, 2½, 5, 10, 20, 25 and 50 escudos. Banknotes: 100, 500, 1,000 and 5,000 escudos. Note: price tags use the $ sign instead of a decimal point. Thus 5 000 $ 00 means 5,000 escudos.

Language: Portuguese. Children study English from the age of 10 and French from 13. Your high-school Spanish will help with signs and menus.

Post offices: Open 9 a.m. to 6.30 p.m. Monday to Friday. Major branch offices also operate till noon on Saturday. The main post office in Praça dos Restauradores works from 8 a.m. to midnight daily.

Restaurants: Lunch from noon until 3 p.m. Dinner from 7.30 to 9.30 p.m. (later in a *casa de fado*).

Shops: Monday to Friday 9 a.m. to 1 p.m. and 3 to 7 p.m., and on Saturday morning from 9 to 1. The new shopping complexes usually stay open until midnight, often on Sundays, as well. Some of the Baixa shops are also open at lunch-time.

Taxis: Every neighbourhood has a taxi rank; you can also find them at railway, Metro and ferry stations. The fare is shown on the meter. Surcharges: 20% at night, 50% for excess baggage.

Tipping: Taxis 10%. Waiters 10% for exceptional service. Porter 50 escudos per bag. Lavatory attendant 25 escudos.

Water: Lisbon's tap water, although strongly flavoured with chemicals, is safe for drinking. Or you can choose from an excellent range of local bottled mineral waters.

LONDON

U.K.

Introduction

You may well fall in love with London—but not at first sight. The world's most habitable great city creeps up on you. No single vista, no instant revelation will bowl you over. Rather, the attractions add up: the sober elegance of a Georgian house, the details of a Victorian pub, a brave show of colour in a windowbox of geraniums. All at once an accumulation of discreet charms will come into focus and you'll find that just being in this immensely civilized city makes you feel good.

Travel from South Kensington to North Kensington and you change environment completely. The pubs and their customers look different; so do the houses.

The diversity of London strikes visitors at once. For the great governmental, financial and cultural centre is not really a city at all, but a juxtaposition of villages—Chiswick, Dulwich, Hampstead, Islington, Chelsea, and so on.

Still, wherever you look you see London's distinctive red pillar boxes, black taxis and umbrella-toting businessmen. And then, of course, there's the weather, a subject dear to the hearts of all Londoners. The sea winds sweep the clouds across the sky, changing the mood from rain to sunshine in a flash. Solution: when the first raindrops spatter down, nip into a museum. By the time you come out there's every chance that it will be clear again.

Yet freezing winter nights are rare, and in summer a heat wave is proclaimed any time City gents actually remove their bowlers and jackets. In other words, the weather is moderate and kind.

And so are the Londoners.

A Brief History

1st–11th centuries	Londinium is founded by Rome in the 1st century, eventually becoming one of the most prosperous towns in the Empire. The Romans abandon the city in the 5th century, and it enters a dark, confused period. The native Celts (by now latinized) first welcome, then are forced to flee Germanic mercenaries—Angles, Saxons, Jutes. The Vikings add to the chaos by staging raids.

Calm and order are restored in the 9th century by King Egbert and his descendants. The Normans, led by William the Conqueror, cross the Channel in 1066, overcoming the English at the Battle of Hastings.

12th–16th centuries

London's influence grows while the English kings are busy elsewhere, warring in France or taking part in the Crusades. Dissenting noblemen force King John to sign the *Magna Carta* at Runnymede in 1215, giving important rights to citizens and special privileges to the city of London.

In the 16th century, Henry VIII breaks with the pope, and England becomes Protestant. The country experiences a golden age under his daughter, Elizabeth I—the era of literary geniuses like Francis Bacon, Ben Jonson, Christopher Marlowe and, above all, William Shakespeare. English naval supremacy is established with the defeat of the Spanish Armada in 1588.

17th–18th centuries

Puritans, led by Oliver Cromwell, seize power briefly in the middle of the 17th century. London suffers two disasters during the reign of Charles II: the Great Plague of 1665, which wipes out one-third of the population and, a year later, a fire that destroys much of the city. The rebuilding emphasizes stately architectural ensembles set around green, open squares. By the end of the 18th century, London has become one of Europe's most important commercial centres.

19th–20th centuries

Admiral Nelson defeats the French fleet at Trafalgar in 1805, assuring Britain's superiority at sea. The Industrial Revolution transforms English society, shifting power to the rising middle classes and giving impetus to London's expansion.

The city is bombed by German dirigibles during World War I, but this is nothing compared to Hitler's firebombs, which gut thousands of buildings and practically destroy London's East End during World War II. The city's indomitable spirit is personified by Winston Churchill, who encourages his hard-pressed people to fight on.

Vast post-war reconstruction adds skyscrapers to London's skyline, while an influx of immigrants from the former colonies and Commonwealth countries contributes to London's cultural diversity.

Sightseeing

Trafalgar Square to Whitehall

The place to start is **Trafalgar Square,** a vast gathering place for tourists and pigeons. It's named after the 1805 Battle of Trafalgar in which Lord Nelson defeated Napoleon's fleet off the Spanish coast. Nelson's statue tops the Corinthian column in the centre of the square.

Just opposite lies the **National Gallery,** one of the world's great museums. Here you'll see masterpieces by Leonardo da Vinci, Raphael, Botticelli, Titian, Rembrandt, Rubens, Velázquez, El Greco, Gainsborough, Hogarth, Reynolds, Turner and Constable, to name just a few.

To the south-west from **Admiralty Arch** there is a magnificent view of the **Mall.** Off to the left stretches St. James' Park, while on the opposite side of the avenue is a series of elegant houses: Nash's Carlton House Terrace, Marlborough House, where the Commonwealth is administered, Clarence House, home of Queen Elizabeth the Queen Mother, and Lancaster House. At the far end of the Mall stands Buckingham Palace.

Have a closer look at **St. James' Palace,** a maze of courtyards and passages, reconstructed many times. From 1698 to 1837 this was a royal residence; Queen Victoria preferred Buckingham Palace, royal residence since then.

Buckingham Palace, behind high iron railings, is interesting not for its architectural beauty but for its role as home of the monarch. The Royal Standard is raised only when the Queen is in residence. Constructed in 1703 for the Duke of Buckingham, the palace was remodelled by Nash in 1825.

You won't want to miss the Changing of the Guard at the palace, the quintessence of British pomp and pageantry. The 30-minute ceremony takes place in front of the main entrance, daily at 11.30 a.m. (alternate days in winter).

You can visit the **Queen's Gallery,** where a selection of pictures from the royal art collection is on view, and the Royal Mews with a display of sumptuous coaches and ceremonial carriages.

The **Houses of Parliament,** officially known as the Palace of Westminster, can be seen from afar thanks to the familiar shape of the clock tower.

This famous belfry, 320 feet (96 m.) high, contains **Big Ben,** a 13½-ton bell which strikes the hours with a chime known round the world.

You may be disappointed to learn that this fine building with neo-Gothic pinnacles and gilded rooftops is a mid-19th-century structure. Most of the ancient palace was destroyed by fire in 1834. In 1941, in the Blitz, the House of Commons was bombed out. It was rebuilt in 1950.

One of the ancient elements still in existence is **Westminster Hall.** Here, the abdication of Edward II was proclaimed, the trial of Charles I took place, and Cromwell was named Lord Protector of the Realm. (Later his head was exhibited here.) In the same hall Guy Fawkes heard his death sentence pronounced for the gunpowder plot.

A flight of steps descends to St. Stephen's Crypt, dating from the 14th century. Unfortunately, its present decoration comes from the Victorian period, the same fate as overtook St. Stephen's Hall.

From the Commons a passage leads to the **House of Lords,** with members' seats arranged around the throne. This hall is the work of the 19th-century architect Pugin, apostle of the neo-Gothic. The Royal Gallery is reserved for the sovereign when she visits the Lords; she hasn't the right to enter the Commons!

The **Jewel Tower,** now a museum, is almost all that remains of the medieval fortress of Westminster.

Much more than just a church, **Westminster Abbey,** only a few steps from the Houses of Parliament, is a place where the sacred and profane, religion and history, are inextricably mixed. From the 14th to the 16th century, the House of Commons met in the abbey and not the Palace of Westminster.

Westminster Abbey was built in stages. The foundations were laid by Edward the Confessor in the 11th century on the site of a chapel which probably existed as early as the 7th century. The body of the king, who was canonized in 1163, rests in a chapel in the apse. In the 13th century another pious king, Henry III Plantagenet, had the abbey reconstructed in the Gothic style.

Henry VII enlarged the abbey in 1503 by adding a new **chapel** in the uniquely English "perpendicular" style. The tomb of Elizabeth I is here. The abbey took on its modern appearance in the 18th century when a pupil of Wren contributed the towers of the façade.

Guided tours are available, but if you prefer to visit the abbey on your own, start by admiring the majestic perspective of the **nave.** More than 500 feet (150 m.) long, it is broken only by a high rood screen. Of the many tombs dispersed throughout the abbey the most notable are in **Poets' Corner.** Here lie Chaucer, Browning, Dickens, Tennyson and Kipling as well as the composer Handel (a longtime London resident though of German origin). The Tomb of the Unknown Soldier is in the abbey, too.

You can also visit the **Great Cloisters** (to the right of the entrance), part of the abbey as it was in the 13th and 14th centuries. The **Norman Undercroft** houses a curious collection of effigies of famous people—as exhibited to the crowds at the time of their funerals.

In the **Chamber of the Pyx,** an ancient chapel remaining from the 11th-century origins of the abbey, were kept the standards for all kinds of money circulating in the realm. The **Chapter House,** with its magnificent tiled floor, dates from the same era. Until 1547 it was the meeting place of the House of Commons.

Whitehall is the sober street of government buildings. Heading from the Houses of Parliament towards Trafalgar Square, the Foreign Office is on the left, the Ministry of Defence on the right. Just beyond the Foreign Office is a dead-end street known to all the world: **Downing Street.** Every tourist seems to want to take a picture of his companions outside Number 10, the office and residence of British prime ministers.

Banqueting House, on the right side of Whitehall, was the scene of many ancient feasts. It is the last vestige of the proud palace of Whitehall built in 1622 for King James I by Inigo Jones. The magnificent ceiling paintings are by Rubens.

Trafalgar Square to the Tower of London

From Trafalgar Square, make your way to St. Paul's Cathedral via the Strand. Along with the Thames, the Strand is the traditional route of all the kings and queens of England.

Farther along the Strand, at Aldwych, American-designed Bush House is the headquarters of the BBC World Service. Temple Bar, at one time the gate to the City, is the site of the **Inns of Court,** tucked away on either side of Fleet Street: The Temple, Lincoln's Inn and Gray's Inn.

As you go along Fleet Street you pass many major newspaper offices—the *Daily Telegraph* and the *Daily Express* on the left. Headquarters of the worldwide Reuters news agency is here, too. The press spills over into the side streets, where you'll also find some venerable old taverns.

On top of Ludgate Hill, **St. Paul's Cathedral** is the masterpiece of Sir Christopher Wren. Having worked on it for 45 years, Wren had the privilege almost always denied a cathedral designer: he saw his work come to fruition in 1710. He is buried in St. Paul's in a modest tomb with the moving Latin epitaph: "Reader, if you seek his monument, look around you."

St. Paul's is the fifth church to be built on this site. The preceding one, an even bigger Gothic structure, was destroyed in the Great Fire of 1666.

The present cathedral, inspired by St. Peter's in Rome, is chiefly remarkable for its

dome (height 365 feet, diameter 112 feet; 110/34 m.). The interior has perhaps fewer historical associations than Westminster Abbey, but it nonetheless contains the tombs of both Nelson and the Duke of Wellington. This was also the scene of the state funeral of Sir Winston Churchill and the wedding of the Prince of Wales.

Don't miss the Whispering Gallery under the dome. Due to a strange acoustical phenomenon, you can hear the slightest whisper from the other side of the gallery.

Leaving St. Paul's, head east through the City of London to the **Tower of London.** It's hard to say which is more famous, the Tower itself or the adjacent **Tower Bridge,** the most celebrated of London's bridges, with its twin towers and roadway that opens to let ships through.

The Tower of London is a fortress constructed around the White Tower which William the Conqueror built in the 11th century. It has been a royal residence, a court of justice and later a prison—and therein lies its fascination, for many a horrible crime has been committed here. Among the celebrated victims: the sons of Edward IV, the Princes in the Tower, murdered in 1483 by order of their uncle, Richard, Duke of Gloucester. Two wives of Henry VIII—Anne Boleyn and Catherine Howard—were also executed here.

The interior of the fortress contains many interesting sights, by no means limited to relics of horror (like the headman's axe, famous swords and notorious dungeons). You can visit the 11th-century Chapel of St. John (said to be the oldest church in London) and see an astonishing collection of armour and the famous **Crown Jewels.** Various crowns are displayed, along with swords, orbs and sceptres.

Stormed by more than two million visitors a year, the Tower of London is valiantly defended by about 40 men in Tudor costume, halberds at the ready. The Yeomen of the Guard are also known as Beefeaters.

The West End

For a Londoner, visiting the West End for shopping in the famous stores, seeing the latest play or film and dining at a distinguished restaurant is "going up to town". A town within a town, the West End is the focus for fashionable living, pleasure and dreams.

For hardy hikers a tour of the West End might start from Tottenham Court Road underground station, heading west along London's busiest shopping street, **Oxford Street.** Huge department stores and smaller fashion stores and boutiques line this thoroughfare for more than a mile to **Marble Arch.**

From here you can see the green expanse of Hyde Park, the site of **Speakers' Corner.** This open space near Marble Arch echoes to unbounded eloquence, mostly on Sunday afternoons. Any orator who has a message—philosophical, religious, ideological, but rarely dull—can face the hecklers here. No theme is too controversial or outrageous to be aired at Speakers' Corner.

Stroll down **Park Lane,** no longer a lane at all but a very busy boulevard with mansions and elegant hotels on one side and the eastern border of Hyde Park on the other. At **Hyde Park Corner,** turn left into **Piccadilly,** an important traffic artery known for its private clubs, discotheques and luxury shops. After Piccadilly crosses Bond Street, you come to Burlington House, home of the Royal Academy of Arts. Just a short way further east and you're in the middle of London's most celebrated traffic circle, **Piccadilly Circus.**

To the north-east is the district which evokes memories of London's early 20th-century literary life, Bloomsbury, home of the internationally renowned **British Museum** (Great Russell Street).

In the British Museum you can admire the celebrated friezes from the Parthenon, known as the Elgin Marbles.

The museum displays incomparable Egyptian, Assyrian, Persian, Greek, Roman and British archaeological treasures plus Eastern and Islamic antiquities. There's a famous exhibition of numismatics. The collection of prints and drawings is one of the finest in the world. In addition, the British Library with its famous domed reading room is a unique research centre. The manuscript collection is overwhelming—from the *Magna Carta* (1215) and a mortgage signed by Shakespeare (1613) to the original manuscript of *Alice in Wonderland.*

For more leisurely sightseeing in the West End you might prefer to take a bus along Oxford Street or Park Lane, with a break here or there for a pub or restaurant. But you still have to explore two West End "villages"—Soho, extending roughly from Charing Cross Road to Regent Street, and Mayfair, between Regent Street and Park Lane.

Soho is a curious mixture of elements: pleasures of all kinds from gourmet restaurants to sordid nightspots.

Just off Oxford Street, by contrast, peaceful Soho Square, a pretty 17th-century meeting place, isolates itself from all the excitement. Shaftesbury Avenue, farther south, is strong on theatres. As for Wardour Street, it might as well be Hollywood, British style: all the big names in the motion-picture industry have offices here. Two streets parallel to Shaftesbury Avenue, Gerrard and Lisle streets, are the heart of London's bustling Chinatown.

Mayfair, on the other side of Regent Street, offers the same pleasures as Soho, but they are more expensive and more respectable. Gambling flourishes in specialized clubs; some discotheques are frequented by young jet-setters.

Mayfair is more varied than Soho. **Old Bond Street** glitters with fashionable stores, art galleries, fine antique shops, and jewellers attracted by the proximity of Sotheby's, the renowned auctioneers. Savile Row outfits the best-dressed men of affairs. An unusual shopping gallery, the exclusive Burlington Arcade, runs through to Piccadilly.

Other Sights

The **Victoria and Albert Museum** is in Cromwell Road. Painting, sculpture, ceramics, furniture, weapons, musical instruments, clocks and costumes fill 145 rooms.

The **Tate Gallery** on Millbank contains examples of English painting from the 16th century to the present; don't miss the works of Turner.

Madame Tussaud's (Marylebone Road). The ever-popular waxworks has been a London tradition since 1802.

With its lake, canal, open-air theatre and zoo, **Regent's Park,** near Madame Tussaud's, is a favourite spot for Londoners. In the 19th century the Prince Regent, the future George IV, wanted to have a country house here. His architect, John Nash, designed a typical English garden in concentric circles and built the baronial terraced houses bordering the park.

Don't miss the **London Zoo,** at the northern end of Regent's Park, one of the most famous in the world.

Eating Out

It may take some hunting to find a restaurant that specializes in traditional English fare.

Appetizers

Potted shrimps, fish pie, jellied eel and game paté.

Soups

Oxtail soup, Scotch broth (a thick mutton, barley and vegetable soup) and cock-a-leekie (a chicken soup strong on leeks).

Main Course

The classic dish is roast beef and Yorkshire pudding. Roast lamb, often served with a mint sauce, can be first-rate. Or sample steak and kidney pie.

England is also renowned for its outstanding fish and seafood: oysters, prawns, salmon and Dover sole. For a takeaway lunch, try the ubiquitous fish and chips. Fillets of cod, plaice, haddock or hake, covered in a rich batter and deep-fried, can also be very good.

Desserts

Look for trifle, a sponge cake smothered in sherry and custard or cream. Fool is a whipped fruit and cream dessert.

Cheeses

The king of English cheeses is Stilton, a strong, blue-veined cheese. Other varieties include Cheddar, Cheshire, Double Gloucester, Lancashire, Leicester and Wensleydale.

Foreign Food

In London you'll have the chance to sample an impressive range of foreign cuisines, especially Indian, Greek and Chinese. London's Chinatown, just south of Shaftesbury Avenue, is jammed with good restaurants.

Breakfast and Tea

The famous English breakfast may consist of fruit juice, cereal, eggs and bacon, sausages or kippers. Along with this goes toast, marmalade, tea or coffee.

The ceremony of afternoon tea is re-enacted in many London hotels. You may be plied with little sandwiches, scones, crumpets or cakes.

Drinks

Wine with dinner and cognac afterwards is the order of the evening in the better restaurants. Beer is taken seriously. Bitter, drawn from the tap, is the biggest seller. Other British brews include mild, stout and lager.

Shopping

Shopping in London can be a pretext for looking over the city and the people.

Special Places

Harrods in Knightsbridge supplies the royal family and the aristocracy of Britain. This vast store caters for everything from theatre tickets to funerals.

Fortnum & Mason in Piccadilly dress their salesmen in frock coats. English tea is celebrated on the premises every afternoon.

Liberty & Co. occupies an extraordinary building fronting Regent Street. The store is noted for an extensive selection of fabrics in silk, Viyella and varuna wool.

Selfridges in Oxford Street boasts some 200 departments, as well as a reputation for good quality and low prices.

Covent Garden, the former fruit-and-vegetable market, has been renovated to house many trendy shops for clothing and accessories.

What to Buy

Antiques. The choice ranges from veritable museum pieces to musty bric-a-brac. Perhaps one of the best places to look is

a street market. Friday mornings, the New Caledonian Antique Market sets up in Bermondsey Street (across Tower Bridge). Saturday is the day for Portobello Road, Monday for Covent Garden's Jubilee Market.

Books. Bibliophiles will want to browse along the Charing Cross Road.

China. England is the home of Wedgwood and other fine makes of china.

Clothing for men. Shop for impeccably tailored suits and raincoats.

Clothing for women. Traditional coats and raincoats, woollens and silks make good buys.

Food. British specialities are: cheeses, marmalades, biscuits, mints, toffees, hard candies, chocolates.

Silverware. Prices are interesting and the British alloy is purer than in Europe.

Teas. Take home a box of something special from India or Sri Lanka.

Textiles and fabrics. The British are still supreme in woollens, cashmeres, tweeds.

Tobacco. Connoisseurs far and wide frequent two famous London shops—Dunhill and Fribourg & Treyer.

Practical Information

Banks and currency exchange: Open 9.30 a.m. to 3.30 p.m., Monday to Friday. Branches at air and rail terminals keep longer hours, weekends included.

Credit cards and traveller's cheques: Major credit cards are widely accepted by most hotels, better restaurants and shops. Traveller's cheques may be refused in some places; it's best to change them at a bank.

Currency: Decimal currency was inaugurated in Britain in 1971; the pound (£) = 100 pence (p). Coins: 1p, 2p, 5p, 10p, 20p, 50p, £1, 2. Notes: £5, £10, £20, £50.

Post offices: Larger post offices are open 9 a.m. to 5.30 or 6 p.m., Monday to Friday and 9 a.m. to 12.30 p.m. on Saturday.

Shops: Generally open 9 a.m. to 5.30 or 6 p.m., Monday to Saturday (10 a.m. to 8 p.m. and Sunday afternoon in Covent Garden). In the West End and the City shops close on Saturday afternoon.

LUCERNE

Switzerland

Introduction

The geographical heart of Switzerland, but more poetically described by Alexandre Dumas as "a pearl in the world's most beautiful oyster", Lucerne is an undeniably magical city. It sits on the shores of the Vierwaldstättersee (Lake of the Four Forest Cantons) at the place where the lake narrows to form the fast-flowing River Reuss.

Over the last 1,000 years Lucerne has grown from a tiny fishing village to a thriving resort, but it has lost none of its natural beauty along the way. Until the 18th century the mountains, which tower over the city and lake, were not considered much of an attraction. However, during the 18th century poets became more sensitive to their beauty and, in turn, this led to a new era for Lucerne.

A steamboat trip around the lake gives visitors a chance to take in the splendid scenery, which includes both mountains and tropical plants. It will also show you, on the one hand, the historical site of the Rütli where the Confederation was formed and, on the other, the site honouring William Tell's legendary leap ashore while escaping a Habsburg overlord.

One of the city's most famous visitors, Richard Wagner, who lived in Lucerne for six years, was moved to say "The sweet warmth of Lucerne's quay is such that it even makes me forget my music!" But he did manage to compose part of *Siegfried* and *Götterdämmerung,* among others, while he lived there.

A Brief History

400 B.C.–9th century A.D.	The Helvetians, a Celtic tribe, settle in Switzerland. The Romans colonize the area and a relatively peaceful coexistence follows. During the 5th century Alemannic tribes invade north-eastern and central Switzerland. The country is divided into two along the River Sarine. The Franks, under Charlemagne, subdue both the Burgundians (in the west), and the Alemanni; Switzerland is incorporated into the Holy Roman Empire.
10th–14th centuries	The Carolingian dynasty dies out in 911 and power struggles break out between the powerful Zähringen,

Kyburg and Habsburg families. The tiny fishing village of Lucerne is run by a Benedictine monastery (owned by the Alsatian Abbey of Murbach). Under its influence Lucerne develops into a market town.

In 1291 three valley communities join together and form a pact against the Habsburgs: the beginning of the Confederation. Also in 1291, Lucerne moves from the monastery's sphere of influence to that of the Habsburg's.

The town feels its independence threatened, so it joins the Confederation in 1332. After the Confederate victory at the Battle of Sempach in 1386, Lucerne is finally free of Habsburg influence.

15th–18th centuries	Lucerne's independence leads to greater prosperity and the town is able to send mercenary soldiers to fight for foreign kings. This produces a flourishing patrician class which reaches its peak during the 17th and 18th centuries. By this time Lucerne is the largest town in the country.
19th–20th centuries	In 1846 the Catholic cantons break away from the Confederation, with Lucerne at the fore. After the reconciliation, Lucerne develops into a peaceful town and popular resort. Caesar Ritz opens the Grand Hotel National in 1870, August Escoffier is head chef.

Sightseeing

A convenient point to start is at the railway station, where you have an overall view of lake, mountains, grand hotels, the river, bridges and the towers of the medieval city.

To your left along the river you'll pass the **Kapellbrücke,** one of the oldest wooden bridges in Europe (around 1330). The wooden bridge's eight-sided stone tower, the Wasserturm, was used as a prison up till the 19th century.

A little further along on the left bank, the **Jesuitenkirche** is one of the earliest and most beautiful Baroque buildings in Switzerland.

Continuing along the Bahnhofstrasse, the simpler **Franziskanerkirche** is a charming contrast to Baroque and Renaissance pomp. Built originally in high-Gothic style (around 1300), the church boasts a richly carved wooden pulpit and choir stalls.

Make your way back to the waterfront, to cross the river at the **Spreuerbrücke** (Mill Bridge). This early 15th-century wooden bridge is colourfully ornamented with "Dance of Death" murals, painted between 1625 and 1632.

The Mühlenplatz leads into the **Weinmarkt.** This was Lucerne's thriving hub in the Middle Ages, crowded with guildhouses, shops and prosperous homes. Its elaborately painted façades still make this spot the most striking part of the old town.

The next square, the **Kornmarkt,** was the town's medieval corn distribution centre. The **Rathaus** (Town Hall), an impressive 17th-century stone building, is still a vital centre of life in Lucerne.

The Kornmarkt leads onto the old hog market, the flag-bedecked **Hirschenplatz.** The splendid antique sign of the Gasthof zum Hirschen (Stag Inn) indicates a hostelry that was a favourite even in the 15th century.

Turn your back on the river now, and make your way up one of the pretty streets leading to the **Museggmauer.** This wall with its nine towers was built around 600 years ago to protect the city. One of Lucerne's most distinctive features, it remains one of the best-preserved and longest (nearly 3,000 ft; 914 m.) wall fortifications in Europe. In season, you can visit the Schirmerturm, the Zytturm (Clock Tower) and walk along the parapet to one of the end towers.

A short walk from the wall by way of Museumplatz and Löwenplatz brings you to the heroic **Löwendenkmal,** the Lion of Lucerne. It was designed by a Danish sculptor, Thorvaldsen.

Just near the Lion Monument is the **Gletschergarten,** an attractive park pockmarked with glacial potholes left by last remnants of the retreating Ice Age 15–20,000 years ago.

Towards the lake along Löwenstrasse stands the elegant **Hofkirche.** The cathedral's two slim towers date back to the 14th century. Note the Tuscan **arcades** surrounding the church before you go in. The remarkably richly carved choir stalls and the beautiful chancel screen inside were made in the mid-17th century.

Make your way back to the station via the busy **Schwanenplatz,** but before crossing the Seebrücke, notice the romantic towered house on the corner of the bridge. The Haus zur Gilgen was named after the knight who built it in the 15th century.

Next door the charming **Kapellplatz** is graced by the little Peterskapelle built no less than 800 years ago.

Further along the street at 21 Furrengasse, the **Am Rhyn Haus** is a beautiful example of a patrician house with its two sections connected by a multi-storeyed arcade.

The Lake...

The most delightful way to see central Switzerland in summer is from one of the lake's "old world" steamboats.

The gentle banks of the central plateau with the 6,980-foot (2,129-m.) Pilatus in the background gradually give way to the lower Alps with their rustic, green pastures, while the great Alps loom majestically over the water at the southern end of the lake.

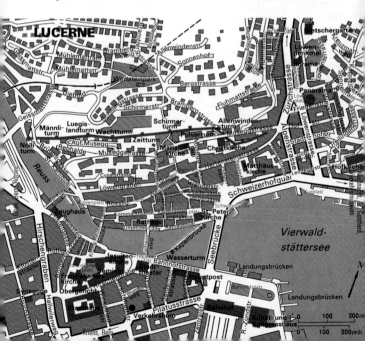

After Meggen on the left, you'll see **Küssnacht bay,** a bright, flowered scene lined with orchards and peak-roofed farmhouses.

The stretch from Hertenstein to Brunnen is so mild that tropical plants flourish on a coastline dotted with resort towns, lush gardens and villas.

High above the lake on the other side perches **Bürgenstock,** once one of the most fashionable resorts in Europe.

Before the ship docks at Brunnen, don't miss **Gersau.** This speck on the atlas was an independent republic, fiercely defending its sovereign rights for 400 years, before it joined the canton of Schwyz in 1817.

Behind the port of Brunnen is the town of **Schwyz** itself, the capital of the canton from which Switzerland derived its name and flag.

Further on, a little green field with a solitary wooden house is the **Rütli.** This famous meadow is the symbol of Swiss unity.

Lake Uri is the most dramatic section of the great lake, with its sheer cliffs plummeting into deep waters.

On the left bank is **Tell's Chapel,** honouring the rock where William Tell leapt ashore to escape from a Habsburg overlord.

Behind the port of **Flüelen** is the capital of the canton of Uri, **Altdorf,** with a huge statue of Tell.

... and the Mountains

Pilatus. This is Lucerne's most striking landmark. Nearly 7,000 feet (2,130 m.) high, it was first climbed in 1555 by a Zurich naturalist.

Rigi. Take a day for this trip, offering great views from nearly 6,000 feet (1,798 m.) with Alpine peaks visible as far as the Jungfrau.

Titlis. This is the highest mountain in central Switzerland (10,625 ft; 3,239 m.). A 22-mile (35-km.) rail or car trip through scenic country brings you to Engelberg, a well-known winter ski resort. The cable-car ride to the summit of Titlis—a perpetual deep-freeze—takes 45 minutes. You can see the awesome glacier from the cable car, wander through an ice grotto and have lunch with a view of the Valaisan Alps and the Bernese Oberland.

Passes

A day trip by car or post bus over the **Susten** and **Brünig passes** offers spectacular summer sightseeing. After a drive along the great lake, you ascend through the High Alps, passing within touching distance of the Stein glacier; then you wend your way back through the broad farming valley of Sarnen with its beautiful old brown wooden houses.

Further south still, the **Furka** and **Grimsel passes** (about 8,000 ft; 2,430 m. and 7,000 ft; 2,165 m. respectively) offer beautiful—though at times, vertiginous and bone-chilling—views.

The famous **St. Gotthard pass** rises to nearly 7,000 feet (2,108 m.) before descending steeply as it winds its way down into the canton of Ticino (Tessin).

Einsiedeln

About an hour's drive from Lucerne is the most magnificent Baroque building in Switzerland. The imposing **Benedictine abbey** is almost incongruous in its gentle, hilly countryside; the small town of Einsiedeln seems overwhelmed by its grandeur.

The present church was built in the 18th century with an extravagant gold and white interior, ornamented by countless figures and paintings. In the midst of this cluttered Baroque wealth stands a tiny **Black Madonna,** the goal of many pilgrimages.

Eating Out

Switzerland is a land of infinite variety of food usually served in vast quantities.

Soups make filling starters and vary from region to region. Lucerne has a favourite called *Brotsuppe* (bread soup)

or try Basle's *Mehlsuppe* (flour soup).

For a meat snack or starter, sample some *Bündnerfleisch* from the Grisons; delicious paper-thin slices of air-dried beef.

Switzerland produces about 45 different types of sausage; specialities include *Schüblig* and *Bratwurst* (pork and veal sausage, respectively). Don't forget to include a portion of *Rösti* (grated fried potatoes) or *Spätzli* (noodle-like dumplings).

For dessert try some *Kirschtorte* (Kirsch brandy cake) from Zug or *Rüeblitorte* made of carrots, eggs, almonds, cinnamon and brandy.

Swiss beer is sold by the bottle or on tap, it's all good. Swiss wine is more expensive but try some of the red Dôle or Pinot Noir, or the white Fendant or Johannisberg.

Shopping

Shopping is expensive, but if you're in the market for some **antiques** such as an Empire clock or piece of Nyon porcelain, then Switzerland could be the place for you. **Paintings** are also available; dealers are used to shipping works of art all over the world.

Look for **embroidery** from St. Gall, extremely well-made **hiking boots** and **Swiss Army knives.** Cuckoo clocks come mostly from Germany, but **watches,** from fashionable Swatches to more expensive traditional timepieces, are all Swiss. **Jewellery** is of a very good quality; try the smaller merchants hidden away in old town neighbourhoods.

Chocolate comes in all shapes and sizes and is delicious.

Practical Information

Banks: Open from 8.30 a.m. to 12.30 p.m., and from 1.30 to 4.30 or 5.30 p.m., Monday to Friday.

Currency: The Swiss *franc* (in German *Franken*), abbreviated *Fr.,* is divided into 100 *centimes* (in German *Rappen*). Coins: 5, 10, 20, 50 centimes, Fr. 1, 2, 5. Banknotes: Fr. 10, 20, 50, 100, 500, 1,000.

LUXEMBOURG

Introduction

The Grand Duchy of Luxembourg lies in the heart of Western Europe, a pocket-sized country of forests and ruins which seems to escape the forces shaping the modern world.

Luxembourg, in fact, owes nothing to fairy stories. Its encounters with the armies tramping their way from east to west and back again are real enough—and more numerous than those of any other European nation. For, in the past, Luxembourg City and its surrounding countryside came to be almost the fulcrum of Europe—a stronghold coveted by great powers anxious to subdue and dominate nations all around.

This historical experience has given Luxembourgers a rare political foresight and pragmatism: Luxembourg's treasured neutrality was unique in the 19th century; and it took the initiative leading to the Benelux union.

Luxembourg, tucked away between France and Germany to the south of Belgium, owes its present boundaries to its former pre-eminence. From Roman times onwards, the strategic significance of the rocky plateaux rising steeply from the Alzette River has never been lost on Europe's military leaders. The fact that Luxembourg City also lies at the junction of the great Paris–Trier and Metz–Aix-la-Chapelle roads only increases its desirability.

Primarily, however, the city's impregnable situation, its cliff faces overhanging numerous tortuous river-courses, made Luxembourg a plum to be grasped in turn by the Romans, Huns, Franks, Burgundians, French, Germans, Spanish and Austrians. Today, you cannot wander through the dramatic countryside without stumbling over the ruins of someone's castle.

Present-day Luxembourg, which covers some 999 square miles (1,610 sq. km.) is divided geographically in two by the River Sûre. Oesling to the north is wild and heavily forested. Here, the terrain is scored by rivers which meander through deep gorges hewn over many millennia. Villages are connected by tunnels through the mountains, their houses clinging improbably to sheer rock. Ruined castles perch on high crags which plunge down a thousand feet. To the south, the Gutland or Bon Pays —both names mean the "Good Land"—is gentle, green countryside, giving way to the industrial and mining region, the Bassin Minier. Iron ore has been mined here since Roman times and the modern steel industry dates from the 19th century.

Despite hundreds of years of foreign occupation, Luxembourgers have a keen sense of national identity, expressed in their national language, "Letzebuergisch", a local dia-

lect of German, although French and German are official languages.

The government comprises a legislative chamber of deputies and an executive cabinet, but the constitutional monarch, Grand Duke Jean of Luxembourg, Duke of Nassau and Prince of Bourbon-Parma, also exercises authority. The royal family are held in high esteem.

A Brief History

53 B.C.	Indutiomar, leader of the Celtic Taeviri, is killed in battle. The victorious Romans, led by Julius Caesar, settle down to an urban existence which lasts 500 years.
5th–9th centuries A.D.	Waves of invading Germanic tribes from eastern Europe—Suevi, Vandals, Huns, Visigoths—obliterate the remains of Roman civilization. The Frankish King Clovis accepts Christian baptism in 496, a watershed for European Christendom.
10th–16th centuries	Count Sigefroi of the Ardennes is granted lands in 963 which include the prehistoric fortifications at Lucilinburch (Lützelburg). He chooses the land bridge known as the Bock on which to build his castle. In 1308, the Count of Luxembourg is elected Holy Roman Emperor, and the royal house occupies the imperial throne until 1437. Luxembourg's territorial domination extends to the frontiers of Muscovy. Luxembourg passes to the Duke of Burgundy.
17th–18th centuries	The city and its land suffer appalling damage during the Thirty Years' War and are again ravaged by the armies of Louis XIV in 1684. Luxembourg changes hands four more times, as it passes from French to Spanish rule, back to the French, then to the Austrians—and finally to Napoleon's empire in 1795.

19th century	At the Treaty of Vienna, 1815, Luxembourg is carved up, the throne going to the Dutch King William I, the Prussians holding Luxembourg City. Not until 1867 are the Prussians displaced: the Treaty of London bestows nationhood and neutrality on what remains of the Grand Duchy. Duke Adolf of Nassau succeeds to the throne in 1890.
20th century	After World War I, Luxembourg votes to restrain its constitutional monarchy; Charlotte is elected Grand Duchess. The Grand Duchy joins the League of Nations and enters into an economic pact with Belgium. Establishment of the Benelux union in 1943 and the Coal and Steel Community seven years later pave the way for the formation of the European Economic Community in 1957.

Sightseeing

Luxembourg City perches high on sharp, rocky escarpments which flank the winding river beds and plunge down again into the deep gorges cut by the Pétrusse and Alzette rivers. At every turn, another superb view unfolds.

The plateaux divide the capital naturally into districts which are connected by 110 bridges and five viaducts. Touring the ramparts and fortifications today, the visitor is gripped still by the awesome sense of distant power, although only a tenth of the original works remains.

The **Rocher du Bock** (Bock Fortress) straddles a long promontory which juts out into a loop cut by the Alzette River.

It was here in 963 that Sigefroi chose to build his fortifications, and from then on the Bock became a focal point for development. All that survives of this one-time impregnable fortress is the base of a circular tower and a belfry on one side and traces of a tower on the other. The town itself grew up in the shadow of the Bock, at the point where the Roman roads crossed, now the **Marché aux Poissons** (Fish Market) where many historic buildings still stand.

The **city walls** were reinforced and extended twice by local rulers. A century after Sigefroi, 15 forts were added —including the Porte de Trois Tours (Gate of Three Towers)— and outer ramparts. Construction in the 14th century included three new forts carved out of the rock face. Successive kings conquered and then lost Luxembourg, leaving behind more works.

The Frenchman Vauban was the most notable of military engineers. Under the auspices of Louis XIV he built the monumental **Citadel of St. Esprit** (on the site of the Convent of the Holy Spirit) to overshadow the lands of the south. Just across the Pétrusse River, pre-dating the citadel by nearly 1,000 years, the **Chapel of St. Quirinus** is one of the oldest Christian shrines in Europe.

Most remarkable of all are the **"casemates"**: a 13-mile (21-km.) network of underground passages hewn from solid rock to link 53 forts. Begun by the Spanish in 1674 and augmented by the Austrians the following century, these echoing chambers housed not only men and horses, but also armories and workshops, abattoirs, bakehouses and kitchens. The casemates are open to the public during the summer months.

The **Corniche,** said to be the most beautiful promenade in Europe, follows the 17th-century ramparts around the edge of the Old City. From this vantage point, the Rham plateau, once the site of Gallo-Roman settlements, is visible. The Corniche leads through numerous gates, some dating back to the 10th century, and barracks with walls 120 feet (36 m.) high. In place of the demolished ramparts, municipal parks now offer a tranquil beauty.

In the Fish Market the ancient buildings that comprise the eclectic **State Museums** have been renovated extensively to accommodate archaeological and natural history collections, popular and industrial art, as well as more conventional—and outstanding—permanent exhibits of art from the Low Countries and the Italian Renaissance.

The Rue de Loge, so characteristic of medieval towns, leads unexpectedly to the magnificent **Grand Ducal Palace.** The oldest section dates from the period of Spanish ascendancy in 1572, when it served as a town hall. The palace bears ample evidence of strong Italian Renaissance influence; additions were made in the 18th century. The 17th-century **Church of St. Michel** has 10th-century foundations: it was first built as the chapel for the castle.

Only a few minutes' walk

away is the **Cathedral of Notre Dame,** built by the Jesuits in the early 1600s. It is a splendid example of late Gothic architecture, but with a curious smattering of Renaissance features.

Soaring 920 feet (280 m.) above the Alzette River, almost as if spanning two worlds, the Grand Duchess Charlotte bridge leads from the ancient Pfaffenthal quarter to the Kirchberg plateau and the **European Centre.**

After sightseeing—or shopping on the busy Grand Rue —aim for the lively **Place d'Armes** at the centre of the Old City. The tree-lined square is an ideal place to pause for coffee or a drink. Afficionados of open markets should not miss the **Place Guillaume** on Wednesdays or Saturdays, where a statue of King William II of the Low Countries and Grand Duke of Luxembourg impassively oversees trading.

Excursions

Even in a country as small as Luxembourg, you would be hard pressed to visit every picturesque town. At least it is possible to tour the Grand Duchy in a relatively short space of time and get a feel for its diversity.

The drive to **Vianden** passes through beautiful, wild hills and valleys, punctuated by ruined castles and glistening rivers. Medieval Vianden, which dates back to the 9th century, has many treasures, including its splendid castle—now restored—and fortifications, a 13th-century Gothic church, and a small museum in the house where Victor Hugo lived in exile.

As you approach **Diekirch,** the splendour of the Ardennes gradually gives way to the gentler terrain of the Bon Pays. Although Luxembourg's tourist industry began in Diekirch, this town, nestled in the Sûre valley, is unspoilt and peaceful. The Romans appreciated its virtues—there are well-preserved mosaics from their villas—as did the Celts, who set up their mysterious dolmens, and the early Christians who built the church here in the 5th century.

Luxembourg's wine-producing region follows the winding Moselle River southwards. Many of the co-operative wine cellars are open to the public, and "Viticultural Circuits" provide a grand tour of vineyards and a visit to the wine-tasting hall.

For those more concerned with the state of their livers, **Mondorf-les-Bains** is a traditional place to take the highly mineralized waters. This pleasant spa, with extensive public gardens and good sports facilities, enjoys a temperate climate as well as beautiful scenery.

Eating Out

Luxembourg has a robust tradition of good eating, with a nod in the direction of Belgian and German cuisine. There is no shortage of good, modestly priced restaurants in both Luxembourg City and the country towns and villages.

Crayfish, pike and trout from the rivers of the Grand Duchy form the basis of some appetizing dishes, while another Luxembourg speciality is *treipen* (black pudding) and sausages, served with mashed potatoes and horseradish.

Many restaurants specialize in delicious Ardennes ham.

Rou tou tou is an unusual vegetable dish made from potatoes and onions, while in the Belgian mode, *frites* (chips) are recommended.

Locally produced cheeses, as well as pastries, make for satisfactory meal endings; a particularly individual pastry is *tarte aux quetsches,* made with small plums.

Shopping

Among souvenirs worth taking home are the cast-iron **miniature firebacks,** called *tak,* which depict castles, arms and other subjects in the Grand Duchy. Delicately decorated **porcelain,** as well as **crystal,** will also make good mementoes, while **earthenware pottery** is another Luxembourg speciality. **Records** of authentic Luxembourg songs and music are available. Since they are often difficult to buy outside the country, a bottle or two of Luxembourg **wine** or **liqueur** will make an enjoyable if ephemeral souvenir. You might also pick up an unusual item or two in the flea markets held regularly in several main towns, as well as every second Saturday in the Place d'Armes, Luxembourg City.

Practical Information

Currency: The Luxembourg unit of currency is the *franc,* with the same value as the Belgian *franc.* The latter currency may be used freely in Luxembourg, but Luxembourg francs are not usually accepted outside the country.

Language: The national language is "Letzebuergisch", a local dialect of German; French and German are official languages.

Shops: Open Monday afternoon and from 9 a.m. to 6 p.m., Tuesday to Saturday. Lunchtime closing from 12 noon for 1 or 2 hours. Certain shops have later evening closing.

MADRID

Spain

Introduction

At an altitude of more than 2,100 feet (650 m.), Madrid on the Castilian plateau is Europe's highest capital. The combination of high altitude and mountain breezes generates a unique atmosphere. The city is alive with light, the sunshine filtering down through a pale sky barely dense enough to float a cloud on.

Like Brasilia, Washington or other "artificial" towns, the city of Madrid is a man-made capital conceived in political compromise. King Philip II promoted Madrid from a provincial town to his national command post in the middle of the 16th century at a time when his empire was still expanding. Since then, the city hasn't stopped growing.

Life starts right down on earth. Madrid is a hospitable hotbed of cafés and restaurants, theatres and nightclubs. This is the world capital of bullfighting. The shops are among the finest in Europe.

The city and its people run to extremes. It could well have something to do with the weather, which is usually either too cold or too hot (roughly one third of the population flees the city every August). The exaggerated contrasts extend to geography as well: the big city ends suddenly in open country, with no semi-detached suburbs to soften the edges. *Madrileños* seem to be bubbling one moment and sulking the next.

They go to church but they go to the striptease, too. At a moment's notice, hand-kissing politeness gives way to the law of the jungle, for instance in the metro, where the train doors slam shut ten seconds after they open, and then, the devil take the hindmost. They may fume about the cost of living, but *Madrileños* never falter in their support of a thriving community of street beggars.

Observe *Madrileños* cramming the bustling promenades and outdoor cafés at the hour of the *paseo,* when the offices begin to empty. Businessmen in wasp-waisted suits escort impeccably coiffed women of all ages. And all those children in tow! Spain's birth rate is nearly double West Germany's.

In its many aspects, historical, architectural, religious and human, Madrid will provide you with an experience that will stay with you long after your final friendly *Adiós!*

A Brief History

Early times	Paleolithic, Neolithic and Bronze Age men roam the Manzanares valley near Madrid.
11th–14th centuries	Christian forces of Alfonso VI capture the Muslim Alcázar fort in 1083. The counter-offensive fails and the Moors are expelled from the region. King Ferdinand IV establishes his Cortes (parliament) in Madrid in 1308. Succeeding monarchs frequent the city—noted for its invigorating air and excellent hunting.
15th–16th centuries	Ferdinand and Isabella (known as the Catholic monarchs) arrive in Madrid in 1477. Spain's Golden Age—a century of Spanish economic and political supremacy accompanied by marvels of art and literature—is ushered in. Charles I succeeds to the throne in 1516; he becomes Charles V and Holy Roman Emperor soon afterwards but is unpopular with his Spanish subjects. He abdicates in favour of his son Philip II in 1556. The construction of the Escorial palace begins. Madrid becomes capital of Spain in 1561. Philip II dies in 1598.
17th–18th centuries	Philip III's reign is short-lived (15 years). Decades of political intrigues at home and abroad follow. A weak economy plus the easily influenced child-kings, Philip IV and Charles II—who accede to the throne at the ages of 16 and five years respectively—contribute to the huge increase in corruption. Charles II dies in 1700 leaving the throne to his daughter Maria-Theresa, married to the French King Louis XIV. He gives the throne in turn to his grandson, Philip V. The Alcázar of Madrid is burnt to the ground in 1734 and new plans are laid for the Royal Palace. Charles III succeeds Philip V. He paves and lights Madrid's streets, installs public fountains, lays out promenades and gardens. His successor, Charles IV, abdicates. Napoleon invades Spain at the end of the century.
19th century	Napoleon pronounces his brother Joseph king. Madrid rises against the interloper in 1808, beginning the Peninsula War. The Spanish succeed in overthrowing Joseph, and the son of Charles IV, Ferdinand VII, is reinstated to the throne in 1814. Power struggles at

home and abroad and the rise of a liberal national party weaken the monarchy. Civil unrest increases.

20th century
King Alfonso XIII goes into exile in 1931. General Franco, with a large section of the army, rises against the Government. The Civil War—lasting until 1939—ensues. Madrid remains in Republican hands for most of the war. After Franco's death in 1975 Prince Juan Carlos, grandson of Alfonso XIII, becomes king.

Sightseeing

If you have time, a good way to begin a visit to Madrid is to sign on for a half-day guided tour to get a general idea of the layout of the town. But it's just as interesting going on your own. Start on foot in the centre of the original Madrid at the **Puerta del Sol** (Gate of the Sun), the radial hub of the city for centuries. All the highways in Spain are measured from here, "Kilometre 0".

Facing all the bustle of a remodelled Puerta del Sol, is a statue based on Madrid's coat of arms. It shows a bear standing against a *madroño* tree (an arbutus, or strawberry tree). This same gourmet bear is seen all over Madrid, on the rear doors of every taxi, for instance.

The neo-classical building on the south side of the square is headquarters of the government of the autonomous community of Madrid.

The **Plaza Mayor** (Main Square), a few blocks away, is an architectural symphony in bold but balanced tones. Broad arcades surround a cobbled rectangle 200 yards long and 100 yards wide. It was built in the beginning of the 17th century, based on the graceful style of Juan de Herrera—symmetry, slate roofs, slender towers. Take a seat at one of the outdoor cafés in the square and enjoy the proportions of Madrid's most elegant architectural ensemble.

Further along Calle Mayor, the old Plaza de la Villa (City Hall Square) juxtaposes stately 16th- and 17th-century buildings of varied style. The **Casa y Torre de los Lujanes** (the House and Tower of the Lujanes), 16th-century Gothic, has an imposing stone portal. The **Casa de Cisneros,** built in the mid-16th century by a nephew of the intrepid inquisitor and warrior, Cardinal Cisneros, belongs to the

a neo-classic design, somewhat curtails the effect of the church's most superlative feature. Once inside, you'll realize that the dome is out of the ordinary. Indeed, its inner diameter of more than 100 feet (30 m.) exceeds the size of the cupolas of St. Paul's (London) and Les Invalides (Paris).

Central Madrid
Except for the intensity of the traffic, the ample **Plaza de la Cibeles** is splendid. The fountain in the centre shows Cybele, a controversial Greek fertility goddess, serenely settled in a chariot pulled by two lions.

The most unavoidable building on the plaza is the cathedral-like Palacio de Comunicaciones (the post office), sarcastically nicknamed *Nuestra Señora de las Comunicaciones* (Our Lady of Communications).

Also facing Plaza de la Cibeles, the headquarters of the Bank of Spain combines neo-classic, Baroque and Rococo styles. It looks about as solid as any bank can be. The financial district, Madrid's City or Wall Street, begins here on **Calle de Alcalá.** Pompous buildings in this very high-rent district contain the head offices or branches of more than

ornate and delicate style of architecture known as Plateresque. Finally, the **Ayuntamiento** (City Hall) represents the Habsburg era, with the towers and slate spires characteristic of the 17th-century official buildings all around Madrid.

In the Calle de Toledo rises the massive dome of the **Catedral de San Isidro.** Cool off inside and visit the relics of the city's patron saint San Isidro Labrador.

Another formidable Madrid church is the 18th-century **Basilica de San Francisco el Grande** (Basilica of St. Francis of Assisi). The curved façade, an original version of

100 banks plus insurance companies, the Finance Ministry and, a few streets away, the **Bolsa de Comercio** (Stock Exchange).

But Calle de Alcalá is not entirely dedicated to Mammon. Next door to the Ministry of Finance is the clumsily named **Museo de la Real Academia de Bellas Artes de San Fernando**—call it the Museum of the Royal Academy. The academy owns a celebrated batch of Goya's paintings,

including the *Burial of the Sardine,* full of action and humour, and a superb self-portrait of the artist in his vigorous old age.

Now let's return to the **Gran Vía,** main east-west thoroughfare and lifeline of modern Madrid. The bustling Gran Vía (Main Avenue) is a mixture of hotels, shops, theatres, nightclubs and cafés—the street for strolling and window-gazing.

You can get your bearings

on the Gran Vía by looking *up*. The highest tower in sight belongs to Madrid's first *rascacielos* (skyscraper), the headquarters of the telephone company, La Telefónica.

At **Plaza del Callao** the pedestrian traffic reaches its peak. This is the centre for department stores, cinemas, cafés and bus stops: yet only a couple of streets south of Callao's turbulence, the **Convent of Descalzas Reales** clings onto a 16th-century tranquillity. Upstairs are heavy timbered ceilings and walls covered with works of art, mostly of religious or royal significance.

From Plaza del Callao, the Gran Vía continues downhill towards the **Plaza de España** through more shopping, strolling and nightlife territory. Two controversial skyscrapers, of 26 and 34 storeys, have changed the atmosphere of the plaza, a sanctuary of grass, flowers, trees and fountains. A favourite sight, especially with visiting photographers, is the Cervantes Monument. A stone sculpture honouring the author looms behind bronze statues of his immortal creations, Don Quixote and Sancho Panza, astride their horse and donkey, respectively.

Calle de la Princesa, which begins at Plaza de España, is actually an extension of the Gran Vía aimed north-west. The house at Calle de la Princesa, 22, is literally palatial; it calls to mind a scaled-down Buckingham Palace. Tucked away in a comfortable park behind high railings, the **Palacio de Líria** is the residence of the Duchess of Alba.

The Prado

The Prado (south of the Plaza de la Cibeles) is undoubtedly one of the world's finest museums. A serious student of art might well plan an entire itinerary around repeated visits to the galleries. But even with only an hour or two you'll be able to appreciate paintings which will almost certainly whet your appetite for a return visit. Look out for Velázquez' *Las Meninas,* Goya's *Naked Maja,* Dürer's *Adam and Eve,* El Greco's *Adoration of the Shepherds* and Rembrandt's *Artemis*—just a tiny selection of the thousands of magnificent works of art on display in the Prado. For your next visit, don't miss the others: Breughel, Bosch, Gainsborough, Murillo, Rubens, Titian, Watteau and many, many more. Picasso's *Guernica* is in the Prado Annex.

Other Museums and Sights

The **Royal Palace** is set among the formal gardens on the bluff overlooking the Manzanares valley. The basic one-hour tour takes in a fraction of the 2,000 rooms, including the **Gasparini Room**—named after its designer. The floor, walls and ceiling swirl with special Rococo effects. The **Ceremonial Dining Room** seats 145 guests. Chandeliers, candelabra and tapestries compete for attention. In the Throne Room, a magnificent Tiepolo ceiling depicts "the greatness of the Spanish monarchy". The austere **Official Office** is occasionally used by the present monarch, Juan Carlos I.

For an extra charge you can see additional sights within the palace including the Crown Jewels, the Museum of Paintings, the Hall of Halberdiers, the Royal Library, Pharmacy and Armoury.

The **Museo de Arte Contemporáneo** (Museum of Contemporary Art), Avenida de Juan de Herrera, Ciudad Universitaria, is warm and attractive inside a somewhat forbidding skyscraper. Beautifully arranged and documented displays show early 20th-century realism to post-pop art.

The **Convento de la Encarnación** (Convent of the Incarnation), Plaza de la Encarnación, was founded in 1611 by Margaret of Austria. This convent-church-museum has accumulated an interesting art collection, with hundreds of religious relics.

The **Museo Arqueológico,** Calle de Serrano, 13, emphasizes the art of the ancient inhabitants of Spain, and includes charming statuettes and jewellery belonging to the 2nd-century B.C. Carthaginian settlers of the island of Ibiza. Miraculously preserved mosaics from 2nd-century A.D. Roman Spain can also be seen here.

The **Museo Nacional de Artes Decorativas,** Calle de Montalbán, 12, is full of the things antique collectors dream of finding at the flea market *(Rastro)*—but here they are real and include the best of old Spanish glassware, woodwork, tapestry, porcelain and jewellery.

Museo Lázaro Galdiano, Calle de Serrano, 122. An astonishingly wide-ranging and priceless private collection bequeathed to the nation.

El Congreso de los Diputados, the Spanish Parliament, occupies a mid-19th-century building very near the Prado Museum. Before the Corinthian columns stand two ornamental lions, cast from the metal of guns captured from some of Spain's 19th-century enemies.

The **Museo de Carruajes** (Carriage Museum), Campo del Moro, is a recent installation, on the far side of the Royal Palace, which houses royal transport of all kinds up to the eve of the age of automobiles. See a 16th-century litter thought to have borne the Emperor Charles V when he was suffering from gout. Much more recent history was made by the gala coach of Alfonso XIII, still showing signs of damage from a 1906 assassination plot. Here are coaches with the evocative Spanish names *berlina, lando, vis-a-vis, faeton* and *milord*. A stage-coach, ancient sedan chairs, sleds and saddles round off the well-organized curiosities.

Excursions

Madrid's central position within Spain makes it an ideal point for day trips to some of Spain's most celebrated and fascinating towns, only an hour or so outside the capital.

Toledo, 43 miles (70 km.) south-west of Madrid. All of Spain—tradition, grandeur and art—is crammed into

this small city set on a Castilian hilltop. If you see only one Spanish city outside Madrid, make it Toledo; and if you visit only one church in Spain make it the **cathedral,** with its quite superb choir, its 750 stained-glass windows, its *transparente* (cupola opened up to seem transparent), its chapter house, treasury room and sacristy. The maze of little streets emerges right out of the Middle Ages, but don't get too lost to visit the historic **Alcázar,** the Plaza de Zocodover, the parish church of Santo Tomé among many others. Nor El Greco's house in his adopted home town.

Segovia, 55 miles (88 km.) north-west of Madrid, boasts a superb **Roman aqueduct,** a work of art and triumph of engineering right in the town centre, plus the **Alcázar,** an incomparable fairy-tale royal castle, and a lovely cathedral. Main feature of **Avila,** 70 miles (112 km.) north-west of Madrid, is its ring of **walls** and an impressive cathedral.

The **Escorial,** 30 miles (49 km.) west of Madrid, is more than a palace; it's an entire royal city—living quarters, church, monastery, mausoleum and museum—all under one roof! Vast and sombre as it may be, Philip II's building

MADRID

leaves no visitor indifferent. It's not only the statistics—by official count the building contains 86 stairways, more than 1,200 doors and 2,600 windows—it's the mood of deep spirituality and the airy setting on a hill at an altitude of 3,460 feet (1,040 m.), in a friendly small township enjoying more than its fair share of hotels, restaurants and bars.

Aranjuez, 31 miles (50 km.) south of Madrid, means a moving guitar concerto to a good many people. It's also a delightful roomy town housing Spain's answer to Versailles, the **Palacio Real.** A visit through the Throne Room, the Porcelain Room, the Chinese Painting Salon among a host of others (some turned into complete museums) provides a revealing cross-section of royal taste in paintings, clocks, pianos, tapestries, sculpture and trinkets.

Eating Out

Plenty of hearty food made with fresh ingredients at reasonable prices: such is the good news awaiting hungry tourists or international gourmets in Madrid.

Cafeterías in Spain are not self-service restaurants, but modern establishments serving fast meals, mostly at a counter.

Tascas are bars serving *tapas,* bite-sized snacks with a variety of fillings and side-dishes ranging from snails and tripe to potato salad and meatballs.

Cafés serve coffee, drinks and snacks, and are almost always open.

Castilian Specialities

Cocido Madrileño may be distinctive to Madrid, but nevertheless resembles the hotpot or stew found in other regions of Spain. The meal often starts with *sopa de cocido* (the broth resulting from boiling the ingredients for the next course), then the *cocido* itself: beef, ham, sausage, chickpeas, cabbage, turnip, onion, garlic, potatoes.

Sopa Castellana is a baked garlic soup, not as strong as it sounds. At the last moment, a raw egg is added; by the time it reaches the table, the egg is well poached.

Callos a la madrileña. By any other name, stewed tripe. But the spicy dark sauce makes all the difference. This is a great local favourite.

Besugo al horno is seabream poached in a wine sauce. *Cochinillo asado* is tender Castilian sucking pig roasted to a golden crispness, while *cordero asado* is roast lamb, often served in a gargantuan helping.

Churros are batter fritters sizzled to a turn in boiling oil. They're favourites for breakfast.

Drinks

The most famous of Spanish wines is sherry from Jerez de la Frontera, which is fortified with the addition of brandy. As an aperitif, try a *fino*. An *oloroso* goes well after dinner.

Sangría, a summertime refresher, is a winecup or a punch made with red wine, fruit juice, brandy and slices of fruit, diluted with soda and plenty of ice.

Spanish beer *(cerveza)* is good and cheap; usually served quite cold.

Finally, look for *horchata de chufa,* a chilled, sweet milky-white drink made from ground-nuts which taste similar to almonds. It's always drunk through a straw.

Shopping

Madrid is Spain's superlative shopping centre, so leave some space in your luggage for gifts and souvenirs.

For a look at the range of handicrafts, covering paperweights to full suits of armour, visit a shop of Artespaña, the official chain of showplaces for Spanish artisans.

For elegance, shop along Calle de Serrano and neighbouring streets; for variety, try the small shops in the Gran Via.

Some best buys are:

Antiques. Madrid's Rastro (flea market) attracts swarms of collectors. In nearby streets are more solid establishments dealing in old *objets d'art*.

Capes. The old-fashioned Madrid *caballeros* sport a slightly sinister black version; women look glamorous in theirs.

Ceramics. Pots, bowls, tiles. Each Spanish region produces its own distinctive shapes, colours and designs, traditional or cheerfully modern.

Damascene. Inlaid gold designs in steel—knives, scissors, thimbles, jewellery. Watch them being made in Toledo.

Embroidery. Good handkerchiefs, napkins, tablecloths, sheets, all embellished with deft needlework.

Fans. The collapsible kind, as fluttered by *señoritas* over the centuries.

Glassware. Blue, green or

amber bowls, glasses, pots and pitchers from Majorca.

Needlework. The traditional lace mantillas for special occasions; or hand-sewn lingerie.

Reproductions. Cheap but handsome copies of great Spanish paintings, on canvas, sold at the Prado and in shops.

Rugs. Inventively designed floor coverings, from tiny throw-rug to full-scale carpet. Some are hand-woven.

Valencian porcelain. Distinctive figurines of traditional or fashionable modern subjects.

Woodcarving. Statues of knights or saints.

Practical Information

Banks: Banking hours in summer are from 8.30 a.m. to 2 p.m. Closed Saturdays. Winter hours are longer. Money can be changed outside normal banking hours at hotels, travel agencies and other businesses displaying a *cambio* sign. Always take your passport with you when changing money.

Currency: The monetary unit of Spain is the *peseta* (abbreviated *pta*.). Coins: 1, 2, 5, 10, 25, 50, 100, 200 and 500 pesetas. Banknotes: 500, 1,000, 2,000, 5,000 and 10,000 pesetas.

Meal times: Lunch rarely begins before 2 p.m. and can go on to 4 or 4.30 p.m. Dinner might be attempted at 9 p.m., but 10 or 10.30 p.m. is the usual hour to start.

Post office hours: Most post offices are open from 9 a.m. to 2 p.m. Madrid's main post office on Plaza de la Cibeles stays open from 9 a.m. to 1.30 p.m. and from 5 to 7 p.m., Monday to Friday; Saturday from 9 a.m. to 2 p.m.

Shops: Department stores open from 10 a.m. to 8 p.m. without a break Mondays to Thursdays, and until 9 p.m. on Fridays and Saturdays. Other shops open from 9.30 a.m. to 1.30 p.m. and 4 or 5 to 8 p.m. Mondays to Fridays, 9.30 a.m. to 2 p.m. on Saturdays.

Tipping: Since a service charge is normally included in restaurant and hotel bills, tipping is optional. However, it is appropriate to give something to porters, lavatory attendants, taxi drivers, tourist guides and so on.

MILAN

Italy

Introduction

Such is the vitality of Milan, that many Milanese feel it should have been the capital of Italy, rather than Rome. But even if the political seat of power lies elsewhere, Milan is certainly the financial, industrial and commercial capital of the country, and one of the most important business centres in Europe.

You'll see its modern face in the centre's skyscraper office blocks and in the sprawling industrial suburbs. And tucked away in its heart you'll find the historic monuments, the cathedral, the massive castle, the churches, palaces and museums that record the great past on which the present is built.

Milan is a city of formidable resilience. Already an important mercantile centre in Roman times, it was destroyed by Huns and Goths, razed to the ground by the Emperor Frederick Barbarossa, fought over by rival powerful families, twice devastated by plague; subjected to foreign rule for nearly five centuries and heavily bombed in World War II. After each setback it sprang to life again with renewed vigour, each time increasing in size and power. Today it is the richest city in Italy and one of the richest in Europe.

Milan owes its pre-eminence not only to the industry and energy of its 1,700,000 inhabitants, but also to its strategic situation at the hub of communications. Railways and motorways radiate north through the Alpine tunnels and passes to France, Switzerland and Germany; south down the spine of Italy; east and west to the Adriatic and Western Mediterranean. Ship canals link the city with the River Po.

But the heart of Milan still lies within its ancient core, between the magnificent cathedral and the grim castle, former stronghold of Visconti and Sforza power. Here you'll find the main banks, stock exchange and smart shopping streets, as well as ancient churches, palaces and the world-famous La Scala opera house.

Not least of Milan's attractions lies in its proximity to five glorious lakes, which nestle in the folds of the Alps, only an hour's drive away— five escapist holiday areas, away from industrial smoke and smog, for bathing, sailing and relaxing against a background of orange trees and snow peaks.

A Brief History

6th century B.C.–3rd century A.D.	Milan is founded by the Gauls around 600 B.C. and becomes the capital of a Celtic tribe, the Insubres. In 222 B.C. the Romans capture the city, then known as Mediolanum. It develops into the second most important city of the Western Roman Empire.
4th–5th centuries	From 305 to 402, the Roman emperors reside in Milan. In 313 Emperor Constantine publishes in Milan his Edict ensuring freedom of worship for Christians. St. Ambrose presides as powerful and eloquent bishop of Milan from 374 to 397.
5th–7th centuries	Attila the Hun devastates Milan in 452. The Goths destroy the city in 539 but it slowly comes to life again and becomes one of the chief cities of the Longobards and then the Franks.
8th–11th centuries	The Milan region is incorporated into the dominions of Charlemagne in 774. The city walls are rebuilt. In the 10th century the archbishops of Milan rule as feudal princes, defying pope and emperor. In 1045 Milan constitutes itself a "commune" with autonomous government and engages in battles for supremacy with Pavia, Cremona, Como and Lodi.
12th century	The Milanese wipe out Lodi and Como. Friederich I Barbarossa brings Milan under the direct authority of the Holy Roman Empire in 1162, after a nine-month siege. Its fortifications are razed and the Milanese forced to seek refuge in the countryside. But the city is promptly rebuilt and the Milanese help defeat Barbarossa's forces and regain their privileges at the Peace of Constance.
13th–15th centuries	An age of economic florescence, with the development of guilds of woollen and armament workers. The Visconti family rises to power and takes the title of Duke of Milan in 1395. After the death of the last Visconti, the castle is razed by the people in 1447 and a republican government set up. But Francesco Sforza, a soldier of fortune married to a Visconti, besieges and takes the city, founding a new dynasty. A period of great prosperity begins, with the introduction of the silk industry and the golden age

of the Renaissance. In 1499 French King Louis XII, descendant of the Viscontis, takes power.

16th–18th centuries

By a peace treaty in 1529, Milan is returned to the Sforzas. In 1535 the entire state of Milan falls under the Austrian Habsburg emperor Charles V, who hands it to his son Philip II of Spain. In 1576 Milan is struck by the plague.

Economic and political stagnation accompanies Spanish rule. Plague ravages the city again in 1630.

The city passes from Spanish to Austrian rule. Neo-classical architecture flourishes. In 1796 Napoleon liberates the city from the Austrians and a Cisalpine Republic is declared.

19th century

In 1805 Milan becomes the capital of the Kingdom of Italy under Napoleon, who crowns himself in the cathedral. But the Austrians return following the defeat of Napoleon in 1815. In 1848, the city rises against the Austrians in the "Cinque Giornate" (five-day) rebellion, remaining free for several months until the Austrians put down the revolt. The "Cinque Giornate" sets off the war of independence, culminating in the liberation of the city after the Battle of Magenta in 1859, when King Vittorio Emanuele II and the French emperor Napoleon III enter the city in triumph.

20th century

In 1919, Mussolini founds the Fascist Party in Milan. At the end of World War II his body is displayed in the Piazza Loreto in April 1945, after he is shot by partisans while fleeing towards Switzerland. With the rapid postwar development of industry, the Communists make Milan one of their political strongholds.

Sightseeing

Start in the very centre of Milan, in the vast Piazza in front of the **Cathedral** *(Duomo)*, one of the biggest churches in Europe and a marvel of Gothic fantasy, expressed in marble turrets, flying buttresses and lacy pinnacles topped with statues. The tallest spire carries a gilded statue of the Madonna. For those who like figures, there are 135 pinnacles and 2,400 statues outside, and another 2,000 statues inside.

The cathedral was begun in

1386 in fulfilment of a vow by a Visconti who hankered for a son. The son was born when the walls were only a few feet high. But the cathedral took nearly five centuries to complete.

The vast interior can easily hold 20,000 people. Fifty-eight immense pillars flank the nave, dimly lit by the light filtering through magnificent stained-glass windows. It was before the altar here that Napoleon crowned himself King of Italy with the iron crown of the Lombards, proclaiming the ancient formula of the Carolingian kings: "God gave it to me, woe to him who

touches it." The iron crown, believed to contain a nail from Christ's crucifixion, is still kept in the cathedral.

In the right transept is a statue of St. Bartholomew (who was flayed alive) carrying his skin over his shoulder.

In the crypt you'll find the tomb of St.Charles Borromeo, archbishop of Milan, who devoted himself to the sick during the plague of 1576.

Take the lift up to the roof for a view of the distant Alps to the north and the Appennines to the south.

In front of the cathedral stands a bronze **statue** of King Vittorio Emanuele on horseback. On the south side of the square lies the former **Royal Palace** (Palazzo Reale) now used for exhibitions.

The high arched entrance of the **Galleria Vittorio Emanuele** opens off the colonnaded north side of the square. You'll enjoy this great shopping arcade, a sheltered place for window-gazing, meeting friends or for sipping an aperitif and watching all Milan stroll by.

The arcade leads right into the Piazza della Scala in front of the world-famous opera house. Burnt out during the war, **La Scala** has been restored in its original 18th-century style, with seats for 3,000 people. It is celebrated for performances of operas by Italian composers Verdi, Rossini, Donizetti and Puccini; among its stars have been conductors such as Toscanini and sopranos such as Maria Callas.

The nearby **Piazza Mercanti** was the merchants' centre of medieval Milan and it is still bordered by ancient buildings—the Romanesque **Palazzo della Ragione,** the **Palazzo Giureconsulti** and the marble Gothic **Loggia degli Osii.**

Behind the Piazza della Scala you will find the **Poldi-Pezzoli Museum,** a sumptuous private palace, enriched by paintings by Botticelli, Cranach and Piero della Francesca, among others, as well as Gobelin tapestries and silver, left to the city by a wealthy 19th-century collector, who died locked by mistake in his own strong-room.

Further north, the **Brera Palace** houses one of Italy's most important collections of paintings, including masterpieces by Mantegna, Crivelli and Titian. A statue of Napoleon by Canova stands in the courtyard.

Cross the busy Piazza Cordusio and take the Via Dante to the **Castello Sforzesco,** a huge square fortress built by the Viscontis, destroyed and rebuilt by the Sforzas and strengthened by the Spanish. Inside its massive walls is the **Museum of Antique Art,** with a notable collection of sculpture, including the Rondanini *Pietà* by Michelangelo. Behind the castle a large park has been laid out in the former gardens of the Dukes of Milan.

Most people make a pilgrimage to the church of **Santa Maria delle Grazie,** south of the castle, specially to see the *Last Supper,* painted by Leonardo da Vinci in 1497 on the wall of the former refectory of a Dominican monastery. At one time badly affected by damp, it has been skilfully restored in recent years.

The church of **Sant'Ambrogio** was founded by St. Ambrose himself in 386 on the site of a temple to Bacchus. St. Augustine was baptized here. Most of the present building

dates from the 12th century, but the porphyry pillars that support the altar canopy come from a Roman temple.

Another building that recalls St. Ambrose is the **Biblioteca Ambrosiana,** a library and art gallery with 600,000 books and precious manuscripts, including the scientific drawings and notes of Leonardo da Vinci, who served the Sforzas and the French in Milan.

You can see working models of some of Leonardo's inventions in the **Museum of Science and Technology,** next to the Church of San Vittore.

Milan's oldest hospital, the **Ospedale Maggiore,** lies

The Saint who Punished an Emperor

The Milanese are known as Ambrosiani, after their patron saint, St. Ambrose (Sant'Ambrogio). The son of a Roman Christian civil servant in Gaul, he became governor of the region round Milan and visited the city in A.D. 374 to see that order was maintained during the election of a new bishop. The Milanese were split by the Arian heresy, which held that Jesus was not equal to God the Father.

Ambrose was trying to calm the crowds when a child suddenly cried out: "Ambrose is the bishop" and the crowd took up the cry, though Ambrose was not even baptized. Within eight days he had become a Christian and was made bishop.

Such was his power and prestige that he excommunicated Emperor Theodosius until he did public penance for having ordered the massacre of 7,000 people in Thessalonica in revenge for a riot. On another occasion St. Ambrose staged a sit-in in his church to prevent its use by Arians. You'll see his symbols in some of Milan's churches—a swarm of honey bees to denote his eloquence and a scourge to portray his suppression of the Arian heresy.

south-east of the Duomo, a long Renaissance building begun in the 15th century, which now houses part of the University of Milan.

The Lakes

To the north and east of Milan, five enchanting lakes stretch like fingers into the Alps: Maggiore, Lugano, Como, Iseo and Garda. They provide glamorous playgrounds for the city-dwellers, all within easy reach for a day's outing.

The westernmost, **Lake Maggiore,** was already a favourite resort for the Romans, who knew it as Lacus Verbanus. It curves almost 40 miles (63 km.) into the mountains, its northernmost end well inside Switzerland. The shores are dotted with picturesque fishing villages; terraced gardens, where camellias and azaleas proliferate, drop down to the blue waters where fishermen angle for trout, pike and perch.

A scenic road runs along the lake shore. Just past the old town of **Arona,** you'll pass an immense copper **statue** of St. Charles Borromeo, Bishop of Milan for 22 years, who was born here in 1538 and whose family owned estates all around the lake. The statue is so big you can climb a spiral staircase into the saint's head.

Stresa is perhaps the most favoured of all the lake resorts. A beautiful town amid orange trees and vineyards, with a fine lakeside promenade, it was a pre-war meeting place of statesmen—perhaps too distractingly beautiful for success: a conference of Britain, France and Italy here in 1935 failed to make a stand against Hitler's rearming of Germany.

Take a boat across to the fabulous **Borromean Islands,** where exotic gardens have been created over the centuries on boatloads of soil ferried over from the mainland. On **Isola Bella,** the Palazzo Borromeo, richly furnished with paintings, tapestries and armour, stands amid terraced gardens of sweet-scented plants, grottoes and statues. Another palace on **Isola Madre** is set among palms and ancient cypresses. On the third island, **Isola dei Pescatori,** is a picturesque fishermen's hamlet.

North of Stresa the road winds through **Baveno** (Queen Victoria stayed here) to **Pallanza,** on a promontory that juts into the lake. The botanical gardens at **Villa Taranto** are the work of a 19th-century Scotsman, who brought plants here from all over the world.

You can ride a cable car up the **Sasso del Ferro** for a magnificent view of the Alps. On the mountain's flank is the hermitage of a 14th-century reformed bandit, precariously overhung by a huge boulder. Pilgrims climb the path to see the rock, which tradition says was stayed by the Madonna just as it was about to fall and crush the hermit; it has remained in suspense ever since.

A car ferry from nearby **Intra** will take you across to **Laveno-Monbello** on the eastern shore. Or you can continue the drive northwards through olive groves along the lake. The mountains close in dramatically as the road reaches **Cannero Riviera.** Those islands just offshore were once a stronghold of brigands; you can still see the jagged ruins of their castles. Beyond **Canobbio** lies the Swiss frontier and the Swiss resorts of Ascona and Locarno.

The road returns down the eastern shore to **Angera,** overhung by a 14th-century Gothic castle at **Rocca,** that was fought over by Viscontis and Borromeos.

Just west of Lake Maggiore

is the small peaceful mountain-girt **Lake Orta,** not one of the main lakes, but a pleasurable place for walking and fishing. The Romanesque basilica of San Giulio lies on an island in the middle. San Giulio is said to have sailed across the lake with his cloak for a sail to rid the island of snakes and dragons before building a sanctuary there.

Lake Lugano (also known as Lago di Ceresio) lies mainly in Switzerland, but the northern and south-western ends are inside Italy, as well as the little enclave of **Campione,** which has a popular casino.

The Romans knew **Lake Como** as Lake Larianus and built luxury villas on its shores. It is the deepest lake in Europe—about a quarter of a mile (nearly half a kilometre) at its deepest. Spurs of the surrounding mountains plunge sheer into the cobalt waters. The green and silver of olive trees alternate with mulberry trees, chestnuts, figs and oleander. Grim castles tower above tiny flowered villages and harbours.

The town of **Como** was already an important outpost of the Gauls when the Romans captured it in 196 B.C. Both the Plinys were born here: Pliny the Elder, who died at Pompei in the eruption of Mount Vesuvius, and his historian nephew, Pliny the Younger. You'll find statues of both, incongruously placed among the saints on the white marble façade of the **cathedral.**

In 1127, the Milanese destroyed Como for having sided with their enemy, the Emperor Friederich Barbarossa. Later it was ruled by the Visconti and Sforza families of Milan and then came under foreign rule before Garibaldi freed it in 1859.

From Como you can travel along the western side of the lake through **Cernobbio,** where the 16th-century Villa d'Este and its gardens have been turned into a top-class hotel.

Between Tremezzo and Cadenabbio lies the **Villa Carlotta,** set in magnificent gardens among cypresses and rhododendrons, approached by an avenue of plane trees known as the Via del Paradiso.

Beyond **Menaggio,** notable for its good tennis and golf, you come to **Dongo.** It was here that Italian partisans caught Mussolini and his mistress Clara Petacci on 27th April 1945, as they were trying to flee to Switzerland in a

German lorry. Both were shot the same day a few miles to the south.

During the 13th century, Dongo and the neighbouring villages of Gravedona and Sorico founded a self-proclaimed republic, too small to be long-lived.

From Musso castle, near **Gravedona,** a 16th-century petty adventurer, nicknamed Il Medichino, terrorized the inhabitants of the lake shores with the connivance of the Sforzas in Milan. He later went to fight in the Netherlands for Emperor Charles V and ended up with the title of Viceroy of Bohemia. You'll find his tomb in Milan cathedral.

Returning down the eastern side of the lake, take a side road round an inlet to see the Romanesque **Abbey of Piona,** with its superb cloister.

The southern part of Lake Como splits into two arms. At **Varenna** you can take a boat across to **Bellagio,** an ideally placed resort on the point where the two arms meet. The rugged shores of the eastern arm run down to **Lecco,** a small industrial town. The western arm runs from Bellagio down to Como, past the **Villa Pliniana** near Turno, believed to be one of several sites where the Plinys had a villa.

Lake Iseo (ancient Lacus Sebinus) is the smallest of the five main lakes, only 15 miles (25 km.) long. But it makes up for this by having the largest island of any lake in Italy, **Monte Isola.** The island is clothed in chestnut and olive trees and the whole lake is a sportsman's paradise for fishing and duck shooting. The name Iseo is believed to have come from the Egyptian goddess Isis, whose temple once stood in a Roman town on its shores.

The beauties of **Lake Garda** (ancient Lacus Benacus) were sung by the Roman poets Virgil, Horace and Catullus. The German poet Goethe also loved the lake and found inspiration here for his drama, *Iphigenia.*

Sirmione, the first town at the foot of the lake, is entered by a narrow bridge and ancient gateway, leading onto a peninsula. The town is dominated by a battlemented castle, built by the Scaliger or della Scala family, one of Italy's great ruling dynasties from Verona, who incidentally gave their name to the church where La Scala opera house now stands in Milan.

Near the castle you can visit the **Grotto of Catullus,** where the poet is believed to have had a villa, near hot sulphur springs.

Driving along the western shore, you come to **Salò,** a town of narrow old streets, where Mussolini set up a puppet government under the Germans after he had been rescued by them from detention in the Abruzzi mountains.

On a hillside near the resort of **Gardone,** you can visit the home of the dashing soldier hero and poet of World War I, Gabriele d'Annunzio. Known as the **Vittoriale,** it is now a museum, both house and garden filled with war relics.

North of Gardone, the mountains grow steeper and terraces of olive trees cling to the slopes. The air is heavy with the scent of lemon trees, fruiting and flowering at the same time. Luxury villas and gardens line the lake shore.

MILAN

The mountains drop so steeply into the water here that the road disappears a score of times into tunnels before reaching **Riva** at the head of the lake. The 13th-century tower above Riva, **La Bastione,** is a symbol of Venetian power that once dominated the region.

The lake was in fact at one time a battleground for the warring fleets of Venetians and Milanese. At **Torbole** the Venetians are said to have launched 30 ships which they had dragged over the mountains from the neighbouring Adige valley to surprise the Visconti fleet. Despite their enterprise, the Venetians lost that particular battle.

At **Malcesine** you'll see an ancient castle built by the Romans, destroyed by the Lombards, rebuilt by Franks and strengthened by the Scaligers. The town became the headquarters of the Venetian fleet on the lake. Take a cable car to **Monte Baldo** for a fine view of the Alps and lake.

Torri del Benace, the chief town on the eastern shore until replaced by Garda, has another 14th-century Scaliger castle, built on the site of one belonging to the Frankish king Berengar I, who styled himself King of Italy.

At **Punta San Vigilio,** where the lake widens out, is a tiny old church surrounded by ancient cypresses, overlooking the bay.

The town of **Garda** lies in an area that has been inhabited since the Stone Age. Prehistoric caves and remnants of lake dwellings have been found here. The first town on the site was built by the Romans. The castle at **Rocca** belonged to the 10th-century King Berengar II. He is said to have imprisoned here a young widow named Adelaide, who refused to marry his son. She escaped, married the Emperor Otto, and saw Berengar roundly defeated in battle.

The vineyards south of Garda are the home of the famous Bardolino wine.

Lazise, just beyond Bardolino, is a picturesque fishing town, enclosed by 11th-century walls, with a Scaliger castle. This was one of the Venetian harbours during the struggles with Milan.

Your round-the-lake trip ends at **Peschiera,** a small town where Pope Leo I is believed to have met Attila the Hun in 452 to persuade him not to attack Rome.

Attila didn't, but Alaric the Goth looted Rome anyway, only a few years later.

Eating Out

The best starter of all, in season, is *prosciutto con melone,* a slice of ice-cold melon with raw Parma ham. Or you can try the *antipasto misto*—salami, olives, radishes, fennel and pickled mushrooms.

The minestrone soup of mixed vegetables and tomato simmered in butter, skilfully blended so that no single taste predominates and sprinkled with grated Parmesan, is a far cry from what passes as minestrone in the fast food stores at home.

To follow, try the lake fish—perch fillets or trout —or the *fritto misto:* seafood fried in batter.

The Po valley is famous for its rice. Don't fail to sample the *risotto alla milanese,* a richly golden dish of rice cooked in chicken broth, flavoured with saffron and sprinkled with cheese. The other staple North Italian dish is *polenta*—cornmeal cooked till it thickens and can be cut into slices and fried. The Milanese eat it with tomato sauce and cheese.

For the meat course there is the *costoletta alla milanese,* veal cutlet dipped in egg and breadcrumbs, fried in butter; or the *osso buco,* thickly cut shin of veal, complete with marrow, cooked gently in tomato sauce and served with the tiniest of peas.

For dessert, try one of the ice-creams for which Milan is renowned, especially the half-frozen ices such as *granita* and sorbets.

There'll be a plentifully stocked cheese-board, with varieties from all over Italy. If you want to try some from the region, go for the *gorgonzola, mascarpone* or *Bel Paese.*

From the wine list choose a Bardolino (red) or Rosatello (rosé) from Lake Garda. Or, if you prefer a sparkle, try the white Asti Spumante from Piedmont.

Shopping

Milan is the place for chic clothes. The designers here are leaders in European taste in men's, women's and children's wear. You'll find excellent shops and boutiques in the Galleria, the Corso Vittorio Emanuele and Corso Venezia. Among the best buys are:

Silks: blouses, shirts, ties, scarves, dresses and dress lengths.

Leather: shoes, handbags, luggage.

Textiles: bed linen, table

linen, towels, lace, hand-finished lingerie.

Tableware: china and porcelain, glassware, silverware.

Jewellery, precious stones, watches and clocks.

Antiques: old furniture, paintings and books, all pricey.

Toys: the cuddliest of dolls and gimmicky electric toys.

Food and Drink: parmesan (parmiggiano), *gorgonzola* and *Bel Paese* cheese; a bottle of Bardolino; and a *pannetone,* the local sweet loaf, flavoured with saffron and studded with candied fruit. It keeps well.

Practical Information

Banks: Opening hours 8.30 a.m. to 1.30 p.m., Mondays to Fridays.

Climate: Warm summers, cold winters. The climate round the lakes is milder than in Milan, which can be very cold and foggy in winter.

Clothing: Light clothes for summer; mediumweight for spring and autumn, with a raincoat. A warm top-coat is needed in winter.

Currency: Italian *lira* (abbr. *L.* or *Lit.*) Coins: L. 5, 10, 20, 50, 100, 200 and 500. Banknotes: L. 1,000, 2,000, 5,000, 10,000, 50,000 and 100,000.

MUNICH

West Germany

Introduction

If the people of Munich differ so much from other Germans it's because, you'll be told, this isn't Germany, it's Bavaria. As the capital of the fervently Catholic and conservative Free State of Bavaria, Munich epitomizes the independent Bavarian spirit. Whole books are filled with jokes at the expense of stiff-necked Prussians. At the annual *Oktoberfest* 5,000,000 visitors consume 4,000,000 litres of beer in an extravaganza appropriate to the oversized image the Bavarians have of their capital.

But it would be wrong to think of life in Munich as one long *Oktoberfest*. The city is undoubtedly the cultural capital of the Federal Republic of Germany: a showcase of classical and modern art, a musical mecca thanks to the opera house and concert halls, a centre for industry, publishing and the West German cinema. No-one who has seen the town's impressive affluence, its dynamic car industry, bril-liantly constructed Olympic sports complex and fine subway system would suggest that Munich's fun-loving attitude was unproductive.

Munich is attached to its historical identity. After the destruction of World War II, many German cities decided to break with the past and build in a completely modern style. But the Bavarian capital preferred to restore and reconstruct painstakingly the great churches and palaces of its past. There are plenty of modern skyscrapers, but the heart of the old city is fast recapturing its former Baroque charm. The inner city is a pedestrian's delight, thanks to an excellent system of public transport and a town plan that keeps much of the traffic circling rather than crossing the city centre.

Munich's genius has always been its ability to combine the Germanic talent for getting things done with a specifically Bavarian need to do them pleasantly—a formula that visitors to Munich won't fail to appreciate!

A Brief History

Middle Ages to 13th century	A few peasants and Benedictine monks settle on the River Isar. (The name "Munich" derives from "*ze den Munichen*", dialect for "the monk's place".) Heinrich

der Löwe, Duke of Saxony, establishes a toll bridge at the site in 1156. The settlement is recognized by the emperor in 1158. The Wittelsbach family take control of the town in 1180 and it becomes the largest in their dominions by the end of the 13th century.

14th century	Duke Ludwig IV is made Holy Roman Emperor in 1328. He establishes his court in Munich. The Black Death sweeps Europe, devastating the city in 1348. High taxes and general penury cause further stresses; citizens split into burgher and patrician factions.
15th–16th centuries	Conditions improve; dissent eases; trade booms in salt, wine and cloth. The Frauenkirche is constructed. Martin Luther's Reformation teaching provokes religious conflict. Struggles for political and economic power continue as do the pomp and circumstance of court life. In 1568 Duke Wilhelm V and his bride Renata of Lorraine hold three-week long wedding celebrations. When Maximilian I (1573–1651) comes to throne, the state coffers are empty.
17th century	In the Thirty Years' War (1618–48) starvation and disease are prevalent. In 1632 Maximilian sets up the Mariansäule (Column of the Virgin Mary). Maximilian II Emanuel returns to Munich after helping Austrians to beat off Turkish attacks in 1683. He brings 296 Turks back with him, thus beginning the city's first *Gastarbeiter* (immigrant worker) community.
18th century	After losing in the War of the Spanish Succession (1701–14), Munich is occupied by Austrians for some ten years. The Wittelsbach family succession falls to Karl Theodor, who has to send in soldiers to quell a starving population in revolutionary times.
19th century	French troops occupy the city in 1800. Napoleon passes through in 1805. The royal wedding festivities of Ludwig I to Theresa of Saxony in October 1810 pave the way for the annual *Oktoberfest*. Ludwig constructs, designs and starts collecting art in a determined effort to reinstate German culture over the French influence. His reputation tarnished by his affair with Lola Montéz, he abdicates, leaving the throne to Maximilian II (1811–64). Ludwig II (1845–80), the last great king of Bavaria, succeeds Maximilian. Ludwig lives out his

time building châteaux and fanciful castles in a fantasy world of his own.

20th century   The Wittlesbach family dynasty ends with World War I. Attempts to found a worker's republic fail and the right-wing *Freikorps* (private armies) gain ground sweeping away the tolerant tradition. Hitler rises to power, becoming the head of the Nazi party. In 1935 Munich is named "Capital of the (Nazi) Movement". Attacks on Jews begin with the looting of the synagogue in June 1938. Heavy bombardments during World War II, especially in 1944, extensively damage the city. After the war, reconstruction takes place on a large scale.

Sightseeing

Innenstadt

The best place to start is **Marienplatz**, right in the centre of town. Until the middle of the 19th century, the wheat market was held here. The square was an obvious site for the town hall, and the place where criminals and other unpopular people were hanged.

Today, Marienplatz is graced with tubs of flowers and outdoor cafés and forms part of an attractive pedestrian zone. Here you'll see the **Marien-säule** (Column of the Virgin Mary), erected in 1632 by Maximilian I in gratitude for the town's deliverance from the Swedes during the Thirty Years' War. The square sports another, more modern monument: the 19th–century Fischbrunnen. Young butchers used to leap into the fountain after completing their apprenticeship; nowadays the tradition is kept up only by an occasional carnival reveller or happy soccer fan.

At the eastern end of Marienplatz stands the almost too picturesque **Altes Rathaus** (Old Town Hall), a gay example of Munich's efforts to reconstruct, rather than replace, the vestiges of its venerable past.

The decorated façade on the northern side of Marienplatz is the 19th-century neo-Gothic **Neues Rathaus** (New Town Hall). From its 260-foot (80-m.) tower you'll be able to admire a splendid **view** of the city and also hear the 43-bell **Glockenspiel** which gives a "concert" of jangling bells, complete with mechanical puppet dancers, every day at 11 a.m.

Continue your walk up Weinstrasse to the **Frauenkirche** (Cathedral Church of Our Lady). This building symbolizes Munich, and its gold-tipped bulbous domes on twin brick towers dominate the skyline. The church was built from 1468 to 1488 by Jörg von Halsbach; the Renaissance domes are an addition of 1524. Inside, the main attractions are the Gothic windows, fine sculptures of the Apostles and prophets and an admirable 16th-century altarpiece. Just outside the church, in Frauenplatz, the granite fountain strikes a modern note.

West of the square via Augustinerstrasse and Neuhauser Strasse is the 16th-century **St. Michael** church, designed by the Netherlands architect Friedrich Sustris, in Italian Renaissance style with Baroque overtones.

Karlstor, a city gate dating from the 14th century, links Neuhauser Strasse to Karlsplatz, popularly known as the **Stachus** after a local innkeeper, which conceals a veritable city of underground shops.

On the surface again, walk north to Lenbachplatz and the **Wittelsbacher Brunnen,** the city's loveliest fountain, built in the 19th century. Further north, turn into Prannerstrasse which leads to the **Erzbischöflisches Palais**. This triumph of Rococo harmony has especially fine stucco work. It is the only 18th-century palace built by Cuvilliés to have survived wholly intact to the present day.

A stroll from Marienplatz in the other direction takes you to **St. Peter's**, the oldest church in Munich, dating from before the foundation of the city itself in 1158. You can climb to the top of the tower for a stunning view of the city.

At the end of Burgstrasse is the **Alter Hof**, a peaceful tree-shaded square offering an exquisite panorama of medieval buildings. The Hof was originally built around 1255 as a defence against foreign invaders.The nearby **Hofbräuhaus** is a beer hall.

Odeonsplatz joins the Inner City to Schwabing and the university. The **Hofgarten** (Court Garden) off the square is planted with chestnut trees, flower beds and fountains. Turn and look south-west across the Hofgarten to capture the delightful vista that helps to give Munich its peculiarly Mediterranean flavour—the twin towers and dome of the splendid **Theatinerkirche**, an Italian Baroque church built from 1663 to 1688 by Agostino Barelli and Enrico Zucalli. The façade was completed by Cuvilliés. The church was built to celebrate the birth of a boy to Princess Henriette Adelaide, and a feeling of jubilation animates the rich decoration: ornamental vines, acanthus leaves and rosettes, and splendid grey and white stucco embellishments.

Across the street, facing Odeonsplatz, is the **Feldherrnhalle** (Hall of the Generals), a 19th-century monument to Bavarian military leaders.

Next door, in Residenzstrasse, stands **Preysing-Palais**, the most richly ornamented of Munich's private Rococo palaces. Begun in 1723 by Joseph Effner, only the Residenzstrasse façade survived World War II, but the restoration of the rest has been masterful. Take a look inside at the imposing ceremonial staircase.

At the other end of Residenzstrasse lies another jewel of 18th-century architecture, the **Hauptpostamt** or Main Post Office, formerly the Palais Törring-Jettenbach. You'll never buy a stamp in a more beautiful setting.

The spacious **Max-Joseph-Platz** is named after the king whose statue sits in the centre. The statue was placed along-side the greatest monument of Max-Joseph's family, the Wittelsbach **Residenz**. Now a museum, the Residenz shows just how wealthy and powerful the Bavarian principality grew to be. To view the exterior, enter from Residenzstrasse and walk through the seven courtyards to the **Cuvilliéstheater**. This is an enchanting playhouse, a tiny 450-seat auditorium basking in a gilded Rococo décor of Greek nymphs, gods and goddesses—and an American Indian girl complete with feathers, bow, arrows and cactus. The acoustics are totally appropriate to the Mozart works played here for the past 200 years.

The walk from Sendlinger Tor takes you through a popular district of the city centre, the busy shopping area of Sendlinger Strasse, and on past the municipal museum to the open-air market beside St. Peter's church. Only two hexagonal towers remain from the picturesque 14th-century **Sendlinger Tor** (City Gate).

Facing north-east, take the left fork along Sendlinger Strasse to **Asamhaus** (number 61) where Egid Quirin Asam, master sculptor and architect of the 18th century, had his home. He was assisted in the decoration of the building by his brother, Cosmas Damian, who specialized in fresco painting. The extraordinary façade happily combines pagan and Christian figures, and a riot of nymphs and satyrs dance around the Muses of Painting, Sculpture and Architecture. The **Asamkirche** next door is also a tribute to the Asam brothers' enthusiasm.

Double back across Sendlinger Strasse passing the Stadtmuseum, to get to the **Viktualienmarkt**. The colours, sights, sounds and smells of the cheerful market will provide a lively lift for a tired spirit.

Königsplatz represents a convergence of the noblest and basest aspirations in the last several hundred years of Munich's history. While still crown prince, Ludwig I visualized the square as a second Acropolis, a vast open space surrounded by classical temples. With Leo von Klenze as his architect, Ludwig made the square a grass-covered, tree-lined haven of tranquillity. A hundred years later, Hitler cut down the trees and paved over the grass for the troops and armoured cars of his military parades. (The pompous Nazi Ehrentempel,

or Temple of Honour, which stood at the eastern end of the square, was deliberately blown up by Allied military engineers in 1945.) Today Königsplatz is returning to its original verdant serenity.

Schwabing

The Schwabing district belongs to that select group of places around the world —London's Chelsea, Paris's Montparnasse, New York's Greenwich Village—of which it's said, often glibly but nonetheless accurately, that it is not so much a place as a state of mind.

Begin your walk symbolically at the **Siegestor** (Victory Gate), which marks the southern boundary of Schwabing. This triumphal arch was designed for Ludwig I as a monument to the Bavarian army. It was damaged in 1944; the new inscription on the south side means "Dedicated to victory, destroyed in war, exhorting to peace". Walk to the entrance of the University and you'll see the little square named Geschwister-Scholl-Platz after the brother and sister who gave their lives in the struggle against Hitler.

At night, the bohemian spirit of Schwabing animates

breezy **Leopoldstrasse**, the street that begins north of Siegestor. The great writers and artists of the past may have gone, but the art galleries and cafés are still going strong. Schwabing now serves as the meeting place for the talents of the New German cinema.

Englischer Garten Area

Opened in 1793, this marvellous landscape garden was mainly the creation of Benjamin Thompson, an American-born adventurer who fought on the British side during the American Revolution. He is known to the Bavarians as Count von Rumsford. The gardens stretch 3 miles (5 km.) to the north, making a lovely walk along the swiftly flowing River Isar. Stroll up to the Kleinhesseloher See, a pond that offers some boating for the more energetic. The little Eisbach, a branch of the Isar, rushes helter-skelter under Tivoli Bridge like a veritable mountain rapid, encouraging a particularly breakneck version of wind-surfing. It's a great spectator sport, but if the mere sight of such activity exhausts you, head for the pretty Japanese Tea House (in the south-west corner), donated by Japan in honour of the 1972 Olympic Games.

Museums

The number and diversity of museums and galleries in Munich attest to the city's importance as a cultural centre. The **Alte Pinakothek**, in Barer Strasse, is one of the world's great art museums. The collection was started in the 17th century by Maximilian I. There is a large number of masterpieces, not only by German artists such as Michael Pacher, Albrecht Dürer and Matthias Grünewald, but

also by the greatest painters of the Flemish, Dutch, Italian, Spanish and French schools. The **Residenzmuseum** is enormous, with 112 rooms, halls and galleries, a monumental Renaissance library, chapels and a treasure chamber full of the riches of the past—all of which can be visited.

The **Deutsches Museum**, in Zweibrückenstrasse, is a scientific and technological museum: a paradise for youngsters and fascinating for their parents. The **Bayerisches Nationalmuseum** (Bavarian National Museum), Prinzregentenstrasse, presents a magnificent survey of German cultural history from the Roman era through the Middle Ages to the 19th century. It emphasizes both religious and secular art and craftmanship.

The **Münchner Stadtmuseum** (Municipal Museum), is in St. Jakobs-Platz. In maps, models and photographs, Munich's personality is distinctly reflected in the city's own museum. There is also a section on marionettes and one on beer-making.

Ancient sculptural glories, especially from Greece, can be seen at the **Glyptothek**, Königsplatz. The **BMW-Museum**, Peutel Ring Autobahn, gives a fascinating insight into the history of the Bavarian Motor Works.

Schloss Nymphenburg was the Wittelsbach's summer refuge. The palace is approached by a long canal with avenues on either bank leading to a semi-circle of lawns, the Schlossrondel, site of the building which houses the royal porcelain factory.

The first pavilion to the south holds the famous **Schönheitengalerie** (Gallery of Beautiful Women). The **Marsstallmuseum**—a dazzling collection of state coaches used for coronations, weddings and other royal frolics —has been installed in the south wing, in what was once the royal stables.

The sumptuous **gardens** contain a splendid hunting lodge, Amalienburg, ponds, promontories, pavilions and pagodas. There's also a cleverly landscaped Arboretum in the **Neuer Botanischer Garten** (New Botanical Gardens) entered from Menzinger Strasse.

Excursions

To take the full measure of Munich, you must visit its hinterland, the beautiful countryside of Bavaria. Go to the lakes, to the little country churches and to Ludwig II's crazy castles. If you don't have

a car, take one of the tours organized by the Munich-Upper Bavaria Tourist Office.

Neuschwanstein, Ludwig II's extraordinary castle, took its inspiration from the medieval castle of Wartburg in Thuringia. The white turreted fantasy is set in the middle of a forest of firs and pine trees overlooking the gorge of Pöllat and Lake Forggen. Wagnerians will recognize the sculptural and painted allusions to *Tannhäuser, The Mastersingers,* and *Tristan and Isolde.*

Pass through Oberammergau, site of the famous 10-yearly Passion Play, to get to Ludwig's second dream palace, **Linderhof,** the embodiment of his most Baroque fantasies. The palace, inspired by the Grand Trianon of Versailles, is opulent inside and out. Quite apart from the carefully tailored landscape of pond and park, you could be excused for believing that the whole romantic Alpine backdrop of the Graswangtal had been conjured up from Ludwig's imagination. But the Venus Grotto, carved out of the mountainside with another Wagnerian motif from *Tannhäuser*, is man-made.

For a change of pace and some fresh air go south to visit the **Ammersee, Starnberger See** and **Chiemsee**—just three of a number of Bavaria's pretty lakes. Ludwig II's most ambitious castle, **Herren-** **chiemsee**, stands on an island at the western end of Chiemsee.

Dachau, 10 ½ miles (17 km.) north of Munich, should be visited. The **Concentration Camp Museum** provides a solemn reminder and challenge to each new generation to refuse extremism of any kind. 31,951 persons were murdered by the Nazis in the camp.

Continue east to **Schloss Schliessheim** and re-enter the sunny Baroque world of Max Emanuel. The Neues Schloss

has a glorious staircase with frescoes by Cosmas Damian Asam. But the gardens are the real triumph: it's sheer joy to walk around the waterfall, canals and flowerbeds designed by Carbonet and Dominique Girard, a discipline of the French master Le Nôtre.

Eating Out

Eating and drinking in Bavaria are major occupations. Conviviality reigns supreme both in the high temples of gastronomy and at the long communal tables of the beer halls and gardens.

The pig and the calf dominate Bavarian main dishes, often in combination. Pork or veal can either be pot-roasted (*Kalbs-* or *Schweinsbraten*) or grilled on a spit (*Kalbs-* or *Schweinshaxen*) with a marvellous crispy, crackling skin. The ultimate in delicious roasts is *Spanferkel,* suckling pig.

Sauerkraut comes beautifully prepared in white wine with juniper berries, caraway seeds and cloves. There's also the sweet-and-sour red cabbage, *Rotkraut,* done with apples, raisins and white vinegar, or a good green cabbage salad (*Weisskrautsalat*).

Desserts are heavy, but delicious; from *Apfelkücherl* (apple cake) and *Zwetschgendatschi* (plum cake) to *Schwarzwälder Kirschtorte* (Black Forest cherry cake) and *Apfelstrudel* from Vienna.

Bavarians appreciate the old saying that there's good beer and better beer, but no bad beer. Not in Bavaria.

Beer *vom Fass* (on tap) can be ordered by the half-litre in restaurants, but elsewhere often only in a one-litre tankard known as the *Masskrug* or simply "*Mass*". Bottled beer comes in several varieties: *Export*, light and smooth; *Pils*, light and stronger; and *Bock,* dark and rich.

Bavarian beer is generally lighter than other German beers, but it has its strong forms, too. If you like it dark with a slightly sweet, malt flavour, order *Dunkles.* This is not served as cold as the more popular light brew, *Helles,* which has an inviting mist on the glass.

Shopping

Munich is an elegant town and there's no lack of chic boutiques, especially on Theatinerstrasse, Maximilianstrasse and Leopoldstrasse.

Some good buys are: leather and sportswear; Nymphenburg porcelain; cutlery, electronic gadgets and linen. Precision binoculars, cameras and telescopes are worth considering, as are records, musical instruments and toys.

The flea markets have a variety of interesting bargains.

Practical Information

Banking hours: From 8.30 a.m. to 12.30 p.m. and 1.45 to 3.30 p.m., Monday to Friday (Thursday until 5.30 p.m.).

Currency: Germany's monetary unit is the *Deutsche Mark* (abbr. *DM*). The mark is divided into 100 *Pfennig* (abbr. *Pf.*). Coins: 1, 2, 5, 10 and 50 Pf. and DM 1, 2, 5 and 10. Notes: DM 5, 10, 20, 50, 100, 500 and 1,000.

Museum hours: Usually from 9 a.m. to 4 p.m. Most museums close on Monday, others on Saturday and/or Sunday. For exact timetables, consult the official *Monatsprogramm* or enquire at the tourist office.

Post offices: Munich's central post office stands just opposite the main railway station, on Bahnhofplatz 1. It remains open 24 hours a day to deal with mail, telegrams and telephone calls. A telex service and currency exchange desk operate from 7 a.m. to 11 p.m.

Shops: Open from 8.30 or 9 a.m. to 6.30 p.m., Monday to Friday, until 2 p.m. (some only till 12.30) on Saturday and 6 p.m. the first Saturday of the month. Shops outside the city centre usually close between 1 and 3 p.m.

Tourist information offices: The airport office operates from 8.30 a.m. to 10 p.m., Monday to Saturday, and from 1 to 9 p.m. on Sundays. The DB-Reisezentrum office in the central railway station opens daily from 6 a.m. to 11 p.m.

Transport: Munich is served by an efficient network of buses, trams, U-Bahn (underground railway) and S-Bahn (suburban railway). The U-Bahn runs north-south through the city; the S-Bahn crosses Munich on an east-west axis and goes out to the surrounding countryside in all directions. All forms of public transport operate from about 5 a.m. to 1 a.m. daily. Free maps and information are available at the tourist offices.

NAPLES

Italy

Introduction

The Bay of Naples—the name unfailingly evokes mandolins and moonlight and triggers familiar songs in your mind. Are they the hackneyed images of a tired romance, or does the queen of Mediterranean cities still cast a spell over all who enter her magnificent bay?

Everyone has his own preconception of Naples—lines heavy with laundry strung between tenements that should have been condemned long ago; mischievous urchins darting through narrow lanes; street vendors gesticulating and shoppers, artisans and restaurateurs shouting down the hooting of scooters and cars and the clanging of trams.

Since the destruction inflicted in World War II, Naples has become a major industrial city, but the irrepressible enthusiasm of the Neapolitans has not changed. Conscious of your expectations, they will do their best to entertain you, by being more Neapolitan than the Neapolitans. Above the hubbub of the city you may even hear a snatch of an aria—Enrico Caruso was, after all, a native of this beautiful city.

However, there can be a darker side to the Neapolitan experience. Although the atmosphere of gaiety, sunshine and colour may mitigate poverty, it is only too real in some quarters of the city.

Memorials of 3,000 years of chequered history are apparent in Naples and the surrounding region of Campania. Ancient civilizations chose the shores of this bay to found colonies of traders who bore the products of the Western Mediterranean and beyond to the markets of the East. The shelter of the bay, the richness of the volcanic soil and the clemency of the weather outweighed the ever-present threat of the mighty volcano that looms over the bay.

Unpredictable Vesuvius destroyed—and preserved—cities which bear witness to a rich and easy life-style of the times when the Roman Empire had reached its height. You will find in Pompeii and Herculaneum ghost cities inhabited by people petrified forever in a cataclysm of two millennia ago.

The area inspired Virgil to write his best poems. Wealthy Romans built their holiday homes here, and emperors chose the island Capri as their favourite resort. And today, however much Naples has changed, the moon still rises over the bay and the strumming of the mandolin can be heard over its calm waters.

A Brief History

8th–4th centuries B.C.	Naples begins as a Rhodian settlement in the 8th century B.C. A century later, inhabitants of the oldest Greek colony in Italy, Cumae, found the nearby "old city" of Palepolis. In the 5th century B.C. a third town (Neapolis—New City) is added on by settlers from the Aegean island of Euboea. The towns amalgamate and join in an alliance with Rome in 326 B.C.
4th century B.C.–5th century A.D.	Naples retains its Greek character well into imperial times, becoming a centre of culture and refined elegance. In A.D. 79 the nearby town of Pompeii, damaged by an earthquake 16 years earlier, and Herculaneum are buried by ash and lava from Vesuvius.
6th–17th centuries	Naples falls to the Goths in 543, but is taken over by Byzantium 10 years later and is able to withstand attacks from the Lombards. In the 12th century it is incorporated into the Norman Kingdom of Sicily. The Hohenstaufen king, Friedrich II, inherits the Norman kingdom and founds the University of Naples in 1224. Charles of Anjou enters Naples in 1266 after defeating the Hohenstaufens at Benevento. The Angevins yield the city to Alfonso of Aragon in 1442 and, from 1503, Naples is ruled by viceroys as part of the Spanish Empire. An eruption of Vesuvius in 1631 ravages the surrounding area.
18th–20th centuries	Excavations begin at Herculaneum in 1737 and at Pompeii in 1748. Naples comes under Bourbon rule in 1748.

Napoleon occupies Naples in 1806 and makes his brother, Joseph Bonaparte, king. After Napoleon's defeat, Naples is put under British protection with the Bourbon, Ferdinand IV, as king. Ferdinand assumes the title of King of the Two Sicilies. Garibaldi wrests the Kingdom of the Two Sicilies from Bourbon rule in 1860, and the Neapolitans vote to join the unified Kingdom of Italy. The city is badly damaged in World War II. Shortly after Allied landings in Sicily in 1943, Neapolitans rise against Fascist rule. After the war the city becomes heavily industrialized, and the harbour area and many parts of the city are reconstructed. |

Sightseeing

The **Piazza Municipio,** a large square of gardens dominated by an equestrian statue of King Vittorio Emanuele II, is the best place to start your sightseeing tour. Most of the important buildings are in the vicinity.

On the south side of the square rise the five massive towers of **Maschio Angioino,** also called Castel Nuovo or New Castle, built 700 years ago by Charles of Anjou. It was later rebuilt to become the residence of the viceroys and kings. Renaissance architects designed the magnificent **triumphal arch** at the entrance

to commemorate Alfonso I of Aragon's arrival in the city.

Treachery took place under the splendid vaults of the **Hall of the Barons** *(Sala dei Baroni)* inside the castle in 1486 when Ferdinand I entertained his rival barons to a banquet and then invited them to attend a mass execution—their own. Nowadays the Naples city council meets here to conduct their business in a slightly more refined manner.

Next door to the Castel Nuovo is undoubtedly the most magnificent of the Neapolitan palaces, the **Royal Palace** *(Palazzo Reale).* The most interesting aspects of the façade are the

eight marble statues of Neapolitan rulers. Inside, the original Bourbon furniture, paintings, statues and porcelain are displayed in sumptuously decorated halls and apartments. It houses the **National Library** started by the Bourbon King Charles V when he took over Naples.

Adjacent to the palace is the **San Carlo Opera** (1737)—one of the largest and most splendid in Europe with nearly 3,000 seats. The French writer Stendhal compared the inside to the palace of an oriental potentate.

The vast **Piazza del Plebiscito** separates the palace and theatre from the colonnaded

Church of San Francesco di Páola built in imitation of the Pantheon in Rome.

Naples' main shopping street, Via Roma, leads north from the square for more than a mile to the **National Archaeological Museum**—one of the world's most important. It is a treasure house of mosaics, statues and other decorations found at Pompeii and Herculaneum, as well as relics of Cumae, thought to be the oldest Greek settlement in Italy.

North of the museum is the **Capodimonte Royal Palace,** set in its own park. It houses a museum of Capodimonte porcelain and rival products from Dresden, Sèvres and Vienna. The **National Gallery** upstairs has a large collection of Titians among its 500 paintings.

Off the Via Capodimonte is one of the most unusual and fascinating sights of Naples— the **Catacombs of San Gennaro.** The gloomy network of tombs and passages on two levels dates back to the 2nd century. Originally the tomb of a noble family, they became the main Christian cemetery of Naples. They contain early Christian paintings.

Three funiculars take you up to the Vómero area on a plateau overlooking the city. Beside the Sant'Elmo Castle is the **San Martino National Museum,** which provides a fascinating look at the history of Naples.

The **Church of Santa Chiara,** originally a Gothic church, was rebuilt in the 18th century in Baroque style. Severe damage during the war enabled it to be restored to its original Gothic. Inside is the tomb of Robert the Wise of Anjou who died in 1343.

A miracle happens twice a year in the **Naples Cathedral** when the blood of San Gennaro liquefies. Martyred by Emperor Diocletian in 305, San Gennaro was Bishop of Beneventum. The saint's relics—two phials of his dried blood and his skull—are kept in a lavishly decorated chapel in the cathedral.

The animated street-life of Naples can best be enjoyed in the evenings in the steep warren of steps and lanes in the **Santa Lucia district.**

Take a stroll along the splendid Via Carácciolo, the favourite seaside promenade of the Neapolitans, to watch the setting sun set fire to the massive walls of the **Castel dell'Ovo,** dominating the harbour, and admire the city skirting the lovely Bay of Naples, all overlooked by the broodling bulk of Vesuvius.

Excursions

Pompeii

The archaeologist's dream, to find an ancient city almost intact, was made possible 1,900 years ago when a volcanic cataclysm buried a thriving community in a burning rain of ash and cinders.

The lost city, rediscovered in the 18th century, has bit by bit revealed a picture of the workaday life of a town at the peak of Roman power.

As you walk through the ruins the bustling life of Pompeii comes readily to your imagination. It is a city grown rich on speculation and profit. The town is swarming with porters, craftsmen, dogs and merchants darting out of the way of carts and picking their way across the streets on stepping stones raised above the rubbish. The walls are scribbled with graffiti—love messages, insults and election notices. Taverns and brothels are doing a brisk trade.

And then you come to the bodies. In 1860, the director of excavations, Giuseppe Fiorelli had the idea of injecting plaster into the spaces that appeared as layers of ash were swept away. The moulds revealed people and animals caught in a final agony as suffocating clouds of dust and ash fell upon the city.

Eating Out

Naples invented the pizza, that fast food standby known the world over. In its home city it is topped with genuine *mozzarella* cheese, made from buffalo milk, and garnished simply with tomatoes, a few anchovies, chopped basil and oregano.

You'll find a variety of seafood soups, each restaurant having its own speciality. Many menus will feature *frittura del golfo,* tiny fish netted in the gulf and deep fried until they are crisp enough to be eaten whole. The king of Tyrrhenian Sea fish is undoubtedly the sea bass *(spigola)* baked with fennel or grilled over charcoal.

Tiny clams *(vongole)* and tomato make a delicious pasta sauce, but more common is the simple *al pomodoro* sauce of tomato garnished with a few leaves of basil. Pasta comes in an extraordinary elaboration of shapes—*ricci di donna* (lady's curls) and *sicchie di prieviti* (priest's ears) are two of the more imaginative.

Many of the local cakes and pastries are associated with festivals. *Struffoli* is for Christmas, *pasteria* for Easter, *sanguinaccio* helps Lent along, *torroni* is eaten at All Saints and the splendid *sfogliatelle* is enjoyed all the time.

Drinks

Lacrima Christi (Christ's tears), a white wine grown on the sulphurous slopes of Vesuvius is ideal with fish. Other volcanic wines include Gragnano, the hearty red Taurasi, Ravello with a sweet aftertaste, and Falerno, the wine celebrated by the poet Horace. Greco di Tufo is a refreshing white.

Some people say the local liqueur, Strega, tastes like hair oil, but it's a taste that is acquired remarkably quickly. Benedictine monks at Montevergine contribute to international well-being with their digestive liqueurs made of herbs, and the brandies of Avellino have won world renown.

Shopping

The craftsmen of Campania are heirs to a centuries-old tradition of fine workmanship, and just about everything that can be made by an artisan is produced in the Naples area.

Since 1771 the Capodimonte School has held its own against the most celebrated porcelain and ceramics manufacturers of Europe. Today its exquisite creations are still eagerly sought after by those who appreciate fine porcelain.

The cheerful colours and homely practicality of the local **pottery** and **terracotta**, may be less refined than the masterpieces of Capodimonte, but they nevertheless have their own artistic value.

The Campania coast has for years been renowned for the manufacture of **coral jewellery**. Torre del Greco is the world centre and there are several exhibition galleries where you can admire the delicate workmanship. Visitors generally stop on the way back from Pompeii to visit a **cameo** workshop and buy examples of the jewellery made there.

Handmade **lace** *(pizzo al tombolo)* and **embroidery** from the small towns of the hinterland are known for their delicacy. Or swathe yourself in **silk** from San Leucio di Caserta.

The craftsmen of Irpina are masters of **copper** and **wrought-iron work,** and the sheer skill that goes into the variety of **sculpted stone** and **wood** objects will astound you.

Typically Neapolitan are the *presepio,* the traditional **Nativity puppets,** beautifully carved by image makers who inherited their craft from their forefathers.

It will be safer to assume that most **antiques** are fakes. But some are excellent and even valuable reproductions of masterpieces found in the ruins of Pompeii and Herculaneum. The *saponari,* are the would-be antique dealers of Naples, but mostly their shops and stalls are filled with bric-a-brac of dubious value.

Practical Information

Banks: Open Monday to Friday from 8.30 a.m. to 1.30 p.m.

Climate and clothing: You may need a jacket or a sweater for winter evenings. Summer temperatures demand lightweight and informal clothing.

Currency: The *lira* (plural: *lire:* abbreviation: *L.* or *Lit.*) Banknotes: L. 1,000, 2,000, 5,000, 10,000, 50,000 and 100,000. Coins: L. 5, 10, 20, 50, 100, 200 and 500.

NICE
AND THE FRENCH RIVIERA

Introduction

The Côte d'Azur, the Riviera, Provence, the Midi—call it what you will, this is the world's dream spot. Celebrated in novels and memoirs, in paintings and on film, it probably has more aura and more money than any other seacoast. Its unofficial capital: Nice.

The Riviera evokes images of the lolling millionaires, pink palaces and long shiny cars of F. Scott Fitzgerald's era. And, from the fabled princes gambling at Monte Carlo to the sleek yachts of St-Tropez, the chic crowd in Cannes or the equally chic undress on the beaches, the lissome women and the debonair men, the coast's legends are still very real. But they are not the whole story.

Beyond the ribbons of golden sand skirting the azure sea and the spectacular scenery of the Corniches, less widely acclaimed sights wait to be discovered. There's the fragrant back country, heady with the scent of mimosa, lavender and thyme; medieval hill towns, many now deserted, others brought back to life by resident artists and artisans; the wild and dramatic valley of the Loup River. To really savour life here, try sitting in a small town square. Be lulled by a gurgling fountain as you watch the desultory social life under the shade of outsized plane trees. And learn how to relax.

Unfortunately, because of its success, the Riviera is not the place to find deserted beaches. The coastal strip is thickly populated and in summer the number of people almost doubles, to say nothing of the traffic.

So just enjoy the Riviera's many blessings—the good food and wine, outgoing people, charming towns, beautiful scenery, sparkling sea and sunny skies. For nowhere else will you find the marvellous blend that makes this the world's most glamorous resort area.

A Brief History

Early times | Ligurians from the south-east settle the south coast of France about 1000 B.C. The Phoceans, Greek traders, arrive four centuries later and found Marseilles, Antibes and Nice, bringing with them olive trees and grape vines. In 125 B.C., the Romans establish Provincia Narbonensis (Provence). They introduce their law and administrative system and build roads and cities. During the last years of Roman rule, Christianity gradually spreads through the region.

5th–10th centuries

Waves of invaders sweep across Provence from the 5th to 7th centuries. A measure of order returns under Charlemagne (771–814), but his heirs squabble over the empire, which is eventually divided three ways. Provence goes to Charlemagne's grandson Lothaire. In the 9th and 10th centuries, the coast is often under attack by Saracens (North Africans).

11th–15th centuries

After the Saracens are driven out, the counts of Provence emerge as rulers. Trade and cultural activity revive. Provence passes from the Counts of Toulouse to the Counts of Barcelona and then the Dukes of Anjou. The reign of the Good King René, the last Duke of Anjou, is a period of prosperity and of artistic and intellectual development. René leaves Provence to his nephew, who dies a short time later naming Louis XI, King of France, his successor.

16th–18th centuries

Thus, in 1481, Provence becomes part of France—but not Nice, which forms an alliance with the House of Savoy. The new political arrangement does not bring peace. Provence becomes embroiled in the bitter conflict between François I of France and Charles V, Holy Roman Emperor. Then, the religious wars of the 16th century bring violence and disruption to the region.

Following the Revolution of 1789, riots, massacres and general lawlessness are common. In 1793, Nice is annexed to France.

19th century

Young General Bonaparte launches his Italian campaign from Nice in 1796. He passes through St-Raphaël after his triumphs in Egypt and again in 1814 on the way to exile in Elba. But Napoleon returns a year later, landing at Golfe-Juan and marching through Cannes and Grasse en route to Paris and his Hundred Days. In 1860, Nice (restored to the House of Savoy after Napoleon's downfall) joins France definitively after a plebiscite.

20th century

The south of France is scarcely affected by World War I. Not so with World War II. In 1940, the

Italians occupy Menton. The rest of the area is under the Vichy regime. In 1942 the Germans take over, but they leave the Côte d'Azur to the Italians. The long-awaited Allied landings begin in August 1944 on the beaches of St-Raphaël and St-Tropez. Within two weeks Provence is free.

The post-war period is brightened by the arrival of the bikini, a Riviera original, which changes the beach scene forever—at least until the advent of the topless craze.

Sightseeing

Nice

Nice is like a rich dowager of simple origins who never lost her common touch. Unofficial capital of the Riviera, Nice is a vibrant, important city, boasting France's second largest airport, an opera house and excellent philharmonic orchestra, a university and several good museums. The city's shops, hotels and restaurants rival the world's best. But the older quarter and its inhabitants have the theatrical, good-natured brawling character of an Italian town.

Any visit to Nice begins along the **Promenade des Anglais,** a splendid palm-lined boulevard stretching 3 miles (5 km.) along the Baie des Anges. It was named for the

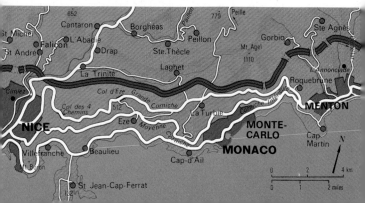

town's English colony, who paid for the street. Along the way, you'll pass landmarks like the legendary Negresco, an imposing hotel with a Rococo façade.

Take time to wander around the **Vieille Ville** (Old Town), stopping by Cours Saleya for the afternoon flower market or the morning fruit and vegetable market, just as picturesque but more aromatic. The open square is surrounded by cheery pizza stalls, cafés and bistros. On the quayside, the little pastel houses where fishermen used to live are mostly restaurants and art galleries now. Showcase of the old town is **Palais Lascaris**, a 17th-century townhouse with a beautifully preserved pharmacy. Guided tours of historical Nice begin here.

Among the other museums in Nice worth mentioning are **Musée Masséna** (35 Promenade des Anglais), known for its collection of Empire furniture and Niçois primitives; **Musée des Beaux-Arts Jules Chéret** (33 Avenue des Baumettes), an outstanding group of Impressionist paintings; **Musée de Terra Amata** (25 Boulevard Carnot), a view of prehistoric man in and around Nice; at **Musée Chagall** (Avenue du Docteur-Ménard), the painter's Old Testament themes are displayed in a modern setting; and **Musée Matisse** (164 Avenue des Arènes) has sketches, paintings and collages of the master, right next door to the Roman baths.

Corniches

Between Nice and Menton the mountains drop to the sea in a changing panorama of spectacular scenery. Three roads wind through this magnificent landscape. Highest is the **Grande Corniche,** built by Napoleon along the Aurelian Way of the Romans; the **Moyenne Corniche** offers a contrast of rocky cliffs and the sea; while the **Corniche Inférieure**—which can be terribly crowded in summer—runs beside the sea.

Four miles (6 km.) east of Nice, **Villefranche** offers instant charm with its yellow, red and pink stucco or brick houses stacked against the hill, its plunging alleyways and the covered Rue Obscure snaking down to the sea. The quayside cafés are well placed for watching the pleasure boats that fill the port today.

The Duke of Savoy had the town's old citadel put up in 1560. Below it, you'll find the 14th-century **Chapelle St-Pierre,** long a fisherman's

chapel, decorated by writer-artist Jean Cocteau in 1956 with drawings of scenes from the life of St. Peter.

A short drive around the rocky, pine-green peninsula **St-Jean-Cap-Ferrat** will convince you that the rich like their privacy. You'll find lots of gates with hints of grandeur behind. The best views are from the upper levels of the **Ile-de-France Museum.** Built in 1912 by Madame Béatrice Ephrussi, née Rothschild, the pink

Italian-style villa contains the delirious assemblage of an insatiable art collector. Though you'll find work here from many periods, the high point of the museum is its collection of Sèvres porcelain, perhaps the world's largest. The gardens surrounding the museum are equally impressive.

The main thing to see in **Beaulieu** is the **Villa Kérylos,** a monument to the glory of Greece built at the turn of the century by scholar-musician-

flock here in all seasons. Amble around the narrow stone streets, lined with souvenir shops, and up to the public gardens filled with cacti.

Monaco

This fairy-tale princedom, an enclave rising from the rocks above the sea, is famed for its casino and wealth. The atmosphere is both big city and miniature operatic—but there are crowds in this paradise with a population density comparable to Hong Kong's and cars jamming thoroughfares all over the hills.

Don't get the idea that gambling is the only local attraction; a mere 5 per cent of the principality's revenue comes from the casino. Many other commercial and cultural activities take precedence—such as music, automobile rallies and flower shows.

All roads here lead to Monte Carlo's **Grand Casino** (and opera). Any resemblance to the Paris Opera is more than coincidental, since architect Charles Garnier designed the two. Inside, look for the delightful Salon Rose, where painted, unclad nymphs float about the ceiling smoking cigarillos. Next door stands the **Hôtel de Paris**, an equally opulent historical monument. The great chef

bibliophile Theodore Reinach. Reinach studied, planned and collected artefacts for years before commissioning an architect to design a Greek villa that would be perfect in every detail.

Highlight of the Moyenne Corniche is the medieval village of **Eze.** It hangs at a dizzying angle above the sea—majestic and deep blue from this perspective—commanding one of the most magnificent vistas on the coast. The town is closed to traffic but not tourists, who

NICE

Escoffier created memorable dishes here for a celebrated clientele.

Up the hill on Monaco Rock, you'll find the **Palais du Prince.** The Grimaldis still live here, but you can visit the palace from June to the middle of October. Any time of year, at 11.55 a.m., you can watch the changing of the guard outside the palace. The five-minute show, complete with fife and drums, is entertaining enough.

Also up on the rock is the **Musée Océanographique,** founded by Prince Albert I in 1910 and now directed by Commandant Jacques-Yves Cousteau, the underwater explorer. The sealife of the Mediterranean is on display in the basement aquarium.

From Nice to Cannes

The first landmark you'll see in **Antibes** is the imposing square fortress, **Fort Carré.** This was the French stronghold against the Dukes of Savoy who controlled Nice, on the other side of the bay. Today, growing flowers is the main local industry, and the hills around Antibes are dotted with glassy greenhouses.

Take a tour around the ramparts, reconstructed by Vauban in the 17th century. The Château Grimaldi, now the **Musée**

Picasso, is a white stone castle with a Romanesque tower built by the lords of Antibes. Apart from classical relics, the museum also has a marvellous Picasso collection, a gift from the artist, who spent six fruitful months working at the castle in 1946.

On the western side of Cap d'Antibes lies the sandy crescent-shaped bay of **Juan-les-Pins.** The resort enjoyed its heyday in the twenties and thirties after American tycoon Frank Jay Gould built a big hotel and casino in the pinewood setting. Sleepy in winter, the town becomes rather wild and racy in summer.

The artisan towns of Vallauris and Biot are only a few minutes' drive from Antibes. **Vallauris** is inevitably associated with Picasso, who worked here after the war, giving new impetus to a dying ceramics and pottery industry. He presented the town with the bronze statue, *Man with a Sheep* (Place Paul-Isnard), and decorated the Romanesque chapel, now the National Picasso Museum, with murals.

Biot, perched on a cone-shaped hill, bulges with artisans' shops. In the local glassworks, you'll see craftsmen fashioning the heavy, tinted glass that Biot is famous for. The light and airy **Fernand Léger Museum** traces the artist's development over his 50-year career.

Going away from the coast, you enter another world. Cypress trees, silvery olive groves and bright mimosa cover the hills of the back country and fields or thyme, rosemary and sage are interspersed with the *garrigues,* an almost impenetrable scrub growth. And tucked away here and there, you'll see half-deserted fortified villages, many dating from Saracen times.

St-Paul-de-Vence is a venerable bastion from a later period, built by François I in the 16th century. Enclosed by spade-shaped walls, it looks out over terraces of vineyards and bougainvillea—and lots of recently constructed villas. Enter the walled city and make a tour of the narrow pedestrian streets, stopping off at the Grande Fontaine and the Gothic church. You'll usually find a lively game of *pétanque* or bowls under the big plane trees of the Place de Gaulle.

Just outside of town, the **Fondation Maeght** displays masterpieces of our time. Full of visual surprises, this brick, steel and glass structure is an ideal place for exhibiting mod-

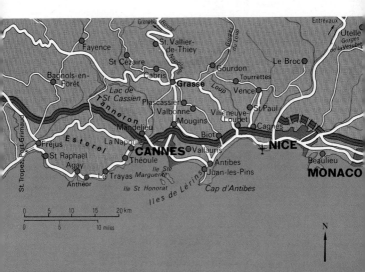

ern art, from the black stabile by Calder at the entry to the bronze figures by Giacometti, stained-glass windows by Braque and paintings and lithographs by many of the great names of 20th-century art.

The **Loup Valley** is a region of singular beauty, of wild and craggy scenery, rugged hill towns, rushing cascades, plummeting gorges and breathtaking views. A tour of the area can be combined with a visit to St-Paul-de-Vence.

Grasse, the world's perfume capital, won't bowl you over with heady scents, but it's hard to miss the enormous signs inviting you to visit the factories. The local industry got its start in the 16th century when the Medici family launched the fashion of scented gloves (Grasse also made gloves). The high price of perfume makes more sense when you discover that it takes a ton of petals to produce 2.2 pounds (1 kilo) of essence.

The most charming spot in town is the friendly, crowded Place aux Aires, with its fountains, arcades and sculptured 18th-century façades. The morning market is a palette of brilliant colours under the shade of locust and plane trees. Local son Fragonard is honoured in the **Musée Fragonard,** an elegant 18th-century townhouse with some nice period furniture and various mementoes and selected works of the artist.

Cannes

Twice a year—during the May film festival and the January record fair—Cannes loses its habitual nonchalance. The rest of the time, the city devotes itself to its touristic vocation as a sleek, cosmopolitan resort in a beautiful setting, with the liveliest pleasure port on the Riviera.

Like Nice's Promenade des Anglais, the **Croisette** is a magnificent showcase of gleaming hotels lining a flowered, seaside boulevard. The golden sand on the beach, by the way, has been imported from a neighbouring town. A few blocks behind the Croisette, you'll find Rue d'Antibes, one of the coast's most glamorous shopping streets.

The old section of town is perched on the hill of **Le Suquet** overlooking Cannes. At night they put dramatic spotlights on the ancient watchtower here, built by the monks of Lérins. The view from Le Suquet is superb. But for an even more spectacular panorama, go to the **observatory** at Super-Cannes.

Just off the coast of Cannes are the two small islands of Lérins. **St-Honorat** with a battlemented 11th-century "château", was the home of the powerful monks who ruled

NICE

Cannes from the 10th to the 18th century. On **Ste-Marguerite,** the main attraction is a dank, smelly dungeon which held a masked prisoner from 1687 to 1698. Some claim the mysterious prisoner was the illegitimate brother of Louis XIV.

West of Cannes

Between Cannes and St-Raphaël lies a mass of porphyry rocks worn down by streams. Though never much

higher than 2,000 feet (610 m.), the landscape of the Esterel appears abrupt and impressive. In the spring, the scrub-herb hills are golden with mimosa.

Focus for the Esterel holiday area, booming **Saint-Raphaël** is an appealing resort built around a port for pleasure boats. In Roman times, it was popular with the people of Fréjus. The modern palmlined seafront boasts a pyramid commemorating Napoleon's triumphant debarkation after his Egyptian campaign of 1799.

St-Tropez barely manages to keep up with its glamorous reputation: its picture-postcard port and charming back streets, its celebrity escapades, fashionable people, "in" spots, chic boutiques and casual nudity on outlying beaches.

But the town weathers its own snobbery while cultivating its legends. It was named after Torpes, a Roman Christian martyred in Pisa in A.D. 68. His headless body, cast adrift in a small boat with a dog and a cock, washed ashore here. Now every May, the town honours St. Tropez with a splendid costumed fête complete with cannons—la Bravade. A second Bravade in June commemorates the day in 1637 when the gallant little fishing village routed a fleet of invading Spanish ships.

Restless crowds converge on St-Tropez's pretty port with its shiny yachts, pastel houses, quayside cafés and the **Musée de l'Annonciade**, a former chapel housing a fine collection of Impressionist and post-Impressionist paintings. Nearby, the plane-tree-shaded Place des Lices abounds with local colour. A food market takes over several mornings a week, but passionate games of *pétanque* (bowls) are the centre of interest in late afternoon. The fine beaches of St-Tropez lie outside of town along a vast sandy crescent that skirts green vineyards.

About 3½ miles (6 kilometres) downhill on the bay of St-Tropez, **Port Grimaud** is a modern French version of Venice. Inaugurated in 1964, this artificial fishing village with canals built on marshland does, surprisingly, have a lot of charm. Besides, the yachts are real.

Eating Out

Marvellous aromas of fresh rosemary or thyme, fragrant olive oil, charcoal-broiled meat and fish, plus the all-pervading bouquet of garlic—these are the keynotes of the cooking of Provence. When you see a dish on the menu prepared *à la provençale,* you can be fairly sure that garlic, tomatoes and lots of herbs went into it.

Soup and Salad

Start off with some *pistou,* a thick vegetable soup perfumed with basil and garlic, or lusty *soupe de poisson,* fish soup served with toast rounds and peppery *rouille,* the tomato-garlic mayonnaise.

Speaking of garlic, you might want to try a bracing *aïoli,* a heavily perfumed mayonnaise in which are dipped boiled cod, potatoes, green beans and so on. The famous *salade niçoise* makes a delightful lunch: tomato, anchovies, green peppers, olives, with the possible addition of tuna, green beans and hard-boiled eggs. Or for a light starter, there's *crudités,* a raw vegetable salad.

Main Dishes

The aristocrat of fish on the Riviera is *loup de mer* (sea bass), often prepared with fennel.

Daurade (sea bream) and *rouget* (red mulllet) are popular local offerings. But *bouillabaisse,* fish stew, is surrounded by enough mystique to fill a Proustian novel. Every chef has his own idea and ingredients vary according to locality. But *bouillabaisse* must contain a Mediterranean fish called *rascasse,* and saffron.

Steaks *(entrecôte, faux filet)* and lamb chops *(côtes d'agneau)* are awfully good grilled with fresh herbs. Chicken might be served *rôti* (spit-roasted) or as *poulet niçoise,* a local fricassee with tomatoes and black olives. Rabbit *(lapin)* is often prepared *à la moutarde* (mustard sauce) or *provençal.*

If you have the chance, order some *ratatouille* with your main course. Tomatoes, onion, aubergine (eggplant), courgette (zucchini) and green peppers are simmered together till they almost meld.

For a sweet finish, spoil yourself with a piece of *tarte tropézienne,* a rich yellow cake filled with custard and dusted with powdered sugar. Or enjoy some of the delicious fruit of the region—the sweet melons of Cavaillon, juicy strawberries, luscious peaches, ripe figs or grapes. You won't go wrong if you pick whatever is in season.

Aperitifs and Wine

The number one drink here-abouts is Pastis, an anise-flavoured liquid that turns milky when you add water.

If you're ordering local wine, you may find you're only offered a choice of colour: *rouge, blanc* or *rosé*. When in doubt, pick the rosé here (though much-maligned by wine snobs). A well-chilled bottle of this light, fruity Provençal wine seems to go with just about anything.

Shopping

The coast is a dazzling bazaar. You can find the best of every-thing French—jewellery, cou-turier clothing, silver, crystal and even furs. In Nice (Rue de France), Cannes (Rue d'An-tibes) and Monte Carlo (around the casino), the shopping is on a par with Paris.

Good buys in the mini-luxury category include silk scarves, perfumes, liqueurs and even scented soaps. Sportswear

is highly recommended, especially for women. You'll see the latest fashions displayed in the many little boutiques. In St-Tropez, you can hardly get through the yards of tee-shirts along the quayside without making a purchase.

Arts and Crafts
You'll find lots of attractive pottery here, particularly around Vallauris, St-Paul-de-Vence and Biot. Anything from simple ashtrays or tiles to entire dinner sets—plain, flowery, contempory, abstract, even some original Picasso designs.

Shop windows are filled with semi-precious stones, often set in jewellery. And in the little towns behind Cannes, you'll see many articles made of olive-wood—tables, stools, salad sets and bracelets.

The famous, attractively flowered Provençal cotton is ubiquitous; you can purchase it in bolts or made up into cushions, bags, skirts or quilts.

Practical Information

Banks: Most open from 8.30 or 9 a.m. to noon and from 1.30 to 5 p.m. Some currency-exchange offices do business evenings and Saturdays.

Clothing: Anything goes on the Riviera but each town has its code. Complete nudity is tolerated on some beaches (notably around St-Tropez); topless sunbathing is permitted almost everywhere.

At night, *tenue correcte* is required in casinos—that is, a jacket and tie for men, dresses or smart trousers for women.

Post offices: Main branches of the *Postes et Télécommunications (P & T)* in cities open from 8 to 5 Monday to Friday; till noon on Saturday. You can also make long-distance calls and send telegrams at the P & T.

Restaurants: Lunch begins about 1, dinner at 8—though the fashionable crowd doesn't appear till 9.30 or so.

Shopping: Most shops open from 8 or 9 a.m. till noon and from 2 to 7 p.m. Tuesday to Saturday. In summer, the shops may close longer in the middle of the day and stay open later in the evening.

OSLO

Norway

Introduction

Geologists come to admire Oslo's foundations, for these ancient rocks are some of the oldest on the face of the earth, dating back hundreds of millions of years. But as European capitals go, Oslo's in fact quite a late-bloomer. Though it was founded more than 900 years ago, at the turn of the 19th century, it had a population even smaller than Norway's second city, Bergen.

Today slightly less than half a million people live in the capital, at the northernmost extremity of the 60-mile-(100-km.-)long Oslo Fjord. Ironically, it's still one of the world's largest cities, with an area of 175 square miles (453 sq.km.), consisting mainly of forests and farmland. Skiers and hikers don't have to leave town to practice, and botanists can study over 1,000 species of plants within the city limits —quite a feat for a capital!

Renaissance fortress of Akershus *dominates Oslo's dynamic harbour.*

A Brief History

9th–11th centuries	Around A.D. 800, Norsemen start exploring, pillaging and exploiting lands overseas. The Norwegian Vikings form settlements in Scotland, Ireland, England, Normandy and later in Iceland and Greenland. In the 10th century Harald Fairhair transforms Norway from an agglomeration of feudal states into a united kingdom. After fighting between Christians and pagans, that destroys Norwegian cohesion, Olav II reunifies the kingdom early in the 11th century. Oslo is founded in 1050 under the rule of Harald Hardråde ("Hard Ruler") on the left bank of the Aker River, but Nidaros (today's Trondheim) continues as the country's capital.
12th–13th centuries	The 12th century is marked by struggles between rival claimants to the throne. Peace and prosperity come with the rule of Håkon IV, crowned in 1217. King Håkon V chooses the town of Oslo as his residence at the end of the 13th century.
14th–16th centuries	Norway grows increasingly dependent on the German merchants of the Hanseatic League, who enjoy great influence and soon control the country's foreign commerce. In 1397, the Union of Kalmar allies Norway, Sweden and Denmark. When Sweden breaks away in 1520, Norway is considered too weak to exist independently, and, in 1536, is incorporated into the Kingdom of Denmark. The same year, the Reformation reaches Denmark, and spreads to the Danish province of Norway. In the late 16th century, the Hanseatic League loses its influence in Norwegian affairs. In 1589, James VI of Scotland (later James I of England) is married to Princess Anne of Denmark in Oslo.
17th–19th centuries	The Danish King Christian IV rebuilds Oslo after the destruction of the town by fire in 1624, moving it to the right bank of the Aker River and naming it Christiania —after himself. The town expands rapidly, overtaking Trondheim and Bergen on account of its timber-trade industry and ship-chandling. After siding with Napoleon, the Danes are forced to cede Norway to the Swedish crown on the defeat of France. At the end of the 19th century, Christiania (Oslo) becomes the centre of a

Norwegian cultural renaissance led by Bjørnstjerne Bjørnson and Henrik Ibsen, and a wave of nationalism sweeps the country.

20th century Norway's parliament votes to end the union with Sweden in 1905; Prince Carl of Denmark, taking the name of Haakon VII, is chosen king, and Christiania (Oslo) becomes capital of the newly independent Kingdom of Norway. In 1925, the capital reverts to its original name of Oslo. In 1940, Norway is invaded by the Germans; the country is liberated by the Allies in 1945, and King Haakon returns to Oslo after five years of exile in London. The post-war period is marked by industrial development and increasing prosperity partly due to North Sea oil.

Sightseeing

For a perspective of the town and a taste of its history, there's no better place to start a tour of Oslo than at Akershus Castle, overlooking the harbour.

Even the names of parts of **Akershus Slott og Festning** conjure up days of derring-do, chivalry and strife: The Daredevil's Tower, the Dark Passage, and Knut's Tower (named after the leader of an unsuccessful revolt, whose body was displayed there as a warning to others). The medieval castle was expanded, renovated and further fortified by Christian IV, who exerted paramount influence over 17th-century Oslo.

Akershus Castle revels in historical and architectural details—secret passages, dungeons, royal halls and the modern royal crypt. The castle is still used for state occasions; the recently restored Olav Hall comfortably seats more than 100 guests at banquets.

Akershus Castle has its museum, **Forsvarsmuseet** (the Armed Forces Museum), that traces the history of the Norwegian military from swords and armour to the jet age.

From the battlements of Akershus, the **view** over the harbour and the centre of Oslo takes in a lively scene of ships' cranes, ferryboats, islands and the unmistakable form of the 20th-century **Rådhuset** (the Town Hall). This controversial building has its friends and enemies. For better or worse, the heavy structure is covered with 1½ million hand-made bricks. All manner of decoration—sculpture, frieze and abstract embellishment—is mobilized to relieve the ponderous effect. Inside, many of the walls are covered with modern narrative murals.

Inland, a few streets behind the Town Hall, the urban scene opens out to reveal public gardens, a spacious strolling zone in the very heart of Oslo. At the western extreme, along with a bandstand and an outdoor café, stands the National Theatre. The statues outside depict two of the country's literary luminaries—Henrik Ibsen and his contemporary, Nobel prizewinner Bjørnstjerne Bjørnson. This area is called **Studenterlunden** (the Students' Grove) because the 19th-century buildings of Oslo University are just across the street, **Karl Johans gate.** This is the main street of the capital and a favourite place for promenades and for shopping. The eastern part of it, beyond the sober-looking Parliament building, becomes a pedestrian precinct (but mind the trams!). There you'll find the Domkirke (Cathedral), consecrated in 1697 and completely restored recently.

At the other end of Karl Johan's Street stands **Slottet,** the Royal Palace on the hill. Without an invitation you can't tour Slottet, but the fine park surrounding the palace is open to the public. The sentries, royal guardsmen with black horsetail plumes on their hats, are always a good subject for a photograph.

The Vigeland Sculpture Park

Vigelandsanlegget, in Frogner Park in west Oslo, is the biggest one-man show you've ever seen—almost all the works ever produced by Gustav Vigeland (1869–1943), a compulsively busy sculptor. In 1921, he gave all his statues to the city in exchange for a studio in which to produce them, some assistants, living quarters and a small stipend.

The studio, outside the park to the south, is now **Vigelandmuseet,** a museum crammed with thousands of his sculptures, drawings and plans.

Bygdøy Museums

Most of Oslo's museums (over 30 of them) deal with Norwegian themes—historical, artistic and maritime. Five of the best are grouped within walking distance of one another on

HOLMENKOLLEN, SKIMUSEET, TRYVANNSTÅRNET

NRK

gate / gata = street
by / kaia = quay
kirke / kirken = church
plass / plassen = square
torg (torv) / torget = market place
vei / veien = road
museum / museet = museum

🚇 tunnelbanestasjon
Underground station

Sørkedalsveien

Slemdalsveien

Essendrops

Middelthuns gt.

Vigelands-
anlegget

Frogner-
parken

Amaldus
Nielsen
plass

Professor
Dahls gate

Kirkeveien

Halvdan Svartes gate

Vigelands-
museet

Camilla Colletts vei

Drammensveien

Slotts-
parken

Bygdøy allé

Colbjørn-
sens gate

Dronningens
Slottet

Blindernveien

Drammensveien

Dronning Blancas vei

Frognerstranda

Drammensveien

Munkedams-
veien

Sjølyst

Frognerkilen

Filipstadveien

Munkedamsveien

FORNEBU LUFTHAVN
HENIE-ONSTAD KUNSTSENTER

Sjølystveien

Bygdøyveien

B Y G D Ø Y

Museumsveien

Frederik

Oslofjord

Norsk
Folkemuseum

Langviksbukten

Vikingskipshuset

Kon-Tiki-
museet

Frammuseet

Norsk
Sjøfartsmuseum

Kavringen

Fredriksborgveien

Bygdøynes

| 0 | 300 | 600 | 900 m |
| 0 | 300 | 600 | 900 yards |

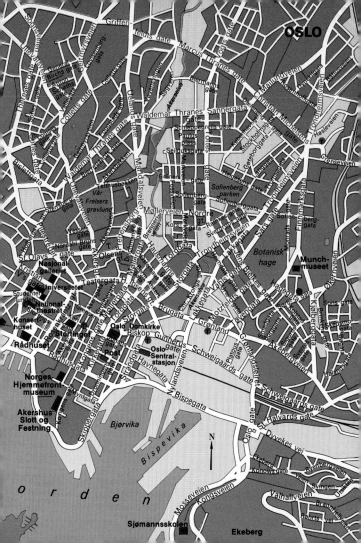

Bygdøy peninsula south-west of central Oslo, easily reached by bus or even better by ferry-boat from the harbour in front of the Town Hall.

Oslo museums record centuries of seafaring, Vikings to Ra II (above).

Vikingskipshuset (the Viking Ship Museum). Built like a severe-looking modern church, this museum enshrines three authentic Viking ships. Bigger and more beautiful than any other relics of the Norsemen, these wooden vessels survived about 1,000 years because they had been forgotten for centuries under airtight layers of stone, clay and dirt. The ships had served as tombs for royal or aristocratic personages. Some of the rich-

est finds are on view in the fourth wing of the museum—haunting sculptures, a wonderfully embellished cart and sleighs.

The low-lying **Oseberg Ship,** built in the early 9th century, was unearthed in 1904. With a length of 70 feet (21 m.), it was designed to be a ceremonial barge or pleasure boat. The precision of the ship-builders, who had to work with Iron Age tools, and the artistry of the wood-carvers are most remarkable.

An even bigger ship, the *Gokstad*, looks less decorative and more seaworthy. And indeed a careful replica was built and sailed across the North Atlantic in 1893 to attend the Chicago World's Fair.

The third ship was excavated in 1867. It was badly damaged by decay. In this case, instead of trying to restore the ship, experts decided to put it on display in its incomplete state to reveal inner details of the construction.

Norsk Folkemuseum (Norwegian Folk Museum), neighbouring the Viking Ship Museum, is a vast permanent exhibition showing the way town and country people lived over recent centuries. More than 150 old buildings have been removed from various parts of the country and reassembled in this attractive park. Here you can see one of the oldest surviving wooden houses in Norway, from the 13th century, with a runic inscription above the door. And here a **stave church** from the same era was restored. Only a couple of dozen of these tall wooden churches still stand in Norway, the survivors of fire, decay or sheer indifference. Several large buildings complement the outdoor exhibit, housing collections on such themes as urban life, peasant and religious art.

The three remaining museums of Bygdøy, all on nautical themes, are clustered on the waterfront, perhaps a 15-minute walk from the Folk Museum.

Kon-Tiki-museet commemorates the voyages of the daring Norwegian ethnographer Thor Heyerdahl. In 1947 he built the primitive balsa raft *Kon-Tiki* in Peru and sailed it to Polynesia, to show that the ancient South Americans could have contributed to the culture of Pacific peoples. *Kon-Tiki* is on display, along with the reed ship *Ra II*, used for Heyerdahl's 1970 expedition across the Atlantic.

Fram-museet. In 1935 the veteran polar exploration ship *Fram* was hauled ashore at Bygdøy and a museum was built around it. In the Fram Museum you can walk around, over and all through this historic 800-tonner, the flagship of two great Norwegian explorers, Fridtjof Nansen and Roald Amundsen.

Norsk Sjøfartsmuseum (Norwegian Maritime Museum), next to the Fram Museum, concentrates on the less glamorous side of the sea—the workaday vessels which have made Norway one of the world's most important fishing and shipping powers. There are ship models galore, graphic details of whaling expeditions, and a model giving Oslo's harbour traffic.

Other Museums

Just behind the University buildings in the centre of town lies **Nasjonalgalleriet** (the National Gallery), containing a cross-section of European art. Predictably the greatest emphasis falls on Norwegian artists. Look for the landscapes of Johan Christian Dahl, the rural landscapes of Erik Werenskiold, the social comment of Harriet Backer and Christian Krohg. Norway's greatest painter, Edvard Munch, is well represented.

Munch-museet (the Munch Museum), in an area of parks in eastern Oslo, is a high-spot for art-lovers. This engaging modern institution contains the life work which Edvard Munch bequeathed to the city. It was opened in 1963 on the centenary of his birth. The reserve of paintings, etchings and lithographs is many times larger than the walls can hold, so exhibitions are periodically changed. But you'll always be able to see a cross-section of the work of this powerful artist on display.

Other Sights

Holmenkollen Ski-Jump. This frighteningly high ski-jump in the hills of western Oslo has a view and history of its own, plus a museum on the premises. For a century Norwegian daredevils have been flying through the air at Holmenkollen, last rebuilt and improved in 1980. For a few kroner you can use the self-service lift to the top of the ski-jump. If you're queasy about heights this may not be for you. The skier's-eye view down the runway into the great beyond might make a competitor prefer to walk back down. Mere sightseers, who can look forward to a safe ride back to earth without shame, will consider the panorama of Oslo and its fjord a good investment in time and money.

Skimuseet, snuggling beneath the jump, displays some unusual evidence to prove that skiing was invented in Norway: a 2,000-year-old ski found at Alvdal, north of Oslo. Other historical exhibits show the rather hit-or-miss evolution of skis, boots, bindings and poles over the years. You can see a 19th-century Lapp sleigh (it was reindeer-propelled), a sled from the Amundsen South Pole expedition and skis used by the Norwegian royal family, who are still avid skiers.

The ski-jump stands within walking distance of the Holmenkollen station on the suburban railway which starts at the underground station just at the back of the National Theatre.

Tryvannstårnet (the Tryvann Tower), just above the Voksenkollen station on the same railway line, has an observation platform, reached by express lift, which boosts your point of view to an altitude of more than 1,900 feet (588 m.) above sea level. The view extends over an area estimated at aboud 11,500 square miles (30,000 sq.km.)— as far as the Swedish border.

Whoops! Daredevil skiers fly through the air at 60 miles (90 km.) per hour from famous Holmenkollen Ski-Jump, scene of popular annual festival.

Eating Out

Some of the best food in Norway comes fresh from the sea, which is only natural in one of the world's leading fishing nations. You can dine on lobster or salmon or pick up a picnic lunch of shrimp and herring.

Norwegian Specialities

The most "national" food of all is what Norwegians call *spekemat* (cured food). Be sure to try *spekeskinke* (cured ham), *spekepølse* (cured sausage), *fenalår* (cured leg of mutton) and *fårepølse* (cured mutton sausage), which all have a long tradition in the country.

Any land with winters like Norway's is bound to develop a hearty repertoire of **soups.** Vegetables feature in some of the favourites: *betasuppe* (a thick meat-and-vegetable soup), almost a dish in itself, and the super-filling *gul ertesuppe* (yellow pea soup) laced with ham. *Fiskesuppe* (fish soup) is a rich brew made richer by the addition of egg yolks and cream.

Snacks

Smørbrød means bread and butter, which is quite an understatement when you consider Scandinavia's reputation for elaborate open sandwiches. Almost anything may turn up on one of these appetizing *smørbrød:* roast beef, ham, shrimp, fried cod roe with bacon, hamburger steak with fried onion, sliced egg with anchovies, and mayonnaise and herring salads.

Cheese is also eaten on open sandwiches, rarely as a separate dish. Be sure to try a *smørbrød* with one of the brown cheeses of goat's milk *(geitost)* or mixed goat's and cow's milk *(gudbrandsdalsost* and *mysost).*

Fish

Among the tastiest, but expensive, fish are salmon *(laks),* trout *(ørret)* and sea trout *(sjøørret).* Boiled cod, often served with its liver *(kokt torsk med lever),* is a great delicacy, as is halibut *(hellefisk). Hvalbiff* (whale steak) is tender and steak-like, with no hint of the sea in its flavour. An exquisite treat as a starter is *gravlaks* (cured salmon).

Meat

Fårikål (lamb or mutton and cabbage stew) is a national tradition. The stew, together with black pepper and a little flour, is cooked in a big pot.

Kjøttkaker (meatballs) are

as popular as they are filling. And *lapskaus* is a tasty stew of chopped meat, potatoes, onion and other vegetables.

Game and fowl are important variations on the menu, as mundane as roast chicken, as unfamiliar as *rugde* (woodcock), *elg* (elk), *rype* (ptarmigan) and *reinsdyrstek* (roast reindeer thinly sliced).

Koldtbord

The Swedish name *smørgåsbord,* is better known than its Norwegian equivalent, *koldtbord* (literally, cold table). Some restaurants and mountain hotels specialize in this bountiful self-service banquet.

Desserts

These often rely on whipped cream and cakes. Examples might be *tilslørte bondepiker* (literally, "veiled farmgirls" —layers of stewed apples, biscuit crumbs, sugar and whipped cream) and *bløtkake* ("soft cake"—a sponge cake filled with fruit and whipped cream).

Norwegians go berserk over berries. The supreme delicacy of this realm is *multer med krem* (Arctic cloudberries with cream).

Drinks

Norwegians often drink plain tap water with their meals.

Alcoholic beverages of any sort are subject to stringent regulations. Spirits are served at most major hotels and restaurants but only from 3 to 11 p.m. or midnight and never on Sunday or holy days; the prices are discouraging, too. Beer and wine are more widely available, Sundays included (from 12 noon). Local beers meet international standards. *Pils* is the generic term for lager, *export* is stronger.

Akevitt (aquavit), the local firewater, is derived from potatoes or barley. Served ice-cold in tiny glasses with meals, it is usually washed down with beer. Delicious, but not to be tippled flippantly.

Skål!

Artisans at work: Lapp women creating typical enchanting jewellery.

Shopping

The Vat, or sales tax, (called "moms") of about 15 per cent will be refunded in cash within four weeks of purchase at the point of departure to non-Scandinavian visitors who buy in shops displaying the red-white-and-blue "Tax free for Tourists" sticker (present your passport). You simply show the Tax-free Shopping Cheque provided by the shop at the departure point.

Best Buys
Here are some of the items to look for:

Cardigans, mittens, scarves and ski-caps are hand-knitted or machine-made in typical Norwegian patterns.

Carvings, painted wooden figurines of Norwegian characters—fishermen, milkmaids, sailors, skiers and Lapps (with reindeer to accompany them).

Cheese slicers, those handy Norwegian implements for producing paper-thin shavings of cheese.

Furs: Norwegian fox and mink pelts are highly esteemed.

Glassware and crystal: glasses, flasks, vases, plates and figurines.

Hunting knives and fishermen's knives in handy scabbards.

Miniature Viking ships of wood, pewter, enamel or silver, with or without sails.

Pewter mugs, glasses, trays and drinking horns, usually with Viking or other traditional motifs in relief.

Reindeer skins, perhaps for use as rugs.

"Rose-painted" wooden articles, such as small boxes, egg cups, plates and miniature bellows.

Sealskin slippers for après-ski or fireside comfort at home. And cuddly little dolls in the form of seals, covered with real seal fur.

Sporting goods: look for the latest designs in skiing, fishing, boating and camping equipment.

Trolls: small enough to pocket or tall as a table, whimsical likenesses of these characters, looking half bear, half leprechaun, are ubiquitous.

Woven goods: tapestry weaving has been an art in Norway since Viking times. There is a fine selection of woven runners, cloths and wall hangings to choose from. Be sure to look, too, at *ryer* rugs, tablecloths and napkins.

Practical Information

Banks and currency exchange: Open from 8.15 a.m. to 3.30 p.m., Monday to Wednesday and on Fridays, until 5 or 6 p.m. on Thursdays. Between June 1 and August 31, however, they close at 3 p.m. (5 or 5.30 p.m. on Thursdays). Oslo Central Railway Station: 8 a.m.–9 p.m., Monday–Friday, till 7 p.m. on Saturdays and until 12 noon on Sundays.

Credit cards and traveller's cheques: Major international credit cards will be honoured in most large restaurants, department stores and tourist shops. Traveller's cheques are easy to cash almost everywhere provided you have proper identification.

Currency: *Krone* (kr) = 100 *øre*. Coins: 10 and 50 øre; kr 1, 5 and 10. Banknotes: kr 50, 100, 500 and 1,000.

Post offices: Oslo's General Post Office, at Dronningens gt. 15 (Oslo 1), is open Monday–Friday from 8 a.m. to 8 p.m., until 3 p.m. on Saturdays. Other post offices open 8 a.m. to 5.30 p.m., Monday–Friday (July 1–mid-August: 4.30 p.m.), and 9 a.m. to 1 p.m. on Saturdays.

Restaurants: Lunch 11 a.m. to 1 p.m., dinner from 7 p.m. A service charge is always included in the bill, so tipping is optional, but good service usually rates an extra 5 to 10% or more.

Shops: Generally open 9 a.m. to 4 or 5 p.m. Monday to Friday, 9 a.m. to 1 or 2 p.m. on Saturdays and days preceding public holidays. Centrally situated kiosks selling newspapers, tobacco, fruit, sweets, and so on, may stay open to as late as 11 p.m.

PARIS

France

Introduction

The city and the people of Paris share a boundless self-confidence that exudes from every stone in its monuments and museums, bistros and boutiques, from every chestnut tree along its avenues and boulevards, from every little street-urchin, fashion model, butcher and baker, from every irate motorist and every charming maître d'hôtel.

Some see it spilling over into arrogance—in the bombast of monumental architecture or in the overbearing attitudes of know-it-all street-philosophers. But looking around, you must admit they have something to be arrogant about. Stand on the Pont-Royal bridge in the late afternoon and gaze down the Seine to the glass-panelled Grand Palais, bathed in the pink-and-blue glow of the river's never tranquil waters. Already you sense that the light in this City of Light is of a very special kind.

The Right Bank conjures up an image of bourgeois respectability. Historically the stronghold of merchants and royalty, it remains the home of commerce and government.

The Left Bank on the other hand has always had a bohemian and intellectual image, dating back to the founding of the university and the monasteries. Today the Sorbonne, the Académie Française, the publishing houses and myriad bookshops continue to exert an intellectual magnetism.

A constant flow and interchange of citizenry from one bank to the other takes place over the 32 bridges of the Seine, a very accessible river well integrated into the town's life.

Paris is a city of people constantly on the move, at all hours of day and night—inevitable, really, since France's capital is one of the most densely populated urban centres in the world.

Paris has the astounding treasures of the Louvre and the ambitious new Beaubourg cultural centre. But it also offers those tiny storefronts on the Rue Jacob for collections of old artistic playing cards and Napoleonic tin soldiers. You can spend a small fortune on the most fabulous evening dress or buy the most stylish tee-shirt—for a thousand times less.

The real bargain is the magic of that light, movement and noise around the Paris streets. That costs just a little shoe-leather.

A Brief History

Early times	Celtic fishermen called Parisii set up home on today's Ile de la Cité. The river protects them against invaders until Romans conquer the town in 52 B.C. The town, called Lutetia, expands to the Left Bank. St. Denis brings Christianity to Paris.
10th–13th centuries	Hugues Capet makes Paris the economic and political centre of France. Louis IX (1226–70) develops the spiritual and intellectual life of Paris, building many colleges, including the Sorbonne.
14th–17th centuries	Charles V, aware of Parisian militancy, builds the Bastille fortress. In 1407 the Duke of Burgundy has the Duke of Orleans murdered—an act which leads to 12 years of strife between the Burgundians and the Armagnacs. The carnage ends with the capture of Paris by the English in 1420. Joan of Arc fails to liberate the town ten years later. King Henry VI of England is crowned King of France. A plague in 1466 fells thousands of Parisians. The religious wars wreak havoc in Paris, starting in 1572 with the Massacre of St. Bartholomew and culminating in the siege of the city by Henri of Navarre in 1589.
	Paris becomes fashionable under Louis XIII. The Royal Printing Press, the Académie Française and other institutions are founded. Louis XIV, the Sun King, moves the court to Versailles.
18th–19th centuries	The Revolution of 1789, largely a revolt by the people against poor living conditions and unfair taxes, destroys many Parisian landmarks and reduces the size of aristocratic families. The city develops under Napoleon. Bourgeois intellectuals, denied the right to publish their newspapers, revolt in 1830. Napoleon III, alarmed by previous uprisings, flattens the most densely populated working-class areas. The Franco-Prussian War cripples Paris in 1870 and leads to the Third Republic. Paris becomes a magnet for writers and artists.
20th century	The Germans occupy Paris during World War II. The Latin Quarter becomes a battleground between students and de Gaulle's Fifth Republic in May 1968. Paris remains a cultural centre as seen by the construction of Beaubourg to encourage art revival.

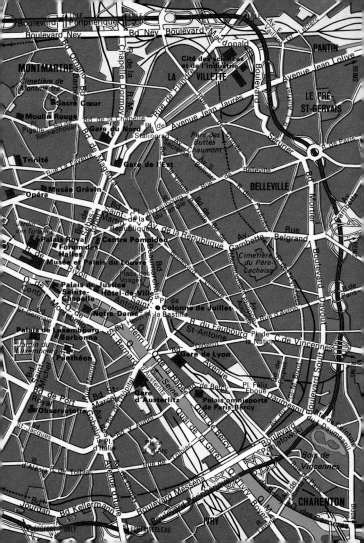

Sightseeing

The Seine is by far the best place to begin to take the measure of Paris. Its mixture of grandeur and intimacy is the very essence of the city.

For that all-important first impression, a **guided boat-trip** on the Seine is unbeatable. You can also take delightful strolls right down by the river between the Pont Sully at the eastern end of the Ile Saint-Louis and the Pont de la Concorde and around the two river-islands.

Right Bank
(Rive Droite)
Any tour of the Right Bank should begin at the **Place de l'Etoile** (officially, Place Charles-de-Gaulle), preferably on top of the **Arc de Triomphe.** One reason for climbing up Napoleon's gigantic triumphal arch (164 feet high, 148 feet wide; 50 × 45 m.) is to get a good view of the 12-pointed star, formed by 12 avenues radiating from the arch in a tour-de-force of geometric planning.

The **Champs-Elysées,** despite extensive commercialization, still deserves the title of the world's most-celebrated avenue. It stretches in an absolutely straight line from the Arc de Triomphe to the Place de la Concorde.

The **Place de la Concorde** has had a hard time earning its name. More than 1,000 people were guillotined here during the Revolution. In 1934, bloody rioting against the government took place here. Ten years later it was the Germans' last hold in Paris.

Cross the Rue de Rivoli to the **Palais-Royal.** There are few pleasanter places to dip back into the history of Paris. Completed in 1639 for the Cardinal Richelieu, this serene arcaded palace with its garden of lime and beech trees and a pond where the young Louis XIV nearly drowned has always been a colourful centre of more or less respectable activity. In the days of Philippe d'Orléans, Regent of France during Louis XV's minority, the Palais-Royal was the scene of notorious orgies. To meet the family's extravagant debts, the ground-floor rooms were turned into boutiques—the last of which still sell old coins, medals, engravings and antiques—and cafés that attracted a fashionable society.

On July 13, 1789, Camille Desmoulins stood on a table at the Palais-Royal's Café de Foy and made the call to arms that set off the French Revolution the next day. At the other end of that era, Prussian General Blücher came to the Palais-Royal after Waterloo to squander 1,500,000 francs in one night at one of the many rambunctious gambling dens.

East of the Palais-Royal, the old food markets of Les Halles have been replaced by gardens, new apartment buildings and the **Forum des Halles,** a rather garish shopping centre.

It's hard to find a more elegant place to work in than the **Place Vendôme,** an airy gracious octagon designed to provide an imposing setting for a statue of Louis XIV. Only his financiers could afford the rents here and nearly 300 years later the situation has not changed much: there are 19 banks (as well as world-famous jewellers, the Ministry of Justice and the Ritz Hotel) encircling the column with which Napoleon replaced the Sun King.

A walk up the Rue de la Paix takes you past jewellers, goldsmiths and furriers to the **Opéra,** the massive epitome of the pretensions of Napoleon III's Second Empire. It takes honours as the world's largest theatre, though it seats only 2,000 people.

Many people are surprised to learn that the **Madeleine** is a church—and, in fact, it did not start out as one. Originally there *was* going to be a church here, and Louis XV even laid its first stone in 1764, but the Revolution halted construction. Then Napoleon decided to put up a huge temple-like structure, Greek on the outside and Roman on the inside. It was variously projected as a stock exchange, the Bank of France, a theatre or a state banquet hall. After Waterloo Louis XVIII reverted to the plan for a church, but with no transept. aisles or bell-tower, or even a cross on the roof.

Montmartre

Montmartre, known locally as "La Butte", has long been famous as the home of artists and bohemian crazies.

Number 13, Place Emile-Goudeau, was the site of the Bateau-Lavoir studio, an unprepossessing glass-roofed loft that burned down in 1970. Here—if in any one place—modern art was born: Picasso, Braque and Juan Gris developed Cubism, while Modigliani worked his mysteries and Apollinaire sang it all in the first surrealistic verses.

Properly respectful of the spirits of the past, make your way around the neighbourhood where the illustrious predecessors of these "upstarts" lived and worked—Renoir, Van Gogh, Gauguin, Utrillo—in the Rue Cortot, Rue de l'Abreuvoir, Rue Saint-Rustique (with the restaurant La Bonne Franquette where Van Gogh painted his famous *La Guinguette*).

At the other end of Rue Saint-Vincent you come around the back of the basilica of the **Sacré-Cœur.** This weird Romano-Byzantine church enjoys a dubious reputation in the city. For many its most attractive feature is the view from the dome, which can be visited, covering a radius of 30 miles (50 km.) on a clear day.

Marais

Built on land reclaimed from the swamps, as the name suggests, the Marais contains some of Europe's most elegant Renaissance-style houses *(hôtels)* now serving as museums and libraries.

Start at the corner of Rue des Archives and **Rue des Francs-Bourgeois,** named after the poor people allowed to live there tax-free in the 14th century. With a fine dramatic sense, the Rue des Francs-Bourgeois ends at what many consider to be the city's most picturesque square, **Place des Vosges.** When Henri IV had the square built in 1605, on the site of a horse-market, it consisted of 36 homes or *pavillons,* each encompassing four arches, nine *pavillons* on each side. The gardens of the square, now a peaceful playground for children, were a favourite spot for the aristocratic duel.

If you are a fan of Victor Hugo, stop by the fascinating **museum** of his manuscripts, artefacts and 350 of his drawings at 6 Place des Vosges.

Ile de la Cité

Shaped like a boat with the Square du Vert-Galant as its prow, the Ile de la Cité is the veritable cradle of the city of Paris.

The site of the cathedral of **Notre-Dame de Paris** has had a religious significance for at least 2,000 years. In Roman times a temple to Jupiter stood here; some stone fragments of the early structure, unearthed in 1711, can be seen in the Cluny Museum.

The cathedral remains an

More than just gardens, the Left Bank's Jardins du Luxembourg are a work of art in themselves.

impressive monument, truly the nation's parish church. It has witnessed, in 1239, Louis IX walking barefoot with his holy treasure, Christ's crown of thorns; in 1430, the humiliation of having Henry VI of England crowned King of France; in 1594, Henri IV attending the mass which sealed his conversion to Catholicism and reinforced his hold on the French throne; in 1804, Napoleon's coronation as emperor, attended by the pope but climaxed by Napoleon crowning himself; and in our own day, the state funerals of military heroes such as Foch, Joffre, Leclerc and de Gaulle.

Left Bank
(Rive Gauche)

To get an idea of what the Left Bank is all about, start at the **Quartier Latin.** Here, facing Notre-Dame, the spirit of inquiry has traditionally been nurtured into protest and outright revolt before subsiding into a lifelong scepticism, as the rebels graduate from the university and move west to the more genteel Faubourg Saint-Germain.

The Latin Quarter's citadel, the **Sorbonne,** was founded in 1253 as a college for poor theological students by Robert de Sorbon, Louis IX's chaplain. The university was taken in hand by Cardinal Richelieu, who financed its reconstruction (1624–42). Around the corner, as a kind of didactic inspiration for the students on what hard work can achieve, stands the gigantic neo-classic **Panthéon,** resting place of the nation's military, political and literary heroes.

Montparnasse is where they invented the cancan in 1845, at the now defunct Grande Chaumière dance hall. In the twenties it took over from Montmartre as the stomping ground of Paris' artistic colony, or at least of its avant-garde.

Saint-Germain-des-Prés is the literary quarter par excellence, home of the major publishing houses, bookshops and literary cafés. In the years following the Liberation it was known as headquarters for Jean-Paul Sartre and his existentialist acolytes.

The **Palais-Bourbon,** seat of the National Assembly, provides a rather formidable riverside façade for the Left Bank's most stately district—the elegant Seventh Arrondissement with its 18th-century foreign embassies, ministries and noble residences *(hôtel particuliers).*

From the quiet intimacy of this area, return to the massively monumental with the **Hôtel des Invalides,** Louis XIV's first vision of grandeur before Versailles, and the work of the same architect, Jules Hardouin-Mansart. Picking up an idea from Henri IV, Louis XIV founded the first national hospital for soldiers wounded in the service of their country. In Napoleon's hands it also became an army museum, another celebration of his victories, and still later the supreme celebration of Napoleon himself, when his body was brought back from the island of St. Helena for burial in the chapel.

There are monuments and there is the **Eiffel Tower.** Some celebrate heroes, commemorate victories, honour kings or saints. The Eiffel Tower is a monument for its own sake, a proud gesture to the world, a witty structure that makes aesthetics irrelevant. Its construction for the World's Fair of 1889 was an astounding engineering achievement—15,000 pieces of metal joined together by 2,500,000 rivets, soaring 984 feet (295 m.) into the air on a base of only 1,400 square feet (130 sq. m.). At the time, it was the tallest structure in the world.

Museums

The collections of the world's most famous museum are housed in the former royal palace. **The Louvre** is so huge that people are sometimes frightened of going in at all. But you do not have to be an art fanatic to realize that to come to Paris without setting foot inside this great palace would be a crime. And you can't miss I.M. Pei's magnificent glass pyramid that covers the new entrance.

François Ier, the Louvre's first art collector, acquired four Raphaels, three Leonardo da Vincis and one Titian (portrait of the king himself).

By 1793 the palace possessed 650 works of art; at the last inventory, in 1933, there were 173,000.

You'll see elegant Greek statues such as the 200 B.C. *Victory of Samothrace* and the 2nd-century B.C. *Venus de Milo,* and outstanding works by Michelangelo, Rembrandt, Leonardo da Vinci (the *Mona Lisa),* Titian, Van Dyck, Rubens, Velázquez, El Greco and Dürer, plus many more.

Though physically part of the Louvre, the **Musée des Arts Décoratifs** is a completely separate museum with its own entrance at 107 Rue de Rivoli. You should look out for the excellent temporary exhibitions devoted to great eras of design history and architecture, styles such as the Jugendstil, Bauhaus, and the American fifties. The permanent collection includes tapestries, lace, furniture, porcelain, and all aspects of domestic and institutional décor.

Right across the river, the 19th-century Orsay railway station has been transformed into the **Musée d'Orsay.** This exciting new museum embraces France's tremendous creativity from 1848 to 1914 in the domains of painting, sculpture, architecture and industrial design, advertising,

Beaubourg—art in action.

newspapers, book publishing, photography and the early years of the cinema. It also displays the collection of Impressionists and their followers transferred from the Jeu de Paume museum, now used for temporary exhibitions.

On the river side of the Tuileries, the **Orangerie** is best known for its ground-floor rooms decorated with Monet's beautiful *Nymphéas* mu-

rals, offering a moment of repose after a hard day's sightseeing.

Another recent addition is the long-awaited **Musée Picasso** (5 Rue de Thorigny in the Marais, Métro Saint-Paul). From the private collections of Picasso's heirs, the museum has received over 200 paintings and 158 sculptures, in addition to hundreds of drawings, engravings, ceramics and models for theatre décors and costumes. It also exhibits the artist's personal collection of masterworks by fellow painters Braque, Matisse, Miró, Degas, Renoir and Rousseau.

Beaubourg, officially Le Centre National d'Art et de Culture Georges Pompidou, is a combination of public library, modern art museum, children's workshop, *cinémathèque,* industrial design centre, experimental music laboratory which aims to make culture readily accessible to all.

One of Beaubourg's simplest pleasures is just going up the escalators in the long glass tubes that run diagonally from the bottom-left to the top-right-hand corner. Watch Paris unfold in front of your eyes with a stunning view of the city's rooftops.

La Villette on the northeast corner of town has been converted from the world's biggest slaughterhouse to a futuristic complex of cultural and scientific activities. **La Cité des sciences et de l'industrie** puts the accent on public participation in all phases of space technology, computers, astronomy and marine biology. Its most attractive symbol is the shining stainless steel **Géode** sphere containing a revolutionary cinema with a wide hemispheric screen.

Excursions

Any excursion outside Paris must include **Versailles** (13 miles/21 km.), where Louis XIV created the most sumptuous royal court Europe had ever seen, partly for his own glory and partly to keep his nobles in impoverished dependency and away from the intrigues of that trouble-making city of Paris. Architects Louis Le Vau and Jules Hardouin-Mansart and landscape-designer André Le Nôtre began their huge undertaking in 1661. It was completed 21 years later. (Closing day: Monday.)

One of the principal attractions of the château is the **Galerie des Glaces.** Here Wilhelm was proclaimed Kaiser of Germany in 1871, after his victorious war against the French, and the peace treaty of World War I was signed in 1919. The most impressive façade is in the west, facing the gardens. Try to be there at 4 p.m. when the fountains begin to play (the first or third Sunday in a month from May to September). You should also see the **Grand Trianon,** the little palace that Louis XIV used to get away from the château, the **Petit Trianon** that Louis XV preferred, and the **Hameau** or "cottages" where

Marie-Antoinette went to get away from everything.

Eating Out

There are some tourists who come to Paris without visiting a single museum or church and who would not dream of "wasting" their time shopping. And yet, they come away with tales of adventure, excitement, poetry and romance— and the feeling they know the city inside out. They have spent their time wining and dining and sleeping in between meals.

Paris has everything except a cuisine of its own. Instead, you can sample food from almost every region of France.

First things first. It's worth trying some of the simplest dishes that do work genuinely as appetizers: *crudités*—a plate of fresh raw vegetables, tomatoes, carrots, celery, cucumber; or just radishes by themselves, served with salt and butter; *charcuterie*—various kinds of sausage or other cold meats, notably the *rosette* sausage from Lyon, *rillettes* (like a soft pâté) and *jambon* from Bayonne or Dijon; or *potages*—rich vegetable soup, with a base of leek and potato, or perhaps a *bisque de homard* (lobster soup).

Fish comes fresh to Paris every day. The trout *(truite)* is delicious *au bleu* (poached absolutely fresh), *meunière* (sautéed in butter) or *aux amandes* (sautéed with almonds). At their best, *quenelles de brochet* (dumplings of ground pike) are simply heavenly—light and airy. The sole and turbot take on a new meaning when served with a *sauce hollandaise,* that miraculous blend of egg-yolks, butter and lemon juice.

For your main dish, expect your meat to be less well-done than in most countries—extra-rare is *bleu,* rare, *saignant,* medium, *à point,* and well-done, *bien cuit* (and frowned upon). Steaks *(entrecôtes* or *tournedos)* are often served with a wine sauce (*marchand de vin* or *bordelaise)* or with shallots *(échalotes).*

It would be a crime not to try at least some of France's 400 cheeses—the blue *Roquefort,* the soft yellow-white, crusted *Camembert* or *Brie* and the myriad of goat cheeses *(fromage de chèvre).*

For dessert you should not miss the chance of a *tarte Tatin* of hot caramelized apples. Or *profiteroles,* delicate ball-shaped éclairs filled with vanilla ice-cream and covered with hot chocolate sauce.

Wine

What is for many people the most intimidating of experiences—ordering a French wine—has in fact far fewer rules than you think. If you happen to like red wine more than white, you can safely and acceptably order red with fish; a light Beaujolais, Morgon or Brouilly chilled goes with both fish and meat. And if you prefer white, you can drink dry Burgundy with fish and Alsatian wine with everything, with impunity. Look, too, for house wine *(vin ouvert)* served by the *quart* (quarter) and *demi* (half) litre, or bottled by the restaurant. It's always cheaper.

Remember, in a Paris restaurant *you* are king. You prefer beer? Go ahead, it goes especially well with Toulouse sausage and Alsatian *choucroute*.

Shopping

Shopping in Paris is a seductive, exotic adventure that turns adults into children and makes the children wish they had the adults' money.

The department stores best equipped for dealing with foreigners are **Galeries Lafayette** and **Au Printemps,** next door to each other on the Boulevard Haussmann. The Galeries have an enormous chinaware department and excellent perfume and luggage sections. Au Printemps is famous for its lingerie and vast toy department.

FNAC, in the younger generation of Parisian department stores (at the Etoile, Montparnasse and the Forum des Halles), has the city's largest selection of books and records.

A strange Parisian phenomenon is **Le Drugstore,** the Frenchman's conception of the American institution of an all-night pharmacy and soda-counter. In French hands it has become a go-go paradise of grocery-store, luxury gifts, news-stand, records, books, perfume, electronic gadgets, expensive luggage, car-rental, theatre-agency—and even a pharmacy.

Paris wouldn't even bother to dispute the title of **fashion** capital of the world with London, New York or Rome. It would just send you to Rue du Faubourg Saint-Honoré and Avenue Montaigne to see the masters of *haute couture:* Balmain, Lanvin, Cardin, Yves Saint-Laurent, Ungaro, Dior, Louis Féraud, Courrèges and Givenchy (on Avenue George-V), to name just a few.

At the second level in price and workmanship, but by no means lagging in creativity, are the chic little boutiques that have sprung up around Saint-Germain, at the Forum des Halles and on the Place des Victoires.

Antique-hunting in Paris takes place on two levels—the high-priced shops grouped mainly in the 6th and 7th *arrondissements* on the Left Bank and the flea markets around the city-limits. You'll find the biggest collection of antique shops in Europe (250 boutiques) at the Louvre des Antiquaires, 2, Place du Palais Royal, open every day except Monday.

The week-end **flea markets** are a well-established Parisian institution. The Marché aux Puces de Saint-Ouen at the Porte de Clignancourt, groups half-a-dozen markets (also open Monday).

Finally there are the markets—all over town—but particularly colourful on the Rue Mouffetard, Maubert-Mutualité and Rue de Seine on the Left Bank and Rue des Martyrs and Passy on the Right Bank.

Practical Information

Banks and currency exchange: Hours vary, but most Paris banks are open from 9. a.m. to 4.30 p.m., Mondays to Fridays. A few banks and currency-exchange offices operate later and on weekends. Always take your passport when you change money.

Currency: The French *franc* (abbreviated F or FF) is divided into 100 *centimes*. Current coins include 5-, 10-, 20- and 50-centime pieces as well as 1-, 2-, 5- and 10-franc pieces. Banknotes come in denominations of 20, 50, 100, 200 and 500 francs.

Post office: You can identify post offices by a sign with a stylized blue bird and the words Postes et Télécommunications *(P & T or PTT)*. Paris post offices are open from 8 a.m. to 7 p.m. Mondays to Fridays and 8 a.m. to noon on Saturdays. The post office at 52, rue du Louvre is open 24 hours a day. Stamps may also be bought at tobacconists.

ROME

Italy

Introduction

Rome overwhelms you by its contrasts. It is at once an incredible mingling of ancient and modern, religious and profane, serene and chaotic. Sprawling today ever farther beyond its original seven hills and the banks of the Tiber, Rome amazes, delights and at times exasperates.

No city in the world is a more complete museum of human endeavour. Stark ruins bear imposing witness to Rome's great empire of centuries long past. In her myriad palaces and churches are found enough artistic treasures to consume a lifetime of sightseeing. Within the ancient city walls, any cobblestoned street reveals a fountain, a marble bust, a fresco, a piazza, a hidden courtyard—each telling a tiny fragment of the intriguing story of the Eternal City.

As the seat of the papacy, Rome is a compelling spiritual magnet for some 550 million Roman Catholics. The influence of the Vatican on the municipality of Rome, which totally surrounds it, is inescapable. The first of the pope's nine titles is Bishop of Rome; priests, nuns, bishops, cardinals and pilgrims are seen throughout the city, which boasts some 500 churches. And yet, Rome today is primarily the secular capital of a struggling nation, caught up in a maelstrom of politics and commerce.

Mostly, today's Romans are indifferent to their magnificent surroundings. Yet they themselves help make the city so fascinating. Gesticulating constantly, hurling harmless insults, religiously staying out of the sun, irreligiously whispering at mass, honking their horns over a football victory, parading in demonstration, triple-parking their Fiats, gulping down espressos, the Romans live and love life to the fullest.

A Brief History

8th–6th centuries B.C.	Founded in 753 B.C. (according to legend, by the twin brothers Romulus and Remus), Rome is ruled by seven Latin and Etruscan kings. The Romans revolt against the Etruscans in 509 B.C. and establish a republic.

5th–2nd centuries B.C.	Rome dominates central Italy. After the Gauls capture and burn the city in 387 B.C., the Romans fortify it. It triumphs over Carthage, winning control of Spain, North Africa and Mediterranean trade.
1st century B.C.	Civil war brings Julius Caesar to the dictatorship, but he is assassinated in 44 B.C. Anarchy ensues until Augustus, Caesar's heir, takes power in 27 B.C. as the first Roman emperor. Rome reaches its peak of glory.
1st–3rd centuries A.D.	The city is burned in Emperor Nero's reign and blame is laid on the Christians, many of whom are martyred. The over-extended empire begins to disintegrate.
4th–8th centuries	Barbarians invade Italy. The emperors flee to Milan and then Ravenna. Alaric the Goth loots Rome in 410. The classical Western Roman Empire collapses. In the Dark Ages of invasions by Goths, Lombards and Franks, Rome becomes a village, its small population subsisting in the Tiber marsh, deserting the seven hills when invaders cut the imperial aqueducts. On Christmas Day, 800, Pope Leo II crowns the Frankish king Charlemagne first emperor of the Holy Roman Empire.
9th–14th centuries	Italy is plagued by the Saracens. In 1095 the pope calls for a crusade against them. Rome degenerates into chaos. The popes move to Avignon in 1309 and remain for 68 years under French protection.
15th–18th centuries	The popes, back in Rome, become patrons of the Renaissance. In 1527 mutinous German and Spanish troops sack Rome, but the city is rebuilt even more magnificently.
19th century	Italian nationalists establish a republic in Rome in 1848, but it is crushed by the French army. Most of Italy is unified in 1860. Rome is captured in 1870 to become capital of the new Kingdom of Italy.
20th century	After World War I, Mussolini seizes power. His Lateran Agreement with the papacy creates the independent state of Vatican City. In World War II, Rome is declared an open city and is captured intact by the Allies in June 1944. The monarchy is abolished in 1946 in favour of a republic.

Sightseeing

Vatican City

(Città del Vaticano)

The tiny sovereign state of Vatican City (108 acres; 44 ha.) contains not only the residence of the pope, the world's largest church and its impressive square, but many of mankind's greatest treasures as well.

Many scholars believe St. Peter was martyred in Nero's circus, where early Christians were tortured and crucified. In the 4th century, Emperor Constantine built the original St. Peter's Basilica above the apostle's tomb. It survived five centuries of barbarian invasions until 846, when it was sacked by Saracens. Pope Leo IV then ordered massive walls to be built around the church and the enclosed area became known as the Leonine City or Vatican City.

Symbolically guarded (since 1506) by an élite corps of Swiss guards, Vatican City has a population of about 300, including the pope and cardinals.

Opening out as if to embrace all mankind, **St. Peter's Square** *(Piazza San Pietro)* was completed in less than 11 years (1656–67) by Rome's leading Baroque sculptor, Gian Lorenzo Bernini. To appreciate the incomparable symmetry of the colonnade, stand on one of the two round, green paving stones flanking the square's central obelisk— the four rows of columns will then appear as a single row.

The largest Catholic church ever built, **St. Peter's Basilica** was consecrated in 1626, a reconstruction and enlargement of Constantine's original edifice. It involved a century of work and the architectural schemes of Bramante, Raphael, Sangallo and Michelangelo.

St. Peter's covers more than 3½ acres (1½ ha.). Beneath the soaring cupola is Bernini's bronze *baldacchino* (canopy), above the high altar at which only a pope may celebrate mass.

Amid the basilica's breathtaking array of gold, mosaic, marble and gilded stucco, the supreme masterpiece is Michelangelo's *Pietà*, a superb marble of the Virgin and the dead Christ.

Near the main altar is the 13th-century bronze **statue of St. Peter**, by Arnolfo di Cambio, its foot worn smooth by the kisses of millions of pilgrims.

Near the entrance, a red porphyry disc marks the spot

where Charlemagne knelt to be crowned Holy Roman Emperor. Markings on the floor indicate the lengths of the world's other large Catholic churches—any one of which would easily fit into St. Peter's.

Nothing in all Rome or, quite possibly, the world, is as fascinating in its immensity as the palatial maze of more than 1,000 rooms and corridors, known as the **Vatican Museum**. There are, in fact, eight museums, five galleries, the apostolic library, the Borgia and Raphael rooms and, of course, the Sistine Chapel.

The **Picture Gallery** (*Pinacoteca Vaticana*) displays many of the world's most famous paintings, dating back more than 1,000 years. The collection includes works by Titian, Giotto, Fra Angelico, Leonardo da Vinci, Rubens and Van Dyck.

In the **Raphael Rooms** don't miss his enormous *Disputation of the Holy Sacrament* and the *School of Athens*, which rank with the greatest art ever produced.

The **Sistine Chapel** is the private chapel of popes and the site of the secret conclaves at which cardinals elect new popes. The awesome vaulted chamber is named after Pope Sixtus IV, who ordered it to be built.

It is covered with superb frescoes by Perugino, Botticelli and Ghirlandaio. From 1508 to 1512, working completely alone, Michelangelo painted the ceiling with the saga of humanity from the Creation to the Flood, the largest work ever accomplished by a single artist. Twenty-three years later, he painted the *Last Judgment* on the Sistine's altar wall.

In the **Pio-Clementine Museum** are housed some of the finest surviving ancient sculptures. Among them are the only copy of the *Aphrodite of Cnidos* by Praxiteles, considered the best Greek statue ever found, and the marble group of *Laocoön,* perhaps the greatest treasure in any Vatican museum.

Classical Rome

Ancient Rome's best-known monument, the **Colosseum** (*Colosseo*) was the scene of unthinkably brutal spectacles. Built by 20,000 slaves and prisoners, the Colosseum was inaugurated in A.D. 80.

The elliptical arena is surrounded by stone tiers which seated 50,000 people. Through the 80 arched passageways, emperors, knights, citizens and slaves thronged in to watch the all-day shows of starving beasts fighting each other: bears, lion, tigers and even elephants. Gladiators fought to the death as the crowd shouted, *Jugula!* ("Slit his throat").

Erected next to the Colosseum in A.D. 315, the **Arch of Constantine** honoured the emperor's victory over pagan Maxentius. It also commemorated the city's conversion to a Christian capital as the result of Constantine's battlefield vision of the cross.

The **Forum** was a glittering complex of marble and gold palaces, temples and pillared markets:

Part of the **Curia,** where the Roman Senate sat for more than 1,000 years, still survives. Beneath a protective shed is the **Lapis Niger,** a black-marble stone installed by Caesar over the presumed site of the grave of Romulus. Here is the oldest Latin inscription ever

found, dating back some six centuries before Christ.

Further on are the remnants of the **Rostra**, the platform for such orators as Cicero and Mark Antony.

Three pillars remain of the **Temple of Castor and Pollux**, dedicated to those legendary brothers of Helen of Troy.

The well-preserved **Arch of Septimius Severus** was built to honour the emperor who died early in the 3rd century at York *(Eboracum)* in England. Farther away, the **Arch of Titus** with its elaborate bas-reliefs commemorated that emperor's sack of Jerusalem in A.D. 70.

Within the circular **Temple of Vesta**, Rome's sacred flame was kept perpetually lit, guarded by six privileged Vestal Virgins, who were to be buried alive if they transgressed their vow of 30 years of chastity.

Just beyond the Forum lies the **Palatine Hill**. This legendary site of Rome's founding is a pleasant place to look out over the **Circus Maximus** where, under the emperors, 200,000 citizens would line tiers of marble seats to watch the chariot races.

In the nearby imperial forums, stands **Trajan's Column**, remarkably intact.

Michelangelo designed the **Capitol Square** *(Piazza del Campidoglio)* on the most sacred site of ancient Rome, where once sacrifices were made before statues of Jupiter and Juno. Today, the mayor of Rome has his office here in the Senatorial Palace.

The bronze statue of the emperor and philosopher Marcus Aurelius in the square is the only imperial Roman equestrian sculpture in existence.

In the **Palazzo dei Conservatori** is kept the hallowed, bronze she-wolf, symbol of the city, superbly sculpted by an Etruscan some six centuries before Christ. The twins Romulus and Remus beneath the wolf were added during the Renaissance. Until recently, a live wolf was kept caged in the bushes next to Michelangelo's huge stairway leading to the Campidoglio. The smaller, steeper stairs rise to the church of **Santa Maria d'Aracoeli** with its magnificent frescoes, relics and gilded ceiling.

South of the Colosseum are the **Baths of Caracalla,** which for 300 years, until barbarians cut the aqueducts, were Rome's finest public baths, accommodating 1,600 bathers at a time. The largest hot-bath room, the *caldarium,* is today

the stage for Rome's outdoor opera performances.

Further south again begins the **Old Appian Way** *(Via Appia Antica)*. Over its paving stones, still visible today, Roman legions rumbled via Capua to Brindisi, to set sail for the Levant and Africa.

Flanking this queen of all the Roman consular roads were sepulchres and tombstones of 20 generations of patrician families. Behind the funereal relics today are the villas of film celebrities and millionaire aristocrats.

During Nero's persecution of the Christians, St. Peter was prevailed upon by his followers to leave Rome. Tradition records that along the Appian Way he encountered Christ and asked, "Domine, quo vadis?" ("Lord, whither goest Thou?"). Christ replied, "Venio iterum crucifigi" ("I come to be crucified again"). Peter turned back to death and martyrdom. The church of St. Sebastian, 1½ miles (2½ km.) along the Appia, contains a stone reputed to bear the footprint of Christ.

Along the Appia are the **Catacombs of St. Callistus**, a vast underground Christian cemetery containing graves of 3rd-century popes. In the **Catacombs of St. Sebastian**, the bodies of the apostles Peter and Paul are said to have been hidden for decades. In the 2nd and 4th centuries Jews were buried in the Jewish Catacombs.

The cylindrical tomb of Cecilia Metella, dominating the Appian landscape, commemorates a wealthy Roman matron.

The Centre

The **Piazza del Popolo** is symmetrically perfect, a 150-year-old spatial masterpiece by Valadier, Napoleon's architect. The obelisk in the centre dates from Pharaoh Rameses II.

At the arched gateway begins the Flaminian Way *(Via Flaminia)*, leading to Rimini on the Adriatic coast.

The **Spanish Steps**, perhaps the world's most famous, ascend from the *Piazza di Spagna* to the major French church in Rome, the twin-belfried Trinità dei Monti. To the right of the steps, the house where John Keats died has been preserved as a museum.

The heart of the country's administration lies in **Piazza Colonna**, where the 1,800-year-old column of Marcus Aurelius stands in front of the Italian Prime Minister's office in the vast Chigi Palace.

On adjacent Parliament Square *(Piazza Montecitorio)*, dominated by a 6th-century B.C. obelisk, stands the Chamber of Deputies, Italy's lower house.

From Piazza Colonna you can window-shop your way along Via del Corso to Piazza Venezia. It's impossible to avoid this huge, traffic-jammed square, the centre of modern Rome. The white marble Vittorio Emanuele monument was aptly nicknamed the "wedding cake" by World War II British soldiers. Built between 1885 and 1911 to honour the unification of Italy and her first king, it contains the Tomb of the Unknown Soldier.

In stunning contrast, the 15th-century **Palazzo Venezia** along one side of the square has been called the finest palace ever built in Christian Rome. Now a museum of Renaissance art, the palace was a papal home, the embassy of the Republic of Venice and later Mussolini's official residence. From its tiny central balcony, *il Duce* delivered his major speeches.

The presidents of Italy normally live in the immense **Quirinal Palace**, formerly the residence of popes. In the Quirinal's Pauline Chapel, conclaves to choose popes were held until 1870. Italian kings, and later presidents, then moved in.

No visitor to Rome misses the **Trevi Fountain**, in a square below the Quirinal Palace. To be sure to come back to Rome, turn your back and toss a coin over your shoulder into the basin.

Old Rome

To stroll through the twisting, cobblestoned streets around Piazza Navona, the Pantheon and Campo de' Fiori is to journey backwards in time. In this quarter with palaces, courtyard fountains and churches, the "feel" of Rome as it was centuries ago still lingers.

Consul Marcus Agrippa first built the **Pantheon**, "temple of all the gods", 2,000 years ago, in 27 B.C. Hadrian reconstructed it after a disastrous fire. It became a church in the 7th century. Its majestic dome, with a diameter (142 ft.; 43 m.) identical to its height, is a triumph of architectural harmony. It's best to visit when the sun is high in the sky—the vault's only light comes through the 30-foot (9-m.) opening in the dome.

Stroll into the **Piazza Navona** nearby. Romans insist

that this is the most beautiful square in the world, and it's easy to agree. It covers the site of the 1st-century A.D. Stadium of Domitian, retaining its exact rectangular dimensions (787 by 213 ft.; 240 by 65 m.).

It's an ideal place for an outdoor meal or drink, allowing time for a leisurely study of Bernini's **Fountain of the Four Rivers**, representing the Nile, Ganges, la Plata and Danube.

The grim circular landmark on the opposite bank of the Tiber is the **Castel Sant'Angelo**, built by Emperor Hadrian as his mausoleum. It was soon converted into a fortress, to which popes fled to safety from invaders along the thick-walled passage connecting it with St. Peter's.

During the last sack of Rome, in 1527, Pope Clement VII held out inside the turreted fortress, watching helplessly as the German and Spanish mutineers ravaged his city.

The castle takes its name from Pope Gregory's miraculous vision in 590 of an angel alighting on its turret, whereupon a plague decimating Rome suddenly vanished.

For a marvellously entertaining glimpse of the Romans being Roman, don't miss bustling **Campo de' Fiori** market. The statue rising above the maze of fruit, vegetable, fish, meat and flower stalls is of Giordano Bruno, a philosopher burned alive here as a heretic in 1600.

Even more crowded, noisy and cheerful is the ancient Roman quarter of **Trastevere**, across the Tiber, with its mystifying maze of cobblestoned streets.

Trastevere surrounds impressive **Santa Maria in Trastevere**, believed to be Rome's oldest church. The basilica was built by Pope Calistus I in the 3rd century A.D., on the spot where legend says oil gushed from the earth to presage the birth of Christ.

The façade's 13th-century gilded mosaics, thoughtfully illuminated at night, attract droves of tourists and Roman jet-setters to the piazza's cafés and restaurants.

Above Trastevere, the **Janiculum** *(Gianicolo)* **Hill** is just the spot for a picnic, a shaded stroll or the best panoramic view of Rome and the surrounding green countryside.

The Churches of Rome

Even if you never go near a church, Rome's the place to make an exception. In addition to St. Peter's, most tourists will want to visit Rome's three other magnificent patriarchal basilicas and some other famous churches.

On the way to the **Basilica of St. Paul's Outside the Walls** (*San Paolo fuori le Mura*) you pass the **Protestant Cemetery**, where Keats is buried and Shelley's ashes are interred.

Looming over the graves is a white **pyramid**, erected in 12 B.C. over the tomb of Roman pretor Gaius Cestius.

St. Paul is believed to have been led down the Ostian Way to his execution where his basilica now stands. The largest in Rome after St. Peter's, the basilica was built by Constantine in 315 and restored after a tragic fire in 1823.

Under the canopied altar the presumed remains of St. Paul are kept in a marble urn. The beautiful **cloister** was undamaged in the fire.

The **Basilica of St. John Lateran** (*San Giovanni in Laterano*) is regarded as the mother cathedral of the Catholic world—it's the seat of the pope as Bishop of Rome. It was also built by Constantine in the 4th century. Popes lived here for a thousand years. On the wooden altar preserved in the basilica's sanctuary, St. Peter is believed to have celebrated mass.

Fires, vandals and earthquakes ruined the Lateran through the centuries. The current basilica, less than 300 years old, is at least the fifth on this site.

Facing the basilica is the ancient edifice that houses the **Scala Santa**, the holy stairway which, according to tradition, Jesus trod in the house of Pontius Pilate. The 28 marble steps may be ascended only on one's knees.

The Egyptian obelisk in the Lateran square is the tallest in the world. It was originally erected at the Temple of Ammon in Thebes in 1449 B.C.

A pilgrim's favourite for centuries, the **Basilica of St. Mary Major** (*Santa Maria Maggiore*) is practically unchanged since it was built on the Esquiline Hill more than 1,500 years ago. The incomparably rich Pauline Chapel has an altar of lapis lazuli, amethyst and agate with a revered painting of the Madonna and Child dating back perhaps 1,200 years.

Santa Maria's ceiling was decorated in the 16th century with the first gold ever brought from America.

The Empress Eudossia founded the church of **St. Peter in Chains** (*San Pietro in Vincoli*) in the 5th century as the sanctuary for the chains which bound St. Peter, which are kept in a bronze reliquary under the altar.

Majestically seated on the tomb of Pope Julius II is Michelangelo's **statue of Moses**, considered by some to be the sculptor's greatest work.

Few churches are as overpowering as the mother church of the Roman Catholic order of Jesuits, **Il Gesù** (The Jesus), which is literally awash in glittering gold, semi-precious stones and mosaics.

Entirely different are the churches of **San Clemente**, in stark Early Christian style, with remnants of a temple to Mithras in the excavations below; and the exquisitely simple church of **Santa Sabina** on the Aventine Hill.

Eating Out

Doing as the Romans do so enthusiastically, visitors should plan to spend a good deal more time at meals than they normally do at home.

Pasta. Pasta comes in myriad forms. But what counts is the sauce, and that's where Roman cooks often excel. Here are a few to try: *bolognese* (or *ragù*): minced meat, tomato, herbs; *carbonara*: beaten egg, diced bacon, cheese, basil; *pesto (genovese)*: basil, oil, pine nuts, cheese, garlic; *pomodoro*: tomato, garlic, parsley.

Main course. The tastiest beef is Florentine T-bone steak *(bistecca alla fiorentina)*, usually charcoal-grilled. Typically Roman are *saltimbocca* ("jump in the mouth"), veal slices rolled round raw ham and sage, fried in butter and sprinkled with Marsala; and *osso buco*, veal shin simmered with garlic, tomato and wine and spiced with anchovy.

Vegetables are a year-round delight in Rome. Spinach *(spinaci)*, courgettes *(zucchine)* and eggplant or aubergine *(melanzana)* are particularly popular.

Cheese: Look for the creamy and tangy *taleggio*, the flavourful *casciotto* from Tuscany or *provolone*.

Dessert. You'll be offered an array of rich pastries, including liquored sponge-cake and creamy custard reminiscent of trifle *(zuppa inglese)*, or rich ice-cream flavoured with crystallized fruit.

Coffee. After all that, an espresso is considered absolutely essential. In summer you may opt for a *granita di caffè*, coffee over crushed ice.

Wine. The white, usually from the Alban Hills south of Rome, is generally known as Frascati or Castelli Romani. It's light, dry and pleasant. The open red wine in Roman restaurants is acceptable. Bottled Tuscan Chiantis are omnipresent, and Barolo, Gattinara and Valpolicella are worth asking for.

Shopping

Rome's international reputation as a marvellous shopping city is unquestionably deserved. All those famous Italian high-fashion brands are on sale at prices often far lower than abroad.

Rome's most fashionable shopping district is found between the Spanish Steps and Via del Corso, notably including Via Condotti, Via Frattina and Via Borgognona.

The flea market at Porta Portese offers incredible bargains in its 2½ miles (4 km.) of cluttered stalls (open Sundays only).

Good Buys

Leather: gloves, shoes, jackets, bags, belts, wallets, desk sets, luggage.

Silk: blouses, shirts, dresses, suits, scarves, ties.

Knitwear, ceramics, costume jewellery, Italian art and antiques, straw goods (but Florence is better), and **Italian wine and spirits.**

Practical Information

Banks: Opening hours 8.30 a.m. to 1.30 p.m. and again for an hour or so in the afternoon, Monday to Friday.

Clothing: Medium- to lightweight in early spring and autumn. Light summer clothing for July and August, which can be uncomfortably hot. Visitors to churches should avoid scanty attire. The Vatican maintains a "decency patrol" at the entrance to St. Peter's to turn back visitors wearing shorts, bare-backed dresses or miniskirts.

Currency: Italian *lira,* plural *lire* (abbr. *L* or *Lit.*). Coins: L. 5, 10, 20, 50, 100, 200, 500; Notes: L. 1,000, 2,000, 5,000, 10,000, 50,000, 100,000.

SALZBURG

Austria

Introduction

A golden city, home of Mozart and a thousand other musical dreams, Salzburg lies in an unequalled natural setting of mountains, hills and forest, along the banks of the River Salzach.

There is something indescribably southern about the town, an air of Florence or Venice. Baroque architecture gives the city a dreamy, poetic charm. Narrow old streets lead into spacious squares, elegant settings for Gothic churches and monasteries and sculptured fountains. Impressive mansions and Renaissance palaces reign over beautiful parks and gardens. It is easy to imagine how the drama and lyricism of these ancient stones, this unique combination of Italian and Germanic, should have influenced the music of one of the world's greatest composers.

Three prince-archbishops of the Renaissance modelled Salzburg, unspoiled to this day. The Old Town is squeezed between the left bank of the river and a high ridge called the Mönchsberg. On top of this is the impregnable fortress of Hohensalzburg, which has protected the city for 900 years.

A Brief History

4th century B.C.–5th century A.D.	Celts found a state with Juvavum as capital, and exploit the local salt mines. Taken over by the Romans in 14 B.C., Juvavum prospers thanks to its favourable position at the crossing of important trade routes. In 477 the town is destroyed by the Gothic chieftain Odoacer, who leads an uprising of the German troops in the Roman army.
6th–9th centuries	Christianity is introduced to the region by Bavarians. The Bishop of Worms, St. Rupert, settles in the ruins of Juvavum in 696 and founds St. Peter's Abbey and a Benedictine convent. The name Salzburg (Castle of Salt) appears in 755. The Irish bishop, St. Virgil, founds the cathedral in 767. Salzburg becomes an archbishopric in 800.
10th century	A time of troubles, marked by struggles against Magyar raids.

11th–12th centuries	The fortress of Hohensalzburg is built in 1077. Friedrich Barbarossa burns down the town in 1167. It is rebuilt, with a new cathedral.
13th century	The town prospers. Archbishop Friedrich II is awarded the title Imperial Prince. Salzburg becomes one of the leading cities of the Holy Roman Empire.
14th–17th centuries	Wars with Bavaria in 1322 and Friedrich III in 1466, and peasant revolt do not hinder development of the city. The salt mines provide the main revenue of the prince-archbishops, who spend it generously on construction. Much of the city is destroyed by fire in 1598. It is rebuilt in Renaissance style by three succeeding Archbishops, Von Raitenau, his nephew Sitticus, and Lodron, who call in Italian architects Scamozzi and Solari to redesign the city, cathedral and ramparts.
18th century	Wolfgang Amadeus Mozart is born in Salzburg in 1756 and lives there until 1777. The town is captured by the French in the Napoleonic Wars (1809), handed over to the Bavarians and returned to Austria in 1816 after Napoleon's defeat.
19th century	A period of economic revival. In 1863 the railway reaches Salzburg. The music academy, the Mozarteum, is founded.
20th century	The Salzburg Festival is established in 1920. The town becomes popular with tourists.

Sightseeing

Since Salzburg offers one of Europe's great urban panoramas, start with an overall view by taking the lift from Gstättengasse up to the terrace of Café Winkler on the **Mönchsberg**. Stroll across to the halfway-station of the funicular railway and go up to **Hohensalzburg**, the archbishop's castle, for a look at the princely life led by Salzburg's aristocratic churchmen. You'll see from the massive walls, towers and dungeons that the castle was a fortress bristling with military defences, rather than a palatial retreat for spiritual meditation. The Salzburg archbishops were rarely popular enough to overcome the fear of civic rebellion.

Guided tours visit the

elegant 16th-century Princes' Rooms *(Fürstenzimmer)*. One of the highlights is the Golden Room *(Goldene Stube)*. The castle museum has a first-class collection of medieval sculpture; also on display are the weapons and instruments of torture used to bolster the archbishops' power.

Back down the Mönchsberg, at the foot of the funicular railway, stands **St. Peterskirche** (St. Peter's Church), richly remodelled in the Baroque style with red and white Salzburg marble. The **cemetery**, shaded by pines and weeping willows, is the elegant, even romantic resting place of Salzburg's noblest families.

The nearby **Franziskanerkirche**, a late Romanesque convent church, has a Gothic steeple. The nave, a model of sobriety, is lightened by the bright Gothic choir. The grand, golden Baroque high altar by the Viennese architect Johann Bernhard Fischer von Erlach frames a poignant 15th-century *Madonna* (the Christ on her lap was added in 1895) by the Tyrol's finest sculptor and painter, Michael Pacher.

Walk past the Festspielhaus to Sigmundsplatz and the **Pferdeschwemme**, a horse trough to end all horse troughs. This grandiose Renaissance structure is orna-

Savour Austrian cakes and pastries in the most elegant of surroundings.

SALZBURG

mented with vigorous sculpture and frescoes of prancing horses.

Kollegienkirche (University Church) figures among the masterpieces of Fischer von Erlach's Baroque architecture. The powerful, twin-towered façade on Universitätsplatz presents an imposing frame for the massive dome looming behind it.

Getreidegasse is *the* great shopping street of Salzburg's old town. Wrought-iron guild signs ornament its Renaissance and Baroque façades. At number 9 is **Mozart's birthplace**—now an enchanting museum. Exhibits include

manuscripts of minuets Mozart wrote when he was five, his counterpoint notebook, paintings of papa Leopold and sister Nannerl. A clavichord bears a note written by wife Constanza: "On this piano my dearly departed husband Mozart composed the Magic Flute".

The early 17th-century **Residenz**, another palace of the archbishops, now serves as an art gallery. The excellent collection of Flemish and Dutch paintings includes a Rembrandt portrait of his mother at prayer and a Rubens portrait of Emperor Charles V.

The south side of the Residenzplatz is dominated by the huge **Dom** (Cathedral), one of the most imposing edifices north of the Alps, executed in Italian Renaissance style, with Baroque overtones. It contains the font where Mozart was christened on 28 January, 1756.

Have a pastry in one of the cafés on **Mozartplatz**, and watch the world go by.

Beyond Salzburg lies the blessedly tranquil **Fuschlsee**. At the west end of this crystal-clear lake is Schloss Fuschl, once the castle-home of Nazi Foreign Minister Joachim von Ribbentrop, now a respectable hotel.

The Festival

The Salzburg Festival, the Mozartian counterpart to Bayreuth's homage to Wagner, is held from the end of July to the end of August. Founded in 1920, this feast of opera, symphony concerts and chamber music recitals is dominated by, but not exclusively devoted to, Mozart. The proceedings begin with an open-air production of Hoffmannsthal's *Jedermann* (Everyman), following a tradition established by Max Reinhardt, the great theatre director and co-founder of the festival.

The geatest artists in the world have considered it a supreme privilege to perform at the Salzburg Festival. It's almost as great a privilege to get tickets. Reservations can be made before the end of November; by the beginning of January, there's very little left.

Your best bet is to aim for the second half of August, when the premières are over and all the honorary guests and journalists have left town. Be sure to couple ticket reservations with a hotel room, since festival regulars bag most of the available space a year in advance. Even if the most popular events are sold out, you can usually find tickets for recitals or chamber concerts, all well worthwhile.

Eating Out

Austrian food is healthy, robust fare, straightforward and unfussy but delicious. The day starts with a substantial breakfast, with a selection of cold meats—ham, salami and liver sausage—and cheese served with bread rolls.

The local custom is to have a solid, hot midday meal, and a light supper of soup, cold meat, ham or sausage and perhaps a salad.

Soups are a regular feature of the meal. The choice includes *Bohnensuppe* (bean soup) and *Knödelsuppe* (dumpling soup). Spicy *Gulaschsuppe*, inherited from Austro-Hungarian days, combines beef, onions, garlic and paprika with tomatoes and celery.

Most menus include a couple of Viennese classics—*Wienerschnitzel*, a large, thinly sliced, breaded cutlet of veal, and *Backhendl*, chicken prepared in the same way. Other dishes to look out for are *Wildschweinbraten*, slices of roast wild boar with bread dumplings and cranberries, and *Bauernschmaus*, a rustic banquet all on one plate— roast pork and boiled ham, sauerkraut and a dumpling.

Goulasch and spicy sausages are sold from roadside stalls until late at night.

As for desserts, apart from dumplings and strudel, the speciality of Salzburg is *Nockerln*, a lemon-flavoured soufflé omelette.

Shopping

Salzburg is well served with shops, ranging from attractive, pedestrian shopping arcades to the lively open-air market at Universitätsplatz, where all the traditional Austrian specialities can be found.

Best buys are **handicrafts:** woodcarvings, petit-point embroidery, glassware, walking sticks, etched and painted glass. The typical **Tyrolean costumes** are popular—dirndl dresses with gay and contrasting colours; *Lederhosen,* the leather shorts that last forever; strong *Loden* coats, now made in a range of bright colours, as well as the traditional olive and grey; knee-length woollen socks, fringed silk scarves, handspun wool.

Among **gastronomic delights**, consider the local liqueurs and schnapps and gingerbread, chocolate, honey and *Sachertorte*.

Practical Information

Banks and currency exchange: Open from 8 a.m. to 12.30 p.m. and 1.30–3 p.m., Monday to Friday, until 5.00 p.m. on Thursday.

Currency: The Austrian *Schilling* (abbr. *S, ÖS* or *Sch.*) is divided into 100 *Groschen* (abbr. *g*). Coins: 10, 50 g, 1, 5, 10 and 20 S. Banknotes: 20, 50, 100, 500 and 1,000 S.

Shops: Generally open from 8 a.m. to 6 p.m., Monday to Friday, and on Saturday until noon.

SEVILLE

Spain

Introduction

In Spain's Golden Age, when galleons carried the treasures of the New World up the Guadalquivir River, people used to say: "Madrid may be the capital of Spain, but Seville is the capital of the world."

The *sevillanos* consider the situation unchanged. When the crowds pour in for the Easter Holy Week ceremonies or for the parades, bullfights and fireworks of the April Fair *(La Feria),* it still seems that Seville is indeed the hub of everything.

For most visitors, the romantic side of Seville predominates: the splendid mansions with wrought-iron balconies, the fountains and orange trees, the Moorish fortress and grandiose cathedral. After all, the city provided the setting for Mozart's *Don Giovanni,* Bizet's *Carmen* and Rossini's *Barber of Seville.*

But Seville is also an important industrial and commercial city, with a population of 600,000, lying in a fertile area of corn and cotton, vineyards and olive groves. Moreover, it is the capital of Andalusia, one of the largest regions in Spain, offering an endless variety of landscape, from the eternal snows of the Sierra Nevada to the sunny beaches of the Costa del Sol.

Phoenicians and Romans first colonized the city, followed by the Vandals (who gave their name to Andalusia) and the Visigoths. A heroic era came during the 500 years of Moorish rule, which saw construction of the Giralda, Seville's most visible landmark. Another glorious epoch followed the return of Christian rule in 1248, when the imposing cathedral was built. Spanish vessels sailed out from Seville to explore the world, and Spanish art and literature flowered.

The historic and artistic interest of the past draws visitors to Seville, the most Spanish of Spain's great cities.

A Brief History

Early times   The Iberian settlement of Hispalis grows up near the site of present-day Seville. Conquered by the Romans around 205 B.C., the town becomes known as Italica. Julius Caesar fortifies it, designating Italica capital of the colony of Baetica. The Roman city boasts a population of 25,000 during its heyday in the 2nd century A.D.

5th–8th centuries
: The Visigoths make Seville their capital for a time, before they transfer their court to Toledo. The Moors take over in 712, christening the city "Yzvilia".

9th–12th centuries
: Christians and Moors battle for possession of Spain. After the fall of Córdoba in the 11th century, Seville becomes the capital of the Almohad kingdom under the aegis of Al Mansur. The Giralda and Golden towers are built, and the city develops into a great cultural centre.

13th–16th centuries
: Seville falls to Ferdinand III of Castile on November 19, 1248. A bastion of Christianity, the city begins construction of its great cathedral in 1401. The port grows in importance with the discovery of the New World. Vespucci and Magellan both sail from Seville on their famous journeys. Designated the port of entry for vessels from the Americas, Seville increases in wealth and prestige. But a slow decline sets in after the defeat of the Spanish Armada (1588).

17th–19th centuries
: The painters Velázquez (1599–1660) and Murillo (1617–82) are born in Seville during Spain's Golden Age of art and literature. In 1628, Zurbaran is appointed the city's official painter. Plague wipes out a third of Seville's population in 1649. Gradually the Guadalquivir silts up, and the city loses its monopoly on American shipping in 1717. Stripped of its wealth, a poor Seville lives through the crises of the 19th century: the War of Independence (1804–14) and the Carlist Wars.

20th century
: At the start of the Civil War, Seville falls to the Nationalists, led by General Franco. After three years of fighting, Franco emerges victorious, bringing Spain under 35 years of Fascist rule. Seville develops as a centre of industry and tourism. With the restoration of the monarchy in 1975, the city gains new prestige as the capital of Andalusia. Seville looks forward to enhanced prosperity with the entry of Spain into the European Economic Community.

Sightseeing

Seville *(Sevilla)*

The city's most famous buildings stand in a cluster at its centre. The 15th-century late Gothic **Cathedral,** built on the site of a mosque, is the third largest in the world (after St. Peter's, Rome, and St. Paul's, London). The immense nave (note the beautifully carved choir stalls and ornamental wrought-iron grille) and numerous side-chapels are filled with art treasures, including works by Murillo, Goya and Andrea della Robbia.

The royal chapel contains the tomb of Ferdinand III of Castile, who liberated Seville from the Moors, while the bones of Christopher Columbus lie in a fine 19th-century monument in the south transept. In the treasury you can see a cross made of gold the explorer brought back from his first voyage to the New World.

Adjoining the cathedral, the tower of the Giralda was originally built by the Moors as a minaret. A marvel of patterned pink brick and stone, the structure was taken over by the Christians, who made it into a bell tower. The mobile figure of Faith *(La Fé)*

Flamenco

After bullfighting, flamenco is Spain's best-known entertainment. Part Moorish, part gypsy, the dances and songs were born in Andalusia.

There are two basic kinds of flamenco—the *cante chico* (light song) accompanied by the clapping of hands, clicking of castanets and tapping of heels, and the anguished *cante jondo* (deep song). The flamenco floor-shows or *tablaos* of Seville feature the more accessible *cante chico,* with elaborately costumed performers. The men wear the slim Cordoban suit, and the women the sweeping, ruffled gypsy dresses that have become the hallmark of flamenco. Authentic *cante jondo* may be heard in numerous bars and clubs frequented by Spaniards, especially those of the Triana district.

at the top serves as a weather vane *(giraldillo)*. You can climb all the way up for a vast view over Seville.

The lovely **Court of the Orange Trees** *(Patio de los Naranjos)* below, the courtyard of the old mosque, provides cool geometric shade.

Across the Plaza de Triunfo stands the **Casa Lonja,** originally the Exchange, designed in the 16th century by Juan de Herrera, architect of the austere Escorial Palace near Madrid. Nowadays the building contains a priceless collection of 36,000 documents on the discovery of the Americas—the Archivo General de Indias—including letters written by Columbus and Magellan.

Horse-drawn carriages line up for passengers in the Plaza de España, to the south-east. Beyond extend the grounds of **Parque de María Luisa** with its fountains and pools of ornamental tile, created for the Ibero-American Exhibition of 1929.

The **Alcázar,** nearby, served as a royal palace for several hundred years. Begun by Pedro the Cruel in the 14th century, it occupies the site of a Moorish citadel. The **Court of the Maidens** *(Patio de las Doncellas),* surrounded by a graceful marble colonnade, leads to the imposing **Hall of the Ambassadors** *(Salón de los Embajadores).* The Moorish arches and decorative motifs are reminiscent of the Alhambra in Granada—the model for the architecture. On the floor above are the former royal apartments, home to Ferdinand II of Aragón and Isabella of Castile. Superb Flemish tapestries hang in the rooms created for Charles V.

Take a stroll among the orange, cypress and palm trees, the rose beds and fountains of the extensive gardens.

Seville is the only inland port in Spain, and 15,000-ton ships still navigate the 62 miles (100 km.) up the River Guadalquivir to the city. It was from the quayside here that Magellan set out to sail round the world in 1519.

Near the river bank stands the neo-classical Maestranza **bullring.** With a capacity of 14,000, it is the largest in Spain, and one of the oldest. Pedro Romero, "father of the Bullfight", appeared here in the 18th century. Further south you'll see the **Torre del Oro** (Golden Tower), a remnant of Seville's Moorish fortifications. The name recalls the colour of the tiles that once covered the structure. A small naval museum lies within.

Across the river sprawls the **Triana** district of Seville, a neighbourhood of artisans and working men known as the cradle of flamenco. Visit bars and clubs here for a taste of the real thing.

Beyond the Alcázar, narrow lanes lead into the **Barrio de Santa Cruz,** the ancient Jewish quarter, a gleaming maze of white houses and flower-filled patios. Seville's

noble families resided here in the 17th century. Now many of Seville's traditional *tapa* bars are to be found here, along with a concentration of bookshops and antique dealers. Be sure to look for Murillo's house at Santa Teresa, No. 8.

You should also visit the impressive **House of Pilate** *(Casa de Pilatos)* of 1540, to the north-east. Built by a Spanish nobleman as a supposed copy of Pilate's house in Jerusalem, the mansion boasts superb stucco work and tile decoration in the best Spanish tradition.

An object of veneration for

pilgrims from all over, the *Macarena Virgin (Nuestra Señora de la Esperanza Macarena)* occupies a small chapel in the district of Macarena, in the north of Seville. The 17th-century sculptor Montañés created the figure, which is carried through the streets to public adulation during Holy Week.

The former convent of La Merced houses the **Museo de las Bellas Artes** (Fine Arts Museum). The emphasis is on the school of Seville and its leading exponents—Pacheco, Zurburan and Murillo.

About 6 miles (10 km.) north-west of Seville lie the Roman ruins of **Italica,** the birthplace of the emperors Hadrian and Trajan. A metropolis of 25,000 inhabitants in its 2nd-century A.D. heyday, Italica preserves one of the largest Roman **amphitheatres** in existence, built to seat 30,000. Numerous private houses have been uncovered, as well as a stretch of road and many mosaic pavements.

Excursions

Perhaps the most interesting outing in the region of Seville is a day's excursion to **Jerez de la Frontera,** the city where sherry wine is made. A visit to Jerez won't be a trip, but a pilgrimage, for Jerez is the home of dozens of companies whose names will make your mouth water if you are a connoisseur; Domecq, Garvey, González Byass, Williams and Humbert, Osborne, Terry and Sandeman are a few of them. There are some 200 different viniculturists in Jerez, and between them they have 20,000 acres of vineyards under cultivation.

The sherry companies export around 19 million gallons of wine each year. The *bodegas,* or cellars, in the town store 700,000 butts, each containing 500 litres and each valued at many thousands of pesetas; as many butts again contain brandy.

Most of the bigger companies welcome visitors and take them on **guided tours** through the cellars. You'll learn all about the fermenting and aging processes, which continue over the course of several months. After the visit, you'll be invited to sample the various types of sherry, and you'll have the opportunity to buy bottles of the wine. Check with the local tourist office to establish times of the tours.

Wine-making may well have been going on in Jerez for 3,000 years. Historians think the vine was brought to south-

ern Spain from the East by the Phoenicians, who probably also settled in Jerez, calling their town *Xera*. Certainly the Romans were here, and documents show that southern Spanish wine was exported to Rome. It was of such good quality that Roman wines couldn't compete, and in A.D. 92 the emperor Domitian ordered that all Spanish vineyards be destroyed. Luckily, this was never carried out.

However, in the 1890s the Jerez vineyards were attacked by *phylloxera,* a kind of louse measuring no more than a millimetre in length, with the capacity to reproduce as many as 25 million during an eight-month period. No wonder the infestation wiped out the Jerez vines in just four years.

Many people thought Jerez was finished, but the determined growers made a study and discovered an American vine with a built-in resistance to the louse.

The Bullfight

Andalusia is the home of the bullfight, the *fiesta brava,* Spain's national sport.

Man against bull, intelligence against instinct, a handful of brains against half a ton of deadly brawn—for the bull the outcome is certain; for the matador less so. You may not like what you see, you may swear never to return to it, or you may become a lifelong *aficionado.*

The bull has been bred to fight in the ring, and the *corrida* is a ritualistic preparation for the bull's death; the *matador* has devoted his life towards finalizing the ritual, and thought of his death has no place in the proceedings.

The fight is divided into *tercios,* or thirds, each act designed to further tire the bull. First the bull charges into the ring, and helpers play it with capes. Then the matador takes over, using the big red and yellow *capote.*

During the second tercio the *picador,* the mounted spearman, uses his lance on the bull's huge shoulder muscles, and the *banderilleros* place darts in the bull's shoulder.

In the third *tercio,* the matador plays the bull with the small, dark red *muleta,* dominating the animal to the point where he can turn his back and casually walk away.

Finally comes the "moment of truth", when the matador lunges with his sword, aiming for a pin-point thrust between the shoulder blades which should kill the bull within seconds.

Depending on the quality and bravery of his performance, the matador is awarded an ear, two ears, perhaps even a tail.

Cuttings from Spanish vines were grafted onto the American plants, and Jerez was back in business.

Other tourist magnets in this city of 150,000 include **La Colegiata,** the biggest church in the city, famed for its Churrigueresque façade. Three miles (5 km.) along the road to Algeciras lies a Carthusian monastery with a fine Gothic church (the exterior is Baroque) and expansive cloisters.

Scene of a famous horse show held every May, Jerez is surrounded by pasturelands where some of the finest animals in Andalusia are raised.

From Jerez you can continue on to the popular tourist town of **Ronda,** one of the most spectacular cities in Spain, situated on the edge of a 600-foot (183-m.) cliff, the rolling hills of the

Serranía de Ronda stretching out before it.

Ronda was at its zenith under the Moors, and the old section of town, **La Ciudad,** remains completely Moorish in character. You'll want to visit the **Palace of the Moorish King** *(Casa del Rey Moro)* built in the 11th century by the local potentate. It's a long climb down to the **Moorish Baths** *(Baños Arabes),* once a place of pleasure and refreshment. Presently under restoration, the **Palacio de Mondragon** offers a splendid view of La Ciudad from a roof-top terrace. But nothing can compete with the view down into the gorge from the **Puente Nuevo** (New Bridge).

Across the bridge in the new quarter, El Mercadillo, you can visit the 200-year-old **bullring,** considered the birthplace of the modern bullfight. It was here that Pedro Romero established the form of the fight in the 18th century.

Eating Out

There is a saying in Spain that "in the south they fry, in the centre they roast and in the north they stew". Andalusia, then, is in frying land—and the Andalusians are expert at it.

Here are some typical dishes:

Ajo blanco (or *sopa de ajo con uvas):* cold garlic soup with almonds and raisins.

Boquerones: fresh anchovies, fried.

Calamares: squid, fried in batter.

Fritura mixta: a selection of fresh fried fish.

Gambas al pil-pil: shrimp cooked in oil with garlic.

Gazpacho andaluz: called a "liquid salad", this soup—always served chilled—incorporates tomatoes, green peppers, cucumber, onions, garlic and breadcrumbs, oil and vinegar.

Huevos a la flamenca: eggs baked with tomato, onion and diced ham; garnished with asparagus tips, red peppers or spicy sausage.

Paella: best-known of all Spanish dishes, *paella* usually combines seafood and chicken or pork, served on a base of saffron-coloured rice with peas, peppers and other vegetables.

Riñones al Jerez: kidneys in sherry sauce.

Sopa de pescado/mariscos: fish/shellfish soup.

Tortilla a la española: potato and onion omelette.

For dessert there is a wide variety of fresh fruit—

oranges, figs, dates, pears. Sweet confections include traditional almond cakes and a kind of brandy-flavoured rolled sponge cake called *brazo de gitano*.

Try at least one *tapa* meal. A *tapa* is a bite-sized morsel of food: roast meat, meat balls, sausage, olives, fried fish, shellfish, Russian salad... it can be anything. The word *tapa* means lid and comes from the old custom of providing a bite of food with a drink, served on a tiny saucer which was placed on top of the glass, like a lid. Some bars specialize in *tapas* to such an extent that you can eat your way down a fantastic line-up of tastily prepared foods, rather like a smorgasbord.

The most famous of all Spanish wines is sherry *(vino de Jerez)*. There are two main types: *fino* and *oloroso*. As an aperitif, try a *fino (manzanillas* and *amontillados*—dry, pale and with rich bouquet —are *finos)*. An *oloroso (brown* and *cream* sherries—heavier and darker—but also the pale, medium-dry

amoroso) makes a good after-dinner drink.

Cooling Sangría combines red wine, brandy, mineral water, orange and lemon juice and sliced fruit.

Most of the better table wines available in Seville are reds from the Rioja region of northern Spain.

Harmonious display of fresh seafood tempts the eye and the palate.

Shopping

You'll find excellent shops along the Calle de Sierpes and in the area of Plaza Nueva, including branches of the best national boutiques. The chain department stores feature good quality, but quite expensive, merchandise. Here are some of Seville's best buys:

Antiques. Interesting items still turn up—usually for a price. Look for hand-carved wooden bowls, ancient keys, ironwork, painted tiles, prints. Most dealers have their premises in the Barrio de Santa Cruz.

Ceramics. Choose from a

selection of enamelled or glazed and simple unglazed earthenware.

Embroidery. Fine needlework embellishes shawls, cushion covers and other articles. Exquisite lacework mantillas and shawls are still produced in the region of Seville.

Flamenco dresses. You can buy the traditional polka-dot gypsy costume, complete with ruffles and train.

Guitars. These are still crafted by hand in Andalusia.

Leather and Suede. Spanish-made shoes, handbags, gloves and articles of clothing are attractive and well styled, if no longer cheap.

Souvenirs. Hand-painted fans, bullfight posters, Arab-style chess sets, the typical Spanish *bota* or soft leather wineskin—Seville's tourist shops stock them all.

Tobacco products. Cigarettes and Havana cigars are available at reasonable prices.

Wrought-iron. Lamps, candlesticks and weather-cocks are just a few of the relatively portable articles you'll see.

Practical Information

Banks: Open 9 a.m. to 2 p.m. Monday to Friday, till 1 p.m. Saturday (9 a.m. to 1 p.m. Monday to Saturday in June, July and August). Money can be changed at establishments displaying a *cambio* sign.

Climate: Seville broils in summer, when temperatures reach up into the 40s Centigrade (100s Fahrenheit). Try to visit in spring or autumn. Winters can be cold and damp.

Currency: The monetary unit of Spain is the *peseta* (abbreviated *pta.*). Coins: 1, 2, 5, 10, 25, 50, 100, 200 and 500 pesetas. Banknotes: 500, 1,000, 2,000, 5,000 and 10,000 pesetas.

Shops: Business is transacted from 9.30 a.m. to 1 p.m. and from 4.30 to 8 p.m. In summer, hours are often extended.

STOCKHOLM

Sweden

Introduction

Though 700 years old, Stockholm only officially became the capital of Sweden in 1634. Today the city is not only the seat of the national parliament, but also the country's financial and business centre. And though there's plenty of elbow room in Sweden, over a seventh of the population lives in the Stockholm area.

Dramatically situated at a point where the cobalt blue of Lake Mälaren meets and clashes with the darker hue of the Baltic Sea, the city has been splendidly endowed by nature. It sprawls gracefully over 14 islands connected by no fewer than 40 bridges.

The different islands and districts that make up Stockholm are often so unlike one another that they create the illusion of a series of miniature and only distantly related cities. Each has its own distinct charm and mood.

A Brief History

–9th century	Nomadic tribes of hunters and fishermen follow the receding ice cap northwards to Sweden. Around 3000 B.C. inhabitants begin to cultivate the land, raise livestock and live together in communities. In A.D. 98 Swedes are mentioned as such for the first time in recorded history by the Roman historian Tacitus.
9th–11th centuries	Viking Age. These extraordinary seamen travel in their long ships as far as England, Iceland, Greenland and even North America. The Swedish Vikings sail towards the east and along the Russian rivers to Novgorod, Kiev and Constantinople. Missionaries begin to spread Christianity in Sweden.
12th–14th centuries	Conquest of Finland begins in 1157 under King Erik IX. The dominant figure in Sweden in the 13th century is Birger Jarl, brother-in-law of the king. He promotes a strong central government and has his son elected heir to the throne after the king's death. He is also credited with the foundation of Stockholm around 1250 as a fort for protection against pirate raids.
14th–16th centuries	In 1397 Sweden, Denmark and Norway – under the single rule of Queen Margrete of Denmark – form the Kalmar Union to counteract the growing power of the German Hanseatic League. In the 1430s Swedes, led by their hero Engelbrekt, rebel against Danish dominance. First Swedish Parliament is assembled in 1435. The unpopular Union of Kalmar collapses after the ruthless execution of scores of Swedish noblemen in 1520 by Christian II of Denmark ("Stockholm Blood Bath"). Gustav I Vasa, with a ragtag army of peasants and foreign mercenaries, succeeds in routing the Danes.
16th–17th centuries	Gustav Vasa is crowned king of Sweden in 1523. He reshapes the nation, reorganizing its administration and stabilizing its finances. Swedish Church breaks with Rome and adopts Lutheranism. King Gustav II Adolf, crowned in 1611, extends the borders of Sweden through conquests in Russia and Poland; Sweden becomes one of the great European powers. The king is killed in battle at Lützen, Germany, in 1632, defending the Protestant cause in the Thirty Years' War. Under the short rule of his

daughter, Kristina, Stockholm evolves from a rustic village into an elegant city. Sweden gains ground in the Baltic and along the German coast, as well as in parts of Denmark and Norway. Karl XII, after a series of brilliant victories in the Great Northern War, is defeated deep in the interior of Russia (1709) and finally killed in Norway (1718). His death marks the end of Sweden's Baltic empire.

18th–19th centuries

The 18th century, a period of uninterrupted peace, is a Golden Age of culture and science. Gustav III, patron of arts and founder of the Swedish Academy, is assassinated in 1792 at a masked ball in the Stockholm Opera House. Sweden becomes involved in the Napoleonic Wars, losing Finland to Russia but taking Norway away from the Danes in compensation. In 1810 Jean-Baptiste Bernadotte, a field marshal under Napoleon, is named heir to the Swedish crown and becomes king in 1818.

19th–20th centuries

By 1850 Stockholm's population numbers around 100,000. Towards the end of the 19th century an agricultural crisis hits Sweden, causing thousands to emigrate to America. Norway declares its independence in 1905. In the 20th century Sweden's economy shifts from farming to industry. Hjalmar Branting becomes the first socialist prime minister in 1920. By adopting a policy of strict neutrality, Sweden keeps out of both world wars. Extensive development brings rapid changes to Stockholm. The country remains a constitutional monarchy, with the king as head of state, but actual power rests with parliament.

Sightseeing

Old Town

Stockholm's past is neatly concentrated in Gamla Stan (the Old Town), known as the "city between the bridges". On this small island—actually four islands—in the heart of the city, Stockholm got its start more than 700 years ago. The cobbled lanes and winding alleys of the Old Town follow the original medieval street plan. Its houses, palaces and soaring spires are steeped in history, and you'll get the impression of being transported back several centuries.

Dominating the northern end of the Old Town is **Kungliga Slottet** (the Royal Palace). It *was* known as the biggest palace in the world where royalty lived (600 rooms), but the king and queen have now decided that Drottningholm, just outside Stockholm, is more suited to family life.

Inside Kungliga Slottet, completed in 1754, you can admire the beautifully preserved Rococo interior of the Royal Chapel or Queen Kristina's silver throne in the Hall of State. The royal jewels, displayed in the **Treasury**, include the king's crown, first used for Erik XIV's coronation in 1561, and the queen's crown, studded with almost 700 diamonds, designed in 1751 for Queen Lovisa Ulrika.

Among the other palace highlights: **royal apartments** and galleries with magnificent Baroque and Rococo interiors, containing priceless 17th-century Gobelin tapestries, paintings, glass, china, jewellery and furniture collected over the centuries by kings and queens. The palace houses three more museums. The

Typical scene in busy Gamla Stan.

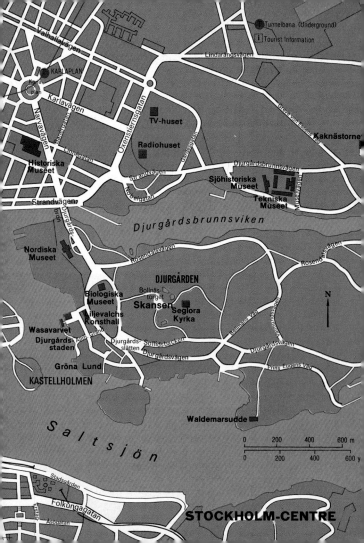

Palace Museum in the cellar contains artefacts from the Middle Ages; the **Museum of Antiquities** displays classical sculpture brought from Italy by King Gustav III during the 1780s; and **Livrustkammaren** is the Royal Armoury which contains a fascinating collection of the weapons and costumes of Swedish kings.

The **changing of the guard,** accompanied by music, takes place in the palace's outer courtyard.

The city's oldest church, **Storkyrkan** (Great Church), stands on Slottsbacken, diagonally across from the south façade of the Royal Palace. It dates back to the 13th century and is the coronation site of most of Sweden's kings. Storkyrkan's dull Baroque exterior gives no hint of the beauty of its late-Gothic interior. Note, especially, the sculptural ensemble *St. George and the Dragon,* a 15th-century masterpiece executed by Bernt Notke, a woodcarver from Lübeck, which symbolizes

St. George and the Dragon, 15th-century sculpture in Storkyrkan.

Sweden's struggles to break free of Denmark.

The tiny island of Riddarholmen (Isle of the Nobility), closely linked to the Old Town, is dominated by the **Riddarholmskyrkan**, unmistakable because of its distinctive cast-iron spire. Founded as an abbey at the end of the 13th century, this church has been the burial place of Swedish kings for some 400 years.

From Riddarholmen quay you get a marvellous **view** of Lake Mälaren.

Skeppsholmen

The enormous collection of the **Östasiatiska Museet** (Museum of Far Eastern Antiquities) covers art from Japan, Korea, India and, most notably, China, from the Stone Age to the 19th century.

The stimulating, trend-setting **Moderna Museet** (Museum of Modern Art), has kept up with the best of contemporary art from the rest of Europe and the United States. The museum's extensive collection of 20th-century art includes Matisse, Braque, Léger, Modigliani, Klee, Rauschenberg, Tinguely and Niki de Saint Phalle, plus top Swedish artists like Isaac Grünewald and Bror Hjorth.

Djurgården

This vast, largely unspoiled island of great natural beauty used to be a royal hunting park (Djurgården means "animal park"). It has miles of woodland trails, magnificent oaks (a few of the oldest go back to Viking times), surprising statuary tucked away in the greenery, outdoor coffee shops and restaurants, and some of the city's most important museums.

In the **Wasavarvet** you will see the world's oldest identified ship, the *Wasa*, Stockholm's number-one tourist attraction. This 17th-century man-of-war capsized and sank in the Stockholm harbour, a few hundred feet from the spot where it was launched on its maiden voyage in 1628. It was discovered only in 1956.

In addition to the well-preserved, elaborately decorated hull, more than 24,000 items from the ship have been recovered. To accomplish this, divers had to sift through some 40,000 cubic yards of mud in the *Wasa's* grave.

The ship is housed in a floating drydock, where visitors can walk round the scaffolding surrounding the hull to watch the fascinating work of preserving and restoring the *Wasa*. Experts were faced with the stupendous task of piecing together 14,000 fragments recovered from the deep. Towards the end of the 1980s when the complete job of restoration is done, the ship will be housed in a permanent museum on Galärvarvet.

Skansen, the world's first and most famous open-air museum, is beautifully situated on a 75-acre (30-ha.) hill. It was created by Artur Hazelius in 1891. The idea was to establish a kind of Sweden in miniature, to show how the people—from farmers to aristocrats—lived and worked during different eras.

Skansen's zoo features northern animals, such as reindeer, seals, wolves and deer, as well as fauna from other parts of the world.

The **Nordiska Museet** (Nordic Museum), also created by Artur Hazelius, shows many aspects of Swedish life – from traditional peasant costumes to an exhibition on the Lapps.

Another Djurgården attraction is **Gröna Lund,** or Tivoli. In this amusement park there are the usual fun things, but also an open-air stage where top artists perform.

Out of the deep, a macabre wooden sculpture retrieved from the warship Wasa that sank in 1628.

The City Hall

Stadshuset, located on Kungsholmen island west of the city centre, was designed by Ragnar Östberg (1923). The building rises gracefully and dramatically on the shore of Lake Mälaren.

The hand-cut brick façades and square tower capped by three golden crowns, the black granite reliefs, pillars and arches—all miraculously blend together to form a unified and coherent whole, almost an architectural hymn to the city.

Highlights include: the **Golden Hall,** covered with striking mosaics; the huge glass-domed Blue Hall (which is actually red), where the Nobel Prize banquets are held; and the Prince's Gallery with murals by Prince Eugen, who died in 1947 at the age of 82.

For a superb **view** of the Old Town and the central parts of Stockholm, go up to the top of the City Hall Tower.

City Centre

Norrmalm, Stockholm's centre, has been almost entirely rebuilt. A bewildering array of shapes and materials characterizes the soaring towers of the new buildings. Old streets have been replaced by modern shopping malls with new restaurants, cinemas and boutiques. This is where the business, banking, shopping and entertainment facilities are concentrated.

A gigantic glass obelisk rising from a fountain will tell you when you have reached **Sergels Torg** (Sergel Square), focal point of the new city centre. The square's lower-level mall, built as a shopping centre, has become a gathering place for angry people, something like the Speaker's Corner of Hyde Park in London. Most protest marches start here.

A short walk from Sergels Torg will bring you to **Hötorget** (Haymarket Square), where the open-air market, selling fresh fruit, vegetables and flowers, adds a touch of colour.

A favourite gathering place for Stockholmers and visitors alike during the warm summer months is **Kungsträdgården** (Royal Gardens), which stretch down from Hamngatan, one of the main shopping streets, to the waters of Strömmen. Established as a royal pleasure garden in the 16th century for the exclusive use of the court and the aristocracy, it now contains refreshment stands, restaurants and amusements of all sorts.

The **Nationalmuseum** (National Museum of Fine Arts), on Blasieholmen, houses a large and impressive collection of paintings, prints, engravings, miniatures, icons, statues and handicrafts. Among the paintings you will find several Rembrandts and important works by Rubens, El Greco and Brueghel, as well as French masters.

To the east of central Stockholm, in the Östermalm area, is situated the **Historiska Museet** (Museum of National Antiquities), where you can see a fascinating collection of items spanning ten thousand years of history.

Further Sights

Millesgården, on the island suburb of Lidingö, is the home, studio and garden of the late Carl Milles, Sweden's famous modern sculptor.

The beautifully terraced gardens overlooking an inlet of the Baltic provide a superb setting for replicas of Milles' best work. Included here are some of his most popular pieces—*Man and Pegasus, Europa and the Bull* and the spectacular *Hand of God.* There is also an important collection of Greek, Roman and more recent sculpture.

Millesgården itself is a work of art, the creation of a man who worshipped beauty. Silver birch and pine trees mingle naturally with statues and fountains, rose beds and urns of flowers blend with marble columns and flights of limestone steps. Carl Milles died in 1955, at the age of 80, and both he and his wife are buried in a small chapel in the garden.

Drottningholm Palace, located on a small island in Lake Mälaren and referred to as the Versailles of Sweden, was built in the late 17th century. Its formal gardens are big and impressive, with statuary, fountains, trees and lawns. Sections of the palace's well-preserved interior—richly decorated with fine tapestries and other works of art—are open to the general public.

Be sure to have a look at the **Chinese Pavilion** *(Kina Slott),* an unusual combination of Rococo and Chinese styles. It was built in the palace grounds in the 1760s as a gift to Queen Lovisa Ulrika.

Best of all is the **Drottningholm Court Theatre,** adjacent to the palace, one of the world's most famous theatrical establishments. This fully restored 18th-century theatre is unique in that its original sets (30 in all), stage machinery and props are in perfect working order and still in use. Except for the lighting—electricity has replaced candlelight—nothing has changed since King Gustav III, the patron of the arts, attended opera performances here.

During the summer months operas by Handel, Gluck, Mozart and others, as well as ballet, are performed in this gem of a theatre.

Eating Out

Sweden's most famous culinary attraction is *smörgåsbord*. It can consist of as many as 100 different dishes and should not be tackled haphazardly. The first thing to remember is not to overload your plate—you can go back to the table as many times as you wish.

Start off by sampling the innumerable herring dishes, taken with boiled potatoes and bread and butter. Then you move on to other seafood, like smoked or boiled salmon, smoked eel, Swedish caviar, shrimps, etc. Next come the delightful egg dishes, cold meats (try the smoked reindeer) and salads. The small warm dishes now loom on the horizon—such as meatballs, fried sausages and omelets —and finally (if you still have room) you end up with cheese and fruit.

Other specialities to be sampled are:

Starters
Västkustsallad is a delicious seafood salad with mushrooms and tomatoes, while *färskrökt lax* is lightly smoked salmon and *sillbord* a herring buffet. *Janssons frestelse* (a casserole of potatoes, sprats, onions and cream), *kräftor* (crayfish) and *gravad lax* (pickled salmon in dill served with mustard sauce) can be eaten either as a starter or main course.

Main Course
Kokt lax is boiled salmon, *kåldolmar* stuffed cabbage rolls; *pytt i panna*, hash served with fried eggs; *kalops*, beef stew; *dillkött*, lamb or veal in dill sauce; *köttbullar*, the famous Swedish meatballs; *strömmingsflundror*, fried herring; and *ärter med fläsk*, yellow pea soup with pork.

Desserts
You could try *våfflor* (crisp waffles served with jam and whipped cream) or *pannkakor med sylt* (pancakes with jam). Fruits such as *smultron* (wild strawberries), *blåbär* (bilberries), *lingon* (red whortleberries) and *hjortron* (Arctic cloudberries) are excellent.

Cheese
There are, reportedly, more than 200 different kinds to choose from. Look for *västerbottenost, herrgårdsost* and *sveciaost*—hard, local cheeses.

Drinks
The Swedish national drink is aquavit, also called *snaps,* distilled from potatoes or grain and flavoured with various herbs and spices. In all, there are 15 varieties. Aquavit should always be consumed with food, especially herring; it should be ice-cold and served in small glasses, taken straight in a grand gulp or two and washed down with beer or mineral water. Aquavit is closely linked to the word *skål,* that universally recognized Scandinavian toast uttered while looking straight into the eyes of your drinking companion.

Other Swedish alcoholic specialities include Punsch (punch), usually served after dinner, well chilled, with coffee. It can also be drunk hot with pea soup.

A joy for shoppers and strollers: the medieval streets of Gamla Stan (mostly car-free) filled with a tantalizing assortment of boutiques.

Shopping

VAT, or sales tax, called "moms" in Sweden, is over 20 per cent on all products and services. This tax will be refunded in cash within seven days of purchase at any point of departure to visitors who buy in shops displaying the blue-and-yellow "Tax-Free Shopping" sticker (present your passport).

Cameras. A good buy in Sweden, they include Hasselblad, the Swedish camera used in space by the American astronauts.

Candles. You'll find them in all imaginable sizes, shapes and colours, and, of course, the variety of candlesticks is equally broad.

Ceramics. Here again, there is a wide choice.

Clogs. Swedish wooden shoes, called *träskor,* have become a fashion hit around the world in recent years.

Furs. Look for the Saga label, the mink world's mark of quality and an outstanding product common to all of the Nordic countries.

Glassware. This is, without doubt, Sweden's most famous design product.

Home Furnishings. Textiles, lamps, and kitchen items are worth looking at.

Lapp Handicrafts. Many shops stock buckles, knife-handles, pouches and other handcrafted Lapp items made from reindeer antlers and skin. They are of exceptionally good quality.

Silver. You can find imaginative jewellery as well as stunning silver bowls, cigarette cases and so on.

Stainless Steel. Another superb Swedish product that has won international recognition.

Suède. Coats, jackets and skirts are excellent buys.

Souvenirs. Among the more worthwhile items are hand-carved Dala horses and hand-made dolls in authentic folk costume.

Practical Information

Banks: Open 9.30 a.m. to 3 p.m. Monday to Friday. A few of the bigger branches close sometime between 4.30 and 6 p.m.

Clothing: The weather in Stockholm in summer is pleasantly warm with low humidity. A sweater or shawl is advised for evenings, and a sturdy pair of shoes for sightseeing.

Credit cards and traveller's cheques: Accepted almost everywhere.

Currency: Swedish *krona (kr)* = 100 *öre*. Coins: 10, 50 öre; 1, 5, 10 kr. Banknotes: 10, 50, 100, 500, 1,000, 10,000 kr.

Restaurants: Lunch is served from 11.30 a.m., dinner from 6 p.m. A service charge is included, but a small extra tip is appreciated.

Shops: Open 9 or 9.30 a.m. to 6 p.m. on weekdays, until 1 p.m. on Saturdays.

Post offices: Open 9 a.m. to 6 p.m. Monday to Friday. Stockholm's main post office (Vasagatan 28–34) is open 8 a.m. to 8 p.m. weekdays, 9 a.m. to 3 p.m. Saturdays. Stamps can also be bought at tobacco shops and kiosks. Postboxes are yellow.

VENICE

Italy

Introduction

Like a glistening gem on a cushion of blue, she lies there in her lagoon, serene in the knowledge of her special place in the sun. Venice is, and always has been, a city apart, a unique blend of West and East. Traces of Byzantium and more distant oriental influence appear everywhere. It's all unlikely—and delightful.

The city rests on a archipelago of 118 islets. Buildings are supported by countless millions of larch poles driven into the sediment. Today about 85,000 Venetians live in the historic centre, but at its peak in the 16th century, the population numbered almost 200,000. Criss-crossing Venice are 177 canals, spanned by 450 bridges (some privately built and owned). The canals are partially flushed out by the tides that sweep in daily from the Adriatic. Venice's fortunes have always been linked to the sea.

Although the city fairly reeks of history and bustles with contemporary commerce, it somehow seems artificial, unreal, a fairy tale. Did people actually live in those incredibly ornate palaces? Can a city function with "streets filled with water"? Understandably, modesty is not a local virtue. "Venice, Queen of the Seas" was the proud slogan of her heyday. Centuries later, Venice continues to marvel at her glories. But few object when Venetians proclaim their city the most beautiful in the world.

Except in winter, much of Venice's energy is devoted to tourism, the modern substitute for the riches once brought home by merchant and warrior fleets. Nowhere else has the practice of relieving visitors of their currency become such a refined art. But the city does offer a lot for the money!

Venice is a tiny stone bridge over a canal with a sleek, black gondola tied up below; it's feeding the pigeons at Piazza San Marco; it's artists showing off their renditions of the city along the quays; honeymooners haggling sheepishly with a gondolier on the Grand Canal; a laundry barge making its daily rounds with stacks of freshly ironed sheets; young boys kicking a soccer ball against the wall of a beautiful Renaissance church; the suggestive glimpse of an enormous, glittering chandelier through the ballroom window of a grandiose Gothic palace; and middle-aged couples holding hands in the world's most romantic moonlight.

A Brief History

Early times
The first Venetians, fishermen and boatmen, are joined by hordes of refugees from the mainland after the Lombard invasion of 568. The lagoon communities elect a doge in 697 to govern under the auspices of Byzantium. In 810 the doge moves the capital to Rivo Alto (Rialto) to escape the invading forces of Charlemagne's son Pépin.

9th–13th centuries
Venice grows, prospers and gains its independence from Byzantium. In the 9th century, she begins a profitable commerce with the Muslims—in defiance of the pope and the Byzantine emperor—and she procures Eastern spices, silks and incense to sell in Europe. Meanwhile, the swift Venetian galleys move down into the Adriatic, secure the Dalmatian coast and eventually sail into the Aegean and Eastern Mediterranean. The city earns the name of "Serenissima, Queen of the Seas".

The Crusades prove a bonanza for the Venetians, who charge extortionate fees to build and outfit ships and equip the knights. During the infamous Fourth Crusade, Doge Enrico Dandolo personally directs the attack on Constantinople that culminates in the brutal sacking and plundering of the city in 1204. The Venetians install a new emperor and receive three-eighths of the defunct empire.

14th century
During much of the 14th century, Venice and her arch rival Genoa battle on the high seas. Overextended, Venice loses ground in the Mediterranean and cedes Dalmatia. At home, a great plague strikes in 1347-48, carrying off about half the population. Then in 1379, the Genoese fleet attacks, burning ships and seizing the important port of Chioggia. On the brink of disaster, Venice saves herself by blockading the lagoon and encircling the Genoans. Recovery comes quickly for the "Queen of the Seas" and for the first time she turns inland, acquiring Padua, Verona, Treviso, Bergamo and Ravenna.

15th–17th centuries
Venice's fortunes finally change. In 1453, the Turks capture Constantinople, cutting off her Eastern trade

routes; in 1498, Vasco da Gama's voyage around the Cape of Good Hope marks the end of her spice-trade monopoly; and closer to home, European powers join the pope in an alliance against Venice, the League of Cambrai. As her fortunes decline, Venice enters a golden age of art and architecture. In the 16th and 17th centuries, as Venice loses vital territory in Italy, Greece and Albania, Ottoman power increases.

18th–19th centuries

When Napoleon Bonaparte arrives in May 1797, he takes Venice without a struggle and deposes the last doge. French troops methodically loot the city. In October, Austria takes over, ruling Venice until Napoleon's return in 1806 and again after Waterloo. The Venetians rise under Daniele Manin in 1848, oust the Austrians and for a brief period restore the Republic. Venice finally regains her freedom in 1866 and joins the new Kingdom of Italy.

20th century

Aside from the collapse of the Campanile of San Marco in 1902, Venetian history of recent years has been unremarkable. The city comes through both world wars without major damage, though the Germans occupy Venice for a time in World War II.

Today, Venice continues to prosper from her traditional enterprises, shipping and tourism. The greatest threats to the "Queen of the Seas" nowadays come from air pollution and water erosion.

Sightseeing

Venice is a maze of waterways and walkways. Though confusing at first, you'll find it surprisingly easy to get your bearings in this small, logically arranged city. Helpful yellow signs are posted everywhere, pointing the way to San Marco (St. Mark's), Rialto and Accademia. As for the *vaporetti* (waterbuses), the mainstay of Venetian public transport, they're an absolute delight with low fares, frequent service and incomparable vistas.

Grand Canal *(Canal Grande)*
Difficult as it is for a visitor to get used to the idea, this compellingly beautiful waterway serves as the main street of Venice. Many tourists ride back and forth on the *vaporetti* for hours, taking it all in. Some

200 palaces built between the 12th and 18th centuries stand along its banks—Byzantine and Gothic, Lombard and Baroque, some carefully restored, others sadly crumbling, a few still inhabited by the grand aristocratic families. Their elegant façades have been imitated the world over. Today, they house municipal offices, hotels and museums.

Spanning the Canal roughly at midpoint is the **Rialto Bridge,** a famous Venetian landmark. Antonio da Ponte built the bridge with its double row of shops in 1588, having won a competition in which designs were also submitted by Sansovino, Palladio and Michelangelo. The Rialto district has always been the city's commercial hub. When Venice was at her peak, it was as important as any financial centre in Europe. Less grandly, the quarter was also noted for its brothels. Today Rialto is the busiest shopping area in Venice. On Rialto Bridge you will find jewellery, clothing, shoes, perfume and souvenir shops, along with hordes of hawkers peddling trinkets. The bridge leads directly down the lively fish and vegetable markets, supplying Venetian kitchens with the freshest fish and produce since 1097.

St. Mark's Square
(Piazza San Marco)
Venetians call it simply the Piazza, since it's always been the only square in town deemed worthy of the name. Splendid processions, unrivalled anywhere, were staged here. Victorious commanders returning home from campaigns abroad were honoured with lavish ceremonies in front of the basilica. European knights and ecclesiastics bought souvenirs and provisions in the Piazza's arcades before setting out on the Crusades. During the years of the Austrian occupation, the hated foreigners took their coffee at Quadri's café, so the Venetians would only patronize Florian's.

St. Mark's Basilica
(Basilica di San Marco)
Mysteriously Eastern, gloriously Western, Venice's cathedral is one of the most incredible buildings the world has ever seen. Although it encompasses a mixture of styles and irregular construction—each of its five domes, for example, has different dimensions and few of its columns match—San Marco somehow conveys the impression of harmonious beauty.

The first church was built in 830 to house the body of St. Mark, stolen from Alexandria

VENICE

N ←

Lido
Punta Sabbioni

Canale di S. Marco

Mestre-Esplanade

Chioggia →

San Giorgio
Maggiore

San Giorgio

Sco. di S. Giorgio
d. Schiavoni

S. Francesco della Vigna

San Michele

Murano
San Michele

Burano
Torcello
Treporti

S. Erasmo

Ospedali

Fondamente Nuove

Parcheggio S. Giuliano

Mestre
Madonna
dell'Orto

S. Alvise

Ponte Tre Archi

Ponte Guglie

Ferrovia

Canale Grande

S. Maria

Piazzale Roma

Parcheggio Isola del Tronchetto

Parcheggio Lido-Punta Sabbioni

S. Simeon

S. Marcuola

R. di Biasio

Ca' d'Oro

Ponte di Rialto

Ca' Foscari

Canal Grande

S. Silvestro

S. Angelo

S. Tomà

Scuola G.
di S. Rocco

Canal Grande

Ponte dell'Accademia

Ca' Rezzonico

S. Samuele

Accademia

Palazzo Ducale
Piazza
S. Marco

Palazzi
Giardinetti

Ponte
dei Sospiri

Coll. F.
Guggenheim

S. M. Sta Maria
d. Salute

Zattere

S. Basilio

Canale della Giudecca

Redentore

La Giudecca

S. Eufemia

Sacca Fisola

Ognissanti

Parcheggio Fusina

Tragnetto Lido-Punta Sabbioni

Vaporetto routes

1	6	12	17
2	8	13	24
4	9	14	
5	10,11	16	

by two Venetian adventurers, and as a chapel for the doges who lived next door. In 976 the largely wooden church burned down and the basilica we know was constructed in the 11th century. As guides shamelessly inform visitors, St. Mark's body was not the only religious treasure "stolen" from the East— almost everything else in the church was brought back as booty from the Levant.

The magical interior of San Marco is covered with about an acre of **mosaics**, the earliest dating back more than 800 years. Among the most beautiful are some on the ceiling of the atrium. Dating from the

13th century, they relate Old Testament stories. Look for a reddish **stone** in front of the main doorway: it marks the spot where in 1177 the doge forced a reconciliation between Pope Alexander III and Friederich Barbarossa, the Holy Roman Emperor.

The **Pala d'Oro**, the shimmering, bejewelled backdrop to the main altar, is one of Christendom's richest treasures. Commissioned by the doge in 976, this masterwork of the goldsmiths of Constantinople contained 2,486 pearls, garnets, sapphires, emeralds, amethysts and rubies—before Napoleon helped himself to a gem or two.

Doges' Palace
(Palazzo Ducale)
For nearly ten centuries, this magnificent palace was the seat of the Republic and residence of most of Venice's doges. It remains almost exactly as it was in the Republic's heyday, rich with reminders of a momentous past. The original 9th-century, fortress-like palace was partially replaced and rebuilt a number of times over the centuries. It took its present form—a unique blend of Byzantine, Gothic and Renaissance elements—in the 15th century.

The **Great Council Chamber** (Sala del Maggior Consiglio), a monument from the early days of Venetian democracy, was the place where the citizens assembled to elect doges and discuss state policies. Later, only

A familiar landmark on the Grand Canal, Santa Maria della Salute.

VENICE

nobles convened in the vast hall. Covering the wall behind the doge's throne is the largest oil painting in the world, **Tintoretto's Paradise.** This monumental work, based on Dante's *Paradiso,* was undertaken by the artist at the age of 70.

The famous **Bridge of Sighs** *(Ponte dei Sospiri)* leads to prison cells in another building. The name supposedly came from the sighs of the inmates as they were led over the bridge to torture or execution.

St. Mark's Bell Tower
(Campanile di San Marco)

Towering over San Marco and the entire city is a bell tower to top all bell towers. It served its Republic proudly as watchtower, beacon, weather vane, gun turret and belfry. The original stood for almost 1,000 years, until about 10 a.m. on July 14, 1902, when it collapsed gracefully into the Piazza below. The city council quickly decided to rebuild the tower "as it was, where it was" *(com'era, dov'era),* a phrase now part of Venetian lore. On April 25, 1912, exactly 1,000 years after the erection of the original Campanile, the almost exact replica was inaugurated. The new one, many hundreds of tons lighter, is believed to be sound enough to last another millennium.

The ride up to the top lasts scarcely a minute. On a clear day, the **view**—of the Adriatic, the *lidi* sheltering Venice, the lagoon islands, the mainland shores and snow-topped Alps to the north—is justly celebrated.

Clock Tower
(Torre dell'Orologio)

Speaking of towers, consider that marvellously colourful example across the Piazza. For nearly five centuries, the two

Moors up there have been hammering the hours on their great bell. Somehow, they've dented it only slightly, as you'll see when you climb the 136 steps that wind up to this landmark. The tower itself features the inevitable winged lion and a splendid zodiac clock which shows the time in Arabic and Roman numerals.

The Art of Venice

The greatest legacy of Venice —aside from the city itself— is its art. The following museums and churches offer outstanding works of the Venetian (and other) masters.

Accademia

This unsurpassed collection of Venetian art includes just about everything. Don't miss Gentile Bellini's *Procession around the Piazza* and Carpaccio's *Miracle of the Holy Cross at the Rialto Bridge* (the earlier bridge)—two of the city's most famous paintings; Giovanni Bellini's beautiful *Madonna and Child* series; Mantegna's *St. George* and Giorgione's lyrical *Tempest; Feast at the House of Levi,* a compelling canvas by Veronese that covers a whole wall; *Presentation* by Titian, considered one of his finest works; and Tintoretto's dazzling *Transport of the Body of St. Mark.*

Scuola Grande di San Rocco

An absolutely breathtaking collection of Tintoretto paintings, 56 in all, displayed in one

Horses on the Move

The bold bronze chargers over the main portal of San Marco must be the world's best-travelled equine team.

Once they crowned Trajan's Arch in Rome, but just where they came from originally remains a mystery. Later on, they graced the imperial hippodrome of Constantinople, until Doge Dandolo took the city and the horses in 1204. In Venice, they guarded the Arsenal for a while and then took their honoured place on San Marco. Napoleon, however, fancied the celebrated *quadriga* and carried it off to Paris; the Austrians brought it back. Finally, during each of the world wars, the horses were sent outside the city for safekeeping.

The Venetians vowed that their horses would not move again. But a different kind of menace caused a minor change in plans. The beloved bronze chargers have been moved inside, safe from the corrosive effects of air pollution, and replicas now stand in for them on the balcony of the basilica.

of the most opulent interiors imaginable. Hire a mirror here to study the stunning sacred works on the ceiling. Tintoretto's monumental *Crucifixion* (in the Sala dell'Albergo) is said to be the painting he considered his masterpiece.

Scuola di San Giorgio degli Schiavoni

Probably nowhere is there so much spectacular painting on view in such a tiny space. Vittore Carpaccio decorated the chapel of the guildhall of the Dalmatian merchants in Venice between 1502 and 1508 with scenes from the lives of St. George and St. Jerome.

Santa Maria Gloriosa dei Frari

Here you'll find two of Titian's most famous paintings—the exquisite *Assumption* (1518) above the high altar and *Madonna di Ca'Pesaro* (1526) over an altar on the left—as well as the great artist's tomb, erected 300 years after his death by the Emperor of Austria. See, too, the fine Bellini triptych of the *Madonna and Saints* (1488) and Donatello's wooden statue of *St. John the Baptist*.

Madonna dell'Orto

This was Tintoretto's parish church and he is buried here with his family near the high

altar. Two of the artist's finest works hang by the altar—*Last Judgement* and the *Worship of the Golden Calf*. His dramatic *Presentation of the Virgin* is over the sacristy door.

Collezione Guggenheim

Here's a chance to visit one of those intriguing Venetian palaces along the Grand Canal. Now a museum, the Palazzo Venier dei Leoni was the home of American expatriate Peggy Guggenheim. She died in 1979, leaving behind one of the best collections of modern art in Europe. Among the outstanding works: a 1910 cubist Picasso, *The Poet;* Constantine Brancusi's often-imitated bronze sculpture, *Bird in Flight,* and Mario Marini's *Horse and Rider,* plus a whole roomful of Jackson Pollock paintings.

Boat Excursions

The Venetian lagoon holds many delights for visitors. You can reach the main attractions either by *vaporetto* or on an organized tour. First stop is bound to be the island of **Murano,** known the world over for its glass blowing. Take a look into one of the factories to see the craftsmen at work, but be prepared for a hard sell. Some of the finest pieces made over the last five centuries can be seen in the glass museum.

Further west is the picturesque island of **Burano,** the pearl of the Venetian lagoon. The people here still live off fishing and lace-making. You'll find that the campanile of San Martino has a decided tilt to it, and the trim little red, blue, yellow and gold houses a great deal of charm.

Torcello, on the other side of Burano, was once a thriving community of 20,000, the seat of a bishop. But as Venice grew, Torcello declined and in time it was abandoned, looted and almost forgotten. Today, all that remains is its cathedral, glowing with superb Byzantine **mosaics** of blue and gold.

The Venetian lagoon is enclosed by long strips of beach known as *litorale.* Closest to Venice proper is the world-renowned **Lido,** a sandy beach lined with a string of luxury hotels. In summer, the municipal casino offers gambling, puts on film festivals and art shows. This resort was the setting for Thomas Mann's *Death in Venice,* but you'll only experience the funereal atmosphere of the novel if you visit off season, when the crowds have disappeared and the mists and fog banks seep in from the sea.

Eating Out

Venice boasts some very good local dishes. Best of all is the superb seafood. And for much of the year you can dine outdoors, enjoying the passing parade as you eat.

Proceeding through the meal Italian style, Venetian restaurants offer a great variety of first courses, such as the antipasto of mixed seafood (*misto* or *frutti di mare*); marinated sardines *(sarde in saor);* ham *(prosciutto)* with melon or figs *(melone* or *fichi).*

Many diners skip this course, starting with a rice dish *(risotto),* a Venetian speciality. Local favourites include *nero di seppie* (squid and its ink), *primavera* (with fresh vegetables) and *risi e bisi* (rice and peas). Spaghetti and many other types of Italian pasta are, of course, served in Venice, but this is really rice country.

The variety of Adriatic seafood seems infinite here. Almost every restaurant offers *San Pietro* (John Dory), a tasty white fish prepared a number of ways; grilled *coda di rospo* (monk fish), *sfogio* (sole), sometimes served in a sweet-and-sour sauce; *anguilla alla veneziana* (eel with tunny sauce) and *scampi* (prawns). If you have trouble deciding which to choose, order the *fritto misto,* (mixed fried fish) for a delicious sampling.

Typical, too, is calves' liver and onions *(fegato alla veneziano)* with *polenta* (maize or cornmeal puree), the omnipresent Venetian side dish.

For those still able to summon an appetite for dessert, restaurants always have a choice of tarts or cakes and several flavours of the exquisite Italian ice-cream. The famous *zuppa inglese,* a sort of creamy trifle, has nothing remotely to do with soup.

The Veneto area produces a number of very pleasant red and white wines. You'll often do as well here with a carafe of open wine. The best local reds are Valpolicella, Valpantena and Bardolino—all light and dry; Soave is the most famous white from the region. From Friuli come Pinot Grigio and Pinot Bianco, two dry whites.

Almost everyone orders mineral water *(acqua minerale)* with meals, either carbonated *(gasata)* or still *(naturale),* though Venetian tap water *(acqua normale),* is perfectly drinkable. If you find the Italian espresso too strong for your taste, ask for a *caffè lungo* (made with more water) or a *cappuccino* with milk. *Buon appetito!*

Shopping

Venice offers a dazzling concentration of shops with enticing window displays. You will find the most exclusive shops around the Piazza, very good shops with more competitive prices along the Merceria, Venice's main shopping street, and budget-priced goods around the Rialto and on the Strada Nuova leading to the railway station. Inevitably, you'll see a good deal of junk in Venice, too, mountains of glass bric-a-brac and cheap souvenirs.

Best Buys

Costume **jewellery** abounds in Venice at reasonable prices. Gold and silver pieces, including some marvellous filigree, are fairly expensive but show the stamp of Venetian craftsmanship.

Italian **leather goods** and fine **silk** scarves, shawls, blouses and ties are definitely worth looking at.

Some distinctly Venetian items: wonderful 17th- or 18th-century theatrical and carnival **masks** of papier-mâché; **gondolier slippers,** normally made of velvet with rope soles, or an inexpensive and authentic **gondolier's straw hat** with coloured band; exquisite items of **lace** made by the women of Burano.

Approach with Caution
Glass: the Murano glassware you see today—and see it you will all over Venice—is not up to the old standards. But with patience, the discerning buyer can find a nice piece. **Italianate antiques:** tourists who aren't specialists should beware of locally produced "Victorian" articles or 1980 copies of 18th-century items. Above all, any pedlars of "original" religious relics should be sternly avoided.

Practical Information

Dress: The general rule is informality, but men usually wear jackets and ties to the best restaurants. Shorts or bare-backed dresses are not suitable attire for visiting churches.

Gondolas, Vaporetti: You may hear that gondola rates are municipally fixed; in practice, some visitors "successfully" bargain the price down slightly—but never to an inexpensive level. *Vaporetti* (Venice's diesel-powered waterbuses), on the other hand, are one of the world's great transport bargains.

Money matters: The currency in Italy is the *lira* (plural *lire,* usually abbreviated *L*). **Currency exchange:** banks, which give the best rate, are open 8.30 a.m.–2 p.m. and 3–4 p.m., Monday to Friday; the *cambio* (exchange offices) reopen after lunch.

Credit cards, traveller's cheques and eurocheques are readily accepted.

Post office: The main branch at Rialto Bridge is open from 8 a.m. to 2 p.m. Monday to Saturday. In the lobby, telegrams, telexes, express and registered letters may be sent 24 hours a day.

Restaurants: Lunch is usually served from 1 p.m., dinner starting at 8 p.m. Your bill will include the tax (IVA) and generally a service charge *(servizio),* but it's customary to leave another 10% or so.

Shops: Open 9–12.30 and 3.30–7.30, Tuesday to Saturday; most businesses close Monday morning.

VIENNA

Austria

Introduction

More than most, Vienna is a city of legends. Part of the adventure of going there is discovering how much is true, how much fantasy.

As the old capital of the Habsburg empire that included not only Slavs and Hungarians but also Germans, Spaniards, Italians and Belgians, Vienna has always been an outpost and gateway of Western civilization. A melting pot long before New York, the city has perpetually defied a simple national label. Its language is German—with a distinctive Viennese touch. But the city and people have too much Balkan and Latin in them to be compared with Hamburg, Berlin or Frankfurt.

Much of the town's 18th-century charm and 19th-century pomp have withstood the onslaught of World War II bombs, post-war building speculation and the inevitable pollution of modern traffic. Its exhilarating tree-lined Ringstrasse, encircling the Innere Stadt (Inner City), compares favourably with the airy sweep of Parisian boulevards. In every sense the heart of the city, the Innere Stadt has Baroque palaces, elegant shops, gay cafés, the illustrious Burgtheater and Staatsoper (State Opera) and narrow medieval streets, winding around the cathedral.

Outside the Ring, the city sprawls through 22 other districts with plentiful parks and even farms and vineyards inside the city limits. Vienna has space to relax, a city in a rural setting that makes the attitude to life of its 1½ million population more easy-going than in most modern cities.

This pleasant atmosphere always comes as a surprise to visitors. Most of the people still seem to have time for the courtesies of the old days. Shopkeepers like to call their regular customers by aristocratic titles that, constitutionally, should have disappeared 60 years ago, or at least by a nicely inflated professional title.

No word better describes the ideal of Viennese life than *Gemütlichkeit*. Literally untranslatable, *gemütlich* means agreeable, comfortable. As unmistakable as a Viennese smile, it is the quality that takes the rough edges off life. And the Viennese protect the *Gemütlichkeit* of their lives with their undying ironic sense of humour. Nothing is so bad that it doesn't have a good side and nothing so good that there isn't a risk somewhere. According to an old joke, "Everything in Vienna is ge- *mütlich* except the wind." "Yes," goes the answer, "and the wind comes only because it's so *gemütlich* here."

A Brief History

1st–3rd centuries	Romans set up a garrison—Vindobona—on the Danube and drive off successive invasions by Teutons, Slavs and other tribes. Emperor Marcus Aurelius leads fighting against the barbarians and dies in Vindobona in 180.
4th–12th centuries	Christianity is introduced; barbarian invasions continue. Huns, Goths, Franks, Avars, Bavarians, Slavs and Magyars burn, plunder and pillage the town. The Magyars are driven out by the Babenberg dynasty around 1000. They are named hereditary Dukes of Austria by the Holy Roman Emperor in 1156.
13th century	Vienna's first "golden age" begins. Art, trade, and handicraft thrive; Scottish and Irish monks establish a monastery; churches, residences and new thoroughfares are built. The era of the minstrels starts the long musical tradition of Vienna. The last of the Babenbergs dies in 1246 and Ottokar II of Bohemia succeeds to the regency. He is supplanted by German King Rudolf von Habsburg in 1278.
14th–16th centuries	Rudolf der Stifter (the Founder) creates the university in 1365. In 1469 Vienna is granted Rome's approval as a bishopric. Hungarian King Matthias Corvinus occupies the city from 1485 to 1490. In 1529 Turks under Suleiman the Magnificent lay siege to the city. The Innere Stadt holds firm and Suleiman retreats. The Reformation reaches Vienna but Catholicism remains predominant. The city emerges as the bulwark of the Church and stands not only against the Muslim Turks but also against the Protestant Swedes who attack the city during the Thirty Years' War.
17th century	Emperor Leopold I ushers Vienna into its glorious Baroque era. The construction of magnificent palaces

	and churches begins. The plague strikes in 1679; the Turks lay a second unsuccessful siege in 1683.
18th century	Emperor Charles VI is succeeded by his daughter Maria Theresa. Her relatively benevolent 40-year reign extends its influence to the capital's citizens and Vienna blooms as a musical city. Concerts, operas, chamber music are performed daily in Viennese woods, palaces, parks and gardens.
19th century	Napoleon's armies arrive in 1805. Emperor Franz I gives his daughter Marie Louise in diplomatic marriage to Napoleon in 1810. The Congress of Vienna completes its territorial discussions in June 1815 and provides Europe with a framework for international diplomacy which is to last a hundred years. The Ringstrasse complex of aristocratic residences is developed. The grand new opera house is built; theatres, concert halls and museums provide a forum for the empire's cultural achievements.
20th century	The Habsburg empire ends with World War I, which leaves Vienna in economic and social ruin. Chancellor Dollfuss is murdered by Austrian Nazis in 1934. Hitler annexes Austria and it becomes a province of "Greater Germany" from 1938 to 1945. After the war Vienna is divided into four sectors under the joint four-power administration of the Americans, Russians, British and French. In 1955 Austria is given independent neutral status and enters a prosperous new period of economic recovery.

Sightseeing

The best way to appreciate the Innere Stadt is on foot, but for a more romantic introduction to the town, try a **Fiaker tour.** The two-horse open carriages have been in business since the 17th century, and their elegantly turned out drivers have a fund of amusing stories to put you in the right mood.

The cathedral, **Stephansdom,** will draw you like a magnet; it is the ideal starting-point for your visit. With its Romanesque western façade, Gothic tower and Baroque altars, the cathedral is a marvellous example of the Viennese genius for harmonious compromise, melding the austerity, dignity and exuberance of those great architectural styles. The Romanesque origins are visible in the Heidentürme and statuary depicting, among others, a griffin and Samson fighting a lion. The transformation into the Gothic structure we see today was carried out mainly in the 14th and 15th centuries.

From the north tower you have a fine view of the city, and of the huge Pummerin bell cast from melted-down Turkish cannons after the 1683 siege was repelled. The present bell is a recast version of the original destroyed during World War II.

Inside the church you should look in the centre aisle for the charming carved Gothic **pulpit** by Anton Pilgram. At the head of the spiral staircase, the sculptor has placed Augustine, Gregory, Jerome and Ambrose, fathers of the Church. He also defied the customary medieval anonymity with a sculpture of himself looking through a window under the staircase.

On the left side of the high altar you'll find the carved wooden **Wiener Neustädter Altar;** on the right side is the impressive marble **tomb** of Emperor Friedrich III, honoured by the Viennese as the man who had the city made a bishopric.

After a long visit to the Stephansdom (and a coffee in one of the pleasant cafés in the area) head for the **Figarohaus** just south-east of the cathedral. Here, from 1784 to 1787, lived Wolfgang Amadeus Mozart; the house is now a museum devoted to the great man. He wrote 11 of his piano concertos here, as well as the *Marriage of Figaro* and many other pieces of music. The composer died, after struggling to finish the *Magic Flute* and the *Requiem,* a few hundred yards away, in the musty Rauhensteingasse. He died a pauper, whose coffin was blessed in an anonymous ceremony for that day's dead.

Stroll back to the **Kärntnerstrasse,** the city's main north-south thoroughfare where many of Vienna's smartest shops can be found. Today it is a traffic-free pedestrian zone with open-air cafés down the middle of the street. At the Stephansdom end of Kärntnerstrasse pass through the Stock-im-Eisen square to the **Graben,** also a pedestrian zone. The **Pestsäule** (Pillar of the Plague) is a somewhat grotesque monument commemorating the town's deliverance from the plague in 1679.

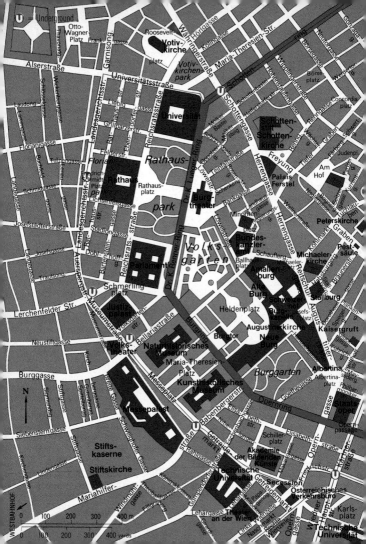

The **Peterskirche** (St. Peter's Church), just off the Graben, provides a splendid example of how Viennese Baroque manages more often than not to be both sumptuous and intimate.

From here you can make your way through the old Jewish quarter and past the solid ivy-covered Ruprechtskirche to the **Hoher Markt** which was the forum of the Roman settlement, Vindobona. A small museum displays the remains of two Roman houses laid bare by a 1945 bombardment.

Go west to Salvatorgasse, past the superb Renaissance porch of the Salvatorkapelle, a happy marriage of Italian design and Austrian late-Gothic sculpture. Beyond it is the slender jewel of 14th-century Gothic, the church of **Maria am Gestade** ("Mary on the banks"—of the River Danube that used to flow directly below it).

Walk back across the Judenplatz—where with luck you may hear an open-air chamber music concert—to the spacious **Platz am Hof,** largest square of the old city. From here make for the **Freyung** triangle flanked by the **Schottenkirche** (Church of the Scots), founded by Scottish and Irish Benedictine monks in the 12th century. The monks had been invited by Duke Heinrich II Jasomirgott who is commemorated by a modern monument on the side of the church.

Ring

Before tackling the Hofburg, it's a good idea to go around the Ring, probably the greatest single urban achievement of Franz Joseph. This boulevard encircling the Innere Stadt was mapped out in the 1860s along the ramparts Joseph II had begun clearing 80 years before.

Start your walk at the west end of the Schottenring, in front of the Votivkirche, a neo-Gothic church built after Franz Joseph survived an assassination attempt in 1853. Next to it are the university and Rathaus (Town Hall) with a pleasant park, but proceed along the Innere Stadt side, past the impressive **Burgtheater,** a high temple of German theatre. Beyond the theatre is the lovely **Volksgarten.** Its cafés and open-air concerts carry on a tradition that began with the café music of the Strauss family.

The **Burggarten,** the park of Hofburg, leads to the **Staatsoper** (State Opera). It's worth taking a guided tour here before attending a performance.

On Karlsplatz, not far from the opera house, stands the huge **Karlskirche,** undoubtedly the most important of the city's Baroque churches.

The church's visual impact has been somewhat diminished since the building of the Ringstrasse. However, the cool, sober interior remains unchanged, with a subdued marble decor and a spacious but gentle oval ground-plan similar to that of the Peterskirche.

In front of the church, a massive Henry Moore sculpture in a reflector pool provides a striking contrast. Also on the Karlsplatz is the fanciful **Stadtbahnpavillon** (Municipal Railway Pavilion) with its graceful green, gold and white Jugendstil motif of sunflowers and tulips.

Palaces

Though the Habsburgs are long gone, Vienna remains an imperial city—an aura enhanced by its palaces. The most imposing is of course the **Hofburg,** home of Austria's rulers since the 13th century.

The vast complex of buildings went through five major stages of construction over six centuries. Start your visit right in the middle at the **Schweizerhof**, named after the Swiss Guard that used to be housed there. Here King Ottokar of Bohemia built a fortress in 1275–76 to defend himself against Rudolf von Habsburg. He wasn't successful and the Habsburgs moved in; they strengthened the fortifications because of the unruly Viennese outside.

The **Burgkapelle** (Castle Chapel), tucked away in the northern corner of the Schweizerhof, was built in 1449. Originally Gothic, it was redone in Baroque style and then partially restored to its original form in 1802. The Wiener Sängerknaben (Vienna Boys' Choir) sing Mass here every Sunday morning except in July, August and September.

Between 1558 and 1565 Ferdinand built the **Stallburg** (outside the main Hofburg complex on the north-east side of Reitschulgasse) as a home for his son Archduke Maximilian.

Still in Renaissance style is Rudolf II's **Amalienburg,** built between 1575 and 1611, mostly by Italian architect Pietro Ferrabosco.

Leopold I launched the city's Baroque era with his **Leopoldinischer Trakt** (Leopold

Wing)—a residence in keeping with the Habsburgs' new role as a world power.

Karl VI carried the Habsburg's new self-confidence proudly forward with the **Reichskanzlei** (Imperial Chancellory), where Franz Joseph was later to have his apartments, the Hofbibliothek (Court—now National—Library) and the Winterreitschule (Winter—better known as the Spanish—Riding School).

The **Josefsplatz** is a marvellously harmonious Baroque square. Inside the old library, a great oval hall with frescoes and walnut shelves, called the **Prunksaal,** is one of the most beautiful workrooms in the world.

Just off the Josefsplatz is the church that the Habsburgs favoured for their great events, the **Augustinerkirche.** The façade of this Gothic and Baroque structure matches the library and Redoutensaal.

On the other hand, the church the Habsburgs chose to be buried in, the Kapuzinerkirche, lies outside of the Hofburg. Its **Kaisergruft** (Imperial Vault) contains about 140 assorted Habsburgs—emperors, empresses, archdukes and less exalted members of the family.

Even if the **Spanish Riding School** *(Spanische Reitschule)* had not claimed the world's attention for the prowess of the Lipizzaner horses, it

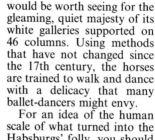

would be worth seeing for the gleaming, quiet majesty of its white galleries supported on 46 columns. Using methods that have not changed since the 17th century, the horses are trained to walk and dance with a delicacy that many ballet-dancers might envy.

For an idea of the human scale of what turned into the Habsburgs' folly, you should take the 45-minute guided tour of the **Imperial Apartments** *(Kaiserappartements),* entrance on Michaelerplatz.

When you leave the Hofburg, take the Schauflergasse to **Ballhausplatz** to see the elegant 18th-century residence of the Austrian chancellors. In the time of Metternich, the world would ask what "the Ballhaus" would do next, just as today it wonders about the thinking of the White House or the Kremlin. Chancellor Dollfuss was assassinated here in July 1934.

If the Hofburg is the oversize expression of a dynasty that outgrew its own virility **Schönbrunn** is the smiling, serene expression of the personality of one woman—Maria Theresa, Archduchess of Austria, Queen of Bohemia and Hungary, as her official titles described her.

To appreciate the emphasis

that Schönbrunn puts on pleasure, rather than imperial pomp, it is best to visit the **gardens** first. The park, laid out in the classical French manner, is dominated by the **Gloriette,** a neo-classical colonnade perched on the crest of a hill. East of the Neptune Fountain are the incredible **"Roman ruins",** actually built in 1778—a half-buried "Roman palace" with bits of Corinthian columns, friezes and archways.

After visiting the gardens head for the **palace** where a guided tour will give you a glimpse of the sumptuous comfort in which Maria Theresa and her successors handled the affairs of state: her breakfast room, decorated with the needlework of the empress and her myriad daughters; the **Spiegelsaal** (Hall of Mirrors) in which the young Mozart gave his first royal recital; the **Chinesisches Rundkabinett** (Chinese Round Room), superbly adorned with lacquered Oriental panels, and also known as Maria Theresa's Konspirationstafelstube (roughly translatable as "top secret dining-room").

You should not miss what is now known as the **Napoleon Room** (though it once was

Maria Theresa's bedroom), where the emperor stayed on his way to the Battle of Austerlitz and where his son, the Duke of Reichstadt, spent his last sad years.

In the adjoining **Wagenburg** museum, you can marvel at a collection of coaches used by the imperial court.

Of all the palaces built by the princes, dukes and barons serving the Habsburgs, the most splendid is certainly the **Belvedere** of Prince Eugene of Savoy. It is regarded as Vienna's finest flowering of Baroque residential architecture. Today the **Unteres Belvedere** and its **Orangerie** together house the admirable collections of Austrian medieval and Baroque art. In the **Oberes** (or Upper) **Belvedere,** the prince held his banquets and other festivities. Nowhere will you get a more delightful view of the city skyline than from the **terrace** of the Oberes Belvedere—little changed since Bellotto-Canaletto painted it in 1760.

The Other Vienna

Beyond the Innere Stadt and outside the Habsburg world of the Hofburg and Schönbrunn, there is another Vienna, the people's Vienna.

Cross the Danube Canal at the junction of Franz-Josefs-Kai and Stubenring over the Aspernbrücke. This takes you to the **Prater** park, Vienna's own non-stop carnival (also accessible by tram or underground). If the Stephansdom had not already become the undisputed symbol of the city, the Prater's **Riesenrad** (giant Ferris wheel) built in 1897 would certainly have laid a claim.

The Riesenrad, with its 14 bright red cabins taking you up for a constantly changing perspective of the city's skyline, is only part of the fair that includes roller-coasters, discotheques, shooting ranges, restaurants and beer halls.

The **Donaupark** linking the old and new Danube is more tranquil than the Prater, laid out with beautiful flower beds, an artificial lake, sports arenas and a chair-lift from which to survey it all. It also features an 827-foot (250-m.) tower, **Donauturm,** with two revolving restaurants and a public terrace featuring a view across the city south to the hills of the Wienerwald and north-west to the Abbey of Klosterneuburg.

Döbling is the most gracious of Vienna's neighbourhoods. Stretching from the Danube Canal back to the undulating slopes of the Wienerwald, Döbling includes Sievering, Grinzing, Heiligenstadt, Nussdorf and Kahlenberg. It has elegant villas, parks, vineyards and, of course, the ever popular Heurigen wine gardens.

A short detour to the north takes in the imposing Augustine Abbey of **Klosterneuburg.** An apocryphal story claims it was founded by Duke Leopold III of Babenberg in 1106 on the spot where the lost veil of his bride was discovered by his hunting dogs. Little of the original edifice remains.

Museums

Vienna's National Gallery, the **Kunsthistorisches Museum,** is outstanding. The magnificent collection contains masterpieces by all of the European great masters—Dutch, Flemish, German and English to the left and Italian, Spanish and French to the right. Austrian art is missing though; that is because it is housed separately at the **Belvedere** in three different galleries: the medieval museum, the Baroque museum and the 19th- and 20th-century gallery.

You can also admire 20th-century works in the **Museum der Modernen Kunst** in the Palais Liechtenstein at Fürstengasse 1.

Most of the vast Habsburg fortune can be seen in the Hofburg. The **Schatzkammer** (Treasury), in the Schweizerhof, contains a dazzling display of the insignia of the old Holy Roman Empire. These include the Imperial Crown of pure unalloyed gold, set with pearls and unpolished emeralds, sapphires and rubies.

The **Hoftafel und Silberkammer** (Court China and Silver Collection) exhibits the priceless Chinese, Japanese, French Sèvres and German Meissen services amassed by the Habsburgs in six centuries.

You can visit the Schubert, Haydn, Beethoven or Mozart museums, but the best arranged of these "personal" museums, but the best arhostility with which most Viennese received him during his lifetime, is the one devoted to **Sigmund Freud.** The house at Berggasse 19 has become a mecca for students—and patients—of psychoanalysis from all over the world.

Eating Out

The emperors, archdukes and generals have gone; not so the Bohemian dumplings, Hungarian goulash, Polish stuffed cabbage and Serbian schaschlik. But there are Austrian specialities too: *Wienerschnitzel,* a large thinly sliced cutlet of veal crisply sautéed in a coating of egg and seasoned breadcrumbs; *Wienerbackhendl,* boned roast chicken prepared like *Wienerschnitzel*; *Tafelspitz,* boiled beef, a Viennese favourite; or *Knödel,* dumplings served with soups and with the meat dish, studded with pieces of liver or bacon, or as a dessert with hot apricot inside *(Marillenknödel)* or with cream cheese *(Topfenknödel).*

Another delicious dessert is *Apfelstrudel,* thinly sliced apple with raisins and cinnamon rolled in an almost transparent, flaky pastry. As for pastries: like "waltz", "woods", and "Danube", the word is almost inseparable from Vienna itself. The variations of cherries, strawberries, hazelnuts, walnuts, apple and chocolate in tarts, pies and cakes are endless. Have them *mit Schlag* (with whipped cream) or without, but have them. And join in the never-ending controversy over the most famous chocolate cake in the world, the *Sachertorte*—whether it should be split and where the apricot jam should go.

Coffee and Wine

Coffee is to Vienna as tea is to England, but you can't just go into a café and ask for "a cup of coffee", as the varieties are endless and there are names for all the shadings from black to white. Ask for *einen kleinen Mokka* and you'll get a small strong black coffee and stamp yourself as someone of French or Italian taste. *Einen Kapuziner,* topped with whipped cream, is already more Viennese; *einen Braunen* with just a dash of milk, entirely Viennese, sophisticated; *eine Melange* (pronounced *"melanksch"*), half milk, half coffee, designed for sensitive stomachs; *einen Einspänner* with whipped cream in a tall glass is for aunts on Sundays; *einen Türkischen,* prepared semi-sweet in a copper pot.

Wine in Vienna is almost always white wine, which the Viennese drink quite happily with meat and fish alike. The best known of Austrian white wines, the Gumpoldskirchner, has the good body and bouquet of its southern vineyards. But the Viennese give equal favour to their own Grinzinger, Nussdorfer, Sieveringer and Neustifter. From the Danube valley, with an extra natural sparkle, come the Kremser, Dürnsteiner and Langenloiser.

Shopping

Not surprisingly, the most important shopping attraction in Vienna—a town preoccupied by its history—is **antiques.** Furniture and objets d'art from all over the old empire have somehow ended up here

in the little shops in the Innere Stadt.

Still in the realm of the past are the great speciality shops for **coin-** and **stamp-**collectors (where else could you expect to find mint-condition Bosnia-Herzegovina issues of 1914?).

The national **Augarten porcelain** workshops still turn out hand-decorated Rococo chinaware, including, of course, the Lipizzaner horses in action. **Petit-point embroidery** is available in the form of handbags, cushions and other items with flower, folk and opera motifs.

You will find the more elegant shops on the Kärntnerstrasse, Graben and Kohlmarkt.

If your taste runs from the exquisite to High Kitsch, try your luck in the Saturday morning flea market on the Naschmarkt.

Practical Information

Banks: Open from 8 a.m. to 3 p.m., Mondays to Fridays (Thursdays until 5.30 p.m.). Branches usually close between 12.30 and 1.30 p.m.

Clothing: Vienna's weather tends to be extreme—very hot in the summer and very cold in the winter—and the wind off the steppes can whip through at any time. Even in summer you should take a cardigan and a raincoat for the suddenly cooler evenings.

The Viennese like to dress up for the theatre, concert and opera, but a dark suit or cocktail dress is nearly always appropriate.

Currency: Austria's monetary unit is the *Schilling,* abbreviated *S, ÖS* or *Sch.,* divided into *Groschen* (abbreviated *g*). Coins: 1, 5, 10 and 20 S, and 10 and 50 g. Be sure you don't confuse the similar 5- and 10-schilling pieces. Banknotes: 20, 50, 100, 500 and 1000 S.

Shops: Most small shops are open from 9 a.m. (food shops an hour earlier) to 6 p.m. with a break for lunch. Major department stores do business from 8 a.m. to 6 p.m. non-stop, but supermarkets close for about two hours at lunch. Saturday afternoons shops are closed.

ZURICH

Switzerland

Introduction

There's much more to Zurich *(Zürich)* than mere gold ingots and bank vaults. The lake and the river are liquid assets that add greatly to the appeal of the city and the general welfare of its inhabitants. The preserved area of guildhalls and medieval houses has great charm. And the modern shopping district glitters as few others can afford to.

Zurich's economic importance—financiers usually put it on a par with New York, London and Paris—may conjure up the idea of an impersonal metropolis. Yet with less than 400,000 inhabitants, the city is manageably sized and easy enough to explore. The "gnomes of Zurich" who wheel and deal in billions of francs' worth of foreign currencies may maintain a hectic pace, but the rest of the citizens are more relaxed. Local people find the time to enjoy the theatres and museums, restaurants and nightclubs, the water sports at the door and the mountains just up the road.

The status of Zurich as a financial capital is little more than a century old: the local stock exchange was founded in 1877. But the city began 2,000 years ago when the Romans established a customs post on a hill overlooking the River Limmat, the Lindenhof, now the city's geographical centre. It took another thousand years before Zurich was recognized as a town, soon to become a prosperous centre of silk-, wool- and linen-weaving industries. In 1351 Zurich joined the Swiss Confederation. The noblemen and merchants had then recently agreed to share power with representatives of the tradesmen's guilds; the guildhalls are still among the most precious landmarks in the old town.

In the 16th century the priest Ulrich Zwingli brought the Reformation to Zurich, adding intellectual renown to the city's growing importance in business and politics. Down through the centuries Zurich has attracted scores of great men, from Goethe and Wagner to Mann and Einstein, James Joyce and Lenin. During World War I, the nihilistic art movement known as Dada was born in what was then Zurich's Café Voltaire.

And today, business and technical knowhow combine with artistic and intellectual vitality to make Zurich an exciting city—with charm.

A Brief History

4th–1st centuries B.C.	The Helvetians, of Celtic origin, settle in Switzerland. In 15 B.C. the Romans establish a customs post—later a fort—on the site of present-day Zurich.
3rd–9th centuries A.D.	With the collapse of the Roman Empire, the Alemanni, a German tribe, settle in eastern Switzerland. The country becomes part of the Holy Roman Empire.
10th–13th centuries	In 1218 Zurich wins independence as an imperial city. Powerful European families struggle for power in Switzerland. In 1291 the cantons of Uri, Schwyz and Unterwalden, south of Zurich, join in a Confederation to resist foreign pressure.
14th century	Zurich's merchants and artisans, grouped in guilds, oust the local aristocratic families from power and, to prevent them returning with Habsburg support, Zurich joins the Confederation in 1351. In 1386 the Swiss decisively defeat the Austrians at the Battle of Sempach, south-west of Zurich.
15th–17th centuries	The Confederation is strengthened by the addition of Berne (1353) and the defeat of the Burgundians in 1476 at the battles of Grandson and Murten (Morat). Zurich becomes a stronghold of the Protestant Reformation. At the Peace of Westphalia, which ends Europe's Thirty Years' War in 1648, the independence of Switzerland is recognized.
18th century	After the French Revolution, France occupies part of Switzerland and sets up a Helvetic Republic.
19th century	Napoleon adds six new cantons, bringing the number to 19. At the Congress of Vienna in 1815, Switzerland's "perpetual neutrality" is restored. A new constitution is proclaimed in 1848 and revised in 1874. Zurich becomes a leading economic centre, prospering in banking, engineering and textiles.
20th century	In two world wars, Switzerland remains neutral, but the army and people are mobilized to defend the country. Banking secrecy develops to foil Hitler's attempts to track down the assets of German Jews.

Sightseeing

The **Bahnhofstrasse** (Railway Station Street), the most elegant shopping street in Switzerland, starts at the station and proceeds to the lake shore. Jewellery and watches, furs and fashions, antiques and objects of art—the shop windows disclose a world of luxury. Much of the street is barred to automobile traffic, making window-shopping even more pleasurable.

The tree-shaded Bahnhofstrasse emerges onto Bürkliplatz at the waterfront. From the nearby bridge, Quaibrücke, you can admire a superb view of the lake.

The venerable **Fraumünster** dominates the west bank of the river. There has been a church here since 853, the year a convent was founded on the site. The present building dates back to the 13th century. Its lovely Romanesque choir has a surprise in store—modern stained-glass windows by Marc Chagall, completed in 1970 when the artist was 83 years old.

Zurich's finest Baroque building, the neighbouring **Zunfthaus zur Meise,** was constructed for the wine merchants' guild in 1757. Now it contains the ceramic collection of the Swiss National Museum.

Narrow old-world streets lined with antique shops and boutiques lead to St. Peterskirche. Set in the 13th-century tower is a huge clock face, one of the largest in Europe, measuring nearly 30 feet (9 m.) in diameter. The Baroque hall, a confection of pink-orange marble pillars, delicate stuccowork and crystal chandeliers, dates from reconstruction of the church in the 18th century.

Picturesque streets lie all around: you may want to wander the winding **Augustinergasse,** leading back to Bahnhofstrasse, or the **Schipfe,** down by the riverside, Zurich's oldest lane.

If you climb the steep steps to the historic **Lindenhof,** you'll enjoy a good view of the Limmat with its flat-roofed river boats. The fountain in this shady square commemorates the women of Zurich, who saved the city from the Habsburgs in 1292. Their ploy was to parade in full battledress, convincing the encircling enemy that Zurich was crowded with defending troops.

Across the river, just opposite the Fraumünster, stands the cathedral, the **Grossmünster,** built between 1100 and 1250 on the site of a 9th-century church. This is the "mother church of the Reformation in German-speaking Switzerland" where Zwingli preached from 1519 until his death on the battlefield in 1531. The cathedral's twin 15th-century towers, capped by 18th-century domes, make it the city's most distinctive landmark. Modern stained-glass windows by Augusto Giacometti light up the stark interior.

More Giacometti windows adorn the **Wasserkirche,** but the most spectacular feature of this late-Gothic church is its riverside situation. Built right on the Limmat, the church once stood on an island where the patron saints of Zurich —Felix and Regula—were said to have been beheaded by the pagan Roman governor.

On the east bank of the river are the historic guildhalls, each one more splendid than the next. Among the most outstanding: **Zunfthaus zum Rüden,** one-time gathering place of the nobility; **Zunfthaus zur Zimmerleuten,** the old carpenters' guildhall of 1708, graced with attractive oriel windows; and **Zunfthaus zur Saffran,** headquarters of the haberdashers' guild. Opposite the latter is the **Rathaus,** the richly ornamented town hall, completed in 1698. Zurich's city and cantonal parliaments still meet here. The entire old town area invites carefree wandering: stroll along **Neumarkt,** one of the best preserved of old Zurich streets, and on to the interesting high-Gothic **Predigerkirche** in Zähringerplatz. Beyond lies Niederdorf, Zurich's red-light district. The bars, restaurants and attractions here comprise the city's hottest nightlife centre.

East of the old town at Heimplatz, the **Kunsthaus** (Fine Arts Museum) surveys European painting (mainly German and French) from the Middle Ages to the 20th century.

Swiss culture, art and history are on display at the **Schweizerisches Landesmuseum** (Swiss National Museum), a vast Victorian structure behind the railway station.

Excursions

For an excellent overall **panorama** of Zurich, its lake and the Alps, take the train from Selnau station—15 minutes by foot from Paradeplatz in the city centre—to Üetliberg, altitude 2,858 feet (871 m.). The ride takes 25 minutes and trains leave every half hour. Or view the city from the perspective of the river. Between April and October glass-topped boats leave every half hour from the Landesmuseum; the tour lasts 50 minutes. You float past the old town houses, guildhalls and churches, out into the lake and on to Zürichhorn park.

Zurich's lake, the **Zürichsee,** extends 25 miles (40 km.) from the end of the Bahnhofstrasse to Schmerikon, on the Obersee. A good way to see the lake is by excursion boat, travelling past pleasant villages, extensive orchards and vineyards, and attractive little inns. The lakeside villages, especially those on the right bank, make up Zurich's wealthier suburbs, known as the "Gold Coast".

You can cruise right along the lake to **Rapperswil,** a pretty medieval town, graced with roses, storybook streets and a 14th-century castle.

Eating Out

Fondues and Raclette
Fondue. The celebrants gather round a bubbly cauldron of cheeses diluted with wine and a dash of cherry-based brandy, into which they dip chunks of bread on long forks.

Fondue bourguignonne. This time the pot is filled with boiling oil, into which the diners dip pieces of meat and flavour them with spicy sauces.

Fondue chinoise. Thinly sliced meat is plunged into simmering stock. The rich broth is served to finish.

Raclette. Melting layers of cheese are scraped from a whole chunk of cheese and eaten with boiled potatoes, pickled onions and gherkins.

Meat. Zurich's speciality is *geschnetzeltes Kalbfleisch* (or to give it the local name, *Züri-Gschnätzlets*), diced veal with mushrooms in a cream and wine sauce. Or try the liver brochettes, with bacon, sage, beans and potatoes; the Zurich-style tripe, with onions, mushrooms, white wine and cumin seed; or *Zouftschrüibertopf,* grilled meat with bacon, mushrooms and vegetables.

Game. Venison, deer, wild boar and hare are served during the September-to-February hunting season. *Rehrücken* (saddle of venison) is roasted and served with red cabbage and a cream sauce.

Potatoes and Noodles. Don't leave Zurich without trying *Rösti,* grated potatoes fried, usually with onion. Another companion to meat (especially game) dishes: *Spätzli,* tiny, noodle-like dumplings.

Shopping

Cheese, chocolate and clocks are the obvious purchases. Some other good buys are:

Antiques. Clocks, china, old silver in antique shops; fascinating junk in the street markets and local fairs.

Art. Galleries abound in Zurich. Dealers are accustomed to shipping paintings and sculpture to the ends of the earth.

Brandies. Potent and portable, made from apples, cherries, grapes, pears, plums and Alpine herbs.

Embroidery and Lace. Hand towels, table cloths, shirts and blouses.

Knives. The Swiss Army pocket knife reveals as many as 13 gadgets, from a corkscrew to a miniature saw.

Souvenirs. Alpenstocks, cow-bells, dolls in regional costumes, alpine fossils and minerals, wooden toys, bowls and plates, music boxes, copper pots, pewter.

Watches. Reliable shops stock all the famous Swiss makes, including the latest cheap version in a variety of styles.

Practical Information

Currency: The Swiss *franc* (in German *Franken*), abbreviated *Fr.,* is divided into 100 *centimes* (in German *Rappen*). Coins: 5, 10, 20, 50 centimes, Fr. 1, 2, 5. Banknotes: Fr. 10, 20, 50, 100, 500, 1,000.

Banks: Open 8.15 a.m.–4.30 p.m. Monday to Friday, with an extension on Monday to 6.30 p.m. in Zurich.

Climate: Cold winters, moderately warm summers. Average midwinter temperature 30 °F (–1 °C); midsummer 63 °F (17 °C).

Clothing: Medium to lightweight in summer. Rainwear may be necessary at any time. In winter a warm overcoat is essential.

Index

An asterisk (*) next to a page number indicates a map reference.

028/906 MUD 80